Handbook of Animation, Cartoon and Multimedia

Handbook of Animation, Cartoon and Multimedia

N. Venkateshwara Rao
Prashant K. Mathur

KANISHKA PUBLISHERS, DISTRIBUTORS
NEW DELHI-110 002

KANISHKA PUBLISHERS, DISTRIBUTORS
4697/5-21A, Ansari Road, Daryaganj
New Delhi-110 002
Phones : 2327 0497, 2328 8285
Fax : 011-2328 8285
e-mail: kanishka_publishing@yahoo.co.in

First Published 2008

ISBN 978-81-8457-095-3

PRINTED IN INDIA

Published by Madan Sachdeva for Kanishka Publishers, Distributors, 4697/5-21A, Ansari Road, Daryaganj, New Delhi-110 002; Typeset by Sunshine Graphics, Delhi, and Printed at Nice Printing Press, Delhi.

Preface

This publication is designed to serve the purpose of a reference book on the said subject areas of animation, cartoon and multimedia. An introduction to the science and arts of animation technology and design is provided with a global perspective, focusing particularly on developments in Europe, America and Asia. The life and work of Prescott Wright is presented as a case study listing his role and contribution in animation based film industry, film festivals, television and related events. Elements, characteristics and design techniques used in animation are described in detail, so has been its impact on western culture and people. Animation variables, such as computer animation, hardware animation, movies amateur and architectural animation, adult and independent animation, slideshow and traditional animation are outlined in detail, so are their various techniques, such as wire frame model, stick figure, etc. Animated poetry is also described in detail. This book survey briefly the contemporary global animation works and makes important case studies, such as, that of "All About Animation", "Picasso Animation Education and Production Centennial's Programs", "Hightech Animation", and "Animation Multimedia Maya Training in India". Various cels of an animation institute are described with focus on fields like edition, publicity, framing, model, background, lithography, prints awareness, etc. Optical toys as the precursor to animation is described in brief. Frequently asked questions about the animation media science and technology are answered and its applications in various fields have been established. The animated cartoons and their evolution have been described in a historical perspective. Select case study w.r.t. India has been made. Similarly, historical development and evolution of multimedia in those world has been outlined systematically. An appendix featuring all important listings in this regard has been given. Select case studies have been made of successful global multimedia projects and companies. The educational and commercial aspects of multimedia has been covered in detail. This book is user friendly and application oriented.

N. Venkateshwara Rao
Prashant K. Mathur

Preface

Contents

Chapter 1

Animation: An Introduction to Its Science and Arts

Animation refers to the process in which each frame of a film or movie is produced individually, whether generated as a computer graphic, or by photographing a series of drawn images (an animated cartoon), or by repeatedly making small changes to a model (see claymation and stop motion), and then photographing the result.

A BASIC SUMMARY: PAST, PRESENT AND FUTURE

The Past

Cave Paintings

Early examples of attempts to capture the phenomenon of motion into a still drawing can be found in paleolithic cave paintings, where animals are depicted with multiple legs in superimposed positions, clearly attempting to convey the perception of motion.

Athens

One of the most earliest successful depictions of an image in motion is evident in the Greek era. Ex. A Parthenon frieze relief which depicts a series of horses that appear to gallop at increasing speeds as they progress.

The Magic Lantern (1671)

The Magic Lantern was classed as the ancestor of the modern day projector. It consisted of a translucent oil painting and a simple lamp. When put together in a darkened room, the image would appear larger on a flat surface. Athanasius Kircher spoke about this originating from China in the 1600's.

Thaumatrope (1824)

A Thaumatrope was a toy used in the Victorian era. It was a disk or card with two different pictures on each side that was attached to two pieces of string. When the strings were twirled quickly between the fingers the two pictures appear to combine into a single image. The creator of this small but yet important invention is clouded. People believe that John Aryton Paris was the creator whereas others believe Charles Babbage was.

Zoetrope (1832)

A Zoetrope is a device which creates the image of a moving picture. This contraption was produced in 1834 by George Horner. The device is basically a cylinder with vertical slits around the sides. Around the inside edge of the cylinder there are a series of pictures on the opposite side to the slits. As the cylinder is spun, the user then looks through the slits producing the illusion of motion.

Praxinoscope (1877)

The Praxinoscope, invented by French scientist Charles-Émile Reynaud, was a more sophisticated version of the zoetrope. It used the same basic mechanism of a strip of images placed on the inside of a spinning cylinder, but instead of viewing it through slits, it was viewed in a series of stationary mirrors around the inside of the cylinder, so that the animation would stay in place, and also provided a clearer image. Reynaud also developed a larger version of the praxinoscope that could be projected onto a screen, called the Théâtre Optique.

Flip Book (1868)

The first flip book was patented in 1868 by a John Barnes Linnet. This was another step closer to the development of animation. Like the Zoetrope, the Flip Book creates the illusion of motion. A set of sequential pictures seen at a high speed creates this effect. The Mutoscope (1894) is essentially a flip book in a box with a crank handle to flip the pages.

The Present

Stop Motion

Stop motion is used for many animation productions using physical objects rather than images, as with traditional animation. An object will be photographed, moved slightly, and then photographed again. When the pictures are played back in normal speed the object will appear to move by itself. This process is used for many productions, for example, clay animations such as *Chicken Run* and *Wallace and Gromit,* as well as animated movies which use poseable figures, such as *The Nightmare Before Christmas* and *James and the Giant Peach.* Sometimes even objects are used, such as with the films of Jan Svankmajer.

Stop motion animation was also commonly used for special effects work in many live-action films, such as The 1933 version of *King Kong* and *The 7th Voyage of Sinbad.*

CGI Animation

Computer-generated imagery changed animated films forever. The first fully computer generated feature film created was *Toy Story,* produced by Pixar Animation Studios in 1995. *Toy Story* proved that companies were slowly making the transition from traditional animation to CGI animation. The process of CGI animation is still very tedious and similar in that sense to traditional animation, and it still adheres to many of the same principles.

A principal difference of CGI animation compared to traditional animation is that drawing is replaced by 3D modeling, though a form of animation that combines the two worlds can be considered to be computer aided animation but on 2D computer drawing (which can be considered close to traditional drawing and sometimes based on it).

The Future

Animated Humans

Most CGI created films are based on animal characters, monsters, machines or cartoon-like humans. Animation studios are now trying to develop ways of creating realistic-looking humans. A film that attempted this was *Final Fantasy: The Spirits Within*, in 2001. However, due to the complexity of the human body functions, emotions and interactions, this method of animation is rarely used. Of principal complexity is the creation of a convincing human face model. Of secondary complexity but still a modern approach are techniques for the production of convincing hair or cloth movement.

Film Animation

The history of film animation began in the 1890s with the earliest days of silent films and continues through the present day. The first animated film was created by Charles-Émile Reynaud, inventor of the praxinoscope, an animation system using loops of 12 pictures. On October 28, 1892 at Musée Grévin in Paris, France he exhibited animations consisting of loops of about 500 frames, using his Théâtre Optique system—similar in principle to a modern film projector.

The first animated work on standard picture film was *Humorous Phases of Funny Faces* (1906) by J. Stuart Blackton. It features a cartoonist drawing faces on a chalkboard, and the faces apparently coming to life.

Fantasmagorie, by the French director Émile Cohl (also called *Émile Courtet*), is also noteworthy. It was screened for the first time on August 17, 1908 at Théâtre du Gymnase in Paris. Émile Courtet later went to Fort Lee, New Jersey near New York City in 1912, where he worked for French studio Éclair and spread its technique in the US.

The first puppet-animated film was *The Beautiful Lukanida* (1912) by the Russian-born (ethnically Polish) director Wladyslaw Starewicz (Ladislas Starevich).

The first animated feature film was *El Apóstol*, made in 1917 by Quirino Cristiani from Argentina. He also directed two other animated feature films, including 1931's *Peludopolis*, the first to use synchronized sound. None of these, however, survive to the present day. The earliest-surviving animated feature, which used colour-tinted scenes, is the silhouette-animated *Adventures of Prince Achmed* (1926) directed by German Lotte Reiniger and French/Hungarian Berthold Bartosch. Walt Disney's *Snow White and the Seven Dwarfs* (1937), often considered to be the first animated feature when in fact at least eight were previously released, was the nevertheless first to use Technicolor and the first to become successful within the English-speaking world.

Europe

Animation before film in 20th century.

History of Czech Animation

- Puppet animation, Jirí Trnka, the Poetic animation school.
- Catalogue of Czech animation.
- Czech animation homepage.

History of Estonian Animation

- 1931—*The Adventures of Juku The Dog,* first Estonian animated short film
- 1950s—founding of puppet animation division of Tallinnfilm by Elbert Tuganov
- 1970s—founding of drawn animation division, Joonisfilm, by *"Rein Raamat"*
- 1999s—I'm a genious

History of French Animation

908-1925, Work of Émile Cohl: The first animated cartoon (1908), and most animation techniques: morphing (1909), puppet animation and color animated cartoon (1910), pixilation (1911), first animated series (*Le chien Flambeau,* 1916).

History of Italian Animation

- The 1970 Italian animated cartoon art and industry (La Linea (cartoon), Caliméro...)
- The 1977 animated Italian classic, *Allegro non troppo,* is both a parody of and homage to Disney's *Fantasia.* This is director Bruno Bozzetto's most ambitious work and his only feature-length animation, although he also directed several notable shorter works including *West and Soda,* an animated spaghetti western.

History of Russian Animation

- 1910-1913 Ladislas Starevich creates puppet animations.
- 1935 First animated feature film in USSR, *The New Gulliver.*
- 1935 Soyuzmultfilm Studio is created, will go on to fund many thousands of short animated films, mostly for kids.
- late 1930s to 1950s—enforced *Socialist Realism* in cartoons (with a few exceptions).
- 1953 Puppet animation division re-founded at Soyuzmultfilm (it was closed shortly after *The New Gulliver* was released).
- 1962 Fyodor Khitruk's short film *History of a Crime* introduces new aesthetic to Soviet animation.
- 1969 First episode of popular series *Nu, Pogodi!*
- 1972 First Cheburashka short is made.
- 1979 Yuriy Norshteyn releases *Tale of Tales,* since then voted twice by a large panel of international critics as the best animated film ever made.
- 1989 Studio Pilot, the first private animation studio in the USSR, is founded.
- 1990s government subsidies shrink dramatically, while the number of studios grows. Soyuzmultfilm is beset by corruption and banditism, slowly loses its dominant place among Russian studios.
- 2000s some high-profile animated features are made. Government diverts some funds to animation again. Nevertheless, many studios experience budget shortfalls and have difficulties finishing their ambitious projects.

History of Animation in Croatia (in Former Yugoslavia)

- The Zagreb school, cf. Zagreb Film.
- The Cakovec school, cf. Škola Animiranog Filma Cakovec.

North and South America

History of Argentinian Animation

World's first two feature-length animated films and first film with sound by Quirino Cristiani;Quirio Cristiani's page (Spanish).

History of Canadian Animation

- Early Work
- Contributions of the National Film Board of Canada's animation department
- Early commercial productions: Contributions of Canadian voice actor recordings
- The 1980s—rise of the major indigenous industry.

History of Cuban Animation

- Vampiros en la Habana
- Festival Internacional del Nuevo Cine Latinoamericano.

History of United States Animation

Beginning of industrial production of animated cartoon.

Because the history of Hollywood animation as an art form has undergone many changes in its hundred-year history, Wikipedia presents four separate chapters in the development of its animation:

Animation in the United States during the Silent Era (1900s through 1920s)

- The beginning of theatrical, the earliest animated cartoons in the era of silent film, ranging from the works of Winsor McCay through *Koko the Clown* and *Felix the Cat.*
- The Bray Studios was the first and foremost cartoon studio, housed in New York City. Many aspiring cartoonists started their careers at Bray, including Paul Terry of "Mighty Mouse" fame, Max Fleischer of "Betty Boop" fame, as well as Walter Lantz of "Woody Woodpecker" fame. The cartoon studio operated from circa 1915 until 1928. Some of the first cartoon stars from the Bray studios were Farmer Alfalfa (by Paul Terry) and Bobby Bumps (by Earl Hurd).
- Max and Dave Fleischer formed their own studio Fleischer Studios, and created the *Koko the Clown*, *Out of the Inkwell*, and *Sound Car-Tunes* series.

The Golden Age of Hollywood Animation (1930s and 1940s)

- The dominance of Walt Disney throughout the 1930s, through revolutionary cartoons Silly Symphonies, Mickey Mouse, and Donald Duck.
- The rise of Warner Bros. and MGM.
- The Fleischer Studios creation of Betty Boop and Popeye cartoons.
- Disney's Snow White and The Seven Dwarfs marks the start of the "Golden Age" at Disney.
- The departure from realism, and UPA.

Animation in the United States in the Television Era (1950s through 1980s)

- The emergence of TV *animated series* from Hanna-Barbera Productions.
- The decline of theatrical cartoons and feature films.
- *Saturday morning cartoons.*
- The attempts at reviving animated features through the 1960s.
- The rise of *adult animation* in the early 1970s.
- The onslaught of commercial cartoons in the 1980s.

Modern Animation of the United States (1980s through Present)

- *Who Framed Roger Rabbit* and the return of Disney.
- Steven Spielberg's collaborations with Warner Bros.
- A flood of newer, bolder animation studios.
- The Simpsons marks the resurgence of adult-oriented animation.
- The mainstream popularization of *anime.*
- The rise of *computer animation.*
- The decline of Saturday morning cartoons, the rise of Nickelodeon and Cartoon Network.
- Cartoon Network's late-night animation block Adult Swim becomes immensely popular and leads to a resurgence in short, adult animation.
- In 2005, Disney closes all facilities for hand-drawn traditional animation, concentrating on *computer animation* for their feature films.

Asia

History of Iranian Animation

The oldest records of animation in Persia (Iran) dates back to 5000 years ago. An animated piece on an earthen goblet that belongs to 5000 years ago was found in Burnt City in Sistan and Baluchestan Province, southeastern Iran. On this ancient piece that can be called the first animation of the world, the artist has portrayed a goat that jumps toward a tree and eats its leaves.

The art of animation as practiced in modern day began in Iran in the 1950s. Iran's animation owes largely to the animator Noureddin Zarrinkelk. Zarrinkelk was instrumental in founding the Institute for Intellectual Development of Children and Young Adults (IIDCYA) in Tehran in collaboration with the late father of Iranian graphics Morteza Momayez and other fellow artists like Farshid Mesghali, Ali Akbar Sadeghi, and Arapik Baghdasarian.

History of Chinese Animation

- 1922 first animation in a commercial Shuzhendong Chinese Typewriter.
- 1926 first animation to showcase technology Uproar in the Studio and acknowledge Wan Laiming and Wan Guchan as pioneers.
- 1935 *The Camel's Dance first chinese animation with sound.*
- 1941 *Princess Iron Fan* first Asian animation of notable length produced in China.
- 1956 *Why is the Crow Black-Coated* first Chinese animation in color.

- 1958 *Pigsy Eats Watermelon* first papercut technique animation.
- 1961, 1964 *Havoc in Heaven* created at the height of the industry with all 4 Wan brothers.
- 1966-1976 the Cultural Revolution would bring the entire industry to a halt.
- 1995 *Cyber Weapon Z* possibly first 3D animation in Hong Kong.
- 2006 *Thru the Moebius Strip* first 3D animation film rendered in mainland China to be shown in United States.

History of Japanese Animation (Anime)

The First Japanese Animation

Found recently in Kyoto, the film depicts a boy wearing a sailor uniform performing a salute. The film dates back to around the year 1900 and is on 35 mm Celluloid, composed of 50 frames put together with paste.

Pre-Tezuka Experiments:

- *Momotaro's Sea Eagles.*
- *Momotaro's Divine Sea Warriors.*

Mushi Productions and Toei Animation

- Osamu Tezuka's *Astro Boy* (1963).
- Isao Takahata's *Hols: Prince of the Sun* (1968), helped by Hayao Miyazaki and Yoichi Kotabe.

1970s

- *Tomorrow's Joe* and the beginning of sports and martial arts anime.
- Rise of the Mecha and Super Robot genres and fall of Japanese film industry.
- Impact of *Gundam* and the beginning of the Real Robot genre.

1980s

- Rise of space operas with *Z Gundam* and *Macross.*
- Rise of Otaku subculture.
- Beginning of Studio Ghibli.
- Rise of fantasy adventures with the Hayao Miyazaki films *Nausicaä of the Valley of the Wind* and *Castle in the Sky.*
- *Dragon Ball* and the rise of martial arts anime.
- Ambitious productions such as *Akira* (1988) and the beginning of cyberpunk and postmodern anime.

1990s

- Decline of domestic industry combined with international growth.
- Rise of harem anime.
- *Dragon Ball Z* and the rise of superhuman martial arts anime.

- *Sailor Moon* and the rise of magical girl anime.
- The impact of *Neon Genesis Evangelion* series and the post-Evangelion trend.
- Critical acclaim in the West and the rise of Moe series domestically.

2000s

- Rise of digital fansubs outside of Japan, particularly among anime fans in the West.
- Revival of sports anime with titles such as *Hajime no Ippo* and *Hikaru no Go.*
- Rise of psychological horrors and psychological thrillers with titles such as *Higurashi no Naku Koro ni* and *Death Note.*
- Rise of 3D computer graphics in anime, including anime titles by Hayao Miyazaki and Katsuhiro Otomo.
- Rise of cel-shading in anime such as *Freedom Project.*
- Revival of Super Robot genre and beginning of anti-Evangelion trend with *Tengen Toppa Gurren Lagann.*

CASE STUDY: PRESCOTT WRIGHT

Prescott J. Wright (b. Bronx, New York 8 May 1935—d. Albuquerque, New Mexico, 28 December 2006) was best known as the longtime producer and film distributor of the annual touring programs of animated films from around the word known as the International Tournée of Animation. In addition, he was one of the founding directors of the Ottawa International Animated Film Festival in Canada, which began in 1976 and which is now held annually, as well as being instrumental in fostering the art of animated films throughout his working life.

Early Life

Prescott Wright was raised in the Bronx, was stationed in the Army at Fort Ord, and went to Monterey Peninsula College. The school had a film series run by Phil Chamberlin and Pres became active with it, running the projectors and helping in other ways. His resume says he was president of the film society and jazz club. In 1963, Chamberlin recommended Prescott, who had recently married, for a job at Brandon Films (also known as Western Cinema Guild) in San Francisco as an assistant and, when the manager left, Prescott became head of the San Francisco office. Brandon was a major 16 mm film distributor of American and foreign features and shorts.

In 1969 he moved to Los Angeles to work at the American Film Institute (AFI). They sent him to New York City in January 1970 to market films produced with AFI grants. In a letter to a friend dated December 1970 he wrote, "By September I had sold about $50 grand worth of films and was applying for my own iron lung. There were some good $$ deals with some major companies if I would stay in New York."

In 1971 he returned to college. He received a BA degree in Communication and the Visual Arts in 1973 from what was then called California State University, San Francisco and a MA degree in Film in 1977 from the renamed San Francisco State University. He was a teaching assistant and then a part-time instructor at SF State from 1972-80. He also taught an extension course in film for the University of California at Berkeley in 1975.

International Tournee of Animation

Taking up an offer to take on distribution of the "Tourney (sic) of Animation" (as it was written), he acquired eight films from KQED-TV and began FilmWright, his small film distribution company, to late 1970.

About 1966 several members of ASIFA-Hollywood (Bill Scott, Bill Littlejohn, Les Goldman and June Foray) decided to put together an international animation program to be shown at the Los Angeles County Museum of Art. Since it was almost impossible to see quality animation in the US at that time, Prescott became active with the group when he joined the AFI in 1969 and, having worked previously in film distribution, he was asked to head the project when they decided to show the program in other cities. Under his guidance, the program became known as the *International Tournee of Animation* and, in late 1970 or early 1971, he began to book the program at the San Francisco Museum of Modern Art, university campuses and other cultural institutions around the country.

FilmWright offered animators an interesting and generous contract when Wright produced the Tournee. As producer, the company received 50 per cent of the gross while the remaining 50 per cent was split among the artists. About half of the money going to the animators was split evenly between each filmmaker and the remaining amount was split based the length of each short film. This meant that a very short film got slightly less than one which was a minute or two longer.

In the 1970s Gary Meyer, who ran the U.C. Theatre in Berkeley, California and became a co-founder Landmark Theatres, convinced Prescott to expand his distribution of the Tournee of Animation to theatres:

> "We needed interesting new programming and approached Prescott about showing the Tournee in theatres. He had only screened at colleges and museums. He took the leap with us and the result was a greatly expanded audience for animated shorts. At a certain point, he was burned out. Assembling a feature length package, distributing it and keeping a couple dozen filmmakers happy is an overwhelming task. Steve Gilula, Terry Thoren and I agreed to buy the Tournee with the understanding that Prescott would continue to provide guidance as we moved forward. And what a mentor he was!"

Author and animation historian Jerry Beck noted:

> "I met Prescott shortly after I moved to L.A. in 1986, when I came to work with Terry Thoren to distribute the Tournee for Expanded Entertainment. Prescott was always friendly, knowledgeable and eager to help us communicate with filmmakers and theatre owners across the country and around the world. Prescott was a pioneer—in those pre-cable, pre-Internet days—in getting independent and international animation showcased and making those films accessible to those unable to attend festivals in far off lands. Without Wright's vision, the Ottawa festival would not be what it is; successor-touring

programs like Spike and Mike's shows and "The Animation Show" would not be, and ASIFA-SF would not be the strong chapter it is."

Involvement with ASIFA Internationally and Locally and with Animated Film Festivals

Between 1975 and 1985, Prescott was on the Board of Directors of ASIFA, the International Animated Film Association, which had over 30 chapters around the world. Until the Iron Curtain collapsed, ASIFA helped bridge the gap between East and West by helping animators from Eastern Europe attend festivals in the West, to visit studios in the Europe and North America, and to show their films in-person. Pres, David Ehrlich, Howard Beckerman, Charles Samu, John Halas, John Hubley and others worked hard to further international relations and to arrange for these screenings in cities with ASIFA chapters.

He was also a founder of ASIFA-San Francisco in 1975. Thanks to his guidance, the chapter grew over the years, and it is known for presenting great programs and having a very informative newsletter.

Prescott served as an advisor to major animation festivals around the world, and regularly attended the ASIFA-sponsored festivals in Annecy, France, and Zagreb, (then in Yugoslavia).

He was a founder and the first International Director of the *Ottawa International Animation Festival* in 1976 and served in that capacity in 1978, 1980, 1982, and also in 1992. In 2004, the Ottawa festival made him an Honorary President of the festival, but he was unable to attend the event due to his health problems. ASIFA-Hollywood has also honored him with the "June Foray Award" for benevolent and significant contributions to the art of animation at the "*Annie Awards.*"

Film Festivals and Television

Pres served a year as director of the Denver International Film Festival (1980/81) and, returning to San Francisco, became the producer of "The Animators", a series of TV programs made in 1982 for KQED-TV in San Francisco which featured Bay Area talent such as Jeff Hale, Bud Luckey, Rudy Zamora, Sally Cruickshank and Marcy Page.

Organized by ASIFA-Hollywood during the Los Angeles Summer Olympic Games of 1984, Prescott was involved, as Director, with the creation and management of the "Olympiad of Animation", which was shown in Los Angeles at the *Academy of Motion Picture Arts and Sciences*' Samuel Goldwyn Theatre. For one program, the organizers polled one hundred animation professionals around the world to determine which animated films were regarded as the greatest of all time; over 30 of the films were shown. He was proud of the fact that he brought the project in under budget.

Other Cultural Events

He also was involved with many other cultural events over the years. These included serving as a member of the Film Arts Foundation Board of Directors in San Francisco from the late 1960s (and as President of the Board from 1978 to 1979), and as Treasurer of the Society for Animation Studies in the late 1980s and early 1990s (with Harvey Deneroff, the founder and first president of that association).

In 1990, Prescott worked for *Disney's* Feature Division as a "Creative Staffing Specialist." He spent 4-months traveling to international animation festivals as a spotter and recruiter of animation talent. He planned to travel to festivals in Hiroshima, Annecy, Zagreb and also in Russia.

After Disney, he worked in both the Philippines and Southern India as an instructor and festival director for emerging animation studios. While he was in India he programmed and managed the first "Week with the Masters" for Toonz India, an emerging animation studio at Trivandrum in October 1999.

ANIME

Anime (アニメ?) pronounced [anime] *listen (help·info)* in Japanese, but typically pronounced /'æntm?/ or /'æntmı/ in English is an abbreviation of the word "animation". Outside Japan, the term most popularly refers to cartoons originating from Japan; and from the Occidental point of view, not all cartoons are considered *anime*. *Anime* is therefore usually considered to be a subset of animation.

Anime is traditionally hand drawn, but like in most animation computer assisted animation techniques have become quite common in recent years. The story-lines of anime represent most major genres of fiction and most motion-picture media (television broadcast, DVD and VHS distribution, and full length motion pictures).

The history of anime begins at the start of the 20th century, when Japanese filmmakers experimented with the *animation* techniques that were being explored in France, Germany, the United States, and Russia. The oldest known anime is in 1907, a three second clip of a sailor boy.

By the 1930s, animation became an alternative format of storytelling compared to the underdeveloped live-action industry in Japan. Unlike America, the live-action industry in Japan remained a small market and suffered from budgeting, location, and casting restrictions. The lack of Western-looking actors, for example, made it next to impossible to shoot films set in Europe, America, or fantasy worlds that do not naturally involve Japan. The varied use of animation allowed artists to create any characters and settings.

Starting with *Snow White, Walt Disney* demonstrated animation's potential as a medium. The success of Disney's works influenced Japanese animators. Osamu Tezukā adapted and simplified many Disney animation precepts to reduce the budget costs and number of frames in the production. This was intended to be a temporary measure to allow him to produce one episode every week with an inexperienced animation staff. Some animators in Japan overcome production budgets by utilizing different techniques than the Disney or the old Tezuka/Otsuka methods of animating anime.

During the 1970s, there was a surge of growth in the popularity of manga—which were often later animated—especially those of Osamu Tezuka, who has been called a "legend" and the "god of manga." As a result of his work and that of other pioneers in the field, anime developed characteristics and genres that are fundamental elements of the art today. The giant *robot* genre (known as "mecha" outside Japan), for instance, took shape under Tezuka, developed under Go Nagai and others, and was revolutionized at the end of the decade by Yoshiyuki Tomino. Robot anime like *Gundam* and *Macross* became instant classics in the 1980s, and the robot genre of anime is still one of the most heard of in Japan and worldwide today. In the 1980s, anime was accepted in the mainstream in Japan, and experienced a boom in production (it should be noticed that manga has significantly more mainstream exposure than anime in Japan). The mid-to-late 1990s, on into the 2000s, saw an increased acceptance of anime in overseas markets.

Terminology

In Japanese, the English term animation is written in katakana as アニメーション (*animeshon,* pronounced [ɑnime：ʔON]). The shortened term, anime (アニメ), emerged in the 1970s. Animation, as well as anime, come from the Latin, *"animare"* meaning "to breathe life into" thus "animated" means to be full of activity, or moving pictures. Both the original and abbreviated forms are valid and interchangeable in Japanese, but as could be expected the shorter form is more commonly used.

The pronunciation of *anime* in Japanese, [ɑnime], differs significantly from English IPA:/'æntmɪ/, which has different vowels and stress. (In Japanese each mora carries equal stress.) As with a few other Japanese words such as *saké, Pokémon,* and *Kobo Abé, anime* is sometimes spelled *animé* in English, with an *acute accent* over the final *e,* to cue the reader that the letter is pronounced, not silent as would be expected for English. However, this accent does not appear in any commonly used system of romanized Japanese.

Word Usage

Linguistically, the anime definition is subject to interpretation. In Japan, the term does not specify an animation's nation of origin or style; instead, it is used as a blanket term to refer to all forms of animation from around the world. In English, main dictionary sources define anime as "a Japanese style of motion-picture animation" or "a style of animation developed in Japan." Common uses of the term is Japanese explicit, among Western audiences. Furthermore, the terms "cartoon" or "animated series" used for most other visual styles, particularly for French, Korean, and American animation. Any non-Japanese works are called anime-influenced animation, if they borrow any stylization from Japanese animation. Even so, some anime are co-productions with non-Japanese companies, like the Cartoon Network and Production IG series IGPX. Yet, a French-Japanese co-production such as Oban Star-Racers is not considered anime.

Anime can be used as a common noun, "Do you watch anime?" or as a suppletive adjective, "The anime Guyver is different from the movie Guyver." It may also be used as a mass noun, as in "How much anime have you collected?" and therefore is never pluralized "animes" (nouns are never pluralized in Japanese). However, in other languages where *anime* has been adopted as a loan word, it is sometimes used as a count noun in singular and in plural as in Danish "Jeg tror, jeg vil se en anime" ("I think I'll watch an anime") and "Hvor mange anime'er har du nu?" ("How many animes do you have now?").

Synonyms

Anime is sometimes referred to as *Japanimation,* but this term has fallen into disuse. *Japanimation* saw the most usage during the 1970s and 1980s and had continued use up until before the mid-1990s anime resurgence. In general, the term now only appears in nostalgic contexts. The term is much more commonly used within Japan to refer to domestic animation. Since *anime* or *animeshon* is used to describe all forms of animation, *Japanimation* is used to distinguish Japanese work from that of the rest of the world.

In more recent years, anime has also frequently been referred to as "manga" in European countries, a practice that may stem from the Japanese usage: In Japan, manga can refer to both animation and comics (although the use of manga to refer to animation is mostly restricted to non-fans). Among English speakers, manga usually has the stricter meaning of "Japanese comics." An alternate explanation is that it is due to the prominence of Manga Entertainment, a distributor of anime to the US and UK markets. Because Manga Entertainment originated in the UK the use of the term is common outside of Japan. The portmanteau "*animanga*" has been used to collectively refer to anime and manga, though it is also a term used to describe comics produced from animation cels.

Visual Characteristics

As an art form, anime places a large emphasis towards visual styles. They can vary from artist to artist or by studio to studio. Some titles make extensive use of common stylization: *FLCL*, for example, is known for its wild, exaggerated stylization. In contrast, titles such as *Only Yesterday* or *Jin-Roh* take much more realistic approaches, featuring few stylistic exaggerations.

While different titles and different artists have their own artistic styles, many stylistic elements have become so common such that they are described as being definitive of anime in general. Another stylistic element is that use of lines. In anime the lines are often influenced more from a stylistic look from brush work, rather than that of the calligrapher's pen. This may be due to the fact that Japanese was traditionally written with a brush and has had a large influence on Japanese art, thus how the lines are treated tend to be different from the Western art. Western lettering was done with a calligrapher's pen. The influences of these things can most influentially be seen in the amount of tapering and thickness of the lines involved.

Anime also tends to borrow many elements from *manga* including text in the background, and borrowing panel layouts from the manga as well. For example, an opening may employ manga panels to tell the story, or to dramatize a point for humorous effect. This is best demonstrated in the anime *Kare Kano*.

Character Design

Body proportions emulated in anime come from proportions of the human body. The height of the head is considered as the base unit of proportion. Head heights can vary as long as the remainder of the body remain proportional. Most anime characters are about seven to eight heads tall, and extreme heights are set around nine heads tall. In comparison, Marvel characters are proportional by eight heads.

With regard to the limbs, both the arms and legs have their joints, the elbows and knees respectively, at the midpoint of their total lengths. The arms range from the shoulders to the midpoint of the thigh. Leg lengths are at least the same as from head to hips. Naturally, the lengths and proportions remain consistent regardless of a characters position and orientation.

Variations to proportion can be modded. Chibi or super deformed characters feature a non-proportionally small body compared to the head. Sometimes specific body parts, like legs, are shortened or elongated for added emphasis. Mostly chibi are three or four heads tall. Some anime works like Crayon Shin-chan completely disregard these proportions. It is enough such that it resembles a Western cartoon. Then, early anime works did not have guidelines on body proportions at all. At the time, the main frame of reference were American cartoons, particularly Disney. For exaggeration, certain body features are increased in proportion.

A common approach is the large eyes style drawn on many anime and *manga* characters. Osamu Tezuka was inspired by the exaggerated features of American cartoon characters such as Betty Boop, Mickey Mouse, and Disney's *Bambi*. Tezuka found that large eyes style allowed his characters to show emotions distinctly. When Tezuka began drawing *Ribbon no Kishi*, the first manga specifically targeted at young girls, Tezuka further exaggerated the size of the characters' eyes. Indeed, through *Ribbon no Kishi*, Tezuka set a stylistic template that later *shojo* artists tended to follow.

Coloring is added to give eyes, particularly the cornea, some depth. The depth is accomplished by applying variable color shading. Generally, a mixture of a light shade, the tone color, and a dark shade is used.

Cultural anthropologist Matt Thorn argues that Japanese animators and audiences do not perceive such stylized eyes as inherently more or less foreign.

However, not all anime have large eyes. For example Hayao Miyazaki is known for not having large eyes and having realistic hair colors on his characters. In addition many other productions also have been known to use smaller eyes. This design tends to have more resemblance to traditional Japanese art. Some characters have even smaller eyes, where simple black dots are used.

A wide variety of facial expressions are used by characters to denote moods and thoughts. Anime uses a different set of facial expressions in comparison to western animation.

Other stylistic elements are common as well; often in comedic anime, characters that are shocked or surprised will perform a "face fault", in which they display an extremely exaggerated expression. Angry characters may exhibit a "vein" or "stressmark" effect, where lines representing bulging veins will appear on their forehead. Angry women will sometimes summon a mallet from nowhere and strike someone with it, leading to the concept of Hammerspace and cartoon physics. Male characters will develop a bloody nose around their female love interests (typically to indicate arousal, based on an old wives' tale). Embarrassed characters either produce a massive sweat-drop (which has become one of the most widely recognized stereotype motifs of anime) or produce a visibly red blush beneath the eyes, especially as a manifestation of repressed romantic feelings. While common, the use of face faults is optional. Some anime, usually with political plots and other more serious subject matters, have abandoned the use of face faults such as Gundam Wing and Teknoman.

Some non-human characters further diversify the array of characters. Some include robots, animals, spirits, and demons. Also, hybrid beings such as catgirls or hanyo are also created. Non-humanoid characters have a very wide variety of shapes and sizes, which can range from miniature characters to those the size of skyscrapers. The use of size proportions will vary. The typical style for non-humans is a dramatization of size for most, or a drastic shrinkage for others. Typical spirits and demons as well as robots and some animals will be shown out of proportion and sometimes the size of skyscrapers and buildings. Often for the purpose of giving the impression of great power or often synched with mecha-anime series in which the main character uses a giant robot to defeat another giant robot or creature. Some robots and animals though are shown to be accurate sized or even miniature for the sake of comical or story important reasons.

Animation Technique

The basics of anime is based on traditional animation. While anime is considered separate from cartoons, anime still uses multiple still images in rapid succession to produce the animated visual effect. Like all animation, the production processes of storyboarding, voice acting, character design, cel production, etc. still apply. With improvements in computer technology, computer animation increased the efficiency of the whole production process.

Anime is often considered a form of limited animation. That means that stylistically, even in bigger productions the conventions of limited animation are used to fool the eye into thinking there is more movement than there is. Many of the techniques used a comprised with cost-cutting measures while working under a set budget.

Anime scenes place emphasis on achieving three-dimensional views. Backgrounds depict the scenes' atmosphere. For example, anime often puts emphasis on changing seasons, as can be seen in numerous anime, such as Tenchi Muyo. Sometimes actual settings have been duplicated into an anime. The backgrounds for the Melancholy of Haruhi Suzumiya are based on various locations within the suburb of Nishinomiya, Hyogo, Japan.

Camera angles, camera movement, and lighting play an important role in scenes. Directors often have the discretion of determining viewing angles for scenes, particularly regarding backgrounds. In addition, camera angles show perspective. Directors can also choose camera effects within cinematography, such as panning, zooming, facial closeup, and panoramic. Lighting effects are used in conjunction with camera effects. For additional three-dimensional effects, various shades of lighting are used.

GENRES

Dragon Ball Z. (1989) is a popular *shonen* anime based on the original manga series which spanned 291 episodes and 13 movies.

Anime has many genres typically found in any mass media form. Such genres include action, adventure, children's stories, comedy, drama, erotica (more specifically ecchi or hentai), medieval fantasy, occult/horror, romance, and science fiction.

Most anime includes content from several different genres, as well as a variety of thematic elements. Thus, some series may be categorized under multiple genres. For example, *Neon Genesis Evangelion* might be considered to fall into the genres of post-apocalyptic, science fiction, mecha, and drama. A show may have a seemingly simple surface plot, but at the same time may feature a far more complex, deeper storyline and character development. It is not uncommon for an action themed anime to also involve humor, romance, and even social commentary. The same can be applied to a romance themed anime in that it may involve an action element, or in some cases brutal violence.

The following is a list of the major genres and designations that are specific to anime and manga:

- *Action/Adventure* primarily focuses on battles, war, and physical competition. Martial arts, weapon fighting, or other action oriented material are usually featured. Examples: *Naruto* or *One Piece.*
- *Drama* primarily has a high degree of character development and emotional themes. Many center around relationship complications. Examples: *Fushigi Yugi* or *InuYasha.*
- *Game Based* primarily revolves around some sort of card or board game. Examples: *Yu-Gi-Oh!* or *Hikaru No Go.*
- *Horror* use darker and/or supernatural themes. Examples: *Vampire Hunter D* series or *Chrono Crusade.*
- *Science fiction* consists of futuristic elements, particularly featuring future science and technology. They can be drawn from current scientific studies and inventions or created to meet the needs of the world. Examples: *Ghost in the Shell* or *Wings of Honneamise.*
- *Progressive* or "Art films" are extremely stylized. Examples: *Sayonara Zetsubo Sensei* or *Byosoku 5 Centimetre.*

Demographic

Demographic describes the intended target audience.

- *Shojo* is Japanese for "young lady" or "little girl." These are generally targeted at girls. Examples: *Fruits Basket* or *Mermaid Melody Pichi Pichi Pitch.*
- *Shonen* is Japanese for "young boy." Examples: *Dragon Ball Z* or *Digimon.*
- *Seinen* is Japanese for "young man" and normally includes teenage or young male adults. Examples: *Oh My Goddess!* or *Cowboy Bebop.*
- *Josei* is Japanese for "young woman." Examples: *Gokusen* or *Honey and Clover.*
- *Kodomo* is Japanese for "child." All children's series fall into this category. Examples: *Hello Kitty.*

Thematic

- ***Bishojo*** is Japanese for "beautiful girl." A blanket term that features pretty girl characters. Sometimes conflated with *Moè.* Examples: *Magic Knight Rayearth* or *Negima.*
- ***Bishonen*** is Japanese for "beautiful boy." A blanket term that can be used to describe any anime that features "pretty" and elegant boys and men. Examples: *Fushigi Yugi* or most CLAMP shows.
- ***Sentai*** is literally a "fighting team" in Japanese. It refers to any show that involves a superhero team. Examples: *Cyborg 009* or *Voltron.*
- **Robot/Mecha** features super robots. Examples: *Mobile Suit Gundam* or *Mazinger Z.*

- **Post-Apocalyptic** simply deals with a post-apocalyptic world. Examples: *Fist of the North Star* or *Nausicaä of the Valley of the Wind.*
- ***Maho shojo*** is a subgenre of *shojo* known for "Magical Girl" stories. Examples: *Sailor Moon* or *Cardcaptor Sakura.*
- ***Maho shonen*** is a male equivalent of *Maho Shojo*. Examples: *D.N. Angel.*
- ***Moé*** features characters with perky, cute, weak, or naivè behaviours. In some way, they are not overly independent. Examples: *A Little Snow Fairy Sugar.*
- **Expertise** specializes with a specific topic in depth. Topics range from sports, the arts, and cooking. Examples: *Eyeshield 21* with football, or *Yakitate! Japan* with bread-making.
- **Lolicon** ("Lolita Complex") is the sexualization of under-aged female characters, the name coming from the titular character of Vladimir Nabokov's *Lolita*. Example: *Kodomo no Jikan.*
- **Shotacon** ("Shotaro Complex") is the sexualization of under-aged male characters, the name coming from the lead child actor from *Tetsujin-nijuhachi-go*. Example: *Papa to Kiss in the Dark.*
- **Harem** is a genre which focuses on a male character surrounded by the romance of multiple female characters. Typically, the male cohabits with at least one female. It is usually marketed as a Shonen or Seinen. Examples: *Ranma ½* or *Love Hina.*
- **Reverse Harem** reverses the gender balance in harem, where a female character is romantically involved with many male characters. It is more often than not a Shojo or Josei Anime. Examples: *Ouran High School Host Club* or *Fruits Basket.*
- **Magical Girlfriend** is more accurately termed **Exotic Girlfriend**. This genre focuses on the romantic relationship (and cohabitation) between a man and at least one woman of extraordinary origins such as alien (*Tenchi Muyo!*, *Urusei Yatsura*), supernatural (*Oh My Goddess!*), or technological (*Chobits*). Often considered a subgenre of Harem.
- ***Ecchi*** is Japanese for "indecent sexuality", derived from the Japanese pronunciation of the letter "H" (the origin of the term is not well known, even in Japan.) Sexual humor and fan service are prevalent. Examples: *Oruchuban Ebichu* or *He Is My Master.*
- ***Hentai*** is Japanese for "abnormal" or "perverted." This term is synonymous to pornography or erotica, as *hentai* content specifically consists of such. Examples: *La Blue Girl* or *Bible Black.*
- ***Shojo-ai or Yuri*** is Japanese for "girl-love." These focus on love and romance between female characters. It is often being replaced by the term "Girls Love" (GL). *Yuri* is like *Shojo-ai,* but sometimes involves older characters or explicit sexual activity. Examples: *Revolutionary Girl Utena* or *Kannazuki no Miko.*
- Shonen-ai is Japanese for 'boy-love.' These focus on love and romance between male characters. The term "Shonen-ai" is being phased out in Japan due to its other meaning of pederasty, and is being replaced by the term "Boys Love" (BL). Examples: *Loveless* or *Gravitation.*
- Yaoi is like "Shonen-ai" but often involving older characters and explicit sexual activity. Examples: *Sensitive Pornograph.*

Distribution

While anime had entered markets beyond Japan in the 1960s, it grew as a major cultural export during its market expansion during the 1980s and 1990s. The anime market for the United States alone is "worth approximately $4.35 billion, according to the Japan External Trade Organization." Anime has also been a commercial success in Asia, Europe and Latin America, where anime has become even more mainstream than in the United States. For example, the *Saint Seiya* video game was released in Europe due to the popularity of the show even years after the series has been off-air.

Anime distribution companies handled the licensing and distribution of anime beyond Japan. Licensed anime is modified by distributors through dubbing into the language of the country and adding language subtitles to the Japanese language track. Using a similar global distribution pattern as Hollywood, the world is divided into five regions.

Some editing of cultural references may occur to better follow the references of the non-Japanese culture. Certain companies may remove any objectionable content, complying with domestic law. This editing process was far more prevalent in the past (e.g. Robotech), but its use has declined because of the demand for anime in its original form. This "light touch" approach to localization has favoured viewers formerly unfamiliar with anime. The use of such methods is evident by the success of Naruto, and Cartoon Network's Adult Swim programming block, both of which employ minor edits.

With the advent of DVD, it was possible to include multiple language tracks into a simple product. This was not the case with VHS cassette, in which separate VHS media were used and with each VHS cassette priced the same as a single DVD. The "light touch" approach also applies to DVD releases as they often include both the dubbed audio and the original Japanese audio with subtitles, typically unedited. Anime edited for television is usually released on DVD "uncut," with all scenes intact.

TV networks regularly broadcast anime programming. In Japan, major national TV networks, such as TV Tokyo broadcast anime regularly. Smaller regional stations broadcast anime under the UHF. In the United States, Cable TV channels such as Cartoon Network, Disney, Sci-Fi, and others dedicate some of their time slots for anime. Then the Anime Network specifically shows anime. Sony based Animax and Disney's Jetix channel broadcast anime within many countries in the world.

Although it is a violation of copyright laws in many countries, some fans add subtitles to anime on their own. These are distributed as fansubs. The ethical implications of producing, distributing, or watching fansubs are topics of much controversy even when fansub groups do not profit from their activities. Once the series has been licensed outside of Japan, fansub groups often cease distribution of their work. In one case, Media Factory Incorporated requested that no fansubs of their material be made, which was respected by the fansub community. In another instance, Bandai specifically thanked fansubbers for their role in helping to make *The Melancholy of Haruhi Suzumiya* popular in the English speaking world.

The Internet had played a significant role in the exposure of anime beyond Japan. Prior to the 1990s, anime has had limited exposure beyond Japan's borders. Coincidentally, as the popularity of the Internet grew, so did for anime. Much of the fandom of anime grew through the Internet. The combination of Internet communities and increasing amounts of anime material, from video to images, helped spur the growth of fandom. As the Internet gained more widespread use, Internet advertising revenues grew from 1.6 billion yen to over 180 billion yen between 1995 and 2005.

Influence on Western Culture

Anime has become commercially profitable in western countries as early commercially successful western adaptations of anime, such as *Astro Boy*, have revealed. The phenomenal success of Nintendo's multi-billion dollar Pokémon franchise was helped greatly by the spin-off anime series that, first broadcast in the late 1990s, is still running worldwide to this day. In doing so, anime has made significant impacts upon Western culture.

Since the 19th century, many Westerners have expressed a particular interest towards Japan. Anime dramatically exposed more Westerners to the culture of Japan. Aside from anime, other facets of Japanese culture increased in popularity. Worldwide, the number of people studying Japanese increased. In 1984, the Japanese Language Profiency test was devised to meet increasing demand.

Anime-influenced animation refers to non-Japanese works of animation that emulate the visual style of anime. Most of these works are created by studios in the United States, Europe, and non-Japanese Asia; and they generally incorporate stylizations, methods, and gags described in anime physics. In the case of *Avatar: The Last Airbender*. Often, production crews either are fans of anime or are required to view anime. Some creators cite anime as a source of inspiration with their own series. Furthermore, a French production team for *Oban Star-Racers* moved to Tokyo to collaborate with a Japanese production team from Hal Film Maker. Critics and the general anime fanbase do not consider them as anime.

Some American animated television series have singled out anime styling with satirical intent, for example *South Park* (with "Chinpokomon" and "Good Times With Weapons"). *South Park* has a notable drawing style, which was itself parodied in "Brittle Bullet", the fifth episode of the anime *FLCL*, released several months after "Chinpokomon" aired. This intent on satirizing anime is the springboard for the basic premise of Kappa Mikey, a Nicktoons Network original cartoon. Even cliches normally found in anime are parodied in Perfect Hair Forever.

Anime conventions began to appear in the early 1990s, starting with Anime Expo, Animethon, Otakon, and JACON. Currently anime conventions are held annually in various cities across North America, Asia, and Europe. Many attendees participate in cosplay, where they dress up as anime characters. Also, guests from Japan ranging from artists, directors, and music groups are invited.

AVAR (ANIMATION VARIABLE)

An *avar* or *animation variable* is a variable controlling the position of part of an animated object, such as a character. The character "Woody" in Pixar's movie Toy Story uses 700 avars (with 100 in the face alone). Successive sets of Avars control all movement of the character from frame to frame. In development, they are used to define the junctions of a stick model. Later, they are incorporated into a full wire frame model or a model built of polygons.

Finally, surfaces are added, requiring a lengthy process of rendering to produce the final scene.

There are several ways of generating the Avar values. Motion capture uses lights or markers on a real person acting out the part, tracked by a video camera. Toy Story uses no motion capture, probably because manual control by a skilled animator can produce effects not easily carried out by a human actor.

Understandings Computer Animation

Computer animation is the art of creating moving images via the use of computers. It is a subfield of computer graphics and animation. Increasingly it is created by means of 3D computer graphics, though 2D computer graphics are still widely used for low bandwidth and faster real-time rendering needs. Sometimes the target of the animation is the computer itself, but it sometimes the target is another medium, such as film. It is also referred to as CGI (Computer-generated imagery or computer-generated imaging), especially when used in films.

To create the illusion of movement, an image is displayed on the computer screen then quickly replaced by a new image that is similar to the previous image, but shifted slightly. This technique is identical to how the illusion of movement is achieved with television and motion pictures.

Computer animation is essentially a digital successor to the art of stop motion animation of 3D models and frame-by-frame animation of 2D illustrations. For 3D animations, objects (models) are built on the computer monitor (modeled) and 3D figures are rigged with a virtual skeleton. For 2D figure animations, separate objects (illustrations) and separate transparent layers are used, with or without a virtual skeleton. Then the limbs, eyes, mouth, clothes, etc. of the figure are moved by the animator on key frames. The differences in appearance between key frames are automatically calculated by the computer in a process known as tweening or morphing. Finally, the animation is rendered.

For 3D animations, all frames must be rendered after modeling is complete. For 2D vector animations, the rendering process is the key frame illustration process, while tweened frames are rendered as needed. For pre-recorded presentations, the rendered frames are transferred to a different format or medium such as film or digital video. The frames may also be rendered in real time as they are presented to the end-user audience. Low bandwidth animations transmitted via the Internet (e.g. 2D Flash, X3D) often use software on the end-users computer to render in real time as an alternative to streaming or pre-loaded high bandwidth animations.

A Simple Example

The screen is blanked to a background color, such as black. Then a goat is drawn on the right of the screen. Next the screen is blanked, but the goat is re-drawn or duplicated slightly to the left of its original position. This process is repeated, each time moving the goat a bit to the left. If this process is repeated fast enough the goat will appear to move smoothly to the left. This basic procedure is used for all moving pictures in films and television.

The moving goat is an example of shifting the location of an object. More complex transformations of object properties such as size, shape, lighting effects and color often require calculations and computer rendering instead of simple re-drawing or duplication.

Explanation

To trick the eye and brain into thinking they are seeing a smoothly moving object, the pictures should be drawn at around 12 frames per second or faster (a frame is one complete image). With rates above 70 frames/s no improvement in realism or smoothness is perceivable due to the way the eye and brain process images. At rates below 12 frames/s most people can detect jerkiness associated with the drawing of new images which detracts from the illusion of realistic movement. Conventional hand-drawn cartoon animation often uses 15 frames per second in order to save on the number of drawings needed, but this is usually accepted because of the stylized nature of cartoons. Because it produces more realistic imagery computer animation demands higher frame rates to reinforce this realism.

The reason no jerkiness is seen at higher speeds is due to "persistence of vision." From moment to moment, the eye and brain working together actually store whatever you look at for a fraction of a second, and automatically "smooth out" minor jumps. Movie film seen in theatres in the United States runs at 24 frames per second, which is sufficient to create this illusion of continuous movement.

Methods of Animating Virtual Characters

In most 3D computer animation systems, an animator creates a simplified representation of a character's anatomy, analogous to a skeleton or stick figure. The position of each segment of the skeletal model is defined by *animation variables,* or Avars.

In human and animal characters, many parts of the skeletal model correspond to actual bones, but skeletal animation is also used to animate other things, such as facial features (though other methods for facial animation exist). The character "Woody" in *Toy Story,* for example, uses 700 Avars, including 100 Avars in the face. The computer does not usually render the skeletal model directly (it is invisible), but uses the skeletal model to compute the exact position and orientation of the character, which is eventually rendered into an image. Thus by changing the values of Avars over time, the animator creates motion by making the character move from frame to frame.

There are several methods for generating the Avar values to obtain realistic motion. Traditionally, animators manipulate the Avars directly. Rather than set Avars for every frame, they usually set Avars at strategic points (frames) in time and let the computer interpolate or 'tween' between them, a process called keyframing. Keyframing puts control in the hands of the animator, and has roots in hand-drawn traditional animation.

In contrast, a newer method called motion capture makes use of live action. When computer animation is driven by motion capture, a real performer acts out the scene as if they were the character to be animated. His or her motion is recorded to a computer using video cameras and markers, and that performance is then applied to the animated character.

Each method has their advantages, and as of 2007, games and films are using either or both of these methods in productions. Keyframe animation can produce motions that would be difficult or impossible to act out, while motion capture can reproduce the subtleties of a particular actor. For example, in the 2006 film Pirates of the Caribbean: Dead Man's Chest, actor Bill Nighy provided the performance for the character Davy Jones. Even though Nighy himself does not appear in the film, the movie benefited from his performance by recording the nuances of his body language, posture, facial expressions, etc. Thus motion capture is appropriate in situations where believable, realistic behaviour and action is required, but the types of characters required exceed what can be done through conventional costuming.

Computer Animation Development Equipment

Computer animation can be created with a computer and animation software. Some examples of animation software are: Amorphium, Art of Illusion, Poser, Ray Dream Studio, Bryce, Maya, Blender, TrueSpace, Lightwave, 3D Studio Max, SoftImage XSI, Alice, and Adobe Flash (2D). There are many more. Prices will vary greatly depending on target market. Some impressive animation can be achieved even with basic programs; however, the rendering can take a lot of time on an ordinary home computer. Because of this, video game animators tend to use low resolution, low polygon count renders, such that the graphics can be rendered in real time on a home computer. Photorealistic animation would be impractical in this context.

Professional animators of movies, television, and video sequences on computer games make photorealistic animation with high detail. This level of quality for movie animation would take tens to hundreds of years to create on a home computer. Many powerful workstation computers are used instead. Graphics workstation computers use two to four processors, and thus are a lot more powerful than a home computer, and are specialized for rendering. A large number of workstations (known as a render farm) are networked together to effectively act as a giant computer. The result is a computer animated movie that can be completed in about one to five years (this process is not comprised solely of rendering, however). A workstation typically costs $2,000 to $16,000, with the more expensive stations being able to render much faster, due to the more technologically advanced hardware that they contain. Pixar's Renderman is rendering software which is widely used as the movie animation industry standard, in competition with Mental Ray. It can be bought at the official Pixar website for about $5,000 to $8,000. It will work on Linux, Mac OS X, and Microsoft Windows based graphics workstations along with an animation program such as Maya and Softimage XSI. Professionals also use digital movie cameras, motion capture or performance capture, bluescreens, film editing software, props, and other tools for movie animation.

Hardware Animation Display Technology

When an image is rendered to the screen, it is normally rendered to something called a back buffer. There the computer can draw the image, making any necessary changes to it before it is done. While the computer is rendering, the screen is showing the contents of what is called the primary or active buffer.

When the image is completed, the computer tells the screen to draw from the back buffer. This can be done in one of two ways: the contents of the back buffer can be copied to the primary buffer (or active buffer—the buffer which is currently being shown) or the computer can switch where it is drawing from and make the back buffer the new primary buffer. In this case, the primary buffer becomes the back buffer. John MacArthur is the one that thought up this process. This process is usually called double buffering or, informally, "flipping," because the computer is flipping its use of primary and back buffers.

This switching should be carried out when it is imperceptible to the user. Therefore it needs to take place during what is called the "v-sync" or vertical retrace. The v-sync, in CRTs, takes place when the electron guns reach the bottom right of the screen and need to reposition the beam to the top left of the screen. This happens very quickly and the image the guns had just projected remain on the screen as they are moving back to their starting position. While the guns are repositioning themselves, the computer has enough time to flip buffers and the new image will be rendered on the screen on the next pass of the guns. The new image will continued to be displayed until the buffers are flipped once more.

When the computer fails to wait for the v-sync, a condition called sprite breakup or image breakup is perceptible. This is highly undesirable and should always be avoided when possible to maintain the illusion of movement.

The Future

One open challenge in computer animation is a photorealistic animation of humans. Currently, most computer-animated movies show animal characters (*Finding Nemo*), fantasy characters (*Shrek, Monsters Inc.*), anthropomorphic machines (*Cars, Robots*) or cartoon-like humans (*The Incredibles*). The movie *Final Fantasy: The Spirits Within* is often cited as the first computer-generated movie to attempt to show realistic-looking humans. However, due to the enormous complexity of the human body, human motion, and human biomechanics, realistic simulation of humans remains largely an open problem. (Of course, all animals have great complexity, but as humans, we are more aware of the nuances in representations of humans.) It is one of the "holy grails" of computer animation. Eventually, the goal is to create software where the animator can generate a movie sequence showing a photorealistic human character, undergoing physically-plausible motion, together with clothes, photorealistic hair, a complicated natural background, and possibly interacting with other simulated human characters. This could be done in a way that the viewer is no longer able to tell if a particular movie sequence is computer-generated, or created using real actors in front of movie-cameras. Complete human realism is not likely to happen very soon, however such concepts obviously bear certain philosophical implications for the future of the film industry.

For the moment it looks like three dimensional computer animation can be divided into two main directions—photorealistic and non-photorealistic rendering. Photorealistic computer animation can itself be divided into two subcategories: real photorealism (where performance capture is used in the creation of the virtual human characters), and stylized photorealism. Real photorealism is what Final Fantasy tried to achieve and will in the future most likely have the ability to give us live action fantasy features as *The Dark Crystal* without having to use advanced puppetry and animatronics, while *Antz* is an example on stylistic photorealism (in the future stylized photorealism will be able to replace traditional stop motion animation as in *Corpse Bride*). None of them are as mentioned perfected yet, but the progress continues.

The non-photorealistic/cartoonish direction is more like an extension of traditional animation, an attempt to make the animation look like a three dimensional version of a cartoon, still using and perfecting the main principles of animation articulated by the Nine Old Men, such as squash and stretch.

While a single frame from a photorealistic computer animated feature will look like a photo if done right, a single frame vector from a cartoonish computer animated feature will look like a painting (not to be confused with cel shading, which produces an ever simpler look).

Detailed Examples and Pseudocode

In 2D computer animation, moving objects are often referred to as "sprites." A sprite is an image that has a location associated with it. The location of the sprite is changed slightly, between each displayed frame, to make the sprite appear to move. The following pseudocode makes a sprite move from left to right:

```
var int x:= 0, y:= screenHeight &div; 2;
while x < screenWidth
drawBackground()
drawSpriteAtXY (x, y) / / draw on top of the background
x : = x + 5 // move to the right
```

Modern (2001) computer animation uses different techniques to produce animations. Most frequently, sophisticated mathematics is used to manipulate complex three dimensional polygons, apply "textures", lighting and other effects to the polygons and finally rendering the complete image. A sophisticated graphical user interface may be used to create the animation and arrange its choreography. Another technique called constructive solid geometry defines objects by conducting boolean operations on regular shapes, and has the advantage that animations may be accurately produced at any resolution.

Let us step through the rendering of a simple image of a room with flat wood walls with a grey pyramid in the center of the room. The pyramid will have a spotlight shining on it. Each wall, the floor and the ceiling is a simple polygon, in this case, a rectangle. Each corner of the rectangle is defined by three values referred to as X, Y and Z. X is how far left and right the point is. Y is how far up and down the point is, and Z is far in and out of the screen the point is. The wall nearest us would be defined by four points: (in the order x, y, z). Below is a representation of how the wall is defined.

(0, 10, 0) (10, 10, 0)
(0,0,0) (10, 0, 0)

The far wall would be:

(0, 10, 20) (10, 10, 20)
(0, 0, 20) (10, 0, 20)

The pyramid is made up of five polygons: the rectangular base, and four triangular sides. To draw this image the computer uses math to calculate how to project this image, defined by three dimensional data, onto a two dimensional computer screen.

First we must also define where our view point is, that is, from what vantage point will the scene be drawn. Our view point is inside the room a bit above the floor, directly in front of the pyramid. First the computer will calculate which polygons are visible. The near wall will not be displayed at all, as it is behind our view point. The far side of the pyramid will also not be drawn as it is hidden by the front of the pyramid.

Next each point is perspective projected onto the screen. The portions of the walls 'farthest' from the view point will appear to be shorter than the nearer areas due to perspective. To make the walls look like wood, a wood pattern, called a texture, will be drawn on them. To accomplish this, a technique called "texture mapping" is often used. A small drawing of wood that can be repeatedly drawn in a matching tiled pattern (like wallpaper) is stretched and drawn onto the walls' final shape. The pyramid is solid grey so its surfaces can just be rendered as grey. But we also have a spotlight. Where its light falls we lighten colors, where objects blocks the light we darken colors.

Next we render the complete scene on the computer screen. If the numbers describing the position of the pyramid were changed and this process repeated, the pyramid would appear to move.

Movies

CGI short films have been produced as independent animation since 1976, though the popularity of computer animation (especially in the field of special effects) skyrocketed during the modern era of U.S. animation. The first completely computer-generated animated movie was *Toy Story*.

Amateur Animation

The popularity of sites such as YouTube, which allows members to upload their own movies for others to view, has created a growing number of what is often considered amateur computer animators. With many free utilities available and programs such as Windows Movie Maker, anyone with the tools can have their animation viewed by thousands. One way to create amateur animation is using the GIF format, which can be uploaded and seen on the web easily. GIF animating software include Beneton Movie GIF, GIF Movie Gear, Ulead GIF Animator, and more.

Architectural Animation

Architects use services from animation companies to create a 3-dimensional models for both the customers and builders. It can be more accurate than traditional drawings. Architectural animation can also be used to see the possible relationship the building will have in relation to the environment and its surrounding buildings.

Adult Animation

Adult animation is animation that is targeted at adults. For western audiences, the primary reason for a program to be described as "adult animation" is adult humor. Popular programs such as FOX's *The Simpsons* and *Family Guy* contain humor that some parents might find unsuitable for children. However, adult humor can be innocuous as well, and simply above an average child's ability to appreciate, as is the case in many early theatrical cartoon series, such as *Looney Tunes* and *Popeye*, as well as in many modern TV cartoon series, such as *Animaniacs*, *The Powerpuff Girls* and *SpongeBob SquarePants*. These cartoons will often contain slapstick comedy for children, but also jokes which can be appreciated only by older audiences, such as pop-culture references, political satire and sexual innuendos. Some animated series, such as Max Fleischer's *Betty Boop* cartoons of the 1930s and Nickelodeon's *Ren and Stimpy* series, walk the line between both types of adult humor.

Graphic violence is a consideration; many Japanese anime contain graphic violence, such as *Akira* and *Neon Genesis Evangelion*, but also some western programs, such as HBO's *Spawn* and MTV's *Æon Flux*, contain violence which is considered unsuitable for children.

Swearing is another reason why programs garner this label. Comedy Central's *South Park* and *Drawn Together* are good examples.

Nudity is not commonplace among American animated programs, but it can be a consideration in some theatrical releases.

Strong sexual content is another template of adult animation. Many films, such as the works of Ralph Bakshi, contain all of these factors, and some examples of "adult animation" were originally released with the X rating in the United States.

Another reason is that a program or movie might contain animated pornography. This is virtually unheard of in American television, but there is a growing section of the population which consumes domestically produced direct-to-video animated pornography, and imported programs and movies from around the world. Animated pornography is produced worldwide, but the best known variety is the Japanese genre, known as Hentai.

It should be noted that prior to the advent of television in the late 1940s, animated films in general were not seen as being primarily for children. In other words, animation that might be viewed upon as "Children's entertainment" today, such as the Disney films or the aforementioned *Looney Tunes* shorts for example, was originally intended for adults and children alike.

Below is a list of programs which might be considered "adult animation" due to one or more of the above reasons. Note that this list only contains programs which are *solely* intended for an adult audience (and are promoted as such) and not programs that are intended for children and adults alike.

Television

"Commissioning Network" mean the network that supplied the bulk of the capital to produce the series, and therefore has a lot of power over it. This is almost always the first network to screen a series.

Name	Commissioning Network	Country of Origin
12 oz. Mouse	Adult Swim (Cartoon Network)	US
2DTV	ITV	UK
3-South	MTV	US
Aaagh! It's the Mr. Hell Show	BBC Two	Canada/UK
Æon Flux	MTV	US
Afro Samurai	Spike TV	Japan
American Dad!	FOX	US
Angry Kid	BBC Three	UK
Aqua Teen Hunger Force	Adult Swim (Cartoon Network)	US
Assy McGee	Adult Swim (Cartoon Network)	US
Baby Blues	The WB	US
Balls (Cartoon)	YouTube	UK
Beavis and Butt-head	MTV	US
Blood+	Adult Swim (Cartoon Network)	Japan
Blue Gender	Adult Swim (Cartoon Network)	Japan
Bob and Margaret	Channel 4 UK	Canada/UK
The Boondocks	Adult Swim (Cartoon Network)	US
The Brak Show	Adult Swim (Cartoon Network)	US
Bromwell High	Channel 4 UK	UK/Canada
The Brothers Grunt	MTV	US
Bro'Town	TV3 NZ	NZ
Celebrity Deathmatch	MTV	US
Chilly Beach	CBC	Canada
Clerks	ABC US	US
Clone High	MTV	Canada/US
Cnex (also Cnex Bach)	S4C	UK
Code Monkeys	G4	US
Cowboy Bebop	Adult Swim (Cartoon Network)	Japan
Crapston Villas	Channel 4 UK	UK
The Critic	ABC, FOX	US
The Cunning Little Vixen	BBC	UK
Daria	MTV	US
Delta State	France 2	France/Canada
Dilbert	UPN	US
Dr. Katz, Professional Therapist	Comedy Central	US
Dogshitter Wants	MTV2	US
Downtown	MTV	US
Drawn Together	Comedy Central	US
The Drinky Crow Show	Adult Swim (Cartoon Network)	US
Duckman	USA Network	US
Earth Girl Arjuna	TV Tokyo, Animax	Japan
Elfen Lied	TV Tokyo	Japan
Ergo Proxy	WOWOW	Japan
Ed, Edd n Eddy	Cartoon Network	US
Family Guy	FOX TBS Adult Swim	US
Father of the Pride	NBC	US
Fat Sluts	Men & Motors	UK
Fish Police	CBS	US
The Flintstones (1960-66)	ABC	US
FLCL	Adult Swim (Cartoon Network)	Japan
Freak Show	Comedy Central	US

(Contd.)

Name	Commissioning Network	Country of Origin
Frisky Dingo	Adult Swim (Cartoon Network)	US
Futurama	FOX	US
G4's Late Night Peepshow	G4	US
Game Over	UPN	US
Gantz	Fuji Television	Japan
Gary & Mike	UPN	US
Gary the Rat	Spike TV	US
Gary Larson's Tales From The Far Side	CBS	US
Ghost in the Shell: Stand Alone Complex	Animax, Cartoon Network	Japan
Ghost in the Shell: S.A.C. 2nd GIG	Nippon TV, Animax, Cartoon Network	Japan
God, The Devil and Bob	NBC	US
The God & Devil Show	Mondo Mini Shows	US
The Groovenians	Adult Swim (Cartoon Network)	US
Happy Tree Friends	G4, self published by Mondo Mini Shows	US
Harvey Birdman, Attorney at Law	Adult Swim (Cartoon Network)	US
The Head	MTV	US
Higurashi no Naku Koro ni	Chiba TV, Kansai TV, Tokai TV	Japan
Hobbies	BBC Three	UK
Home Movies	UPN	US
The House of Morecock	Self Published	US
Human Contraptions	ABC Australia	Australia
I Am Not an Animal	BBC Two	UK
King of the Hill	FOX	US
Korgoth of Barbaria	Adult Swim (Cartoon Network)	US
Lil' Bush	Comedy Central	US
Liquid Television	MTV	US
Little Johnny Show	Self Published	US
Lucy, the Daughter of the Devil	Adult Swim (Cartoon Network)	US
Macross	Mainichi Broadcasting	Japan
Macross 7	Mainichi Broadcasting	Japan
Macross Plus	Studio Nue	Japan
Malcom and Melvin	Cartoon Network	US
The Maxx	MTV	US
Metalocalypse	Adult Swim (Cartoon Network)	US
Minoriteam	Adult Swim (Cartoon Network)	US
Mission Hill	The WB/Adult Swim (Cartoon Network)	US
Monkey Dust	BBC Three	UK
Moral Orel	Adult Swim (Cartoon Network)	US
Neon Genesis Evangelion	TV Tokyo	Japan
The Oblongs	The WB	US
Paranoia Agent	Adult Swim (Cartoon Network)	Japan
Penguins Behind Bars	Adult Swim (Cartoon Network)	US
Perfect Hair Forever	Adult Swim (Cartoon Network)	US
The PJs	FOX, The WB	US
Pond Life	Channel 4 UK	UK
Popetown	BBC Three	UK
Problems	DR2	Danmark
Quads!	SBS Australia	Australia/Canada
Queer Duck	Icebox.com, Showtime US	US
RahXephon	Fuji Television	Japan
Record of Lodoss War	Bandai Visual, TV Tokyo	Japan
Reign: The Conqueror	Adult Swim (Cartoon Network)	Japan

(Contd.)

Name	*Commissioning Network*	*Country of Origin*
The Ripping Friends	Adult Swim (Cartoon Network)	US
The Ren and Stimpy Show	Nickelodeon	US
Ren and Stimpy Adult Party Cartoon	Spike TV	US
Rex the Runt	BBC Two	UK
Robot Chicken	Adult Swim (Cartoon Network)	US
Robotech	Television syndication	US/Japan
Rocko's Modern Life	Nickelodeon	US
Samurai Champloo	Adult Swim (Cartoon Network)	Japan
s-CRY-ed	Adult Swim (Cartoon Network)	Japan
Saddle Rash	Adult Swim (Cartoon Network)	US
Sealab 2021	Adult Swim (Cartoon Network)	US
Shorties Watchin' Shorties	Comedy Central	US
The Simpsons	FOX	US
Sons of Butcher	The Detour (Teletoon)	Canada
South Park	Comedy Central	US
Space Ghost Coast to Coast	Adult Swim (Cartoon Network)	US
Spawn	HBO	US
Spicy City	HBO	US
Shin Chan	Jetix UK/Adult Swim	UK/US/Japan
Squidbillies	Adult Swim (Cartoon Network)	US
Starveillance	E!	US
Station X	The Detour (Teletoon)	Canada
Stressed Eric	BBC Two	UK
Stripperella	Spike TV	US
Stroker and Hoop	Adult Swim (Cartoon Network)	US
Superjail	Adult Swim (Cartoon Network)	US
The Super Milk-chan Show	Adult Swim (Cartoon Network)	US
SuperNews	Current TV	US
Texhnolyze	Fuji Television, Animax	Japan
That Crook'd 'Sipp	Adult Swim (Cartoon Network)	US
This Just In!	Spike TV	US
Tokko	Kodansha	Japan
Tom Goes to the Mayor	Adult Swim (Cartoon Network)	US
Tomorrow's Joe	Fuji Television	Japan
Trigun	TV Tokyo, Cartoon Network	Japan
Trinity Blood	Adult Swim (Cartoon Network)	Japan
Tripping the Rift	Sci Fi Channel	US
TV Funhouse	NBC, Comedy Central	US
Two Posh Old Men	UKTV	UK
The Grim Adventures of Billy and Mandy	Cartoon Network	US
Undergrads	MTV	US
The Venture Bros.	Adult Swim (Cartoon Network)	US
VH1 ILL-ustrated	VH1	US
Welcome to the NHK	Various Japanese Broadcast Networks	Japan
Welcome to Eltingville	Adult Swim (Cartoon Network)	US
Where My Dogs At?	MTV2	US
Who I Am And What I Want	Channel 4	UK
Witch Hunter Robin	Adult Swim (Cartoon Network)	Japan
Wonder Showzen	MTV2	US
The Wrong Coast	The Movie Network	Canada
Yukikaze	Animax	Japan

(Contd.)

Name	Commissioning Network	Country of Origin
YuYu Hakusho	Adult Swim (Cartoon Network)	Japan
Zeroman	The Detour (Teletoon)	Canada

Movies

Country	Name	Year
US	Eveready Harton in Buried Treasure	c. 1928
US	Betty Boop	1932-1939
US	Coal Black and de Sebben Dwarfs	1943
UK	Animal Farm	1954
Italy	West and Soda	1965
Japan	One Thousand and One Arabian Nights	1969
Japan	Kureopatora	1970
US	Fritz the Cat	1972
US	Erotic Cartoon Festival	1973
US	Heavy Traffic	1973
US	The Nine Lives of Fritz the Cat	1974
US	Down and Dirty Duck	1974
Belgium	Tarzoon: Shame of the Jungle	1975
US	Coonskin	1975
US	Bucky Beaver's Triple XXX Rated Cartoon Show!	1928-1970s
US	Once Upon a Girl	1976
US	Wizards	1977
Italy	Allegro non troppo	1977
UK	Watership Down	1978
Hungary	Foam Bath	1979
Belgium	B.C. Rock	1980
US	Chuck Vincent's Erotic Animation Festival	1980
Canada	Heavy Metal	1981
France	Time Masters	1981
US	American Pop	1981
Australia	Grendel Grendel Grendel	1981
US	Hey Good Looking	1982
Italy	Little Dick, The Mighty Midget	1982
UK	The Plague Dogs	1982
US	Fire and Ice	1983
Japan	Golgo 13	1983
Canada	Rock & Rule	1983
Cuba	Vampires in Havana	1985
Czechoslovakia	Krysar	1985
UK	When the Wind Blows	1986
US	The Amazing Mr. Bickford	1987
Belgium	The Big Bang	1987
USSR	Laughter and Grief by the White Sea	1987
Japan	Wicked City	1987
Japan	Akira	1988
Japan	Grave of the Fireflies	1988
France	Light Years	1988
US	Who Framed Roger Rabbit	1988
Germany	Werner-Leg Hard!	1990

(Contd.)

Country	Name	Year
US	Spike and Mike's Sick and Twisted Festival of Animation	1990
Ukraine	Eneida	1991
US	Cool World	1992
Japan	La Blue Girl	1992
US	The Tune	1992
Japan	Ninja Scroll	1993
US	The Thief and the Cobbler (original version)	1993
South Korea	Blue Seagull	1994
Germany	Felidae	1994
Japan	Ghost in the Shell	1995
Germany	Werner-Eat My Dust!!!	1996
US	Beavis and Butt-Head Do America	1996
Japan	Neon Genesis Evangelion: Death and Rebirtn	1997
Japan	The End of Evangelion	1997
Germany	The Little Bastard	1997
US	I Married a Strange Person!	1997
US	Mondo Plympton	1997
Japan	Perfect Blue	1997
France	The Perfume of the Invisible One	1997
Japan	Kite	1998
Japan	Jin-Roh	1998
US	South Park: Bigger, Longer & Uncut	1999
US	Gonad The Barbarian/Search For Uranus	1999
Germany	Werner-Volles Rooäää!!!	1999
Japan	Blood: The Last Vampire	2000
US	Heavy Metal 2000	2000
Japan	Vampire Hunter D: Bloodlust	2000
Japan	Metropolis	2001
US	Mutant Aliens	2001
US	Waking Life	2001
US	Star Ballz: The Movie	2001
Japan	Cowboy Bebop: The Movie	2001
US	Eight Crazy Nights	2002
Japan	Mezzo Forte	2001
US	Private Ninn: 2Funky4U	2002
US	Twisted Tales of Erotic 3D Animation	2002
Canada, France	The Triplets of Belleville	2003
US	The Dream-Quest of Unknown Kadath	2003
Japan	Appleseed	2004
Hungary	The District!	2004
US	Hair High	2004
US	PornoMation	2004
US	Carnal Cartoons	2004
US	Dirty Cartoons	2004
Denmark	Terkel in Trouble	2004
US	Stormy Bangs Betty!	2005
US	Disaster!	2005
Estonia	Frank and Wendy	2005
US	Stewie Griffin: The Untold Story	2005
US	The Princess Has Come of Age	2005
US	Sweet Cheeks	2005
US	A Scanner Darkly	2006

(Contd.)

Country	Name	Year
US	Blood Tea and Red String	2006
Norway	Free Jimmy	2006
US	Queer Duck: The Movie	2006
Germany	The Little Bastard and the Old Fart: Death Sucks	2006
US	Live Freaky! Die Freaky!	2006
Japan	Paprika	2006
Denmark	Princess	2006
Russia	Prince Vladimir	2006
France	Renaissance	2006
Brazil	Wood & Stock: Sexo, Orégano e Rock'n'Roll	2006
US	Aqua Teen Hunger Force Colon Movie Film for Theatres	2007
Czech Republic	One Night in One City Jedné noci v jednom meste	2007
France	Persepolis	2007
US	The Simpsons Movie	2007
US	Beowulf	2007
US	Futurama: Bender's Big Score	2007

Upcoming

Country	Name	Year
Russia	Alien Pile	2007
US	Idiots and Angels	2007
Russia	Krakatuk	2007
US	Futurama: The Beast with a Billion Backs	2008
US	Futurama: Bender's Game	2008
US	Futurama: Into the Wild Green Yonder	2008
US	The Haunted World of El Superbeasto	In Production
UK	Grass Roots	In Production
US	Last Days of Coney Island	In Production
Russia	The Overcoat	In Production
Russia	A Robot Story, or Shoot, Mofucka, Shoot!	In Production

Independent Animation

Independent animation is a term used to describe animated short cartoons and feature films produced outside the professional Hollywood animation industry.

The history of animation is as old as the film industry itself. Independent animators have produced innovative, often experimental, shorts since the silent era.

Because animation is very time-consuming and expensive to produce, the vast majority of animated productions are made by professional studios. When the Hollywood animation industry entered a decline during the 1960s (*see* Hollywood Animation: The TV Era), a small but steady number of independent animation producers kept the art of animation alive. They produced a number of experimental films that pushed the boundaries of the medium, experimenting in ways that Hanna-Barbera and Disney did not dare to consider. A number of independent animation producers went on to produce mainstream animation, and they became successful in their own right.

Many independent animation short films are largely unknown; they are rarely seen outside of independent "art house" movie theatres. Collections of independent films have been gathered for theatrical viewing, and video release, under such titles as the International Tournee of Animation (which existed between about 1966 and the late 1990s) and Spike and Mike's *Classic Festival of Animation* (1977 to 1990) and Spike and Mike's Sick and Twisted Festival of Animation since 1990.

The rise of the Internet in the 1990s and 2000s saw an exponential increase in the production of independent animation. Personal computer power increased to the point where it was possible for a single person to produce an animated cartoon on a home computer, using software such as *Macromedia Flash* or *Autodesk,* and distribute these short films over the World Wide Web. Independently produced Internet cartoons flourished as the popularity of the Web grew, and a number of strange, often hilarious short cartoons were produced for the Web.

In the late 1990s, an independent animated short film called *The Spirit of Christmas* was produced for under $2,000 by two artists, Matt Stone and Trey Parker. This film was widely distributed on the Internet as a pirated cartoon, and its phenomenal popularity gave rise to the popular TV animated series *South Park.*

1930s

- *Spook Short (1939)* by Mary Ellen Bute.

1940s

- *Radio Dynamics (1942)* by Oskar Fischinger.

1950s

- *Color City (1952)* by Len Lye.

1960s

- *The Critic (1963)* by Mel Brooks.
- *Mothlight (1963)* by Stan Brakhage.
- *The Nose (1963)* by Alexander Alexeieff and Claire Parker.
- *Breathdeath (1964)* by Stan Vanderbeek.
- *Cibernetik 5.3 (1960-65)* by John Stehura.
- *Bambi Meets Godzilla* by Marv Newland.

1970s

- *Synchromy (1971)* by Norman McLaren.
- *Train Landscape (1974)* by Jules Engel.
- *Sunstone (1979)* by Ed Emshwiller.
- *Closed Mondays* by Will Vinton.

1980s

- *Calculated Movements (1985)* by Larry Cuba.

- *Luxo Jr. (1986)* by John Lasseter.
- *Tin Toy (1988)* by John Lasseter.
- *Your Face (1987)* by Bill Plympton.
- *A Grand Day Out (1989)* by Nick Park.

1990s

- *Panspermia (1990)* by Karl Sims.
- *Eggy (1991)* by Yoichiro Kawaguchi.
- *Triangle (1994)* by Erica Russell.
- *Third Interpolation (1999)* by Dylan Kendle.
- *Sink (1999)* by Tomioka Satoshi.
- *The Wolfman (1999)* by Tim Hope.

2000s

- *In Absentia (2000)* by Brothers Quay.
- *Monocodes (2000)* by Alexander Rutterford.
- *Bleip: No (2001)* by Pleix.
- *Flow (2001)* by Han Hoogerbrugge.
- *Eyen (2001)* by Jean-Luc Chansay.
- *Aug 16th (2001)* by InsertSilence.
- *Full Moon (2001)* by Paul Glabicki.
- *Homestar Runner* by The Brothers Chaps.
- *Kaze Ghost Warrior* by Timothy Albee.
- *We Are the Strange* by "M dot Strange".

Slideshow Animation

Slideshow animation is a type of animation using images synchronized to music. This is primarily used for comedy tracks.

Traditional Animation

Traditional animation, also referred to as *classical animation, cel animation,* or *hand-drawn animation,* is the oldest and historically the most popular form of animation. In a traditionally-animated cartoon, each frame is drawn by hand.

Storyboards

Traditionally-animated productions, just like other forms of animation, usually begin life as a *storyboard,* which is a script of sorts written with images as well as words, similar to a giant comic strip. The images allow the animation team to plan the flow of the plot and the composition of the imagery. The *storyboard artists* will have regular meetings with the director, and may have to redraw or "re-board" a sequence many times before it meets final approval.

Voice Recording

Before true animation begins, a preliminary soundtrack or "scratch track" is recorded, so that the animation may be more precisely synchronized to the soundtrack. Given the slow, methodical manner in which traditional animation is produced, it is almost always easier to synchronize animation to a pre-existing soundtrack than it is to synchronize a soundtrack to pre-existing animation. A completed cartoon soundtrack will feature music, sound effects, and dialogue performed by voice actors. However, the scratch track used during animation typically contains just the voices, any vocal songs that the characters must sing along to, and temporary musical score tracks; the final score and sound effects are added in post-production.

In the case of most pre-1930 sound animated cartoons, the sound was *post-synched;* that is, the sound track was recorded after the film elements were finished by watching the film and performing the dialogue, music, and sound effects required. Some studios, most notably Fleischer Studios, continued to post-synch their cartoons later, which allowed for the presence of the "muttered ad-libs" present in many *Popeye the Sailor* and *Betty Boop* cartoons. Although virtually all American animation is now pre-synched (and has been since the 1930s), nearly all Japanese animation *(anime)* is post-synched.

Animatics

Often, an *animatic* or *story reel* is made after the soundtrack is created, but before full animation begins. An animatic typically consists of pictures of the storyboard synchronized with the soundtrack. This allows the animators and directors to work out any script and timing issues that may exist with the current storyboard. The storyboard and soundtrack are amended if necessary, and a new animatic may be created and reviewed with the director until the storyboard is perfected. Editing the film at the animatic stage prevents the animation of scenes that would be edited out of the film; as traditional animation is a very expensive and time-consuming process, creating scenes that will eventually be edited out of the completed cartoon is strictly avoided.

In the mid 1970's these were known as Videomatics and used primarily for test commercial projects.

Advertising agencies today employ the use of animatics to test their commercials before they are made into full up spots. Animatics use drawn artwork, with moving pieces (for example, an arm that reaches for a product, or a head that turns). Video storyboards are the same thing as animatics, but do not have moving pieces. Photomatics are another option when creating test spots, but instead of using drawn artwork, there is a shoot in which hundreds of digital photographs are taken. The large amount of images to choose from may make the process of creating a test commercial a bit easier, as opposed to creating an animatic, because changes to drawn art take time and money. Photomatics generally cost more than animatics, as they require a shoot, and on-camera talent.

Design and Timing

Once the animatic has been approved, it and the storyboards are sent to the design departments. Character designers prepare *model sheets* for all important characters and props in the film. These model sheets will show how a character or object looks from a variety of angles with a variety of poses and expressions, so that all artists working on the project can deliver consistent work. Sometimes, small statues known as *maquettes* may be produced, so that an animator can see what a character looks like in three dimensions. At the same time, the *background stylists* will do similar work for the settings and locations in the project, and the *art directors* and *color stylists* will determine the art style and color schemes to be used.

While design is going on, the *timing director* (who in many cases will be the main director) takes the animatic and analyzes exactly what poses, drawings, and lip movements will be needed on what frames. An *exposure sheet* (or *X-sheet* for short) is created; this is a printed table that breaks down the action, dialogue, and sound frame-by-frame as a guide for the animators. If a film is based more strongly in music, a *bar sheet* may be prepared in addition to or instead of an X-sheet. Bar sheets show the relationship between the on-screen action, the dialogue, and the actual musical notation used in the score.

Layout

Layout begins after the designs are completed and approved by the director. The layout process is the same as the blocking out of shots by a cinematographer on a live-action film. It is here that the background layout artists determine the camera angles, camera paths, lighting, and shading of the scene. Character layout artists will determine the major poses for the characters in the scene, and will make a drawing to indicate each pose. For short films, character layouts are often the responsibility of the director.

The layout drawings are spliced into the animatic, using the X-sheet as a guide. Once the animatic is made up of all layout drawings, it is called a *Leica reel*. The term originates from the Disney Studio in the 1930s, from the frame format used by Leica cameras.

Animation

Once the Leica reel is finally approved by the director, animation begins. In the traditional animation process, animators will begin by drawing sequences of animation on sheets of paper perforated to fit the peg bars in their desks, often using colored pencils, one picture or "frame" at a time. A *key animator* or *lead animator* will draw the key drawings in a scene, using the character layouts as a guide. The key animator draws enough of the frames to get across the major points of the action; in a sequence of a character jumping across a gap, the key animator may draw a frame of the character as he is about to leap, two or more frames as the character is flying through the air, and the frame for the character landing on the other side of the gap.

Timing is important for the animators drawing these frames; each frame must match exactly what is going on in the soundtrack at the moment the frame will appear, or else the discrepancy between sound and visual will be distracting to the audience. For example, in high-budget productions, extensive effort is given in making sure a speaking character's mouth matches in shape the sound that character's actor is producing as he or she speaks. (Try making "ah," "ooh" and "ee" sounds out loud, and note how your mouth will subconsciously form a different shape for each sound; good animators must pay attention to such seemingly trivial things).

As they are working on a scene, a key animator will usually prepare a *pencil test* of the scene. A pencil test is a preliminary version of the final animated scene; the pencil drawings are quickly photographed or scanned and synced with the necessary soundtracks. This allows the animation to be reviewed and improved upon before passing the work on to his *assistant animators,* who will go add details and some of the missing frames in the scene. The work of the assistant animators is reviewed, pencil-tested, and corrected until the lead animator is ready to meet with the director and have his scene *sweatboxed,* or reviewed by the director, producer, and other key creative team members. Similar to the storyboarding stage, an animator may be required to re-do a scene many times before the director will approve it.

In high-budget animated productions, often each major character will have an animator or group of animators solely dedicated to drawing that character. The group will be made up of one supervising animator, a small group of key animators, and a larger group of assistant animators. For scenes where two characters interact, the key animators for both characters will decide which character is "leading" the scene, and that character will be drawn first. The second character will be animated to react to and support the actions of the "leading" character.

Once the key animation is approved, the lead animator forwards the scene on to the *clean-up department,* made up of the *clean-up animators* and the *inbetweeners.* The clean-up animators take the lead and assistant animators' drawings and trace them onto a new sheet of paper, taking care in including all of the details present on the original model sheets, so that it appears that one person animated the entire film. The *inbetweeners* will draw in whatever frames are still missing *in between* the other animators' drawings. This procedure is called tweening. The resulting drawings are again pencil-tested and sweatboxed until they meet approval.

At each stage during pencil animation, approved artwork is spliced into the Leica reel.

This process is the same for both *character animation* and *special effects animation,* which on most high-budget productions are done in separate departments. *Effects animators* animate anything that moves and is not a character, including props, vehicles, machinery and phenomena such as fire, rain, and explosions. Sometimes, instead of drawings, a number of special processes are used to produce special effects in animated films; rain, for example, has been created in Disney films since the late-1930s by filming slow-motion footage of water in front of a black background, with the resulting film superimposed over the animation.

Backgrounds

While the animation is being done, the *background artists* will paint the sets over which the action of each animated sequence will take place. These backgrounds are generally done in gouache or acrylic paint, although some animated productions have used backgrounds done in watercolor, oil paint, or even crayon. Background artists follow very closely the work of the background layout artists and color stylists (which is usually compiled into a workbook for their use), so that the resulting backgrounds are harmonious in tone with the character designs.

Traditional Ink-and-Paint and Camera

Once the clean-ups and in between drawings for a sequence are completed, they are prepared for photography, a process known as *ink-and-paint.* Each drawing is then transferred from paper to a thin, clear sheet of plastic called a *cel,* so called because they were once made out of cellulose nitrate (cellulose acetate is now used). The outline of the drawing is inked or photocopied onto the cel, and gouache or a similar type of paint is used on the reverse sides of the cels to add colors in the appropriate shades. In many cases, characters will have more than one color scheme assigned to them; the usage of each one depends upon the mood and lighting of each scene. The transparent quality of the cel allows for each character or object in a frame to be animated on different cels, as the cel of one character can be seen underneath the cel of another; and the opaque background will be seen beneath all of the cels.

When an entire sequence has been transferred to cels, the photography process begins. Each cel involved in a frame of a sequence is laid on top of each other, with the background at the bottom of the stack. A piece of glass is lowered onto the artwork in order to flatten any irregularities, and the composite image is then photographed by a special animation camera, also called rostrum camera. The cels are removed, and the process repeats for the next frame until each frame in the sequence has been photographed. Each cel has *registration holes,* small holes along the top or bottom edge of the cel, which allow the cel to be placed on corresponding peg bars before the camera to ensure that each cel aligns with the one before it; if the cells are not aligned in such a manner, the animation, when played at full speed, will appear "jittery." Sometimes, frames may need to be photographed more than once, in order to implement superimpositions and other camera effects. Pans are created by either moving the cels or backgrounds one step at a time over a succession of frames (the camera does not pan; it only zooms in and out).

As the scenes come out of final photography, they are spliced into the Leica reel, taking the place of the pencil animation. Once every sequence in the production has been photographed, the final film is sent for development and processing, while the final music and sound effects are added to the soundtrack. Again, editing is generally not done in animation, but if it is required it is done at this time, before the final print of the film is ready for duplication or broadcast.

Digital Ink and Paint

It should be noted that the actual "traditional" ink-and-paint process is no longer in use by any major animated productions at present. The current process, termed "digital ink and paint," is the same as traditional ink and paint until after the animation drawings are completed; instead of being transferred to cels, the animators' drawings are scanned into a computer, where they are colored and processed using one or more of a variety of software packages. The resulting drawings are composited in the computer over their respective backgrounds, which have also been scanned into the computer (if not digitally painted), and the computer outputs the final film by either exporting a digital video file, using a video cassette recorder, or printing to film using a high-resolution output device. Use of computers allows for easier exchange of artwork between departments, studios, and even countries and continents (in most low-budget animated productions, the bulk of the animation is actually done by animators working in other countries, including Korea, Japan, Singapore, and India).

The last major feature film to use traditional ink and paint was Studio Ghibli's *Princess Mononoke* (1997); the last animated series to do so was *Ed, Edd n Eddy*. Minor productions such as Hair High (2004) by Bill Plympton have used traditional cels long after the introduction of digital techniques. Digital ink and paint has been in use at Walt Disney Feature Animation since 1989, where it was used for the final rainbow shot in *The Little Mermaid.* All subsequent Disney animated features were digitally inked-and-painted, using Disney's proprietary CAPS (Computer Animation Production System) technology, developed primarily by Pixar (the last Disney feature using CAPS was *Home on the Range*). Most other studios use one of a number of other high-end software packages such as Toonz or Toon Boom Studio, Animo, US Animation and even consumer-level applications such as Macromedia Flash.

Computers and Video Cameras

Computers and video cameras in traditional cel animation can also be used as tools without affecting the film directly, assisting the animators in their work and making the whole process faster and easier. Doing the layouts on a computer is much more effective than doing it the old original way. And video cameras gives the opportunity to see a "sneak preview" of the scenes and how they will look when finished, enabling the animators to correct and improve them without having to complete them first. This can be considered a digital form of *pencil testing*.

Techniques

The Cel and Limited Animation

The cel is an important innovation to traditional animation, as it allows some parts of each frame to be repeated from frame to frame, thus saving labour. A simple example would be a scene with two characters on screen, one of which is talking and the other standing silently. Since the latter character is not moving, it can be displayed in this scene using only one drawing, on one cel, while multiple drawings on multiple cels will be used to animate the speaking character.

For a more complex example, consider, a sequence in which a girl sets a plate upon a table. The table will stay still for the entire sequence, so it can be drawn as part of the background. The plate can be drawn along with the character as the character places it on the table. However, after the plate is on the table, the plate will no longer move, although the girl will continue to move as she draws her arm away from the plate. In this example, after the girl puts the plate down, the plate can then be drawn on a separate cel from the girl. Further frames will feature new cels of the girl, but the plate does not have to be redrawn as it is not moving; the same cel of the plate can be used in each remaining frame that it is still upon the table. The cel paints were actually manufactured in shaded versions of each color to compensate for the extra layer of cel added between the image and the camera, in this example the still plate would be painted slightly brighter to compensate for being moved one layer down.

In very early cartoons made before the use of the cel, such as *Gertie the Dinosaur* (1914), the entire frame, including the background and all characters and items, were drawn on a single sheet of paper, then photographed. Everything had to be redrawn for each frame containing movements. This led to a "jittery" appearance; imagine seeing a sequence of drawings of a mountain, each one slightly different from the one proceeding it. The pre-cel animation was later improved by using techniques like the slash and tear system invented by Raoul Barre; the background and the animated objects were drawn on separate papers. A frame was made by removing all the blank parts of the papers where the objects were drawn before being placed on top of the backgrounds and finally photographed. The cel animation process was invented by Earl Hurd and John Bray in 1915.

In lower-budget productions, this "shortcut" is used in a greater capacity. For example, in a scene in which a man is sitting in a chair and talking, the chair and the body of the man may be the same in every frame; only his head is redrawn, or perhaps even his head stays the same while only his mouth moves. This is known as *limited animation.* The process was popularized in theatrical cartoons by UPA and used in most television animation, especially that of Hanna-Barbera. The end result does not look very lifelike, but is inexpensive to produce, and therefore allows cartoons to be made on small television budgets.

"Shooting on Twos"

Moving characters are often shot "on twos", that is to say, one drawing is shown for every two frames of film (which usually runs at 24 frames per second), meaning there are only 12 drawings per second. Even though the image update rate is low, the fluidity is satisfactory for most subjects. However, when a character is required to perform a quick movement, it is usually necessary to revert to animating "on ones", as "twos" are too slow to convey the motion adequately. A blend of the two techniques keeps the eye fooled without unnecessary production cost.

Animation for most "Saturday morning cartoons" is produced as cheaply as possible, and is most often shot on "threes", or even "fours", i.e. three or four frames per drawing. This translates to only 8 or 6 drawings per second.

Animation Loops

Creating *animation loops* or *animation cycles* is a labour-saving technique for animating repetitive motions, such as a character walking or a breeze blowing through the trees. In the case of walking, the character is animated taking a step with their right foot, then a step with their left foot. The loop is created so that, when the sequence repeats, the motion is seamless. However, since an animation loop essentially uses the same bit of animation over and over again, they are easily detected and can in fact become distracting to an audience. In general, they are used only sparingly by productions with moderate or high budgets.

Ryan Larkin's 1969 Academy Award nominated National Film Board of Canada short *Walking* makes creative use of loops. In addition, a promotional music video featuring the Soul Coughing song "Circles" poked fun at animation loops as they are often seen in *The Flintstones,* in which Fred and Barney, supposedly walking in a house, wonder why they keep passing the same table and vase over and over again.

Multiplane Camera

The multiplane camera is a tool used to add depth to scenes in 2D animated movies, called the multiplane effect. This visual phenomena is also called the parallax process. The art are placed on different layers of glass plates; in this way, realistic backgrounds and foregrounds can be made. The panorama views in *Pinocchio* are examples of the effects a multiplane camera can achieve. Different versions of the camera have been made through time, but the most famous is the one used by the Walt Disney Studio. Another one, called a tabletop, was made by Fleischer Studios. Miniature sets made of paper cutouts were placed in front of the camera, and the cels between them, creating visually realistic scenes. Others who made their own multiplane camera include Ub Iwerks and Don Bluth.

Hand Inking

Originally the cels were inked by hand by first laying them over the artists drawings, and then the inkers traced the outlines of the artwork onto the cels, using different colors. With the invention of xerography (below), hand inking was no longer needed, and this was reflected by the animation's visual style.

Xerography

Applied to animation by Ub Iwerks, the electrostatic copying technique called xerography allowed the drawings to be copied directly onto the cels, leaving only the coloring to the inkers. This saved time and money, and it also made it possible to put in more details and to control the size of the xeroxed objects and characters (this replaced the little known, and seldom used, photographic lines technique at Disney, used to reduce the size of animation when needed). At first it resulted in a more sketchy look, but the method was improved later. Instead of using black lines only, cels with lines in different colors were also possible, using colored toner powder.

The xerographic method was first used by Disney in the short film *Goliath II*, while the first feature using this process was *One Hundred and One Dalmatians* (1961). The graphic style of this film was strongly influenced by the process. Some hand inking was still used together with xerography in this and subsequent films when distinct colored lines were needed. Later, colored toners became available, and several distinct line colors could be used, even simultaneously. For instance, in *The Rescuers* the characters outlines are gray. White and blue toners were used for special effects, such as snow and water.

The APT Process

Invented by David W. Spencer (aka Dave Spencer) for the movie *The Black Cauldron*, the APT (Animation Photo Transfer) process was a new breakthrough in how to transfer the animators' art onto cels. Compared to Xerography, it looked visually better. Basically, the process was a modification of a repro-photographic process; the artists' work were photographed on high-contrast "litho" film, and the image on the resulting negative was then transferred to a cel covered with a layer of light sensitive dye by making a "sandwich" of the negative and the cel and expose the negative to light. The layer of dye was sandwiched between the other two elements and exposed to the light through the transparent areas of the negative. Because it was actually divided into thinner layers of dye, each in a different color and sensitive to a specific wavelength of light, it was exposed to the relevant wavelengths one at the time. The light caused it to harden and fuse to the surface of the cel, and chemicals were then used to remove the unexposed portion, leaving the drawings in a variety of colors (photo emulsion). Small and delicate details were still inked by hand if needed. Spencer received a Technical award from the Motion Picture Academy for developing this process.

Cel Overlay

A cel with inanimate objects made to make the impression of a foreground when laid on top of a ready frame. This creates the illusion of depth, but not as much as a multiplane camera would. A special version of cel overlay is called line overlay, made to complete the background instead of making the foreground, and was invented to deal with the sketchy appearance of xeroxed drawings. The background was first painted as shapes and figures in flat colors, containing rather few details. Next a cel with detailed black lines was laid directly over it, each line drawn to add more information to the underlaying shape or figure, giving the background the complexity it needed. In this way the visual style of the background will match the visual style of the xeroxed parts of the animation. As the xerographic process evolved, line overlay was left behind.

Computers and Traditional Animation

The methods so far describes the techniques of an animation process who originally depended on cels in its final stages, but painted cels are rare today as the computer moves into the animation studio, and the outline drawings are usually scanned into the computer and filled with digital paint instead of being transferred to cels and then colored by hand. The drawings are composited in a computer program on many transparent "layers" much the same way as they are with cels, and made into a sequence of images which may then be transferred onto film or converted to a digital video format. It is now also possible for animators to draw directly into a computer using a graphics tablet, cintiq or a similar device, where the outline drawings are done in a similar manner as they would be on paper. The development of paperless handdrawn animation is likely to replace the traditional pencil and paper not too far into the future, just as cels and traditional paint was replaced when digital ink and paint was fully introduced in the 1990's. For instance the Goofy short How To Hook Up Your Home Theatre represents Disney's first project based on the paperless technology available today. Some of the advantages are the possibility and potential of controlling the size of the drawings while working on them, drawing directly on a multiplane background and eliminating the need of photographing line tests and scanning.

Though traditional animation is now commonly done with computers, it is important to differentiate computer-assisted traditional animation from 3D computer animation, such as *Toy Story* and *ReBoot.* However, often traditional animation and 3D computer animation will be used together, as in Don Bluth's *Titan A.E.* and Disney's *Tarzan* and *Treasure Planet.* DreamWorks executive Jeffrey Katzenberg coined the term "tradigital animation" to describe films produced by his studio which incorporated elements of traditional and computer animation equally, such as *Spirit: Stallion of the Cimarron* and *Sinbad: Legend of the Seven Seas.*

Interestingly, many modern video games such as *Viewtiful Joe, The Legend of Zelda: The Wind Waker* and others use "cel-shading" animation filters to make their full 3D animation appear as though it were drawn in a traditional cel style. This technique was also used in the animated movie *Appleseed,* and was integrated with cel animation in the FOX animated series *Futurama.*

Rotoscoping

Rotoscoping is a method of traditional animation invented by Max Fleischer in 1915, in which animation is "traced" over actual film footage of actors and scenery. Traditionally, the live action will be printed out frame by frame and registered. Another piece of paper is then placed over the live action printouts and the action is traced frame by frame using a lightbox. The end result still looks hand drawn but the motion will be remarkably lifelike. *Waking Life* is a full-length, rotoscoped animated movie, as is *American Pop* by Ralph Bakshi. The popular music video for A-ha's song "Take On Me" also featured rotoscoped animation, along with live action. In most cases, rotoscoping is mainly used as a guide to aid the animation of realistically rendered human beings, as in *Snow White and the Seven Dwarfs, Sleeping Beauty, Pocahontas,* and *Anastasia.*

A method that is related to conventional rotoscoping was later invented. If the movie was supposed to contain inanimate objects like a car or a boat, a small live action model of the object(s) was built and painted white, while the edges of the model were painted with thin black lines. In the next stage the object was filmed like it was supposed to move in the animated scene, either by moving the model or filming it while the camera was sweeping over or around it, or using a combination of both. The film frames were then printed on paper, showing a model made up of the painted black lines. After the artists had added details to the object not present in the live action version of the model, it was xeroxed onto cels. (A notable example is Cruella's car in *One Hundred and One Dalmatians.*) The process of transferring 3D objects to cels was greatly improved when computer graphics advanced enough to allow the creation of three dimensional computer generated objects (wire frame models) that could be manipulated in any way the animators wanted, and then print the outlines on paper before being copied onto cels using Xerography or the APT process. Even if the use of cels has been left by the majority of animators, computer animated objects in traditional animation has come to stay.

Related to rotoscoping are the methods of vectorizing live-action footage, in order to achieve a very graphical look, like in Richard Linklater's film *A Scanner Darkly;* and motion-capturing actor's movements to use the data in 3D-animation, as in Robert Zemeckis's 2005 film *The Polar Express.*

Live-Action Hybrids

Similar to the computer animation and traditional animation hybrids described above, occasionally a production will marry both live-action and animated footage. The live-action parts of these productions are usually filmed first, the actors pretending that they are interacting with the animated characters, props, or scenery; animation will then be added into the footage later to make it appear as if it has always been there. Like rotoscoping, this method is rarely used, but when it is, it can be done to terrific effect, immersing the audience in a fantasy world where humans and cartoons co-exist. Early examples include the silent *Out of the Inkwell* (begun in 1919) cartoons by Max Fleischer and Walt Disney's *Alice Comedies* (begun in 1923). Live-action and animation were later combined to successful effect in features such as *The Three Caballeros* (1945), *Anchors Aweigh* (1945), *Song of the South* (1946), *Mary Poppins* (1964), *Bedknobs and Broomsticks* (1971), *Heavy Traffic* (1973), *Coonskin* (1975) *Pete's Dragon* (1977), *Who Framed Roger Rabbit* (1988), *Cool World* (1993), *The Pagemaster* (1994) and *Space Jam* (1996). Other significant live-action hybrids include the music video for Paula Abdul's hit song "Opposites Attract" and numerous television commercials, including those for cereals such as Honey Nut Cheerios, Trix, and Rice Krispies.

Special Effects Animation

Besides traditional animated characters, objects and backgrounds, many other techniques are used to create special elements such as smoke, lightning and "magic", and to give the animation in general a distinct visual appearance.

Notable examples can be found in movies such as *Fantasia, Wizards (film), The Lord Of The Rings (1978 film), The Little Mermaid* and *The Secret of NIMH*. Today the special effects are mostly done with computers, but earlier they had to be done by hand. To produce these effects, the animators used different techniques, such as drybrush, airbrush, charcoal, grease pencil, backlit animation or, during shooting, the cameraman used multiple exposures with diffusing screens, filters or gels. For instance, the *Nutcracker Suite* segment in *Fantasia* has a fairy sequence where stippled cels are used, creating a soft pastel look.

Wire Frame Model

A *wire frame model* is a visual presentation of an electronic representation of a three dimensional or physical object used in 3D computer graphics. It is created by specifying each edge of the physical object where two mathematically continuous smooth surfaces meet, or by connecting an object's constituent vertices using straight lines or curves. The object is projected onto the computer screen by drawing lines at the location of each edge.

Using a wire frame model allows visualization of the underlying design structure of a 3D model. Traditional 2-dimensional views and drawings can be created by appropriate rotation of the object and selection of hidden line removal via cutting planes.

Since wire frame renderings are relatively simple and fast to calculate, they are often used in cases where a high screen frame rate is needed (for instance, when working with a particularly complex 3D model, or in real-time systems that model exterior phenomena). When greater graphical detail is desired, surface textures can be added automatically after completion of the initial rendering of the wire frame. This allows the designer to quickly review changes or rotate the object to new desired views without long delays associated with more realistic rendering.

The wire frame format is also well suited and widely used in programming tool paths for DNC (Direct Numerical Control) machine tools.

Stick Figure

A *stick figure* is a very simple type of drawing, generally of the human form, although stick figures of other types of animals are possible (for example, a stick figure dog). In a stick figure, the head is represented by a circle, sometimes embellished with details such as eyes or crudely-scratched-out hair. The neck, arms, legs and torso are all represented by single straight lines (thus the name). The neck and torso are different segments of one straight line.

Generally, stick figures are drawn by hand with a pen or pencil and have hard, defined edges. Though not displaying very much detail, what is drawn is generally required. For instance, if one was to draw a person, the person's eyebrows would generally only be drawn to provide a sort of facial expression, be it of anger or shame.

Stick figures have proven effective as a source of advertising, entertainment and as a form of storyboarding and practice for filmwork. This is especially crucial for creating "animatics", as a film special effects team is then able to visually display the outcome of a scene by using stick figures, but saving in money, time and effort of providing a completed shot, but only having to have the necessary information provided. Stick figures are sometimes associated with violence.

Flash

Stick figures are often used in Adobe Flash animations. Stick figures are easy to draw and can be traditionally animated a lot quicker than full drawings. Well known stick figure flash animations include *Xiao Xiao, Joe Zombie, Killing Spree,* and *Castle*. They are also used on Google and other websites.

PowerPoint

Microsoft PowerPoint has also been used to make stick figure movies. By creating a slide with a stick figure in it, copying and pasting a new slide and changing the new slide users can create a movie, although it is a much more labourious process.

Cutout Pro Stickman

Cutout Pro Stickman is specifically designed for stick figure animation. Each figure is controlled with control points and key frames and saves drawing inbetweens. When an arm is moved, the whole body gets affected using skeleton simulation.

Pivot Stick Figure Animator

Pivot Stick Figure Animator is also designed for stick figure animation. Just like Cutout Pro Stickman you control with key points/joints and it also allows the user to load images (sprites) and animate them.

This is Stick Figure Animation Software (TISFAT)

TISFAT is tween-based stick figure animation software, allowing the user to create any kinds of figures and objects, that are animated in layers by keyframes, between which the program does the animation for the user. You can easily share your stick figures too, export your movies in AVI, SWF, SIF and even executable in the older versions, that will play in the standalone TISFAT movie player.

ANIMERAMA

Animerama is a series of Japanese adult animated films produced by Osamu Tezuka's Mushi Production studio from the late 1960s to early 1970s.

All are directed, at least in part, by Eiichi Yamamoto, and the first two also feature contributions from Tezuka himself. The first, *A Thousand & One Nights*, was the first erotic animated feature film (pre-dating Ralph Bakshi's 1972 film *Fritz the Cat*) and at 130 minutes, it remains one of the longest ever animated films.

The three films in the trilogy are:

- *A Thousand & One Nights* (1969).
- *Cleopatra* (1970).
- *Belladonna* (1973).

All three where released onto DVD by the video division of Columbia Music Entertainment, both separately and as a box set, in 2004 in Japan, and re-released in 2006.

Animated Poetry

Animated poetry is most simply described as an art form in which the artist renders a text poem using moving or animated words. Abstract, descriptive or allegorical animated images may also be used instead of, or with, the moving text.

Animated poetry need not consist of only moving or animated text, it is often composed of several media types, including sound/music, animation, photography/videography, written text and spoken words. The images, sounds, motion and the viewer's visual perception of the poem are an integral part of animated poetry, as important as the text itself. The elements of animated poetry combine to form a unified artistic expression, expressing a concept, idea, event or emotion much like traditional poetry.

Music Videos, such as those seen on MTV can be considered a form of animated poetry, that uses audio and video elements to express the song's lyrics.

Chapter 2

Contemporary Global Animation Works: Selected Case Studies

CASE STUDY : ALL ABOUT ANIMATION

All About Animation is a three-pronged effort at animation awareness, education and encouragement, in the form of a *website, blog* and soon-to-be-launched monthly *E-Magazine*. It is dedicated to enabling animation lovers in India to educate themselves on every aspect of animation, interact with its exponents and truly appreciate this art form in all its glory.

- *Awareness*—for those enjoy viewing animation but know little or nothing of it.
- *Education*—for those who know a little bit about animation and are interested in learning more.
- *Encouragement*—for those who are already a part of the Indian animation community, either as students or professionals, and need nurturing, support and motivation.

AIMS

- to create one single, unified information destination; for anybody and everybody in India who is interested in animation.
- to acquaint young Indian animation enthusiasts with global animation; its history, evolution, varying styles and techniques.
- to raise awareness as well as interest levels; what is animation? what are visual effects? what is gaming?
- to assist and guide students both prospective and current; recommend schools, list resources, solve problems.
- to discuss issues affecting the Indian animation industry; attrition, acute shortage of talent, lack of awareness and training.
- to showcase good animation; by students, independent animators as well as studios.
- to provide a free platform for students to display their creations and for people to view student work.
- to elucidate career options; creative, technological and business.

Types of Animation Art

Animation is a beautiful and highly collectible art form that is growing in popularity all across the world. Enjoy original works of Art of all your favorites cartoons from Disney, Warner Bros., Hanna-Barbera®, Chuck Jones, The Simpsons and many more. The Cartoon Factory would like to help introduce you to this fascinating and fulfilling collectible.

As you first look into collecting Animation Art, you may find many of the descriptions we use difficult, if not impossible, to decipher. This is a list of terms you are likely to encounter as you explore the world of animation art collecting. As you consider collecting animation art, as with any purchase, it is important you understand *exactly* what you are dealing with. While this glossary is by no means definitive, it should give you a firm background in the semantics of Animation.

CEL

A broad term that encompasses most types of animation art. In its strictest interpretation, a cel is the plastic sheet, either cellulose acetate or cellulose nitrate, that animated characters are painted on. In practice, the term cel has come to mean that plastic sheet in combination with the outline and coloring of a character, object, and/or special effect. Outlines can be either hand-inked or Xerographically transferred to the sheet of plastic. Those outlines are then filled with color, either by hand-painting or a serigraphic process, to complete the cel.

12 or 16 Field

These terms are used to describe the size of a particular cel. They come from the size of the "field" of view of the camera photographing the artwork. For rough use, consider a twelve-field cel roughly 10" × 12", and a sixteen-field cel approximately 14" × 16". The actual framed size may differ.

Original Production Cel

These are the cels actually used in the production of a cartoon. They can have either Xerographed or hand-inked outlines, and are hand-painted at the studio. These cels are one-of-a-kind pieces of art, and their rarity makes them highly sought after by collectors. Because these cels were created to make an actual cartoon, each cel is a component part of a larger movement. Different cels from the same scene may be more or less desirable depending on a variety of factors: size, profile and expression of the character, any damage to inking or paint, and overall visual appeal.

Limited Edition Cel

As with production cels, limiteds can have either hand-inked or xerographic outlines, and are also hand-painted. The major difference, as its name implies, is that the limited editions are created in limited quantities, generally in runs of 250 to 500 cels. Because of these small edition sizes, limiteds can also be very collectible. Some limiteds are exact reproductions of the frames of the film they represent. Others are based on contemporary interpretations of classic characters or scenes by their animators—Chuck Jones limiteds, for instance. Limited editions are always hand-numbered on the cel, and many are signed by the artists.

If you would like to learn more about how hand-painted limited edition cels are made, we invite you to drop by our online Creating a Limited Edition cel presentation.

Sericels

Sometimes called serigraph cels. The serigraphy process involves silk-screening each individual color to the cel, one at a time. Every distinct shade is a separate screen, and a separate pass in the procedure. As a result of this fine art operation, each color is flawlessly reproduced. Sericels are also created in limited quantities, typically 2500 to 5000 pieces. Because of their larger edition size, sericels are the most affordable type of animation art, ideal for the beginning collector.

If you would like to learn more about how sericels are made, we invite you to drop by our online Creating a Limited Edition Sericel presentation.

Publicity Cel

A cel, usually hand-painted, not actually used in a film or created for collectors, but made for publicity or promotional purposes.

Cel Set-Up

A combination of cels presented together. If the combination of cels match exactly, it is referred to as a KEY SET-UP.

Animation Drawing

These are the original, one-of-a-kind drawings, penciled by the animator, that cels are eventually made from. Drawings can be rough, or the more refined CLEAN-UP drawings. Sometimes, set-ups are available with matching drawings and the cel that was made from it.

Storyboard Drawing

A drawing or story sketch made for the storyboard, which conveys visually the plot and action of a scene or shot. The storyboard serves as a preliminary guide for the artists.

Model Sheets

Drawings, or studio reproductions of a character in a variety of actions used as reference by the animators during production.

Original Production Background

This covers a wide range of backgrounds that are original paintings, and were used in the production of a cartoon. It is important to note that it does not necessarily mean it is the *same* production that the cel is from. It may not even be from the same *studio* as the cel. If you see this term used, you will want to know what production the background is from.

Key Master Set-Up

This is the ultimate set-up, and the most rare. A key master set-up combines the original cel, or a key set-up of cels, *with the background they were originally photographed over.* When framed, this will look exactly as it did in the actual film or short.

Presentation or Hand-Painted Background

This type of background was specially prepared to complement the cel by an independent artist. Generally, it will be in the style of the original. Although it may enhance the visual appeal of the set-up, it adds little value or collectibility to the cel (unless the artist is famous in his or her own right).

Reproduction Background

This is the most common type of background. It is, as the name implies, a copy of a background. The reproduction can be by color Xerox, lithography, serigraphy or photography. In many cases, it is a reproduction of the original background.

Lithographs/Lithography

Lithography owes it existence to the chemical principal that oil and water do not mix. The artist draws the image to be printed on a flat slab of limestone, metal, or plastic using a greasy crayon. The surface is then chemically fixed and wet with water, which does not adhere to the greasy image areas. When the surface is inked with a roller, ink adheres only to the greasy areas and not the wet area. Paper is then positioned over the plate and the press is manually operated to produce one impression. The process must be repeated for each color. It is not unusual for fine lithographs to be printed from 15 or more plates.

Giclée Prints

Creating Giclée fine art prints requires the utmost care and attention to detail. *Harvest Productions, LTD.*, who produce all of the Giclée's for *Linda Jones Enterprises*, customize the color settings for each image so that each print is truly what the artist had in mind. The French term "Giclée", literally meaning "spray of ink," is used to describe these prints. Four precision nozzles spray up to a million microscopic droplets per second on to fine art paper. Then, each piece of paper is individually hand-mounted. Displaying a full color spectrum, the prints are lush and velvety, capturing the subtle nuances of the original artwork.

Pix-Cel Prints

The pix-cel is a trademarked product developed by Acme (Producrs of Simpson Artwork) and Epson utilizing proprietary technology to give a fully rendered continuous tone 3-D image directly from digital production files onto clear acetate and positioned on a giclee background also from a digital production file.

The Persistence of Vision

All film is essentially an optical illusion, a trick of the eye, which is known as 'persistence of vision'. When the human eye sees an image, it retains it for a fraction of a second. If in that tiny space of time, one image can be substituted by another which is slightly different, then there appears to be movement! What you really see when watching a 'movie' is NOT really a 'moving' picture at all but a series of 'still' pictures being shown in rapid succession. At the rate of 24 frames per second, the eye is easily deceived.

Animated film-making is fundamentally different from live-action film-making. The live-action camera captures a scene moving in real-time and freezes it into individual still 'frames' which are then projected onto the screen. In animation, there is no pre-existing motion. The camera captures stills that are either drawn, sculpted or created in a digital environment.

Animation is a complex and immersive art, with science as its backbone. It takes a great deal of practice and dedication for an artist to master it.

Animation Boom ...or Doom?

The media has been touting animation as the 'hottest new career' and the billion dollar figures being flashed around are enticing hordes of people into the industry. Many youngsters are looking at animation as a viable career option but do they really know what they are getting into? Do they have the basic talent needed? Studios complain about the lack of talented animators, institutes are blamed for trying to make a quick buck off students without really training them... the finger pointing goes on. The demand for animators is certainly very high but unless they are trained well enough to meet the demands, the industry will flounder. What is the solution?

Awareness

The best way to tackle any problem is awareness. And that is what this site has set out to do. The *Animation A-B-C section* will cover various topics that are essential for any budding animator to know. Right from the basics of animation, the skills required, the temperament and attitude that an animator should possess, in short, all that one needs to know about!

Art in Motion

The desire to animate is as old as art itself. Early man drew pictures on cave walls, attempting to depict motion by showing animals with multiple superimposed legs. The vases of ancient Greece with their gods and heroesand the friezes of Rome with their battling warriors and galloping steeds, also sought to capture, in static images, the dynamics of action. It was only in the 19th century, in the years leading up to the invention of the motion picture, that animated pictures became a real possibility.

Here is an extract from the book "Animation Art" that sums up the origin and evoltion of Animation as we know it now.

The early days of animation were filled with invention and novelty—on screen and behind the scenes. This was an era of experimentation, where techniques being created and refined. Brave newspaper cartoonists attempted to adapt their pen and ink creations to the moving screen—and most of them succeeded beyond their wildest dreams.

Standardization of production methods was quickly established, and then the storytellers, artists and film-makers took over. At first they told jokes, then proceeded to telling stories with original characters, classic fables and comic-strip adaptations. They tried live-action combined with animation, stop-motion, pixilation, silhouette animation, sound cartoons and color. They then made documentaries, instructional films and pure visual art. But it was not easy...

Winsor McCay drew complete scenes—background settings and moving characters—for every frame of motion-picture film, and there were 24 frames per second. Earl Hurd improved upon this by drawing characters individually on celluloid (cels) over static background paintings. Raoul Barre created registration pegs so animator's drawings would align under the camera. Otto Mesmer arrimated characters that could think, while Walt Disney and Ub Iwerks gave their cartoon drawings real personality.

It was the beginning of a new visual medium where anything was possible. In these pioneer days before sound, the artists sharpened their skills and created an industry.

OPTICAL TOYS—THE PRECURSOR TO ANIMATION

In the 17th to 19th centuries, simple animation devices were invented long before film projectors: the Thaumatrope, Phenakistoscope, Praxinoscope, Zoetrope, Stroboscope, Magic Lantern and Mutoscope. These were more complex versions of the flip book, often using drawings, paintings, photos, or slides on rotating card/s or cylinder. These "optical toys" tricked the eye into believing that the images were moving. The light source was often an oil lamp, light bulb, or none (natural light).

The Magic Lantern (1671)

The Magic Lantern was classed as the ancestor of the modern day projector. It consisted of a translucent oil painting and a simple lamp. When put together in a darkened room, the image would appear larger on a flat surface. Athanasius Kircher spoke about this originating from China in the 1600's.

Thaumatrope (1824)

A Thaumatrope was a toy used in the Victorian era. It was a disk or card with two different pictures on each side is attached to two pieces of string. When the strings were twirled quickly between the fingers the two pictures appear to combine into a single image. The creator of this small but yet important invention is clouded. People believe that John Aryton Paris was the creator whereas others believe Charles Babbage was.

Phenakistoscope (1831)

One variant of the phenakistoscope was a spinning disc mounted vertically on a handle.

Around the center of the disc a series of pictures was drawn corresponding to frames of the animation; around its circumference was a series of radial slits. The user would spin the disc and look through the moving slits at the disc's reflection in a mirror.

Zoetrope (1832)

A Zoetrope is a device which creates the image of a moving picture. This contraption was produced in 1834 by George Horner. The device is basically a cylinder with vertical slits around the sides. Around the inside edge of the cylinder there are a series of pictures on the opposite side to the slits. As the cylinder is spun, the user then looks through the slits producing the illusion of motion.

Praxinoscope (1877)

The Praxinoscope, invented by French scientist Charles-Émile Reynaud, was a more sophisticated version of the zoetrope. It used the same basic mechanism of a strip of images placed on the inside of a spinning cylinder, but instead of viewing it through slits, it was viewed in a series of stationary mirrors around the inside of the cylinder, so that the animation would stay in place, and also provided a clearer image. Reynaud also developed a larger version of the praxinoscope that could be projected onto a screen, called the Théâtre Optique.

Flip Book (1868)

The first flip book was patented in 1868 by John Barnes Linnet. This was another step closer to the development of animation. Like the Zoetrope, the Flip Book creates the illusion of motion. A set of sequential pictures seen at a high speed creates this effect.

Film Animation

The history of film animation began in the 1890s with the earliest days of silent films and continues through the present day. The first animated film was created by Charles-Émile Reynaud, inventor of the praxinoscope, an animation system using loops of 12 pictures. On October 28, 1892 at Musée Grévin in Paris, France he exhibited animations consisting of loops of about 500 frames, using his Théâtre Optique system—similar in principle to a modern film projector. This day is now observed as *International Animation Day* around the world.

The first animated work on standard picture film was Humorous Phases of Funny Faces (1906) by J. Stuart Blackton. It features a cartoonist drawing faces on a chalkboard, and the faces apparently coming to life.

Fantasmagorie, by the French director Émile Cohl (also called Émile Courtet), is also noteworthy. It was screened for the first time on August 17, 1908 at Théâtre du Gymnase in Paris. Émile Courtet later went to Fort Lee, New Jersey near New York City in 1912, where he worked for French studio Éclair and spread its technique in the US.

The first puppet-animated film was The Beautiful Lukanida (1912) by the Russian-born (ethnically Polish) director Wladyslaw Starewicz (Ladislas Starevich).

The first animated feature film was El Apóstol, made in 1917 by Quirino Cristiani from Argentina. He also directed two other animated feature films, including 1931's Peludopolis, the first to use synchronized sound. None of these, however, survive to the present day. The earliest-surviving animated feature, which used color-tinted scenes, is the silhouette-animated Adventures of Prince Achmed (1926) directed by German Lotte Reiniger and French/Hungarian Berthold Bartosch. Walt Disney's Snow White and the Seven Dwarfs (1937), often considered to be the first animated feature when in fact at least eight were previously released, was the nevertheless first to use Technicolor and the first to become successful within the English-speaking world.

Traditional/Cel Animation

Traditional animation, also known as cel animation, was the process used for most animated films of the 20th century. The individual frames of a traditionally animated film are photographs of drawings, which are first drawn on paper. To create the illusion of movement, each drawing differs slightly from the one before it. The animators' drawings are traced or photocopied onto transparent acetate sheets called cels (from where the phrase *'cel animation'* has been dervied) which are filled in with paints in assigned colors or tones on the side opposite the line drawings. The completed character cels are photographed one-by-one onto motion picture film against a painted background by a rostrum camera.

This process became obsolete by the beginning of the 21st century. Today, animators' drawings and the backgrounds are either scanned into or drawn directly into a computer system. Various software programs are used to color the drawings and simulate camera movement and effects. The final animated piece is output to one of several delivery mediums, including traditional 35 mm film and newer media such as digital video.

Full animation refers to the process of producing high-quality traditionally animated films, which regularly use detailed drawings and plausible movement. Films produced by Walt Disney studios are full animation films.

Limited animation involves the use of less detailed and/or more stylized drawings and methods of movement. Pioneered by the artists at the American studio United Productions of America, limited animation can be used as a method of stylized artistic expression. The Hannah Barbera cartoons are examples of limited animation.

Rotoscoping is a technique, patented by Max Fleischer in 1917, where animators trace live-action movement, frame by frame. The source film can be directly copyed from actors' outlines into animated drawings, as in The Lord of the Rings (US, 1978), used as a basis and inspiration for character animation, as in most Disney films, or used in a stylized and expressive manner, as in Waking Life (US, 2001) and A Scanner Darkly (film) (US, 2006).

Stop Motion

Clay Animation

In this technique figures made of clay or a similar malleable material are used to create stop-motion animation. The figures may have an armature or wire frame inside of them, similar to the related puppet animation (below), that can be manipulated in order to pose the figures. Alternatively, the figures may be made entirely of clay, such as in the films of Bruce Bickford, where clay creatures morph into a variety of different shapes.

Examples of Clay Animation—Most of the Aardman Studios films including the Wallace and Grommit series and Chicken Run.

Cutout Animation

This is a type of stop-motion animation produced by moving 2-dimensional pieces of material such as paper or cloth on a flat surface or in a digital environment. Example of Cutout Animation—South Park and Nickelodeon's popular kid's program—Blue's Clues.

Silhouette Animation

This is a monochrome variant of cutout animation in which the characters are only visible as black silhouettes. Example of Silhouette Animation—The Adventures of Prince Achmed by Lotte Reiniger.

Graphic Animation

This style uses non-drawn flat visual graphic material (photographs, newspaper clippings, magazines, etc.) which are sometimes manipulated frame-by-frame to create movement. At other times, the graphics remain stationary, while the stop-motion camera is moved to create on-screen action.

Model Animation

This technique has stop-motion animation created to interact with and exist as a part of a live-action world. Intercutting, matte effects, and split screens are often employed to blend stop-motion characters or objects with live actors and settings. Examples of Model Animation—Ray Harryhausen's Jason and the Argonauts and the King Kong films.

Object Animation

This style refers to the use of regular inanimate objects in stop-motion animation, as opposed to specially created items. Example of Object Animation—Ishu Patel's Beadgame.

Pixillation

This is a specialized technique for animating people. The camera records occasional frames of some natural or real-time event, but because of the intermittent filming, the effect of the resulting film is that of an unnatural movement somewhat like in an old silent movie. A stationary camera records a stationary posed subject, shooting on twos. Between exposures, the character moves to a new position. The process is low, tiring and requires a great amount of patience. Because the subject in pixillation is usually a living person, complete control of the pose is difficult. Trial and error rules pixillation. Example of Pixillation—Norman McLaren's Oscar-winning film Neighbours.

Puppet Animation

This kind of animation typically involves stop-motion puppet figures interacting with each other in a constructed environment, in contrast to the real-world interaction in model animation. The puppets generally have an armature inside of them to keep them still and steady as well as constraining them to move at particular joints. Examples of Puppet Animation—Tim Burton's Nightmare Before Christmas and Corpse Bride.

Experimental Animation

Drawn on Film Animation

A technique where footage is produced by creating the images directly on film stock, for example by Norman McLaren and Len Lye.

Sand Animation

Sand is moved around on a backlighted or frontlighted piece of glass to create each frame for an animated film. This creates an interesting effect when animated because of the light contrast.

Paint on Glass Animation

A technique for making animated films by manipulating slow drying oil paints on sheets of glass.

Pinscreen Animation

This technique makes use of a screen filled with movable pins, which can be moved in or out by pressing an object onto the screen. The screen is lit from the side so that the pins cast shadows. The technique has been used to create animated films with a range of textural effects difficult to achieve with traditional cel animation.

Computer Animation

- 2D-Analog computer Animation.
- 2D-Flash Animation.
- 3D Animation.

Motion Capture

Also known as MOCAP, it is the creation of a 3D representation of a live performance. We will have a detailed section on Motion Capture soon which will cover topics like:

- What is Motion Capture?
- Systems used for Motion Capture.
- The Hardware and Software.
- Studios in India specializing in Motion Capture.
- Implications and Controversies—is Motion Capture truly Animation or not?

There are innumerable great artists who have created animation magic through the years. Disney may be the only household name in India when it comes to animation, but we must honour the thousands of others who pushed the envelope and took the art form to newer and far greater heights.

Here you will find a list of names from all over the world, artists from varying backgrounds, all working towards the same goal—to create animated masterpieces. Over time we shall provide detailed information on each and every one of them. As of now, do take some time to search the net or scout your local library or bookstore for books on the life and art of these inspirational masters. You will find something to learn from each one of them.

Alexandre Alexeieff
Andrew Stanton
Barry Purves
Berthold Barthosch
Bill Plympton
Bill Tytla
Bob Clampett
Brad Bird
Bruno Bozetto
Caroline Leaf
Charles Mintz
Chuck Jones
Cordell Baker
Craig McCracken
Dave Sproxton
Don Bluth
Emile Cohl
Emile Reynaud
Frederic Back
Friz Freleng
Gene Deitch
George Dunning
George Griffin
George Pal
Georges Melies
Hans Fischerkoesen
Hayao Miyazaki
Ishu Patel
J. Stuart Blackton
Jan Svankmajer
Jim Henson
Jiri Trnka
JHoanna Priestly
Joanna Quinn
John Canemaker
John Randolph Bray
Joseph Barbera
Joy Batchelor
Koji Yamamura
Ladislaw Starewitch
Lotte Reiniger
Marv Newland
Max Fleischer
Michael Dudok de Wit
Norman McLaren
Nick Park
Osamu Tezuka
Oskar Fischinger
Otto Mesmer
Paul Driessen
Paul Grimault
Paul Terry
Peter Lord
Ralph Bakshi
Raoul Barre
Ray Harryhausen
Rene Laloux
Richard Williams
Robert McKimson
Shamus Culhane
Stephen Quay
Terry Gilliam
Tex Avery
Timothy Quay
Ube Iwerks
Victor Bergdahl
Viking Eggeling
Walt Disney
Walter Lantz
Wendy Tilby

John Grierson
John Halas
John Hubley
John Lasseter
Will Vinton
William Hannah
Winsor Mcay

TASI—The Animation Society of India

The Animation Society of India (TASI) has been formed with a view to increase awareness of the medium of animation in India. It aims to educate the emerging generation and the public at large and at the same time provide a platform for the exchange of creative and technical information within the Indian art and animation fraternity in order to strengthen existing talent and encourage growth by educating and guiding prospective artists in India.

NASSCOM—National Association of Software and Service Companies

NASSCOM is India's premier trade body and the chamber of commerce of the IT software and services industry in India, with over 1100 members, of which over 250 are global companies from the US, UK, EU, Japan and China. NASSCOM's member companies are in the business of software development, software services, software products, IT-enabled/ BPO services and e-commerce.

ASIFA (INDIA)—Association of International Du Film D' Animation, India

The Association of International Du Film D' Animation, officially called ASIFA, is a professional body, recognized by UNESCO, devoted to developing film animation both as an art and also as an effective means of communication. ASIFA today enjoys a representation from over 55 countries.

ASIFA India received its official charter on November 25, 2000, and it aspires to the same ideals and goals as the international organization. By staying true to the spirit and upholding one of its mottos of blending art and technology, making available invaluable knowledge and information, ASIFA India throughout the year, arranges several free workshops, namely the CG-Meetup. The chapter also recognizes the best animation in India through the ASIFA India Awards of Excellence. In addition to this ASIFA India also extends its support to other community building events.

WIA (INDIA)—Women In Animation

Women In Animation is a professional, non-profit organization established in 1994 in US to foster the dignity, concerns and advancement of women who are involved in any and all aspects of the art and industry of animation. WIA is also an educational organization. Through our workshops, meetings and panels you are bound to gain valuable insight into the industry, opportunities available to you and other educational resources in your area.

Women In Animation is currently in the process of starting its Indian chapter and is actively looking for volunteers to help launch this organization at a grass roots level. The Indian chapter is led by Saraswathi Balgam with help from Rekha Thorat. All interested individuals should please send an email to info@womeninanimation.in and you will be notified soon about the first get together to establish and formalize the organization.

ABAI—Association of Bangalore Animation Industry

ABAI was formed by like minded people to have an association that would regulate the Animation business activities in Bangalore and contribute towards the greater good of the regional animation industry. Their vision is to create a platform and bridge the gap between production facilities and qualified manpower, and to promote Animation, Gaming and VFX professionals and production houses in Bangalore. The association will constantly encourage talent to enhance artistic and digital skills qualitatively.

CASE STUDY: PICASSO ANIMATION EDUCATION AND PRODUCTION CENTENNIAL'S PROGRAMS

Canada's one of the oldest and respected college: Centennial College, Toronto is now in its 38th year of imparting Quality Education. It has a record of exemplary teaching, innovative programming and extensive partnership building. Centennial is recognized as one of the most culturally diverse post-secondary institutions in Canada. Centennial offer more than 100 programs and has approximately 12,000 full-time and 40,000 part-time students on rolls. Centennial College boasts of award-winning animators and production professionals as instructors and supervised workshops. Focusing on animation principles, students are trained in the key areas of animation production and earned the reputation in the animation industry. Now Centennial's famous animation programs are available in India through Picasso Centennial Animation College.

His Holiness, Maharishi Mahesh Yogi, brought to the world in 1957 the simple, natural and effortless technique of Transcendental Meditation (TM) to unfold the full creative potential of higher consciousness latent in every individual. This knowledge proclaims solutions to the problems of life through the development of higher states of consciousness.

Maharishi Group, besides many philanthropic activities, runs several successful business entities with professional management in diverse areas and large number of educational institutes worldwide. Our diversity reflects the mature and broad based corporate skills and commitment to quality education.

Maharishi Group's Corporate Entities:

- Age of Enlightenment Publications.
- Maharishi Ayurveda Corporation Pvt. Ltd.
- Cosmic Softech Ltd.
- Picasso Digital Media Pvt. Ltd.
- Maharishi Ayurveda Products Ltd.
- Maharishi Solar Technology Pvt. Ltd.
- Star Granites Pvt. Ltd.
- Ram Rajya Clothing Pvt. Ltd.
- Global Diamonds Pvt. Ltd.
- Maharishi Ayurveda Arogya Sansthan.
- Multiple TV channels telecast from Holland for European and North American TV viewers.

Maharishi University of Management, 272 acre campus is located 50 miles west of Mississippi river, a few hours from Chicago, St Louis, Kansas city, Madison and Minneapolis. Iowa city, home of University of Iowa lies an hour to the north. Students find it a wholesome and dynamic environment to study in this 1.2 m sft. of teaching, research, recreation and living space. There is ample space for learning and plenty of room for fun.

Secondary Education

Maharishi group runs over 200 schools and colleges throughout India. Group also runs a unique chain of schools for girls called Maharishi Ideal Girls Schools in India and USA.

Picasso Digital Media: Founded by Mr. ABRP Reddy, veteran IT and education professional, Picasso Digital Media has launched Picasso Animation College with international alliances. Its vision is to bring in the global standards to Indian animation industry to put India on the top of the global animation map. To facilitate this at fast pace, it brought best international standards and practices to India by setting up international alliances. Its collaboration with Centennial Collage, Toronto, Canada is a fine example in this direction. The systematic approach of this group helped in achieving the outstanding results for the students. While animation education institutes recorded only 13 per cent placements for their students nationally, Picasso achieved 133 per cent on campus placements consistently.

The core management team of Picasso consists of Indian and Canadian professionals from animation, entertainment, fine arts and education industry. They include:

- *Philip Edward Alexy*: Worked for projects such as STAR WARS, Casper, Flubber, Jumanji, 101 Dalmatians and directors such as George Lucas and Steven Spielberg.
- *Prof Shaun McKenna*: Taught for over 15 years in Canada and guided many prize winning animation projects of youth in Canada.
- *Amit Khanna*: Graduate from Sheridan College, Canada; worked in Singapore and India.
- *Rajan Dhesinghu*: Worked with studios such as Prana, Maya Entertainment.
- *Suraj Dhar*: Worked with studios such as Moving Pictures and DQ entertainment as creative supervisor.

"At Picasso, we have a compelling vision: to nurture talent in India in line with international animation industry standards. If you are looking for dynamic and stimulating environment with international standards that can launch you into the exciting world of digital animation, Picasso is for you."

ABRP Reddy
MD and CEO of Picasso Digital Media
(Formerly COO of NIIT Middle East;
Head of Education,
NIIT Europe;
MD of Informatics India)

APPLICATION FORM

WEB-DOWNLOAD

www.picasso.co.in

PICASSO ANIMATION
A Maharishi Group Company

in partnership with

CENTENNIAL COLLEGE
Toronto, Canada

Please Paste your recent passport-sized photograph here

PICASSO CENTENNIAL CANADIAN ANIMATION COLLEGE
B-1/E-11, MCIE, Mathura Road, New Delhi-110044 INDIA Tel (Board): 011-65644778, 09212504425
E-mail: delhi@picasso.co.in Webside: www.picasso.com

ACADEMIC RECORDS *(Do not enclose any Certificates)*

Examination Level	Qualification	Major Subjects	Medium of Instruction	Board/ University	Marks (%)/ Grade	Year of Passing
Senior Secondary School (10+2)						
Others						
Others						

- Please read the instructions carefully before filling up the form.
- Please retain a photocopy of the application form with you.
- Write in CAPITAL LETTERS (USE BLACK INK only)
- Send the form, duly filled in, along with a Demand Draft/Banker's Cheque/ Pay Order for Rs. 250/- in favour of **Picasso Digital Media Pvt. Ltd.** payable at New Delhi

COURSE APPLIED FOR

- Art & Design Foundation
- Digital Animation
- Integrated Design & Digital Animation Programme

PERSONAL DETAILS

Name : Mr./Ms...

Date of Birth...
(Specify Date/Month/Year)

Correspondence Address:...

City.............................State.............................Pincode.............................

Phone (STD code No.).............................Mobile.............................

E-mail...

Permanent Address :...

City.............................State.............................Pincode.............................

Phone (STD code No.).............................Mobile.............................

Father's/ Guardian's Name...

Profession of Guardian ....Annual Household Income.............................

DECLARATION

I hereby declare that I satisfy the eligibility requirements of the Programme as stated in the Prospectus of the Picasso Animation College and have furnished correct information. I also declare that I have read all the rules and regulations governing admission and fee payable to Picasso Animation College and agree to abide by the same, if selected. I also understand that the decision of the Admission Committee regarding my selection will be final and binding on me. I have enclosed DD No.

....

..........Dated .... for Rs. ....250/-..........

on Bank...

Signature of Applicant

PICASSO CENTENNIAL CANADIAN ANIMATION COLLEGE
B-1/E-11, MCIE, Mathura Road, New Delhi-110044 INDIA
E-mail: delhi@picasso.co in Webside: www.picasso.com

APPLICATION FORM

www.picasso.co.in
PICASSO ANIMATION
A Maharishi Group Company

in partnership with
CENTENNIAL COLLEGE
Toronto, Canada

Please Paste your recent passport-sized photograph here

PICASSO ANIMATION COLLEGE
B-1/E-11, MCIE, Mathura Road, New Delhi-110044 INDIA Tel (Board): 011-65644778, 09212504425
E-mail: delhi@picasso.co.in Webside: www.picasso.com

ACADEMIC RECORDS *(Do not enclose any Certificates)*

Examination Level	Qualification	Major Subjects	Medium of Instruction	Board/ University	Marks (%)/ Grade	Year of Passing
High School (10th)						
Senior Secondary School (10+2)						
Others						

- Please read the instructions carefully before filling up the form.
- Please retain a photocopy of the application form with you.
- Write in CAPITAL LETTERS (USE BLACK INK only)
- Send the form, duly filled in, along with a Demand Draft/Banker's Cheque/ Pay Order for Rs. 500/- in favour of **Picasso Digital Media Pvt. Ltd.** payable at New Delhi

COURSE APPLIED FOR: Integrated B.Sc multimedia & animation (Film & TV)

PERSONAL DETAILS

Name : Mr./Ms. :..

Date of Birth..(Specify Date/Month/Year)

Correspondence Address:..

....

City..State..Pincode..

Phone (STD Code No.)..Mobile..

E-mail ....

Permanent Address : ....

....

City..State..Pincode..

Phone (STD Code No.)..Mobile..

Father's/ Guardian's Name : ....

Profession of Guardian ....Annual Household Income ....

DECLARATION

I hereby declare that I satisfy the eligibility requirements of the Programme as stated in the Prospectus of the Picasso Animation College and have furnished correct information. I also declare that I have read all the rules and regulations governing admission and fee payable to Picasso Animation College and agree to abide by the same, if selected. I also understand that the decision of the Admission Committee regarding my selection will be final and binding on me. I have enclosed DD No. ....

Dated .... for Rs. ....500/-........................... on

Bank...

Signature of Applicant

FOR OFFICIAL USE ONLY

Date of receipt of application..

Written Test on..

Result..

Interview on ....By...

Result..

Admission details...

....

....

....

PICASSO ANIMATION COLLEGE
B-1/E-11, MCIE, Mathura Road, New Delhi-110044 INDIA
E-mail: delhi@picasso.co.in, Webside: www.picasso.com

Picasso Digital Media made pioneering steps to bring the world class animation education to India in partnership with Centennial College, Toronto and set up Picasso Centennial Animation College at Delhi.

In order to address the need of the Indian animation industry for a comprehensive degree program of international standard, Integrated Bachelors Program, BSc has been designed. The inputs for this program were collected from Indian studios involved in outsourcing work/international projects and industry experts. This program for the first time integrates Indian University degree with an international qualification delivering industry demanded skills in a comprehensive and seamless manner.

Student at the end of this 3-year intensive full time program gains:

- Art and Design Foundation Program from Centennial College, Canada during year I
- Digital Animation Program from Centennial College, Canada during year II
- Industry Internship in a multimedia/animation studio during year III
- Academic head from Centennial College during year I and Year II
- Lead faculty from Canada for Digital Animation Program
- UGC recognized degree from Indian University
- Option of credit transfers to Canadian and American Universities at the end of 1st year
- A demo reel comprising of student's own animation film and projects done during various stages of the program. This becomes the passport for a bright career in animation industry for the student
- Campus recruitment facility
- *Eligibility*: 10+2 or equivalent.

To apply:

Please send Rs. 500 for prospectus and application form
or
Download the application form and send along with a DD for Rs. 500 to
Admissions Manager
Picasso Centennial Animation College
B-1/E-11, Mohan Co-operative Industrial Estate
Mathura Road
New Delhi- 110044
DD should be in favor of Picasso Digital Media Pvt. Ltd.,
Payable at New Delhi.

Digital Animation

This program is aimed at offering high-end 3D animation for the applicant who has a portfolio already. This program provides a dynamic combination of both creative and technical production skills that keeps our graduates always ahead of others.

Integrated Digital Animation with Foundation

This program addresses the needs of students applying for Digital Animation Program without formal training/portfolio in any creative field. Students go through rigorous training in Art and Design studies and build up the portfolio which is a pre-requisite for our coveted Digital Animation Program.

Art and Design Foundation Studies

This program is a unique blending of traditional and digital art media and meet the requirements of selected universities and institutions in Canada/USA for special studies including Digital Animation, New Media Design etc.

Objective

These programs help students emerge as high-end 3D experts in the areas of Modeling, Rigging, Texturing, Lighting, Character Animation, Rendering, advanced editing and cutting edge composting techniques.

Highlights

- Lead Faculty who are industry professionals from Canada.
- State of the art facilities with Apple G5, High end Intel workstations, Servers with dual processors.
- Programs that are widely recognized worldwide for quality of the students.
- Production-style environment.
- Project-based learning environment.
- Utilizes industry-standard methodology that will be very familiar to our graduates once they hit the workforce.
- Placement Facility for all students.
- Opportunity to work as project interns in 3D production studios in India (available for select meritorious students).

Career Courses for College Going Students and Working Executives

Picasso offers several programs for those who wish to prepare for a career in the exciting world of 3D Animation. These courses are intensive and yet paced in such a way suitable for those who cannot devote full time attention. Designed by experts from the industry, Picasso's programs addresses the need for industry ready professionals made available at the campus itself.

Animation Film Making with Internship (18 months)

This program is designed to equip the young minds to develop their skills and become the most sought-after animation professional in the industry. This program will conclude on completion of 3 months studio internship by the student.

Professional Video Editing and Compositing (6 months)

This extensively researched program enables the student to step into a career as a Professional Editor/Compositor in TV Studio, Production Houses, Advertising Agencies, Documentary Film Making Agencies, or can start as a (self-employed) freelance compositor, editor and rendering expert.

3D Animation for Beginners (3 months)

After completion of the Foundation Program in 3D Animation, a student gets the knowledge of how the special effects for the movies are generated. Student gets hands on experience in developing his/her own models and animating them. Student will also be ready to take up a serious career courses in the line of animation and modeling.

Mastering 3DS Max (6 months)

The objective of the program is to enable the student master the 3D animation using the popular software 3Ds Max. At the end of the course, students are capable of handling the requirements for commercials, visual effects, logo designing, walk-through, interior designing, modeling and animation.

Compositing with Combustion (2.5 months)

This Program will focus on a comprehensive learning of the Combustion toolset providing him/her cutting edge skills. These techniques will build knowledge on creating a complete Compositing for Film, Video, or Web Output.

Composting with Shake (2.5 months)

This is an advanced course covering the concepts of compositing for both broadcast and films on shake. Students gain extensive knowledge of Shake on Apple Platform and ready to take up assignments in entertainment industry.

Video Editing with FCP (1.5 months)

This program covers Final Cut Pro extensively on Apple platform which will enable the student to gain expertize in the field of editing special effects and prepares him/her ready for video editing assignments.

Animation Film Making with Internship (18 months)

It is designed to equip the young minds to develop their skills and become the most sought-after animation professionals in the industry. This program will conclude with 3 months studio internship.

Personal Attention

Picasso offers the student far more teaching hours on par with most of the internationally acclaimed colleges.

The project-based learning environment utilizes international industry-standard methodology. Students do multiple projects during the program that makes learning effective and interesting.

Picasso's mission is to build STARs for global animation projects: India needs STARs with creative story tellers as animators, not software technicians. Our STAR rated programs comply with criterion such as:

- Curricula on par with international standards
- Project based learning
- Creativity focused
- Faculty with project experience
- Internship/live project as part of program.

Contents of Star Program

- *Creative Foundation* prepares students to develop and unleash their creative potential.
- *Character Development Projects*: Through various assignments students are taken into animation production pipeline which include modeling, texturing, lighting, and character setup.
- *Character Animation Projects*: Students are given extensive assignments and projects to master the principles of animation.
- *Specilization and Show Reel:* Students choose an area of specialization and build up their skills further and develop their own show reel using latest tools and techniques.
- *Internship/Live Project:* Students are provided with the unique opportunity of working in a studio as project intern with the opportunity of participating in a live project for a minimum period of 3 months.

India's only Animation College with Full Time Canadian Experts

- UGC Recognized Degree and Diploma Programs.
- International Studio Quality infrastructure.
- Project oriented approach.
- Curriculum in line with international standards and practices.
- 133 per cent on campus job offer record.
- Short Animation Film by each student.
- Live Project/industry Internship.

Admission Notification

Admissions for Feb/June 2008 intake

Entrance exam on 22nd December 2007 for:

- Integrated B.Sc. with multimedia and animation (Students appearing Class XII may also apply).

Picasso Animation College

Information Request Form

PLEASE FILL IN YOUR DETAILS

- To apply for admission or
- Enrolling for free workshops or
- For any specific information required.

Fields marked with asterisk (*) are mandatory

YOUR CONTACT INFORMATION:

Name:*		Age: (yrs)	
Street Address:		State /City:	
Mobile:		Phone:* (Ex: 91-427-245521)	
Your Email: *	*(If you don't have email id type* student@picasso.co.in	Occupation	(Student / Housewife /Business/Employed)
Educational Qualification:		If Student:	(Arts /Science/Commerce/Fine Arts/ Professional /Engineering /Others)
Year of Study	*year (1 /2 /3)*	How did you come to know of our website? *	

Details of Technical / Fine Arts Training

S.No	Course Name	Duration(yrs)	Institute
1			
2			
3			
4			

The Digital Animation Program is an intensive, project-based training experience. Internationally recognized by the commercial animation and effects industry, this program is designed for tomorrow's talented animators for the film, television and interactive gaming world.

This program produces creative thinkers with relevant production training—not software technicians.

- Duration: 10 months (full time)
- Admission Requirements:
  - Eligibility: (BFA/Alpha Level Programs/Diploma in Animation/Multimedia)
  - Student's Portfolio in illustration/photography/2D or 3D animation/music/ Performance Art/Publishing or Art and Design Foundation Program Centennial College
  - Proficiency in English.

CASE STUDY: HITECH ANIMATION

Hitech Animation is a part of Hitech Group, one of the major Business Process Outsourcing (BPO) firm in Gujarat, India. Since its initial set up in early 2004, the company prides itself in offering quality services in the field of 3D Animation, Game assets creations, Architectural visualization, Product modeling.

Services

Hitech Animation offers 3D animation services targeted for Broadcast animation. The company has technical, creative and production division to create modern animated feature films, documentaries, short films, and animated advertisements.

- Modeling
- Texturing
- Lighting
- Animation
- Bio Medical
- Forensic
- CAD Engineering
- Product Concepts.

Infrastructure

Hitech Animation executes Animation Projects at a fraction of the production cost *vis-a-vis* the U.S., while maintaining high standards of quality. Its talented 3D Animation and Modeling professionals with impressive track records will transform vision and imagination to virtual realities of the client.

Through an industrious team of talented and skilled employees, Hitech animation has successfully maintained long-term business relationships with the international clients assuring them higher quality standard in a specific turn around time. Hitech Animation is committed to deliver best offshore animation services to its clients with dedicated and skilled business personnel, sound infrastructure and strong financial foundation.

Vision

To be one of the leading Multimedia service providers by assisting its clients with flexible solutions enabling them a smooth functioning in the global business.

Mission

- To provide unmatched creative animation services.
- To provide healthy and creative working environment to the employees.
- To become the best in the animation industry with unique expertize.

3D Animation

Hitech Animation offers 3D animation services targeted for Broadcast animation. The company has technical, creative and production division to create modern animated feature films, documentaries, short films, and animated advertisements.

Game Assets Creation

Hitech Animation offers the best-in-class Game Assets Projects and Animation services. It specializes in 3D character modeling, texturing, and animation services targeted mainly for gaming industry. We proud to create a new generation computer games by providing exceptional quality within a client-specific turn around time.

Architectural Visualization

Hitech Animation specializes in creating presentations of architectural projects and designed objects. We targets architects, real estate developers, facility owners, city planners, interior designers, and landscape architects who require quality renderings benefit from our realistic presentations.

Product Modeling

Hitech Animation has expertize in creating 3D Product Modeling and stunning digital effects targeted for the entertainment industries, advertising agencies and commercial production houses. We use high-end technologies to provide the best quality animation. The product modeling animation will be the best solution for online brand marketing and for interactive agencies.

CASE STUDY: ANIMATION MULTIMEDIA MAYA TRAINING IN INDIA

MIDDS has been established with the concept of providing state of the art animation/VFX, Game development, Graphic design and Interior Design courses to people who aspire to establish a career in the respective fields.

There is a need for a platform where students can learn and acquire the technical knowledge and artistic skill-set required to become world-class designers. The Design industry has been brewing in India for a while. Now is the time when some very significant mile-stone developments have started to take place in this space and when Hollywood and Japanese Entertainment industries are seriously looking at India as the next hotbed for Animation and Special Effects work. In addition, Indian market itself is growing by such leaps and bounds that almost all well-established animation/design studios are desperately looking to expand. Animation/Design is one of the very few industries that can boast starting salaries that are way above the industry average, and the analysts report this industry to be the next biggest boom in India after Information Technology.

MIDDS was started to provide the world with international standard animators who are highly creative and know the technique and not just the software. It is a platform where aspiring animators can learn and acquire the technical knowledge and the skill-set required to become animators that have the technical as well as the artistic eye to be world-class animators.

MIDDS offers Diploma in Film Animation, Diploma in Game Designing, Diploma in Virtual Reality, and short-term courses.

- Diploma in Film Animation is for 14 months

- Diploma in Game Design is for 1 year
- Diploma in Virtual Reality is for 6 months

A candidate has to be at least 10+2 and also has to clear an entrance exam. Exceptions are made for students who demonstrate exceptional creativity and knack for this field.

There are following multifold reasons:

1. World-class trained faculty.
2. A curriculum that has been crafted by some of the best animators in the world.
3. Auditorium where movie screenings are done every week to teach and inspire students with some of the best Animation and SFX work done in the world.
4. Studio visits.
5. Guest Lectures by Top Notch professionals of the industry. MIDDS has been proud to host professionals from Rhythm and Hues, Animation Express, Crest Studios, UTV, Prana, etc.
6. Practice labs available 24 hours.
7. Fully equipped state of art Library including books and CD's for student's reference. There are books and publications available in our library on all different topics of Animation, VFX, Game Design, Virtual Reality, Story Writing, Cinematography, Lighting, etc.
8. Workshops on Personality Development.
9. Workshops on Marketing yourself as an Animator.

MIDDS courses have been designed to fulfill the perceived needs of a new entrant to the field of 3D animation film-making.

MIDDS puts a lot of stress on practical training. Eighty per cent of the training and education is practical in nature.

MIDDS assists the outstation students to get a PG accommodation or a flat on sharing basis.

If the work of the student is as per the international standards, getting a job is not an issue in this industry.

Animation is one of the very few industries that can boast starting salaries that are way above the industry averages, and the analysts report this industry to be the next biggest boom in India after Information Technology.

Capacity of the school is 280 students per year, 8-10 students per class.

In case of 2D Animation, yes but MIDDS offers a Diploma in Film Animation, which focuses on 3D animation while covering aspects of 2D Animation as well. So, drawing and sketching skills are not at all required. However, the knowledge of it do give you an edge.

MIDDS has the following sister concerns:

- Meteor International (www.meteorinternational.com)
- Meteor Studios (www.meteor-studios.com)

MIDDS was established as an educational institution dedicated to the professional design disciplines of 3D, 2D design, Animation, Multimedia, and Game Development Technology. It is the leading private design education provider with its headquarters in Mumbai, the financial capital of the country.

Offering an expeditious pathway to an Advanced Diploma to students within 15 months of graduating from high school, our curriculum is constantly reviewed to keep our students at the forefront of 3D and 2D design education and training.

Always at the cutting edge, MIDDS prides itself in grooming individuals to award-winners. That is why our program is totally focused towards preparing our students for the REAL WORLD. We consider ourselves a Professional Institute before an Academic Institute. Today MIDDS has strategic tie-ups with Bank of India, Oriental Bank of Commerce, Sir JJ Institute of Applied Arts, National College, and Northumbria University to name a few. The synergies arising from these partnerships go a long way towards helping our students financially as well as having opportunities to interact and gain from some of the finest Design institutes in the world.

MIDDS continues to strive for excellence in delivering high quality education and providing an enriching learning experience. A unique combination of academic theory and hands-on experience ensures that all graduates possess the skills and knowledge required by employers worldwide as well as a sound foundation for advanced study. MIDDS encourages its students to gain practical training during its curriculum during which students establish networks with companies, which very often become their future employers.

Lecturers are professional practitioners in their respective fields. They offer a wealth of technical knowledge and experience which they impart with commitment, creating an international learning environment that is rich in creativity.

MIDDS, INDIA Currently Offers the Following Courses

Diploma Courses

- Advanced Diploma in Animated Film Making (15 months)
- Advanced Diploma in Game Design (15 months)
- Advanced Diploma in Interior Design (15 months)

Certification Courses

- Multimedia and Graphic Design (4 months)
- Web Design (4 months)
- Maya/Photoshop (5 months)
- Max/Photoshop (3 months)
- Compositing/Editing (2 months)

The DIPLOMA Courses at MIDDS have the following Value Additions

- Weekly Animated/VFX movie screenings in Private Theatre
- Communication and Personality Development
- Marketing yourself as an Animator and Showreel preparation
- 24 hr. practice labs
- Sketching Workshops
- Clay Modeling Workshops
- Guest Lectures from Animation/VFX industry
- Studio Visit

- Audio Video Reference Tutorials
- Strong Placement Assistance

Admission Criteria

The minimum criteria for applying for the course is 10+2 and the applicant also has to clear an Entrance Exam to get admission. Students completing the 1-year Diploma course will also have the option of taking additional classes and do an advanced Diploma in Film Animation. These students will be eligible to enroll directly into the third year at Northumbria University, UK.

MIDDS, India emphasizes on complete development of an animator instead of just teaching the software. Hence, all programs will include classes in script-writing, concept design, storyboarding, style design, digital cinematography, sound, background music, and post-production.

MIDDS is in the heart of Bollywood in the posh Lokhandwala Complex of Mumbai. Our facilities include:

Classrooms: Classrooms are equipped with:

- Plasma Screens.
- Individual computers for all students.
- Universal audio-video connectivity and conferencing facilities.

Library: A library with wealth of information in form of books, manuals, magazines, journals, publications, catalogs, DVDs, CD ROMs, press kits, etc.

Auditorium: MIDDS has provided its students with a state of the art fully acoustically engineered auditorium for movie viewings and guest lectures. This facility has:

- A high resolution projection system.
- Is fully equipped for audio-video conferencing for guest lectures from around the world.
- Can be used to shoot Green/Blue screens.
- The facility is used for group discussions, conducting seminars, and movie screenings.

Practice Lab: Practice labs are available 24 hours a day, 7 days a week for practice and project work.

Sketching Facilities: MIDDS School's philosophy is to inculcate creativity in its students. We pay special emphasis on making sure that our students do not ignore sketching as part of their experience at MIDDS. So, we have arranged for easels and donkeys that are constantly used by students to hone their sketching abilities.

Meeting Rooms: Meeting rooms are generally used for counseling sessions and group discussions.

Chapter 3

Frequently Asked Questions about Animation: A Case Study

INTRODUCTION

Computer animation is a large and growing field, and people want different things from it; this FAQ tries to cover all bases, and as a result is rather thin on many of them! So feel free to contribute, or to offer suggestions—the FAQ will never be complete or free of errors, but your help will make it better.

Should I Post to comp.graphics.animation?

'comp.graphics.animation' is a forum for discussion of all things relating to computer animation. This includes, but is not limited to the following: (these are general guidelines ONLY!):

- Computer animation research
- Implementation of animation systems
- Animation software packages
- Animation-related hardware
- Computer animation in film and TV
- Working in the animation industry
- Net-accessible animation.

If you did like to see the original charter for the group, as it first appeared in the usenet Call For Votes, you can find it at: URL: ftp://ftp.uu.net/usenet/control/comp/comp.graphics.animation.Z. If your post is not of general interest (to 'comp.graphics.animation'), but you think 'c.g.anim' is the most specific, the most appropriate, or is likely to be the most fruitful forum—do not hesitate to post. But 'c.g.anim' is not for discussion of things for which there *are* more specific resources available (i.e. newsgroups, mailing lists, etc.) and which are not of *general* *interest* to 'c.g.anim' readers.

If you are not sure, you may as well post—the group's not moderated, and is frequented by mostly polite people—you are not likely to get flamed, but please do spare a moment's thought before you post.

Availability/Distribution

The most current version of the FAQ in all its different formats is always available by FTP in URL: ftp://avalon.viewpoint.com/pub/FAQs/cga-faq/ and the latest HTML version is at URL: http://www.ridgecrest.ca.us/fx/cga-faq.html

The plain-text version of the FAQ is posted the first week of every month on comp.graphics.animation, and the article (like all other 'official' FAQs) is archived on 'rtfm' URL: ftp://rtfm.mit.edu/pub/usenet-by-group/news.answers/graphics/animation-faq

All official FAQs, and then some, are available on the WWW (plaintext and/or HTML-ized) at: URL: http://www.cis.ohio-state.edu/hypertext/faq/usenet/FAQ-List.html

Related Resources

...or, does my post really belong in 'comp.graphics.animation'?

Computer animation, like its progenitor computer graphics, abouts on a large number of fields. There are a lot of crossover topics, and a lot of related resources other than this newsgroup. Please try and direct your questions to the most appropriate place!

Graphics/Animation Newsgroups

- comp.graphics.misc — *general image generation, modeling*
- comp.graphics.algorithms — *algorithms for graphics*
- comp.graphics.animation — *you're looking at the FAQ right now!*
- comp.graphics.raytracing — *bouncing light around*
- comp.graphics.visualization — *scientific/data visualization*
- comp.graphics.apps.wavefront — *CG software from Wavefront*
- comp.graphics.apps.alias — *CG software from Alias Research*
- comp.graphics.apps.lightwave — *CG software from NewTek*
- comp.graphics.apps.softimage — *CG software from Softimage*
- comp.graphics.apps.photoshop — *Adobe Photoshop*
- comp.graphics.packages.3dstudio — *CG package from AutoDesk*
- comp.graphics.rendering.raytracing — *Raytracing software (POV, etc.)*
- comp.graphics.rendering.renderman — *rendering via Renderman*
- comp.graphics.rendering.misc — *misc rendering discussions*
- comp.sys.XXX.graphics
- comp.sys.XXX
- comp.sys.XXX.hardware.video
- comp.os.ms-windows.*
- comp.windows.*

  } *how do I do YYY on/under XXX*
- comp.multimedia — *sound and text and vision*
- alt.3d — *SIRDS, holograms, etc. 3d perception*
- alt.movies.visual-effects — *SFX for film and TV*
- alt.graphics.pixutils — *picture manipulation, conversion*
- rec.arts.animation — *discussion of traditional animation*
- rec.arts.disney.animation — *discussion of Disney's animation*
- rec.arts.anime* — *discussion of Japanese animation*

- alt.animation.warner-bros — *Chuck Jones and mates*
- rec.video.{desktop, production} — *video, desktop video*
- sci.image.processing — *sophisticated image manipulation*
- sci.virtual-worlds* — *anything about VR*
- comp.compression — *compression issues (JPEG, MPEG, etc.)*
- alt.ascii-art.animation — *yes, vt100 animation*
- alt.binaries.pictures.* — *posts of pictures, anims, utils, etc.*
- fj.rec.animation — *discussion of anime (in Japanese)*
- *.test (misc.test, etc.) — *test postings (some people...)*
- comp.*.advocacy — Mac vs PC vs SGI vs Amiga, etc...

Web Resources

These references are specific sources of information in various broad areas relevant to this FAQ. If you do not understand the syntax used here to specify where to reach these resources on the net, check out the 'About Box' section of the FAQ for information on Resource Specifications.

3DSite

3DSite (URL: http://www.3dsite.com/3dsite/): a great CGI/animation WWW site. Industry resumes (submit yours!) and job offers, information on CGI production houses. Literature, references, discussion for animation (not just computer animation). Information on relevant hardware and software firms, software packages. Pointers to CGI organizations, labs, projects, and some VR pointers. IRC panels on animation and more. Maintained by Daniele Colajacomo (*daniele@netcom.com*).

GWEB

GWEB (URL: http://www2.cinenet.net/GWEB/): An informal trade journal for the computer animation industry. Includes monthly interviews with industry luminaries, job postings, and information on production houses. Also information on relevant hardware and software. Maintained by Rob and Sharil (*gweb@cinenet.net*).

Avalon

This FTP/Website was created to be a 3D repository site for the 'net. It is primarily a stockpile of free 3D objects and models in various different formats, along with file format descriptions, conversion/display/plug-in utilities, and some textures and demo software. Although FTP access is still available, Viewpoint asks anyone with web-browsing capabilities to access the site through their home page (URL: http://www.viewpoint.com/) for a *much* better interface to the archive.

Comp.Graphics.Misc FAQ

The 'comp.graphics.misc' FAQ: graphics references, groups, standards, various algorithms, etc. HTML version available at URL: http://www.primenet.com/~grieggs/cg_faq.html Maintained by John T. Grieggs (*grieggs@netcom.com*).

Other graphics-related FAQs can be found at: ®URL: http://www.cis.ohio-state.edu/hypertext/faq/usenet/graphics/top.html

More Specific Resources

More specific resources are scattered throughout the FAQ in the sections dealing with the specific topic, so for instance for resources concerning animation file formats, see 'Animation File Formats', and for resources concerning individual software packages.

Miscellaneous Questions

Here are some of the FAQ's that are not answered elsewhere in this document. If there are any questions that you feel belong here, or wish to add to any of the answers, please do not hesitate to contact me.

1. *Is it ok to post job offers to this newsgroup?*

Although not specifically mentioned in the charter, and there *is* a newsgroup for job offers (misc.jobs.offered), the general concensus is that yes, they are welcome.

2. *Is it ok to post advertisements for software, services, etc. to the newsgroup?*

Gray area. For the most part, this is bad netiquette. However, posting a short message with a pointer (e-mail address, web page, etc.) so those who actually want more information can go and find it without flooding the group, is ok.

3. *I want to study [CG] animation for a career. Are there any good schools?*

Craig Slagel (*Craig@craig5.demon.co.uk*) has put together a "computer animation schools FAQ", which includes excerpts from many responses that have been posted to this question. It is posted to the newsgroup, and it is available via ftp at: **URL:** ftp://avalon.viewpoint.com/pub/FAQs/computer.animation.school.faq

Also, GWEB (**URL:** http://www2.cinenet.net/GWEB/) has a nice page of schools, indexed by general locations.

4. *What should I put on a demo reel?*

Quick answer: your best stuff. Keep it short (3-10 minutes max). Show the kind of thing you want to get a job doing (i.e., be careful about including flying logos unless that is what you want to do).

5. *How much should I charge for my work?*

Quick answer: how much are you worth, and how much are your clients willing to pay you? If you just want experience, you can charge little (or nothing), but your client(s) *will* get used to it, and it will be harder for you to convince them to pay you later if you want to do it as a business. Since the amount of work varies from one animation job to another, there is no clear-cut figure to give. Variables to consider are time needed to do the job, and what resources are required.

6. *What is the best system for CG/animation?*

Flammable topic! Don't ask. If you must ask, be more specific... what type of CG/animation work do you want to do, what quality, will you be doing work with any other H/W and/or specific S/W package, and how much are you willing to spend in both time and money. Even so, every system has strengths, weaknesses, and advocates. Don't expect a concensus. Your best bet is to try out as many different ones as you can firsthand, and make your own decision.

7. *What is the best software package for CG/animation?*

See above.

8. *How do I contact ILM (Industrial Light & Magic)? Is there an e-mail address?*

You don't, they call you:) ...actually, they do have a P.O. Box number (probably more than one, really): P.O. Box 2009, San Rafael, CA 94912. They also have a net connection, but it's not "advertised", and those who know it are not going to give details. They wish to remain as anonymous as possible on the net... *please* respect their privacy.

9. *What about ILM/Lucasfilm internships for students?*

(from the rec.arts.movies.production FAQ): Both Lucasfilm and ILM run an intership program three times a year for several months. Only the summer program is available to those who reside outside the United States.

10. *Has anyone seen or know anything about the cartoon "Reboot"?*

Reboot is produced by Alliance Communications and BLT Productions in Vancouver. They use SGI hardware and Softimage software (along with their own propietary stuff for facial animation and lip sync). They do not use motion capture. They started production in 1994 (though the show's copyright lists a 1991 date), and the show just finished its second season. An "Unofficial" Reboot home page is at: URL: http://www.inwap.com/Reboot.html

Note: Word is that a third season of Reboot will be produced and shown in Canada (starting in September), but ABC has decided to drop it from its Saturday morning lineup. No information has surfaced yet on who might pick up the series for US distribution in the fall...

11. *I need an object/model/mesh of...*

See the 'Related Resources' section of the FAQ as well as the specific sections for each software package below for info on FTP sites for freely available models.

Additionally, there are several companies which sell ready-made or custom-made models in most formats. They usually advertise in some of the magazines listed in the "Journals" section (below). Here are a few of the well-known ones and where to find them on the web:

- *Viewpoint Datalabs*—URL: http://www.viewpoint.com/ In addition to having their catalog online, Viewpoint also hosts the Avalon archive for the largest collection of free 3D models on the net (now with a cool HTML interface!)
- *Acuris—URL:* http://www.acuris.com/

- *3Name3D—URL*: http://www.ywd.com/
- *3DSite* (URL: http://www.3dsite.com/3dsite/) also has a "model market" service available from their web page, and another similar service is Richard Tilmann's "MeshMart" (URL: http://cedar.cic.net/~rtilmann/mm/index.htm), and visit Harry H. Chang's home page at URL: http://www.loop.com/~hhc/ for some cool Star Wars objects (3DStudio format).

12. *I need an image/texture/picture of...*

There are a few textures at avalon.viewpoint.com. There is also a huge collection of pictures (though most are not tileable) at URL: ftp://wuarchive.wustl.edu/multimedia/images

There is a growing collection of textures available at URL: http://www.meat.com/textures/ (a number of mirror sites are listed on that page), and if you are using the POV raytracer, check out URL: http://www.eskimo.com/~scott/povtext.html for some neat stuff.

There are numerous other ftp sites with clumps of pictures and textures out there... too many to list. Additionally, there are also several CD-ROM's out with tileable texturemaps and other images in most popular formats.

13. *What is motion capture?*

Motion capture is a technique by which a performer's movements can be recorded digitally, and reproduced by a CG character either in real-time or after the data has been processed (depending on how the data is sampled). This allows for more realistic and natural motion in character animation. A variation of this technique uses an armature instead of a performer, and movements are made and keyframed the same way that stop-motion animators have been doing it for many years.

14. *What resolution should I render my animations in?*

That depends greatly on what the final media will be. If it is going to remain on a computer screen (MPEG, Quicktime, etc.), then factors to consider are disk space, playback speed, and memory requirements. If it will be transferred to video or film, best to ask whoever will be recording it for you, because it might depend on the recording device.

15. *So what do you know about Toy Story?*

The Pixar movie "Toy Story" is currently playing in theatres in the US. They have a deal with Disney to produce two more movies (and are reportedly already working on the next one). What the next one will be about is still a closely-guarded secret.

There is a lot of inside jokes in the movie, mainly in the brands and company names seen, as well as references to several of the animators and Pixar's previous works in the titles of the books in Andy's room. For some more info on the movie, visit the website HTTP: http://www.toystory.com/. For information on the technical aspects of the film (resolution, number of objects, etc.) see the August 1995 issue of Computer Graphics World. Another good article about the movie appears in the December 1995 issue of Cinefex.

One last note: According to CNN, "Toy Story" came out as the #3 movie for US domestic box office performance in 1995 (behind "Batman Forever" and "Apollo 13", but ahead of Disney's "Pocahontas"). Congrats Pixar!

16. Where can I get the Pixar videos?

Pixar reportedly sells them directly (in VHS format). Call 510-236-4000 and follow the instructions, or you can try them at 1001 West Cutting Blvd., Richmond CA 94804. Fax: 510-236-0388. They are not currently available on Laserdisc except for a few bits here and there in general CG animation collections.

Additionally, there are at least two (*unconfirmed*) sources for the video which includes "Red's Dream", "Luxo, Jr.", "Tin Toy", and "Knick-Knack":

Expanded Entertainment
1-800-996-TOON extension 125 (Mon-Fri 9am-6pm Pacific)
$25 plus S&H

Media Magic
1-800-882-8284 (credit card orders)
(order #v145) for $25

17. Is there a program to convert {MPEG, FLI, MOV, QT, AVI, single images, etc.} to {single images, AVI, QT, MOV, FLI, MPEG, etc.}?

Stephane Woillez (*wos@prism.uvsq.fr*) has put together a web page (URL: http://www.prism.uvsq.fr/public/wos/multimedia/) with several conversion utilities available for downloading. So far, this is the best single collection of such tools I know of.

Mainactor (for Amiga) available on Aminet (in 'gfx/edit', will read 14 formats including GIF, IFF-ILBM, IFF-ANIM[5,7,8], MPEG, FL[CI], and write most of these (not GIF or MPEG) You can add sound effects and edit your animations too.

18. Is computer art "cheating"?

The overwhelming opinion (of the informed public) is that no, it is not. Computer art is simply a new form, much like photography was when it was first introduced. Computers do little more than sit there and take up space unless a human uses them to create something. It is just a bad misconception when the media reports something was done "by" a computer, when it was a really a human being using a computer the way a painter uses a paintbrush. The computer is just a tool.

Using Animation

This section is for those who simply want to see the results of others' hard labour—animation file formats and conversions, animation players and sites. Much of the information here is presented much better in the graphics file formats FAQ: URL: ftp://rtfm.mit.edu/pub/usenet/news.answers/graphics/fileformats-faq.

Animation File Formats

For code that reads: DL, FLI, FLC, GIF, IFF, MovieSetter, PFX, Quicktime, and RLE animation formats, see the 'xanim' entry in 'Players', below. Other players' source may also be useful for these and other formats.

- *AVI (PC):* Resources: URL: ftp://ftp.microsoft.com/ (RIFF AVI format. does not include compression format).
- DL: ??
- *FLI, FLC (Autodesk) (PC)*: FLI support is for 320x200 images, and is a series of images and deltas. The color map can be changed during the animation. FLC has a few additional chunks and supports larger image sizes. Resources: FLC article in DDJ'93—'ftp://simtel20.../graphic/...' and URL: ftp://avalon.viewpoint.com/pub/format_specs/Autodesk_fli_and_flc_format.txt (specification of format).
- *GIF (PC)*: A GIF file consists of a screen color map and a series of images, each with an optional color map. The images do not have to be at the origin and can be any size smaller than the screen size. This allows GIF animations to be created that only update the part of the screen that changes. GIFs (including transparent GIFs) are also discussed in the Comp.Graphics.Misc FAQ.
- *GL (PC)*: (not to be confused with SGI's GL programming language).
- *IFF ANIM (Amiga)*: The Amiga's IFF format was designed as a universal (extensible) data format. Many different data types and chunks can be found in IFF ANIMs. Many ANIMs include sound chunks or color cycling. There are a plethora of compression techniques (with different tradeoffs) used. Most IFF ANIMs are meant to be double-buffered, with deltas applying to frames two distant. A looping ANIM means the last two deltas produce images that are the same as the first two. The Amiga has a large number of display modes (a couple of them, EHB and HAM are unusual; HAM is the hardest to emulate). Resources: (specification of format) URL: ftp://avalon.viewpoint.com/pub/format_specs/iffspecs.lzh
- *MovieSetter (GoldDisk) (Amiga)*: A very flexible animation format. Animations are stored as a bunch of backgrounds, sounds and sets. Sets are smaller images that get placed on top of the background (with transparent pixels). A frame list at the end describes each frame. Each frame specifies which background to use (backgrounds can also scroll in different directions and speeds), and a list of sets to put on that background with depth information so characters can pass behind or in front of each other. Sound information is contained here as well to sync it up to the action. There is also color cycling and specialty fades and wipes. Can come as one file or as three directories and a control file.
- *MPEG (lossy)*: Resources: 'faq://graphics/mpeg-faq', also in germany ftp://ftp.cs.tu-berlin.de/pub/msdos/dos/graphics/mpegfa??.zip' (covers specification, future, software (players, &c), hardware, incl. pointers to other information...); 'post://alt.binaries.pictures.utilities/"WHERE TO GET MPEG UTILS"'; Luigi's MPEG FAQ (URL: http://www.crs4.it/~luigi/MPEG/mpegfaq.html); another WWW MPEG site (URL: http://w3.eeb.ele.tue.nl/mpeg/index.html); URL: ftp://ftp.crs4.it/ (MPEG, and other image compression techniques).
- *PFX (PageFlipper Plus F/X) (Amiga)*: A series of deltas with a play list at the end. Supports color map changes, nested loops and dynamic timing.
- *RLE (URT) (Unix)*: One or more runlength encoded images, viewable with an X11 viewing program. Tools for creating consistent color maps and for many other operations are part of the toolkit.

Players

'display' v1.84 (PC) (Jih-Shin Ho). AVI, DL, FLC, GL, MPEG.

'ftp://nctuccca.edu.tw/PC/graphics/disp*' (also on 'simtel20')

MPEG players for IBM, Mac, Unix, VMS, Next.

See 'post://alt.binaries.pictures.utilities/"WHERE TO GET MPEG UTILS"', or the MPEG FAQ at URL: http://www.cs.tu-berlin.de/~phade/mpegfaq/

MPEG player for Atari, X11, IBM

URL: http://w3.eeb.ele.tue.nl/mpeg/index.html

'xanim' (X-Windows) (Mark Podlipec).

DL, FLI, FLC, GIF, IFF, MovieSetter, PFX, Quicktime, RLE Official FTP site: 'ftp://ftp.x.org/contrib/applications/xanim???.tar.Z'. WWW page URL: http://www.univ-rennes1.fr/ASTRO/fra/xanim.html

DFV

From the same person who gave you DTA (Dave's Targa Animator), comes Dave's Flic Viewer (?). Available in URL: ftp://ftp.povray.org/pub/povray/utilities

For animation file format converters, see the 'Miscellaneous Questions' section.

Animation Sites

URL: ftp://ftp.univ-rennes1.fr/Images/ASTRO/anim/—Space anims

URL: ftp://ftp.cnam.fr/pub/Fractals/anim/—Fractal anims

URL: http://w3.eeb.ele.tue.nl/mpeg/index.html—Various MPEG anims

URL: ftp://ftp.wustl.edu/pub/aminet/gfx/anim/Kinetic.lha (**DOWN**)—Various Amiga anims (also on other aminet sites)

URL: ftp://ftp.povray.org/—POV-anims (and all other things POV...)

URL: http://www.cs.ubc.ca/nest/imager/imager.html—MPEG animations done using hierarchical b-splines. For more on the modeller see 'Dragon'.

URL: http://archpropplan.auckland.ac.nz/People/Mat/gallery/animations.html—Mat Carr's animations

URL: ftp://ftp.ridgecrest.ca.us/pub/users/dejesus/rednightmare.mpg—Red's Nightmare (a nice take on Red's Dream—3.6MB)

URL: http://animation.filmtv.ucla.edu/—UCLA Animation Workshop

URL: http://www.aw.sgi.com/Product/library/Animation_Gallery.html—Animation Gallery at the Alias|Wavefront Site (lots of cool stuff)

URL: http://www.eecs.wsu.edu/IRL/ANIM/Anim.html—WSU Computer Animations

"Grinning Evil Death" (featuring a cockroach and a breakfast cereal superhero) and other computer animation is available in video stores as "The Computer Animation Festival, Volume 1". See 3DSite (URL: http://www.3dsite.com/3dsite/) for more sites.

Hobby Animation

This is for those who want to make their own animations for fun.

Animation Process [by charles king and angus]

Things do not necessarily have to happen in this order (or at all), and there is room for plenty of feedback between them, especially in computer animation, but here is the basic flow. Although it is an advantage (both for the animator and the software) to integrate as many stages as possible in the one package, and most 'animation' packages do so, in practice all packages have their relative merits and work may be swapped from package to package to exploit their strengths, especially in 'high end' studios. This sequence assumes that the animation has already been scripted.

Model Design
  input
    script
tool
    Modeller
task
    making the models to be animated
output
    models
Animation Design
  input
    models, script
tool
    Animation Package
task
    planning and tuning sequences of motion, action, interaction, lighting (very important!), etc...
output
    animation script
Production/Rendering
  input
    models, animation script
tools
    Renderer front-end, Renderer
task
    generating images from which the animation is to be constructed
output
    images
Post-Production
  input
    images, script

tools

Editor, Compositor, Paint, Image Processing, other SFX

Packages

task

modifying, compositing, sequencing the images

output

final sequence of images

Transfer

input

sequence of images

tools

various media, media i/o hardware

task

transferring the frames to the desired medium

output

the product Venues

Conferences and other Events

Siggraph

ACM's Special Interest Group on Computer Graphics. Annual conference includes courses, vendor shows and demos, displays of the year's best animations, paper presentations, etc. SIGGRAPH '95 will be held in Los Angeles, California, August 6-11. There are numerous local chapters, and meetings held in each region. For more information, ftp to ftp://ftp.siggraph.org/ or check out their home page at URL: http://www.siggraph.org/

Prix Ars Electronica: International Competition for the Computer Arts.

This is an annual event. Information follows:

~$80k US in prizes for the animation category alone!

General Info '94: (Peter Schoeber) mail: ORF-Prix Ars Electronica, Europaplatz 3, A-4010 Linz, Austria. phone: +43 (732) 6900-267, fax: -270, telex: +21616 e-mail: `*schoeber@jk.uni-linz.ac.at*' (if you have trouble reaching that address, try *rito@rito.com*).

Animation Info '96: (Christine Schpf) phone: +43 (732) 6900-218.

For more info, check out their web page: URL: http://www.rito.com/prix/index.htm

Imagina, EG w'shop (eg), CGI (cgs), Computer Animation (cgs), Graphics Interface.

Animation Media

This section is about the various media an animation might end up on, and how to get it there.

Both GWEB (URL: http://www2.cinenet.net/GWEB/) and 3DSite (URL: http://www.3dsite.com/3dsite/) have information on animation hardware and software.

Media Properties

Video

(NTSC PAL SECAM HDTV fields composite component synch RGB analog digital...)

Video Formats

format	*by*	*use*	*A/D comp*	*other*
VHS	JVC	home analog	composite	1/2"
Video8/8mm	Sony	home	analog ...	8mm
Betamax	Sony	home	analog ...	composite 1/2"
SVHS	JVC	prosumer	analog ...	1/2"
Hi-8	Sony	prosumer	analog ...	8mm
ED Beta	Sony	prosumer?	analog component	—
M	(M1)?	Matsu	industrial?	analog —
U-Matic 3/4" Sony?	industrial	analog	composite	3/4"
Betacam	Sony	industrial?	analog component	1/2"
Digital Betacam	Sony	broadcast	digital component	compressed
M2	Matsu	broadcast?	analog	component —
U-Matic SP	Sony?	broadcast?	analog —	—
Betacam SP	Sony	broadcast	analog component	—
D-3	Matsu	broadcast	digital composite	—
DCT	Ampex	broadcast	digital component	compressed
D-2	Ampex	master on-air	digital composite	
uncompressed?				
D-1	Sony	master RGB	digital component	uncompressed

other formats?
other properties (image encoding techniques, sound quality, effective number of 'lines', ...)
notes: D-1 endorsed by SMPTE committee
Matsu == Matsushita == Panasonic

Film

(8mm super-8 16,32,72mm anamorphic stock ...) normal film grain ~2500 lpi resolution. slow film <-> higher resolution. **32mm: 0.875" x 1.3125" (2:3)**

Media I/O (VCRs Genlocks Frame-Stores Film-Scanners)

Film Recorders: most film recorders have at least 2000 lpi resolution, 4000 is typical. For optimum quality, your image should be a little over twice the resolution of the recording medium.

Screen-To-Camera: a cheap (but surprisingly effective) option for images that can be displayed at full resolution on your monitor is to photograph the screen directly using a single-framing camera. Film better than super-8 is likely to be overkill. Any lights on your monitor should be taped over, and the whole lot should be put under a black hood (made of cardboard or anything else handy). A slow film (100 ASA or slower, the slower the better), f8 exposure, and loong exposures should eliminate any scanline artifacts.

Resolution/Aspect film recorders: 2000+ lpi (4000 typical).
35mm: ~2500 lpi at .875" x 1.3125" ~= 2200 x 3300 pixels. (2:3)
lpi == lines per inch.

Career Animation

This section is for those who want to make a career of computer animation.

(See 'Hobby Animation' for Animation Process, Software, Venues)

3DSite (URL: http://www.3dsite.com/3dsite/) holds resumes, and has information on job offers, CGI production houses, organizations, laboratories and projects.

GWEB (URL: http://www2.cinenet.net/GWEB/) has industry interviews, information on production houses, and job listings.

Your Union

The Motion Picture Screen Cartoonists and Affiliated Optical Electronic and Graphic Arts, Local 839 IATSE (California) has an ftp site with copies of their negotiated awards, news, courses, etc: URL: ftp://ftp.netcom.com/pub/mp/mpsc839/ (e-mail '*mpsc@netcom.com*' for more info).

Animation Theory

This chapter covers the basics of what computer animation is about according to graphics academics (well, it is meant to).

Types of Computer Animation

2-D

Most computer animation takes place in the 3-D world, as our world is itself basically 3-D, and model interpolation becomes a problem in fewer dimensions, due to a lack of context. 2-D animation packages mostly replicate the processes of cel-based animation, where "key-frames" are used to plot the course of the animation, and the "inbetweens" (interpolating the keys) are filled in later (by an animator, not the computer). The main difference is that the images are created using pixel-based, rather than oil-based techniques. "Morphing" is probably the major 2-D animation technique in use today. Like most other computer work used for SFX in film (wire-removal, compositing, other retouching, etc.), it is largely a matter of image manipulation (image processing) rather than image creation (computer graphics), although morphing *is* an animated technique, unlike many other SFX 'graphics' techniques.

A good starter on morphing by Valerie Hall (1992) is at URL: ftp://marsh.cs.curtin.edu.au/pub/graphics/bibliography/Morph/morph_intro.ps.Z. It references more detailed works for those interested, and she is also written a morphing article in DDJ (1993).

3-D

Almost all 'computer animation' done today is done within the "event-based" or, interchangeably, "track-based" computer animation paradigm, which is based loosely on the key-framing system used in cel-based animation. Most computer animation systems today are built around time-varying parameters, known as "tracks", which determine the state of the animation world at any time. Tracks take the place of the variables which determine the state of a static scene: they are 'animation variables'. A track's value at a given time depends on the "events" (<time, value> tuples) that define the track's state, and on the interpolation technique being used [see 'Interpolation']. Events are conceptually similar to the key-frames of cel-based animation, but allow much more flexibility due to their finer grain (state-variable, rather than world-state). Although tracks may not be independant, they may usefully be treated as such, leading to the "hierarchical animation" technique espoused by Lasseter, where the gross motion of a model is animated first, followed by animation of progressively finer detail. The number of tracks that need to be dealt with, and their often complicated interdependencies, make animating anything of reasonable complexity a big job both in terms of time and effort. Hence most of the subsequent research in computer animation.

Particle System

A particle system is usually different than a track/keyframe-based animation system, and more like a state machine. They are particularly good for simulating and animating natural phenomena, such as rain, fire, smoke, etc.

Particle systems work by defining states and rules of behaviour for each particle or group of particles. A particle can usually be anything, from a point to an object. Objects and particles can usually emit other particles, and thus you can go to a new level of complexity that is not feasible with keyframing. Instead of exploding an object into five large pieces, a particle system makes it simple to blow it up into hundreds or thousands of smaller pieces, without having to define individual motion for each one. The pieces can emit other particles, so they can have smoke trails, etc.

Particle systems are also a good way to animate groups of animals such as herds and flocks of birds, by treating each individual member as a particle and defining actions such as "follow the first particle" and having forces that make each particle repel each other at a close distance. Throw in a little randomness and other general rules and you start to get group motion that looks realistic. If you want the group to move through a specific path, you could just keyframe the "leader" particle, as opposed to keyframing hundreds of individual elements.

Inverse Kinematics

"Kinematics" is the science of movement: position, velocity, acceleration, and their rotational equivalents. "Forward kinematics", used in the context of an articulated structure (something with joints), is determining the positions of the links given the joint angles between them—i.e. starting at the `top' of the hierarchy, we work our way along it, applying the relevant transformations, until the end-positions are known—it is easy for the programmer, and it is the way things are normally done. However, it is quite difficult for an animator who simply wants the hand of a model to be `here', or `there'—what the animator has to do is adjust each of the joints in the structure in order to arrive at the desired position. "Inverse kinematics" reverses the situation, making things easy for the animator by allowing an end-effector to be dragged wherever desired, but hard for the programmer/computer because the problem is underconstrained (many configurations of the joints may produce the desired end-position, which one is used?) and ill-conditioned (small changes in the end-position can mean large changes in the joints).

Rotoscoping

[NOTE: *These are two replies to a question specifically asking about the rotoscoping techniques used for the Lightsabers in the "Star Wars" movies and do not go into detail about current digital methods, but the principles are basically the same*].

From Craig Good (*good@pixar.com*): Rotoscoping is animating directly to live action footage. One way to do it is to make blowup prints of each frame from a shot and lay the animation cell over the top. It is then a matter of "tracing" or matching your effect to the picture. It is essentially painting the light saber into Luke's hand in every frame.

Sometimes the rotoscope animation effect is not directly seen on the screen. In "Return of the Jedi" it was impossible to use blue screen in the dark, glossy Emperor's throne room, so mattes were hand drawn to hold out the windows where stars and ships would be composited in. Look at it some time and think about tracing all of those "dental tools" and googaws hanging from the ceiling which pass in front of the windows during long tracking shots. I heard that the animator who did that sequence nearly went insane.

Another technique which gets called Rotoscope these days is matching a 3-D computer graphics element to a live action plate, frame by frame by eye. Generically it refers to just about any kind of animation effect being matched to live action by direct reference to the image in the frame.

It has also been used in animated films since very nearly the beginning. Ralph Bakshi relied on it heavily in "Lord of the Rings", and you can find examples of it in Warner Brothers classic cartoons and in many others. It always looks different than free-hand drawn animation, standing out as looking "too smooth" and a little too life-like. It is a cheap way to produce certain kinds of animation, but usually not a very good way.

From Hal Hickel (*hal@pixar.com*): The type of Rotoscoping referred to here is done in the following way: A positive registered print is made from the original negative for the scene that fx animation will be added to. The registered print is loaded into the camera of an animtion stand (often an Oxberry or Mechanical Concepts, or a dedicated roto stand). The camera has been fitted with a light source and prism which make the camera function as a projector, projecting the image from the print down onto the table top of the stand. So basically you have got the equivalent of a really big darkroom enlarger. The camera can be advanced one frame at a time in either direction. The rotoscoper places a cel or piece of punched paper down on the pegs on the table top, and can see the image of the first frame projected onto the paper. He/she can then create artwork that matches exactly to that frame. Then he/she advances the camera one frame and puts down a new cel. When the artwork is complete, the print, prism, and lamp are removed from the camera, it is loaded up with raw stock and the artwork is shot just like any other drawn animation. What that artwork is depends on the effect that is desired and how it will be added to the live action plates. It can be simple black on white (ink on paper) drawings that will be reversed in optical and burned in with diffusion, or it could be back-lit artwork that is colored and diffused right on the animation stand. Of course much of what is described here is the old fashioned way.

Interpolation

To be done:

- 1-d interpolation

- 3-d rotation interpolation
- euler angles and gimbal lock
- quaternions

References

For general computer graphics references, check out the comp.graphics FAQ. In particular, "Computer Graphics: Principles and Practice" and "Digital Image Warping" both have relevance.

For information on animation (computer and general) books, try DeBry (URL: http://www.xmission.com/~grue/animate/index.html) and 3DSite (URL: http://www.3dsite.com/3dsite/)

A recently started collection of off-the-cuff reviews of animation books is at: URL: http://www.cs.monash.edu.au/~aland/reviews/reviews.index.html

Information about a mailing list for animators (of all persuasions) and wannabees is at URL: http://www.xmission.com/~grue/animate/index.html

A good place for information and papers on Collision Detection is at URL: http://www.cs.unc.edu/~manocha/collide.html

Books (Industry)

Morrison, Mike, "*Becoming a Computer Animator*", Prentice-Hall, 1994.

Covers computer animation history, technology (and how to keep up with it), techniques. with tutorials, interviews with industry luminaries, buyer's guide (s/w and h/w), how to find work, getting an education. a chapter *i.e.* on: television, motion pictures, visualization, forensic, games. incl. 600Mb CD-ROM of PC & Mac animation and software.

"International Directory of Computer Animation Producers", Pixel, 1994.

800+ separate listings of producers in 44 countries. listings include company profiles, also lists animation schools. See Pixel, in 'Organizations', below, for ordering info.

"The Roncarelli Report on the Computer Animation Industry", *Pixel, 1993.*

Market status and strategic analysis for the global computer animation industry: an annual.

Shaddock, Philip, "*3d Modeling Lab*", Waite Group, 1994.

Includes disk with v2.0 of Imagine (see 'Impulse—Imagine').

Books (Computer Animation)

Leister, W, M\"uller, H, and St\"o\3er, "*Fotorealistische Computeranimation*", Springer-Verlag, 1991. ISBN 3-540-53234-X. Text in German. Introductory text for both artists and computer scientists. Covers: animation, modeling, rendering, video, post-production. Includes 60-page glossary. [thanks Wolfgang Leister].

Vince, John, "3D Computer Animation", Addison-Wesley, 1992.

Introductory animation theory for programming. Watt, Alan and Watt, Mark

"*Advanced Animation and Rendering Techniques*", Addison-Wesley, 1992. an excellent text, covering important implementation theory and details.

Whitney, John, "*Digital Harmony*".
?. storyboarding.

Books (Animation)

Arijon, Daniel, "*The Grammar of the Film Language*" ?. storyboarding.

Culhane, Shamus, "*Animation: from script to screen*", St. Martin's Press, 1988. ex-disney animator describes the whole animation process including production details, setting up a studio, storyboards, character animation, and more. Culhane manages to fit a lot into relatively small book.

Halas, John, "*Visual Scripting*". ?. storyboarding.

Hoffer, Thomas, "*Animation: a reference guide*", Greenwood Press, 1993.

Muybridge, Eadweard, "*The Human Figure in Motion*", Dover Press. ISBN 0-486-20204-6.

Muybride, Eadweard, "*Animals in Motion*", Dover Press. ISBN 0-486-20203-8 muybridge spent years taking sequences of strobe photos of animal and human movement. The photos are a great help for anyone trying to make something move properly. Some more good books for the coffee table Russet, Robert, and Starr, Cecile, "*Experimental Animation*".?. storyboarding.

Thomas, Frank and Johnston, Ollie "*Disney Animation: The Illusion of Life*", Abbeville Press, NY, 1981. A look at many of the techniques and approaches used by the Disney studios. Occasionally referred to as 'The Animation Bible' (due to its size and the value of its contents). The Disney 'rules of animation' and many other useful rules-of-thumb are included. Lots of pretty piccies make it good for your coffee table, too!

Foley, Don and Melora "*So you want to be an Animator*" and "*Animation and 3D Modeling on the Mac*". Macintosh-oriented. Excerpts can be found at: URL: http://www.idsonline.com/business/3dfoley/home.html

Journals

Cinefex. The special-effects industry magazine, with reviews of how the SFX in major films were done. Increasingly, this means computer animation.

"*Computer Artist*". "*Computer Graphics*", ACM/SIGGRAPH.

SIGGRAPH's journal. Proc. SIGGRAPH is published in one issue. Some special issues are also of note.

"*Computer Graphics Forum*", Eurographics (EG). Eurographics' journal. Proc. Eurographics is published in one issue. Rarely contains anything of note for animation.

"*Computer Graphics World*", CGW. A graphics industry magazine. Product reviews, industry news. Web page at URL: http://www.cgw.com/

"*The Journal of Visualization and Computer Animation*", ?.

"*Pixel—the computer animation newsletter*", Pixel.

'inside' news on the computer animation industry.

Proc. "*Computer Animation*", Springer-Verlag/CGS.

Proceedings of CGS's computer animation conference

Proc. "*Computer Graphics International*", Springer-Verlag/CGS.

Proceedings of the second-largest graphics conference

Proc. *"Eurographics", see "Computer Graphics Forum"*. Proc. *"Eurographics Workshop on Animation and Simulation"*, Eurographics. Proc. *"Graphics Interface"* proceedings of an important graphics conference. Proc. *"SIGGRAPH"*, Addison-Wesley/ACM Press/ACM/SIGGRAPH, see "Computer Graphics". Proceedings of the largest graphics conference

"3D Artist", Columbine, Inc. desktop 3d graphics for and by independent artists: tips and tricks, 3d news, reviews, classifieds. Web page at URL: http://www.3dartist.com/

"The Visual Computer", Computer Graphics Society (CGS). A good graphics journal. Web page at URL: http://www-ci.u-aizu.ac.jp/VisualComputer/ An extensive list of computer graphics journals, including ordering and other information is available from Ville Walveranta (*vvw@netcom.com*).

Organizations

ACM/SIGGRAPH—The ACM Special Interest Group on Graphics.

Home page at URL: http://www.siggraph.org/

Computer Graphics Society.

Eurographics.

Pixel—the computer animation news people, inc.

109 Vanderhoof Ave, Suite 2, Toronto, ON, Canada M4G 2H7. (416) 424-4657. (Fax) 424-1812. PO Box 1674 5325 Sheridan Drive, Williamsville, NY, USA 14231-1674.

Papers

Lasseter, John, *"Principles of Traditional Animation Applied to 3D Computer Animation"*

Computer Graphics, July 1987, Proc. SIGGRAPH '87. Lasseter relates the disney principles of animation (see Thomas and Johnston, above) to computer animation, and introduces 'hierarchical' animation while here is at it.

Course notes from *"Animation Tricks"* (course offered at SIGGRAPH 1994).

Lecturers were Chris Wedge, John Lasseter, Jim Blinn, and Ken Perlin.

Shoemake, Ken, *"Animating Rotation with Quaternion Curves"*

Computer Graphics, July 1985, Proc. SIGGRAPH '85. an early quaternion paper. There are probably better ones, anyone?

Animation Software

GWEB (URL: http://www2.cinenet.net/GWEB/) and 3DSite (URL: http://www.3dsite.com/3dsite/) both have information on animation software. SGI's WWW site (URL: http://www.sgi.com/) has pointers to applications that run on their machines.

The following fields in the product listings have been excised in the posted version for the sake of brevity: Platform, Company, Cost, Notes. A separate post follows with the full software listings.

3-D Package Reviews

Reviews of the following six high-end UNIX animation packages are now available by ftp from avalon: ftp://avalon.viewpoint.com/pub/misc/six-anim-reviews.gz Originally published in Computer Graphics World Oct-Nov 1993, Internet distribution thanks to Chris Williams January, 1994.

- Alias Animator (see 'Alias—Animator')
- ElectroGIG 3DGO (see 'ElectroGIG—3DGO')
- Softimage Creative Environment (see 'Softimage—Creative Environment')
- TDI Explore (see 'TDI—Explore')
- Vertigo Revolution (see 'Vertigo—Revolution')
- Wavefront Advanced Visualizer (see 'Wavefront—Advanced Visualizer')

3D Choreographer

Home page at URL: http://www.spadion.com/anicom/

3D/EYE *TriSpectives*

Home page at URL: http://www.eye.com/

AERO

AERO web page. URL: http://www.informatik.uni-stuttgart.de/ipvr/bv/aero/aero.html. Available by FTP at URL: ftp://ftp.informatik.uni-stuttgart.de/pub/AERO/

Alias | Wavefront *PowerAnimator*

The Alias | Wavefront Website: URL: http://www.aw.sgi.com/

An Independent Alias WWW Site: (in German?)

URL: http://www.uni-wuppertal.de/computer/software/grafik/Alias/, and associated ftp site. URL: ftp://ftp.uni-wuppertal.de/pub/graphics/Alias/

The Alias FAQs at:

URL: http://www.uni-wuppertal.de/computer/software/grafik/Alias/FAQ/welcome.english.html

The 'comp.graphics.apps.alias' newsgroup.

For a review, see '3-D Package Reviews'.

To subscribe to the mailing list: 'mailto://listserv@uga.cc.uga.edu//"subscribe alias-l Your_Name"'.

Alias | Wavefront *Advanced Visualizer*

For a review, see '3-D Package Reviews'. The 'comp.graphics.apps.wavefront' newsgroup.

To subscribe to the mailing list: 'mail://listserv@psuvm.cac.psu.edu//"subscribe wavefr-l <yournamehere>"'.

There is a 2-way gateway between the mailing list and the newsgroup.

A WWW site at URL: http://www.aw.sgi.com/

Alias | Wavefront *Explore*

ex TDI *Explore* (see 'TDI—Explore')

For a review of TDI Explore see '3-D Package Reviews'. The 'comp.graphics.apps. wavefront' newsgroup, which is predominantly concerned with the Advanced Visualizer.

*Autodesk *3D Studio**

To subscribe to the mailing list: 'mailto://majordomo@autodesk.com//"subscribe 3dstudio-L <your-full-e-mail-address> (Your Real Name)"'.

'comp.graphics.packages.3dstudio' newsgroup

There's an occasional FAQ: 'post://comp.graphics.animation/"3DS FAQ"'.

You can find objects here: URL: ftp://avalon.viewpoint.com/pub/objects/3ds/

And utilities (IPAS plug-ins, etc.) here: URL: ftp://avalon.viewpoint.com/pub/utils/3ds/

*Caligari *TrueSpace**

ex Octree *Caligari* on the Amiga

A home page under construction is at: URL: http://www.netnet.net/users/truespace/ There is a Compuserve forum. The mailing list: send SUBSCRIBE to '*truespace-request@cs.uregina.ca*' Caligari is '<caligari@aol.com>'.

Mike Morrison's 'Becoming a Computer Animator' [see 'Books (Industry)'] includes a CD-ROM with the v2.0 demo version on it. There is a demo version and some other stuff available by FTP here: URL: ftp://ftp.netnet.net/pub/mirrors/truespace/

*ComputerEasy *3-D Design Plus**

Digital Creations *DCTV*

To subscribe to the mailing list: 'mail://DCTV-request@nova.cc.purdue.edu//'.

Dragon

Get the modeller (SGI binary only) and some models from URL: ftp://ftp.cs.ubc.ca/pub/pickup/forsey/ Some animations using the modeller are here URL: http://www.cs.ubc.ca/nest/imager/imager.html.

*EAI *Vislab**

WWW page at URL: http://www.eai.com/ (**DOWN**) (still under construction?)

ElectricImage

WWW page at URL: http://guppie.cac.psu.edu/EIAS/EIASwelcome.html

*ElectroGIG *3DGO**

For a review, see '3-D Package Reviews'. ElectroGIG's WWW page at URL: http://www.gig.nl/1/Online/

*Hash *Animation Master**

ex Playmation, ex Animation Journeyman (Playmation still sells). For direct help/information e-mail '*animmaster@aol.com*'. To subscribe to the mailing list: 'mail://listserv@netcom.com//"subscribe animaster-l"'. A WWW URL: ftp://ftp.netcom.com/pub/ga/gavingav/Home.html

A more current Web page: URL: http://www.hash.com/~hashinc/
FTP some information URL: ftp://ftp.netcom.com/pub/ga/gavingav/Hash_Info
Or simply FTP around at URL: ftp://ftp.netcom.com/pub/ga/gavingav/
There is also stuff here URL: http://www.xmission.com/~gastown/animation/index.html

Impulse *Imagine*

To subscribe to the mailing list, send a message to:
Listserv@sjuvm.stjohns.edu ...with the following body:
SUBSCRIBE IMAGINE [First Name] [Last Name]
(Do not include Brackets)
Philip Shaddock's '3D Modeling Lab' [see 'Books (Computer Animation)'] includes a copy of v2.0 on disk.
A demo of the current (4.0) version of Imagine is available for downloading from the Website: URL:http://www.coolfun.com/NatPix *Blizzard*

A WWW site URL: ftp://ftp.netcom.com/pub/na/natpix/html/natpix.html Get the demo version by FTP URL: ftp://ftp.netcom.com/pub/na/natpix/blizdemo.2.9.tar.Z

NewTeK *Lightwave 3D*

A WWW site URL: http://www.newtek.com/ An FTP site at URL: ftp://tomahawk.welch.jhu.edu/pub/LW newsgroup: comp.graphics.apps.lightwave

To subscribe to the mailing list: mail://lightwave-request@bobsbox.rent.com//subscribe lightwave-l <your-e-mail-address> (<your-real-name>).

ObjViewer

Get a Macintosh binary over the WWW. URL: http://www.hut.fi/~jmunkki/ObjViewer.sea.bin

Radiance *Movieola*

*RealSoft *Real 3D**

Home page at: http://ns1.win.net/~real3d/

There is a demo and other goodies at URL: ftp://uunorth.north.net/pub/realsoft/

*Renderize *Live/Visual Reality**

Platform: PC Win (Visual Reality), UNIX (Renderize)

Company: Visual Software Inc. 21731 Ventura Blvd., Ste. 310, Woodland Hills, CA 91364 USA.

Cost: about $259 US for the PC version, Notes, Resources: URL: http://www.vissoft.com/ Compuserve GO VISSOFT.

Side Effects *PRISMS*

SoftF/X for Windows

Web page at URL: http://bytebybyte.com/

*Softimage *Creative Environment**

For a review, see '3-D Package Reviews'.

There are a number of softimage-related mailing lists at 'softimage.co.uk'. These are the lists: '2d, 3d, discussion, eddie, mental, particles, pfx'. To subscribe, mail to the listname with '-request' added to it, with the subject 'subscribe'. For example, to subscribe to the '3d' list, use: 'mail://3d-request@softimage.co.uk/subscribe/'.

There is also a Website URL: http://delphi.beckman.uiuc.edu/softimage/

Specular *Infini-D*

*Strata *StudioPro**

*Symbolics *S-Products**

S-Dynamics, S-Geometry, S-Render, S-Paint, S-Record, S-Colorize, ...

*TripleI *ARKAttack**

TurboSilver

*Vertigo *Revolution**

For a review, see '3-D Package Reviews'.

*Vision Images *Revelation 3D**

Wavefront (see Alias/Wavefront)

2-D Packages

2-D packages included here are for 2-D animation, and multimedia and video presentation and editing. NOTE: There is reportedly a review/comparison of several 2-D packages in the July 1995 issue of NewMedia magazine. Here is a short list forwarded to me by *artsbox@aol.com* (thanks!):

{good}
3D Choreographer—$149 - (919)967-2890
Animation Paintbox - $199 - (310)981-2771
Animator Pro - $595 - (800)879-4233
Animation Works - $495 - (408)982-0200
{better}
Animator Studio - $795 - (800)879-4233
AXA Animation Series - $4,280 - (714)757-1500

*Autodesk *Animator Pro**

aka Animator Studio (?)

AXA

*CAS *Animo**

Now available on the SGI and soon under Windows NT. Contact CAS as *'admin@cam-ani-co.uk'*. URL: http://www.animo.com/

Deluxe Paint

*Disney *Animation Studio**

Fantavision

*Gold Disk *Animation Works**

*Hanna-Barbera *Animation Workshop**

Linker

*Macromedia *Action!**

*MetroLight *Annie**

*MotionWorks *ProMotion**

*Vision Images *Animator Broadcast**

*Softimage *Toons**

Morph Packages

DMorph

Find it by FTP as this URL: ftp://ftp.povray.org/pub/povray/old-incoming/utilities/dmorf112.zip

*Elastic Reality *Morph Plus**

SPMorph

Order full version from Scott Pultz (*scott@eskimo.com*). Available from: URL: http://www.eskimo.com/~scott/spmorf.html, URL: ftp://ftp.eskimo.com/u/s/scott/spmorf20.zip

RMorph

Available by FTP from: URL: ftp://ftp.demon.co.uk/pub/ibmpc/dos/apps/rmorf/rmorf3.zip

WinMorph

Available by FTP in 'ftp://phoenix.oulu.fi/...' and also on 'garbo.uwasa.fi' and 'ftp.funic.fi'.

Xmorph

Available from the X11R6 contrib applications directory.

Renderer Front & Back Ends

'3DPATH.ZIP'. Define several control points and the number of frames between the points, and it would generate an animation based on that info by changing the camera position.

SIPP rendering library -> PPM frames. ['ppm' toolkit] -> 'GIF or something'. ['fbmtofli'] -> FLI animation. Find them all with 'archie'.

link GIF, TGA, PCX images together to make a FLI or FLC anim: Dave's, Targa Animator (DTA), available from: URL: ftp://ftp.povray.org/pub/povray/utilities and on other sites (find one near you with 'archie').

Chapter 4

Analysing Animated Cartoons and Their Evolution

ANIMATED CARTOON

An *animated cartoon* is a short, hand-drawn (or made with computers to look similar to something hand-drawn) film for the cinema, television or computer screen, featuring some kind of story or plot (even if it is a very short one). This section is not about animated films in general, but only about ones which follow the above definition. Although cartoons can use many different types of animation, they all fall under the *traditional animation* category.

History

Early examples of attempts to capture the phenomenon of motion into a still drawing can be found in paleolithic cave paintings, where animals are depicted with multiple legs in superimposed positions, clearly attempting to convey the perception of motion.

The phenakistoscope, zoetrope and praxinoscope, as well as the common flip book, were early animation devices to produce movement from sequential drawings using technological means, but animation did not really develop much further until the advent of motion picture film.

The first animated cartoon (in the traditional sense, i.e. on film) was *"Fantasmagorie"* by the French director Émile Cohl. Released in 1908.

One of the very first successful animated cartoons was "Gertie the Dinosaur" by Winsor McCay. It is considered the first example of true character animation.

In the 1930s to 1960s, theatrical cartoons were produced in huge numbers, and usually shown before a feature film in a movie theatre. MGM, Disney, Paramount and Warner Brothers were the largest studios producing these 5 to 10-minute "shorts."

Competition from television drew audiences away from movie theatres in the late 1950s, and the theatrical cartoon began its decline. Today, animated cartoons are produced mostly for television.

Technologies

The advent of film technology opened opportunities to develop the art of animation. The basic animation process is described in the topic Animation, and the classic, hand-drawn technology in Traditional animation.

At first, animated cartoons were black-and-white and silent. Felix the cat is a notable example.

The first cartoon with synchronized sound is often identified as Walt Disney's Steamboat Willie, starring Mickey Mouse in 1928, but Max Fleischer's 1926 My Old Kentucky Home is less popularly but more correctly credited with this innovation. Fleischer also patented rotoscoping, whereby animation could be traced from a live action film.

With the advent of sound film, musical themes were often used. Animated characters usually performed the action in "loops", i.e., drawings were repeated over and over, synchronized with the music.

Disney also produced the first full-color cartoon in Technicolor, "Flowers and Trees", in 1931, although other producers had earlier made films using inferior, 2-color processes instead of the 3-color process offered by Technicolor.

Later, other movie technologies were adapted for use in animation, such as multiplane cameras, stereophonic sound in Disney's Fantasia in 1941, and later, widescreen processes (e.g. CinemaScope), and even 3D.

Today, animation is commonly produced with computers, giving the animator new tools not available in hand-drawn traditional animation. See Computer animation for further information of the specific technologies. However, many types of animation cannot be called "cartoons", which implies something that resembles drawings. Most forms of 3D computer animation, as well as clay animation and other forms of stop motion filming, are not cartoons in the strict sense of the word.

An animated cartoon created using Adobe Flash is sometimes called a webtoon.

Feature Films

The name "animated cartoon" is generally not used when referring to full-length animated productions, since the term more or less implies a "short." This section will focus on traditionally-animated feature films which would have been called cartoons had they had a shorter running time.

The first feature-length animated film (of any type) was Quirino Cristiani's traditionally-animated *El Apóstol,* made in 1917 in Argentina to resounding critical acclaim and popular success. That film is now lost, as is Cristiani's *Sin dejar rastros,* released a year later. The earliest surviving animated feature film is Lotte Reiniger's The Adventures of Prince Achmed, made in the Weimar Republic in 1926. It used intricate black paper cut-outs and scenes were tinted in various colors. However, it cannot be called a "cartoon" because it used a type of 2D stop motion animation. The first animated feature film with synchronized sound was Cristiani's 1931 traditionally-animated *Peludòpolis,* which is also lost.

Snow White and the Seven Dwarfs (released in 1937) is the first animated feature film to use a Technicolor process and the first to go into worldwide release. To date, Disney has produced 44 "Classic" hand-drawn animated features. For a while it appeared that no more would be produced, since the studio had closed all its facilities for this type of animation (choosing instead to make only computer-animated features). However, there have been recent news that John Lasseter, the new head of Disney's animation division, is attempting to revive the studio's 2-D wing, and has approved to upcoming feature *The Frog Princess* to be made using traditional animation.

Other studios also produced huge numbers of animated features; a list of those released in the United States can be found here.

Notable Artists and Producers

- Stephen Hillenburg
- Tex Avery
- Ralph Bakshi
- Hanna-Barbera
- Don Bluth
- Quirino Cristiani
- Walt Disney
- Max Fleischer
- Paul Grimault
- Ivan Ivanov-Vano
- Chuck Jones
- Walter Lantz
- Matt Stone
- Hayao Miyazaki
- John Lasseter
- Matt Groening
- Mike Judge
- Brad Bird
- Bob Clampett
- Trey Parker
- John Kricfalusi
- Joe Murray
- Jay Ward
- Fred Quimby

Television

American television animation of the 1950s featured quite limited animation styles, highlighted by the work of Jay Ward on *Crusader Rabbit*. Chuck Jones coined the term "illustrated radio" to refer to the shoddy style of most television cartoons that depended more on their soundtracks than visuals. Other notable 1950s programs include UPA's *Gerald McBoing Boing*, Hanna-Barbera's *Huckleberry Hound* and *Quick Draw McGraw*, and rebroadcast of many classic theatrical cartoons from Warner Brothers, MGM, and Disney.

Hanna-Barbera's show, *The Flintstones* was the first successful primetime animated series in the United States, running from 1960-66 (and in reruns since). While many networks followed the show's success by scheduling other primetime cartoons in the early 1960s, including *The Jetsons*, *Top Cat*, and *The Alvin Show*, none of these programs survived more than a year in primetime. However, networks found success by running these failed shows as Saturday morning cartoons, reaching smaller audiences with more demographic unity among children. Television animation for children flourished on Saturday morning, on cable channels like Nickelodeon and Cartoon Network, and in syndicated afternoon timeslots.

Primetime cartoons were virtually non-existent until 1990s hit *The Simpsons* ushered in a new era of *adult animation*.

Commercial Animation

Animation has been very popular in television commercials, both due to its graphic appeal, and the humor it can provide. Some animated characters in commercials have survived for decades, such as Snap, Crackle and Pop in advertisements for Kellogg's cereals.

The legendary animation director Tex Avery was the producer of the first Raid "Kills Bugs Dead" commercials in 1966, which were very successful for the company. The concept has been used in many countries since.

Genres of Animated Cartoons

Funny Animals

The first animated cartoons often depicted funny animals in various adventures. This was the mainstream genre in the United States from the early 1900s until the 1940s, and the backbone of Disney's series of cartoons.

Zany Humor

Bugs Bunny, Daffy Duck of Warner Brothers, and the various films of Tex Avery at MGM introduced this popular form of animated cartoons. It usually involves surreal acts such as characters being crushed by massive boulders or going over the edge of a cliff but floating in mid air for a few seconds. The *Road Runner* cartoons are great examples of these actions. The article Cartoon physics describes typical antics of zany cartoon characters. Disney has, to a lesser extent, applied this to some of their cartoons. Although they never really mastered the genre.

Sophistication

As the medium matured, more sophistication was introduced, albeit keeping the humorous touch. Classical music was often spoofed, a notable example is "What's Opera, Doc" by Chuck Jones. European animation sometimes followed a very different path from American animation. In the Soviet Union, the late 1930s saw the enforcement of socialist realism in animation, a style which lasted throughout the Stalinist era. The animations themselves were mostly for kids, and based on traditional fairy tales.

Limited Animation

In the 1950s, UPA and other studios refined the art aspects of animation, by using extremely limited animation as a means of expression.

Modernism

Graphic styles continued to change in the late 1950s and 1960s. At this point, the design of the characters became more angular, while the quality of the character animation declined.

Animated Music Videos

Popular with the advent of MTV and similar music channels, music videos often contain animation, sometimes rotoscoped (see: *Take on Me*), i.e., based on live action performers. Cartoons animated to music go at least as far back as Disney's 1929 *The Skeleton Dance*. These are now popular with the animated band Gorillaz.

Trivia

An episode of Disney Cartoon series hero Bonkers has Bonkers and Friends saving an old fashioned hand-drawn cartoon studio. Ironically about 10 years after this episode, Disney changed from hand drawn to computer animation.

CASE STUDY: CARTOONS PROMPT DEBATE IN INDIA

The absence of strict blasphemy laws in India—unlike those in Pakistan—allowed for a more open discussion of the Prophet cartoon within the press and a harsher condemnation of violent responses than elsewhere in the subcontinent. The cartoon controversy prompted some Muslim clerics in India to demand a stronger blasphemy law (UPI) both domestically and internationally.

Article 19-4(c) of the Indian Constitution places "reasonable restrictions" on the freedoms of speech and expression "in the interests of the sovereignty and integrity of India or public order or morality."

However, this restriction has generally not interfered with the press, except during the 1975 emergency when Prime Minister Indira Gandhi's Government suspended civil liberties for a two-year period.

The press in India continues to be aggressive, and religious issues can generally be discussed in the public sphere unaffected by the limitations of Article 19. The cartoon controversy thus prompted stronger debates in the pages of India's newspapers than evident elsewhere in the subcontinent.

Leaders Respond

A prominent Islamic leader in India, the *Shahi Imam* of Delhi's Jama Masjid mosque, criticized Prime Minister Manmohan Singh's United Progressive Alliance (UPA) Government for its mild response to the Prophet cartoons:

> "The entire Muslim world is protesting the blasphemy, but this so-called progressive and secular UPA Government is not taking a bit of pain while leading a country where 200 million Muslims live," he said.

The UPA Government later issued a statement, unreservedly condemning the cartoons, but also strongly criticizing violent protests:

"We have greatest respect for all religions. India's commitment to tolerance and upholding religious harmony is unshakeable, but statements by some sections of our people are not acceptable," Prime Minister Manmohan Singh said. "I am sure that all our political and religious leaders would do nothing to inflame public opinion and will exercise the utmost restraint."

Singh also said India had conveyed its outrage to the Danish government and that the offending newspapers should tender an apology and ensure such acts were not repeated.

"The government condemns the action of any country to offend the sentiments of any community. The publication of cartoons had offended Muslims worldwide," Singh said.

Game Platforms, Types of Games and Links

List of Game Platforms

(*i*) Gameboy
(*ii*) GameCube
(*iii*) Mobile
(*iv*) N-Gage
(*v*) Nintendo DS
(*vi*) Nintendo Wii
(*vii*) Online
(*viii*) PC
(*ix*) PS2—Playstation2
(*x*) PS3—Playstation3
(*xi*) PSP—Playstation Portable
(*xii*) Xbox
(*xiii*) Xbox 360

Overview of Types of Games

- *Action:* Action games tend to have a large amount of violence due to their fast-paced nature. This is the category that most "M" (mature-rated) games fall under which are inappropriate for children. Some games are milder but may contain suggestive themes. Action games may pit person against person or person against animal/alien. Some examples of such problematic games include Halo, Star Wars: Jedi Knight and Enter the Matrix.
- *Arcade:* Arcade games can be almost anything from the violent Street Fighter to the classic Pacman. This category includes games that cover the entire spectrum of ratings. Many oider arcade games have been updated and turned 3-D. Some examples are Pacman, Soul Caliber 2 and Frogger.
- *First Person Shooters (FPS):* First person shooters are more popular amongst the multiplayer world than the single player world. Albeit, some single player FPS games have captured our attention as well. Some fine examples of FPS games would

be Half-Life, Counter-Strike, Doom, Castle Wolfenstein and many other types. A first person shooter puts you into the role of a single character toting many weapons and the common goal of reaching the end, escaping doom and all such fun stuff.

- *Multiplayer Online Shooters:* First-person shooters have come a long way since Quake demonstrated the potential for online play in a 3D action game. Today multiplayer shooters are played on consoles as well as PCs, and they encompass everything from realistic counter-terrorist settings to extreme science fiction. When playing in a multiplayer game, you can play in a FFA (Free For All), Team game or any other varieties.
- *Real Time Strategy (RTS):* The role of a real time strategy game is to put the strategic part of your mind into the views of a fast paced environment. Typically your goal in a RTS game would be to defeat the opposing army with an army of yours that you have to build up by getting resources. Fine examples of RTS games would be Starcraft, Warcraft, Total Annihilation, Command and Conquer and many other varieties of games as well.
- *Multiplayer Strategy:* The ability to compete online with other players is becoming a common feature in recent strategy and sports games. Strategy games give you control of entire armies and empires, rather than just a single avatar.
- *Role Playing Game (RPG):* A role playing game is typically a game that is very long and drawn in. There are too many RPG's out there that does not require over 20+ hours of your life. Some fine examples of RPG's are Final Fantasy, Dragon Warrior, Breath of Fire, Secret of Mana and other many varieties. Typically a RPG involves a group of characters that you need to build up or develop to reach a common end goal. To get to this goal, you will need to strengthen your character by leveling him up or gathering new equipment. Some roleplaying games are ideally suited to small groups of players who want exclusive encounters, while others feature large persistent online worlds with hundreds of players running around.
- *Racing Games:* These are real fun and typically revolve around one of the following: stunts, speed, tricks, collisions, or combinations of some or all of these. Off-road Racing and Need for Speed are fine examples. It can be trucks, snowboards, skateboarding, dune buggies, sports cars. Games in this genre include Need for Speed, Moto Racer, Off-road Racing and other titles as well.
- *Simulation:* Simulation games are often aircraft simulations. You get to fly a jet or a helicopter. Most have nothing more to them other than the destruction of enemies; rarely they use excessive language. Some games in this category include Secret Weapons Over Normandy and SimCity.
- *Sports Games:* This genre typically denotes those sports at which you can play in real life. Sports like, skateboarding, snowboarding, tennis, basketball, football and likewise. They feature real life pro teams and put you 'into' the game. Some good examples of games like this would be Madden NFL, Cool Boarders, NBA Slam, and many others such as PGA Tour Golf, Tiger Woods Golf, Brunswick Bowling. Sports games let you guide your team to glory, or test your driving skills against others on the track.
- *Puzzlers:* Puzzle games are another variety that is very popular. Your typical puzzle

game can include everything from chess and checkers to your lonely Marble Madness. Puzzle games are almost never rated higher than 'E' (for everyone). They all take thinking and logic skills. A common puzzle game is Tetris. Many others are Tetris-like or involve color matching skills. Many games incorporate puzzle aspects but are not true puzzles. Some of the puzzle-incorporating games fall under Action or Role-Playing.

Popular Links

International Game Developers Association

Excellent site for learning resources and information on Gaming:

(*i*) Video Games
(*ii*) Video Game Industry
(*iii*) History of Video Games

GAMETRAILERS.COM—A Great Site for Viewing Game Trailers

From its humble beginnings in 2002, Gametrailers.com has evolved into the leading Internet broadcaster for the video game industry. Gametrailers.com was started by gamers who were tired of waiting in line for slow downloads of small, boring gameplay footage. The result of their hard work is what you see today; a vast library of unmarked, high-resolution video game trailers and gameplay that users can download or stream immediately to their computer.

The site, which re-launched in December of 2004, serves millions of trailers a month to media-starved gamers. New features include user registration, game tracking, platform sorting, expanded forums, fan movies, user ratings and the Gametrailer Top20 that ranks the most popular game trailers according to user feedback and number of views.

GAMASUTRA.COM—The Art and Science of Making Games

International Gaming Industry Resource. It has got an amazing amount of information on the videogame industry. If you are looking to enter the field this is the first stop on your journey. Articles on design, news on the state of the industry, resume database, events calendar and lots more.

GAMESPOT.COM—Online Magazine on Computer Games

A part of CNET networks, huge website with lots of previews, cheats, demos, betas, interviews and best of all, user submittable game reviews. Produced in conjunction with Computer Gaming World.

Other CNET Game-Related sites

(*i*) gamerankings.com
(*ii*) sportsgamer.com
(*iii*) gamefaqs.com
(*iv*) metacritic.com

Other Cool Game-Related Sites

(*i*) The Dot Eaters
(*ii*) Game oldies
(*iii*) Gamespy
(*iv*) IGN

Mobygames

Incredible, ongoing database of classic (and recent) computer games, along with lots of box cover images, screen shots, technical info, and interesting trivia tid-bits. Add your own entries, rate the games that are there, read informative articles, and enjoy.

Online Games

- *PC Gameworld:* For PC Games, downloads, reviews, cheats and lots more.
- *Video Games 101*: A very interesting series of articles on classic home game consoles; nicely written and quite indepth.
- *Videogamespot's History of Video Games:* A quick walk-through of the industry's history.

Chapter 5

Multimedia: Historical Development and Evolution

MULTIMEDIA

Multimedia (Lat. Multum + Medium) is media that utilizes a combination of different content forms. The term can be used as a noun (a medium with multiple content forms) or as an adjective describing a medium as having multiple content forms. The term is used in contrast to media which only utilize traditional forms of printed or hand-produced text and still graphics. In general, multimedia includes a combination of text, audio, still images, animation, video, and interactivity content forms.

Multimedia is usually recorded and played, displayed or accessed by information content processing devices, such as computerized and electronic devices, but can also be part of a live performance. *Multimedia* (as an adjective) also describes electronic media devices used to store and experience multimedia content. Multimedia is similar to traditional mixed media in fine art, but with a broader scope. The term "rich media" is synonymous for interactive multimedia. Hypermedia can be considered one particular multimedia application.

Categorization

Multimedia may be broadly divided into linear and non-linear categories. Linear active content progresses without any navigation control for the viewer such as a cinema presentation. Non-linear content offers user interactivity to control progress as used with a computer game or used in self-paced computer based training. Non-linear content is also known as hypermedia content.

Multimedia presentations can be live or recorded. A recorded presentation may allow interactivity via a navigation system. A live multimedia presentation may allow interactivity via interaction with the presenter or performer.

Features

Multimedia presentations may be viewed in person on stage, projected, transmitted, or played locally with a media player. A broadcast may be a live or recorded multimedia presentation.

Broadcasts and recordings can be either analog or digital electronic media technology. Digital online multimedia may be downloaded or streamed. Streaming multimedia may be live or on-demand.

Multimedia games and simulations may be used in a physical environment with special effects, with multiple users in an online network, or locally with an offline computer, game system, or simulator.

The various formats of technological or digital multimedia may be intended to enhance the users experience, for example to make it easier and faster to convey information. Or in entertainment or art, to transcend everyday experience.

Enhanced levels of interactivity are made possible by combining multiple forms of media content. Online multimedia is increasingly becoming object-oriented and data-driven, enabling applications with collaborative end-user innovation and personalization on multiple forms of content over time. Examples of these range from multiple forms of content on web-sites like photo galleries with both images (pictures) and title (text) user-updated, to simulations whose co-efficients, events, illustrations, animations or videos are modifiable, allowing the multimedia "experience" to be altered without reprogramming. In addition to seeing and hearing, Haptic technology enables virtual objects to be felt. Emerging technology involving illusions of taste and smell may also enhance the multimedia experience.

Terminology

History of the Term

In 1965 the term Multi-media was used to describe the *Exploding Plastic Inevitable*, a performance that combined live rock music, cinema, experimental lighting and performance art.

In the intervening forty years the word has taken on different meanings. In the late 1970s the term was used to describe presentations consisting of multi-projector slide shows timed to an audio track. In the 1990s it took on its current meaning. In common usage the term multimedia refers to an electronically delivered combination of media including video, still images, audio, text in such a way that can be accessed interactively. Much of the content on the web today falls within this definition as understood by millions.

Some computers which were marketed in the 1990s were called "multimedia" computers because they incorporated a CD-ROM drive, which allowed for the delivery of several hundred megabytes of video, picture, and audio data.

Word Usage and Context

Since media is the plural of medium, the term "multimedia" is a pleonasm if "multi" is used to describe multiple occurrences of only one form of media such as a collection of audio CDs. This is why it is important that the word "multimedia" is used exclusively to describe *multiple forms* of media.

The term "multimedia" is also ambiguous. Static content (such as a paper book) may be considered multimedia if it contains both pictures and text or may be considered interactive if the user interacts by turning pages at will. Books may also be considered non-linear if the pages are accessed non-sequentially. The term "video", if not used exclusively to describe motion photography, is ambiguous in multimedia terminology. *Video* is often used to describe the file format, delivery format, or presentation format instead of *"footage"* which is used to distinguish motion photography from *"animation"*, motion illustrations. Multiple forms of information content are often not considered multimedia if they do not contain modern forms of presentation such as audio or video. Likewise, single forms of information content with single methods of information processing (e.g. non-interactive audio) are often called multimedia, perhaps to distinguish static media from active media.

Usage

Multimedia finds its application in various areas including, but not limited to, advertisements, art, education, entertainment, engineering, medicine, mathematics, business, scientific research and spatial temporal applications. Several examples are as follows:

Professional

Creative Industries

Creative industries use multimedia for a variety of purposes ranging from fine arts, to entertainment, to commercial art, to journalism, to media and software services provided for any of the industries listed below. An individual multimedia designer may cover the spectrum throughout their career. Request for their skills range from technical, to analytical, to creative.

Commercial

Much of the electronic old and new media utilized by commercial artists is multimedia. Exciting presentations are used to grab and keep attention in advertising. Industrial, business to business, and interoffice communications are often developed by creative services firms for advanced multimedia presentations beyond simple slide shows to sell ideas or liven-up training. Commercial multimedia developers may be hired to design for governmental services and nonprofit services applications as well.

Entertainment and Fine Arts

In addition, multimedia is heavily used in the entertainment industry, especially to develop special effects in movies and animations. Multimedia games are a popular pastime and are software programs available either as CD-ROMs or online. Some video games also use multimedia features. Multimedia applications that allow users to actively participate instead of just sitting by as passive recipients of information are called *Interactive Multimedia*. In the Arts there are multimedia artists, whose minds are able to blend techniques using different media that in some way incorporates interaction with the viewer. One of the most relevant could be Peter Greenaway who is melding Cinema with Opera and all sorts of digital media. Another approach entails the creation of multimedia that can be displayed in a traditional fine arts arena, such as an art gallery. Although multimedia display material may be volatile, the survivability of the content is as strong as any traditional media. Digital recording material may be just as durable and infinitely reproducible with perfect copies every time.

Education

In Education, multimedia is used to produce computer-based training courses (popularly called CBTs) and reference books like encyclopedia and almanacs. A CBT lets the user go through a series of presentations, text about a particular topic, and associated illustrations in various information formats. Edutainment is an informal term used to describe combining education with entertainment, especially multimedia entertainment.

Learning theory in the past decade has expanded dramatically because of the introduction of multimedia. Several lines of research have evolved (e.g. Cognitive load, Multimedia learning, and the list goes on). The possibilities for learning and instruction are nearly endless.

Engineering

Software engineers may use multimedia in Computer Simulations for anything from entertainment to training such as military or industrial training. Multimedia for software interfaces are often done as a collaboration between creative professionals and software engineers.

Industry

In the Industrial sector, multimedia is used as a way to help present information to shareholders, superiors and coworkers. Multimedia is also helpful for providing employee training, advertising and selling products all over the world via virtually unlimited web-based technologies.

Mathematical and Scientific Research

In Mathematical and Scientific Research, multimedia are mainly used for modeling and simulation. For example, a scientist can look at a molecular model of a particular substance and manipulate it to arrive at a new substance. Representative research can be found in journals such as the Journal of Multimedia.

Medicine

In Medicine, doctors can get trained by looking at a virtual surgery or they can simulate how the human body is affected by diseases spread by viruses and bacteria and then develop techniques to prevent it.

Miscellaneous

In Europe, the reference organization for Multimedia industry is the European Multimedia Associations Convention (EMMAC).

An observatory for jobs in the multimedia industry provides surveys and analysis about multimedia and ITC jobs.

Structuring Information in a Multimedia Form

Multimedia represents the convergence of text, pictures, video and sound into a single form. The power of multimedia and the Internet lies in the way in which information is linked.

Multimedia and the Internet require a completely new approach to writing. The style of writing that is appropriate for the 'on-line world' is highly optimized and designed to be able to be quickly scanned by readers.

A good site must be made with a specific purpose in mind and a site with good interactivity and new technology can also be useful for attracting visitors. The site must be attractive and innovative in its design, function in terms of its purpose, easy to navigate, frequently updated and fast to download.

When users view a page, they can only view one page at a time. As a result, multimedia users must create a 'mental model of information structure.'

Patrick Lynch, author of the Yale University Web Style Manual, states that users need predictability and structure, with clear functional and graphical continuity between the various components and subsections of the multimedia production. In this way, the home page of any multimedia production should always be a landmark, able to accessed from anywhere within a multimedia piece.

Conferences

There are a large number of multimedia conferences, the two main scholarly scientific conferences being:

- ACM Multimedia;
- IEEE ICME, International Conference on Multimedia and Expo.

Historical Development and Evolution

Today multimedia might be defined as the seamless digital integration of text, graphics, animation, audio, still images and motion video in a way that provides individual users with high levels of control and interaction. The evolution of multimedia is a story of the emergence and convergence of these technologies.

As these technologies developed along separate paths for disparate purposes, visionaries saw the possibilities for the sum of the parts as well potential personal application in the broader societal context. This section highlights visionaries and technological developments from the development of the printing press to the emergence of the world-wide web (www).

> *"The historian, with a vast chronological account of a people, parallels it with a skip trail which stops only at the salient items, and can follow at any time contemporary trails which lead him all over civilization at a particular epoch. There is a new profession of trailblazers, those who find delight in the task of establishing useful trails through the enormous mass of the common record. The inheritance from the master becomes, not only his additions to the world's record, but for his disciples the entire scaffolding by which they were erected."*
>
> Vannevar Bush (1945).

This section is constructed around five themes developed over a time line, presented within an interactive timeline framework.

- *Visionaries:* From the ingenious idea of the programmable computer, trace the innovations of the outstanding thinkers that had a direct impact on the explosion of the technological age.
- *Text, Processing and Software:* Inventions and innovations that spawned the development of software enabling computers to move from mathematical processing to technology that creates and delivers multimedia.
- *Computers:* From the printing press through the exclusive military and academic and corporate worlds trace computer development into the ubiquitous role of the desktop personal computer of today.
- *Audio and Communication:* From the telegraph signal to cellular telephones, follow the development from signal transmission to digital transmission of voice.
- *Video and Animation:* From manually manipulated negative film and hand drawn sketches, video and animation develops to sophisticated digital creation and rendering of motion.

Time & Vision	*Text, Processing & Software*	*Computers*	*Audio & Telecommunication*	*Video & Animation*
Pre20th Century				
1455	Printing Press Gutenberg and Caxton, movable type printing			
1780 FRANKLIN		Franklin discovers electricity		
1822 BABBAGE		Charles Babbage designs the Difference Engine		
1833 LADY BYRON		Babbage designs Analytical Machine, often considered to be the fist general-purpose computer. Lady Byron writes programs for the machine		
1837 MORSE			Telegraph receiver and transmitter	
1839				Daguerreotype: photographs produced using a paper negative
1854 BOOLE		George Boole: develops binary mathematical language of 1's and 0's (Boolean Algebra)		
1858			Transatlantic cable laid	
1867	Remington Manual Typewriter			
1876 BELL			Telephone	
1879 EDISON			Granted a phonograph patent	

(Contd.)

Time & Vision	*Text, Processing & Software*	*Computers*	*Audio & Telecommunication*	*Video & Animation*
1886		Burroughs: First commercially successful adding machine.		
1888			Mood Music for Film: Musical scores sent along for organ accompaniment Gramophone: disks manually rotated @ 70 rpm	Film: Sequential photographs with sprockets manually pulled through a projector
1890 HOLLERITH		Tabulating Machine for the U.S. Govt. Census using punch cards. The tabulating machine later became IBM.		
1900-1933				
1920			Commercial radio: KDKA Pittsburgh	
1925			Electronically recorded sound discs AT&T's Bell labs allow recording of whole symphonies	
1927			"Talkies": The first commercial talkie film using optical sound recording.	"The Jazz Singer" starring Al Jolsen.
			Juke Box: Automatic Music Instrument Company—coin operated phonograph Telephone becomes operational between London and New York.	First public demonstration of T.V.
1928 DISNEY				"Steamboat Willie" first cartoon with a fully synchronized soundtrack
1931 ZUSE		Conrad Zuse First calculator.		
1932			Magnetic tape BASF introduces magnetic tape recording	
1933			Dudley	
			Vocoder—voice coder	
1934-1945				
1936 TURING		"Turing's Machine" defined as capable of computing any calculable function		
1937				"Snow White and the Seven Dwarfs" the first full-length animation is released.
1939 ATANASOFF		John Atanasoff and Clifford Berry design a prototype of the ABC computer (the first automated digital computer).		
1940				First color T.V. broadcast.

(Contd.)

Time & Vision	*Text, Processing & Software*	*Computers*	*Audio & Telecommunication*	*Video & Animation*
1941		"Colossus" built for the British military from Alan Turing's design		
1943		Zuse—Z3: First machine to work on a binary system rather than decimal system.		
1945 BUSH	"*As we may think*" in the Atlantic Monthly	Memex		
1946-1956				
1946 MAUCHLY		ENIAC Electronic Numerator Integrator and Calculator the first successful high speed digital computer. However, it used the same concepts that Atanasoff and Berry used to build the ABC computer.		
1948		Shockley, Bardeen and Brattain develop the transistor. More reliable and cheaper to run than vacuum tubes.	Open reel tape recorder by Magnecord	
1951		UNIVAC Computer used magnetic tape for buffer memory.		
1952		IBM 701: First electronic stored computer that used vacuum tubes, RAM, punch cards and was the size of a piano.		
1953	Electric typewriter			
1954			Transistor radio: First commercial use of transistor radio developed in 1947 © Bell labs	
1956			First Transaltantic telephone cable	CBS broadcast First network broadcast using video tape.
1957-1964				
1957			Sputnik launched	
1958		CRAY: Builds the CDC 1604 for Control Data Corporation. The first fully transistorized supercomputer. Texas Instruments develops the first Integrated Circuit. Solves the problems of speed, size and wiring.		

(*Contd.*)

Time & Vision	*Text, Processing & Software*	*Computers*	*Audio & Telecommunication*	*Video & Animation*
1959		Second generation computer introduced by IBM. Used transistors instead of vacuum tubes.		
1960		Removable disks Paul Baran sees a communications network different than the traditional point to point links. He envisioned a "fishnet network".		
1963		CAD (Computer Aided Design) Sketchpad uses the first light pen.	Phillips first compact audio cassette.	First home video tape recording
1964 McLUHAN	"*Understanding Media*" postulates the global village.	Third generation of computers included the photo printing of conductive circuit boards to eliminate wiring.		
1965-1974				
1965 NELSON	Xanadu hypertext project			
1969 VanDAM	Development of hypertext editing system		Dolby labs produces Dolby noise reduction for prerecorded tapes	
1970		Fourth generation computer by IBM uses chips to reduce size and cost.		
1971		Intel 4004 chip developed by Hoff. Computers can'now be owned by individuals.		
1972				Phillips laserdisc playback only deck PONG, first commercial video game
1973	Metcalf outlines ideas for ethernet		Kahn & Cerf present ideas for structure of Internet	
1974		Intel 8080 microprocessor which was to be used in many PC's.		
1975-1979				
1975 GATES		Microsoft is founded by Bill Gates.	DND takes over ARPANET	SONY Betamax VCR with a one hour, ½ inch video cassette tape.
1976				JVC introduces VHS format.
1977 JOBS & WOZNIAK		Apple was founded by Steven Jobs and Steve Wozniak	E-mail provided to 100 researchers	

(Contd.)

Time & Vision	*Text, Processing & Software*	*Computers*	*Audio & Telecommunication*	*Video & Animation*
1978			First commercially available cell phone	
1979	VisiCalc: the first spreadsheet		Walkman: SONY introduces a portable audio cassette player.	
	Wordstar: word processing package is released.		First MUD, MUD1, by Richard Bartle and Roy Trubshaw at U of Essex Beginning of on-line services with CompuServe and The Source.	
1980-1989				
1980	Word Processing Machine Single purpose machine with limited storage on magnetic material			SONY introduces the consumer camcorder
1981	The MS-DOS, or Microsoft Disk Operating System	Adam Osborne completed the first portable computer	Apollo Computer unveiled the first work station	
1982	Lotus 1-2-3, software writes directly into the video system of the IBM PC		First digital audio 5" compact disc.	Computer-generated graphics in movies step forward with Disney's "Tron."
1983		First PC clone	Musical Instrument Digital Interface (MIDI) introduced Internet is born TCP/IP protocol	
1984 ENGLEBART	W. Gibson in *Neuromancer* coins the term "cyberspace."	Apple Computers introduces the Macintosh with the first mouse driven GUI (Graphical User Interface).	3½ inch "microfloppy" diskette DNS: domain name server introduced voicemail developed	
1985	Desktop publishing Aldus PageMaker for the Macintosh		NSFNET: linking five university supercomputer centers (550 mg) CD-ROMs evolve from CDs on which music is recorded.	
1986		Optical transistor patented, a component central to digital optical computing.		SONY Betamax removed from consumer shelves
1987	Hypercard: Apple (1987) actually hypermedia (nonsequential links to documents) includes authoring system—tool for building interactive hypermedia documents (Authorware Model, Linkway)		First digital audio tape players	
1988	Robert Morris' worm flooded the ARPANET.			3D Graphics: 3D graphical supercomputers Pixar's "Tin Toy": the first computer-animated film to win an Academy Award.

(Contd.)

Time & Vision	Text, Processing & Software	Computers	Audio & Telecommunication	Video & Animation
1989	Handwriting recognition is introduced by grid with a touch sensitive pad on a lap top computers.	Battery powered, fully functional notebook computer.	Corporation for Research and Education Networking (CREN) is formed by merging CSNET into BITNET	Maxis released SimCity, a sophisticated video game launching a new genre 'simulation'.
1990-date				
1990	IBM, Tandy AT &T, and others announce the software specifications for multimedia platforms. ARCHIE	IBM, Tandy AT &T, and others announce the hardware specifications for multimedia platforms.	The birth of the World Wide Web Tim Berners-Lee, develops HTML (HyperText Markup Language)	
1991	GOPHER PGP encryption released by Phillip Zimmerman		National Science Foundation lifts ban on commerce on the Internet.	
1992 BERNERS LEE	VERONICA		World Wide Web	
1993	Mosaic developed by M. Andreessen		Internet	
1994			Internet goes interactive; shopping, banking, live concerts, radio broadcasting, spamming	
1995			Private ISP becomes big business Netscape goes public	

"Our failure to place affection and empathy at the center of the educational process says something very grave about us, and I do not think it will be of much value for us to persevere unless we can learn to love our technology less and ourselves more." ... Neil Postman (1996)

*"In order that the picture may not be too commonplace, by reason of sticking to present-day patterns, it may be well to mention one such possibility, not to prophesy but merely to suggest, for prophecy based on extension of the known has substance, while prophecy founded on the unknown is only a doubly involved guess."*Vannevar Bush (1945)

Before you become too entranced with gorgeous gadgets and mesmerizing video displays, let me remind you that information is not knowledge, knowledge is not wisdom and wisdom is not foresight. Each grow out of the other and we need them all. Arthur C. Clark (1997)

Interactive Multimedia at TCNJ

Definition of Interactive Multimedia

Interactive multimedia refers to the use of several media in learning where learners are able to process information through multiple sensory channels including auditory, visual and kinesthetic manipulation. The advantages of interactive multimedia in learning include visualizing abstract and concrete ideas by creating images, diagrams, or animations, reducing cognitive load in learning, facilitating mental representation of external objects, and improving cognitive learning for low spatial ability learners.

Overview

The program in Interactive Multimedia is a transdisciplinary undergraduate education, providing a national exemplar of educating students to be "successful, ethical, and visionary leaders in a multicultural, highly technological, and increasingly global world." The program is a cutting-edge, collaborative work to prepare students for the next generation of innovation in technology and communication. It is specifically targeted to students who are talented across disciplines, those whose gifts are broad-based and whose potential lies in developing skills to integrate ideas from a variety of perspectives. The program is unique and explicitly designed as an undergraduate experience. It is the only program of its type in the country (undergraduate or graduate) that combines in a balanced manner with emphasis on interaction and collaboration, the three areas of Digital Media, Interactive Computing, and Professional Writing.

Students may specialize in one of the above areas, each one leading to a different option to be indicated on their transcript. Due to the inherent transdisciplinary nature of Interactive Multimedia, students in one area continue to take intermediate and advanced courses in each of the other two areas. Students also work with others from all three areas, in order to develop an approach that represents an intellectual synthesis within their discipline.

Students who complete the major are prepared to work in such diverse fields as web design and production, technical writing, instructional technology, as well as print, online, interactive, or broadcast media. The Interactive Multimedia program can be effectively coupled with an array of existing majors and minors, including English, Music, Computer Science, Art, Marketing, Information Systems, Women and Gender Studies, African American Studies, Communications, History, Psychology and Sociology. Courses in departments such as Art and Music are shared among the programs. Not only will minors and dual majors be available to students in these programs, but students will be able to take various courses taught in other programs as a part of their major.

The on-going mission of the Interactive Multimedia program is to bring students and faculty together from disparate, although converging, fields with the expectation that they work together, collaboratively and as individual creators, with respect and understanding for varying points of view, vision, and contributions; meaning...

- To be one of the earliest leading and innovative programs that support and nurture this attitude of creativity among and across disciplines;
- To have faculty and students working together in a collaborative environment, where they can effectively pursue and share their research and creative goals;
- To foster:
  - — Depth of investigation into underlying structures, principles and processes;
  - — Quality of communication and realization of output/projects;
  - — Concern for the social implications and effects of the results of this work; and
  - — A place where learning is both significant and enjoyable.

Multimedia Esperanto

Multimedia Esperanto is a formal artificial language for the modeling of multimedia content. The name derives from Esperanto and emphasizes the ambition to foster accessibility and semantic understanding of multimedia contents for every human independently on sensual or cognitive deficiencies and disabilities or cultural origin. It allows to provide every human with a uniform semantic and artistic impression of an arbitrary multimedia content.

The grammar and vocabulary are based on multimedia structures like certain color sequences and specific pattern arrangements *(Visual Archetypes)*. As an artificial language, Multimedia Esperanto is not genealogically related to any ethnic language.

Originally defined by Philipp E. Haindl and further developed by a group of French and Austrian students, Multimedia Esperanto now is a versatile and universally applicable modeling language, which harnesses the human's individualities for its constant enhancement and expansion.

History

The foundations of Multimedia Esperanto go back to the theory of archetypes of the Swiss psychiatrist Carl Gustav Jung and Ludwig Wittgenstein's *picture theory of language*, which became known as propositions 1-3 of his famous work Tractatus logico-philosophicus.

Both theories are mainly based upon visual symbols for prototypes of ideas and are linked with the semantics of observed information. Following Jung's theory they subsequently become involved in the semantic interpretation of information, whereas L. Wittgenstein's theory expects visual symbols to possess the same logical structure as the semantics being associated with the related visual information.

By 2004, a prototype of a visual alphabet for the computation of visual symbols was developed, which combined the aspects of both theories to evaluate if images follow a visual grammar similar to their semantics. This prototype was intended to ease the computation of classifiers for machine learning applications allowing the computer to grasp the meaning and implication of an image *(machine image understanding)*.

The visual symbols being computed with the prototype were evaluated for their mathematical uniqueness in the full set of possible symbols and the proband's unambiguous connection between the symbol and the regarding semantics with the ambition to trace single visual symbols in imagery. Assuming that a single image incorporates multiple visual symbols following a logical order, the prototype was later improved to also detect multiple symbols in images, which are jointly associated with the images' semantics.

In spring 2005, the prototype was extended to also regard the geometrical dependencies of visual symbols in an image as well as the correlation between proper recognition of visual symbols and surrounding color situation. In contrast to former versions, which contained a fixed set of visual symbols and language elements, it allowed the computation of these symbols and elements on demand by different communities of people.

Asking different communities to compute their own visual symbols and language elements was one of the major steps in supporting perception and culture dependent semantics of visual symbols and made Multimedia Esperanto a versatile language, which, though open to user's diversities, also respects the individual demands for being universally applicable.

Language Features

Just like any other language, Multimedia Esperanto is based upon an alphabet and a grammar prescribing the way letters must be arranged to form a sentence. In this context, letters are composed of specific, auxiliary visual patterns, called *Visual Archetypes*, and the grammar is derived from Wittgenstein's theory of visual language. As any other language, Multimedia Esperanto is a means to convey information simply by forming or translating sentences (represented by visual contents augmented with specific visual patterns), which mediate certain semantics and propositions to the beholder and thus facilitate to recognize a visual information's semantic proposition.

Color Equivalents

Color equivalents are ordinary colors, which are computed representatives for specific sets of similar colors not singly distinguishable by the human eye. These color equivalents are equally perceivable by every human independently on sensual constraints and can thus provide the same impression for everybody. They can be imagined as visual «common denominators» for similar colors, which would otherwise be perceived differently and should thus be substituted.

Visual Archetypes

The theory of archetypes was first described by the Swiss psychiatrist Carl Gustav Jung, who was also the founder of Analytical Psychology. The main proposition of Jung's theory is that archetypes are innate prototypes for ideas, which may subsequently become involved in the interpretation of observed information. Archetypes can be imagined as a sort of psychological organs, directly analogous to our physical, bodily organs: both being morphological givens for the species and both arising at least partially through evolutionary processes. They are symbols, which occur in our consciousness and link sensual information with certain sensual impressions and images in our minds.

Visual Archetypes build an interface between Jung's theory and modern informatics and facilitate understanding of visual contents by intensively mediating its semantic proposition, which notably supports people with cognitive deficiencies to perceive digital artistic contents more tangible.

Exhibitions

International exhibitions and festivals of Multimedia Esperanto projects:

- Linz (October 2005, Lange Nacht der Forschung)
- Paris (March 2006, Spring Technology Briefing)
- Berlin (May 2006, Spring Technology Workshop)
- Linz (July 2006, 10th International Conference on Computers Helping People with Special Needs)
- Washington (expected November 2007, Winter Developer Symposium)

Multimedia Messaging Service

Multimedia Messaging Service (MMS) is a standard for telephony messaging systems that allows sending messages that include multimedia objects (images, audio, video, rich text) and not just text as in Short Message Service (SMS). It is mainly deployed in cellular networks along with other messaging systems like SMS, Mobile Instant Messaging and Mobile E-mail. Its main standardization effort is done by 3GPP, 3GPP2 and Open Mobile Alliance (OMA).

Basics

MMS is the evolution of *Short Message Service* (SMS, which is a text-only messaging technology for mobile networks). It allows the sending and receiving of multimedia messages such as graphics, video and audio clips. It has been designed to work with mobile packet data services such as GPRS and 1x/EVDO.

Methods of Delivery

There are two modes of delivery in MMS: *immediate* or *deferred*:

- *Immediate delivery*: When the MMS client on the mobile phone receives the MMS notification, it then immediately (without user intervention or knowledge) retrieves the MMS message from the Multimedia Messaging Service Center (MMSC) that sent the notification. After retrieval, the subscriber is alerted to the presence of a newly arrived MMS message.
- *Deferred delivery*: The MMS client alerts the subscriber that an MMS message is available, and allows the subscriber to choose if and when to retrieve the MMS message.

As with the MMS submission, the MMS retrieval request, whether immediate or deferred, occurs with an HTTP request. The MMSC responds by transmitting the MMS message in an HTTP response to the MMS client, after which the subscriber is finally alerted that the MMS message is available.

The essential difference between immediate and deferred delivery is that the former hides the network latencies from the subscriber, while the latter does not. Immediate or deferred delivery are handset dependent modes, which means that the handset manufacturer can provide the handset in one mode or the other or let the user decide his/her preference.

Application

MMS-enabled mobile phones enable subscribers to compose and send messages with one or more multimedia parts. Multimedia parts may include text, images, audio and video. These content types should conform to the MMS Standards. For example your phone can send an MPEG-4 video in AVI format, but the other party who is receiving the MMS may not be able to interpret it. To avoid this, all mobiles should follow the standards defined by OMA. Mobile phones with built-in or attached cameras, or with built-in MP3 players are very likely to also have an MMS messaging client—a software program that interacts with the mobile subscriber to compose, address, send, receive, and view MMS messages.

History

MMS was originally developed within the *Third-Generation Partnership Program* (3GPP), a standards organization focused on standards for the UMTS/GSM networks.

Since then, MMS has been deployed world-wide and across both GSM/GPRS and CDMA networks.

MMS has also been standardized within the *Third-Generation Partnership Program 2* (3GPP2), a standards organization focused on specifications for CDMA2000 networks.

As with most 3GPP standards, the MMS standards have three stages:

- *Stage* 1—Requirements (3GPP TS 22.140)
- *Stage* 2—System Functions (3GPP TS 23.140)
- *Stage* 3—Technical Realizations.

Both 3GPP and 3GPP2 have delegated the development of the Stage 3 Technical Realizations to the OMA, a standards organization focused on specifications for the mobile wireless networks.

Challenges Faced by MMS

There are some interesting challenges with MMS that do not exist with SMS:

- *Content adaptation*: Multimedia content created by one brand of MMS phone may not be entirely compatible with the capabilities of the recipients' MMS phone. In the MMS architecture, the recipient MMSC is responsible for providing for *content adaptation* (e.g., image resizing, audio codec transcoding, etc.), if this feature is enabled by the mobile network operator. When content adaptation is supported by a network operator, its MMS subscribers enjoy compatibility with a larger network of MMS users than would otherwise be available.
- *Distribution lists*: Current MMS specifications do not include distribution lists nor methods by which large numbers of recipients can be conveniently addressed, particularly by content providers, called *Value Added Service Providers* (VASPs) in 3GPP. Since most SMSC vendors have adopted FTP as an ad-hoc method by which large distribution lists are transferred to the SMSC prior to being used in a bulk-messaging SMS submission, it is expected that MMSC vendors will also adopt FTP.
- *Bulk messaging*: The flow of *peer-to-peer* MMS messaging involves several over-the-air transactions that become inefficient when MMS is used to send messages to large numbers of subscribers, as is typically the case for VASPs. For example, when one MMS message is submitted to a very large number of recipients, it is possible to receive a *delivery report* and *read-reply report* for each and every recipient. Future MMS specification work is likely to optimize and reduce the transactional overhead for the bulk-messaging case.
- *Handset configuration*: Unlike SMS, MMS requires a number of handset parameters to be set. Poor handset configuration is often blamed as the first point of failure for many users. Service settings are sometimes preconfigured on the handset, but mobile operators are now looking at new device management technologies as a means of delivering the necessary settings for data services (MMS, WAP, etc.) via over-the-air programming (OTA).
- *WAP push*: Few mobile network operators offer direct connectivity to their MMSCs for content providers. This has resulted in many content providers using WAP push

as the only method available to deliver 'rich content' to mobile handsets. WAP push enables 'rich content' to be delivered to a handset by specifying the URL (via binary SMS) of a pre-compiled MMS hosted on a content provider's web server. A downside of WAP push is that from a billing perspective this content is typically billed at data rates rather than as an MMS. These charges can be significant and result in 'bill shock' for consumers.

MMS should not be confused with Enhanced Messaging Service (EMS), which is simply Short Message Service (SMS) with additional payload capabilities, allowing a mobile phone to send and receive messages that have special text formatting (such as bold or color), animations, pictures, icons, sound effects, and special ring tones.

MMSC Vendors

- Openwave
- Ericsson

Protocols

- EAIF—Nokia's External Application Interface.
- MM1—the 3GPP interface between MMS User Agent and MMS Center.
- MM2—the 3GPP interface between MMS Relay and MMS Server.
- MM3—the 3GPP interface between MMS Center and external servers.
- MM4—the 3GPP interface between MMS Centers.
- MM5—the 3GPP interface between MMS Center and HLR.
- MM6—the 3GPP interface between MMS Center and user databases.
- MM7—the 3GPP interface between MMS VAS applications and MMS Center.
- MM8—the 3GPP interface between MMS Center and the billing systems.
- MM9—the 3GPP interface between MMS Center and an online charging system.
- MM10—the 3GPP interface between MMS Center and a message service control function.
- MM11—the 3GPP interface between MMS Center and an external transcoder.

Multimedia Literacy

Multimedia literacy is a new aspect of literacy that is being recognized as technology expands the way people communicate. The concept of Literacy emerged as a measure of the ability to read and write. In modern context, the word means reading and writing at a level adequate for written communication. A more fundamental meaning is now needed to cope with the numerous media in use, perhaps meaning a level that enables one to successfully function at certain levels of a society. Multimedia is the use of several different forms of media to convey information. Several are already a part of the canon of global communication and publication: (text, audio, graphics, animation, video, and interactivity). Others, such as virtual reality, computer programming and robotics are possible candidates for future inclusion. With widespread use of computers, the basic literacy of 'reading' and 'writing' are often done via a computer, providing a foundation stone for more advanced levels of multimedia literacy.

Definition Wars

Critics of the concept of multimedia literacy question whether the term literacy can be extended beyond its original definition. Others question whether the 'literacy' skills and concepts in multimedia literacy are new at all, being found in the theatre, film, radio etc. for many years. The expansion of basic literacy through history and across geography provides perspective on those seeking to draw hard lines about what literacy is and is not.

Thousands of years ago, a few early cultures invented the skills and technologies of reading and writing. Many languages today still have no written form. Of those with the invention of writing, only a small percentage of the citizens of these early cultures needed literacy. Each culture and time decides its needed technologies of thought and communication. Those who teach in a society respond to these needs. All societies have relatively recently (in the last 200 years) found that traditional literacy is essential. Not all have achieved it yet. Today there is a very rapid growth in forms of literacy, largely due to the arrival of the personal computer and the Internet.

There was a tipping point in the demand for universal (reading and writing) literacy as an effect of the Industrial Revolution. Paper, writing instruments and printing also became much cheaper at about this time. Today there is a revolution in the development of new communication media. There is a demand for literate people to become skilled in the new literacies related to the use of a variety of online tools—blogs, social networking, video and audio sharing and so on. The impact of these Internet related media is different from that of the earlier multimedia revolution when film and radio became widespread. These media were powerful, but were largely in the hands of a small number of people with the mass of the population being a passive audience. The new media, particularly those described as Web 2.0 tools tend to actively involve the users in responding and creating material.

There is considerable debate in progress about the nature and significance of these new media. Traditionalist educators may argue that the long standing media form of text has and will continue to be the foundation of learning. Others will argue that the new forms are displacing the old forms of literacy and that schools must teach the full range of multimedia literacies.

Changing Digital Technology

As personal computers and their software become more powerful they have the capacity to not only record and edit text, sound, still images, motion pictures and manage interactivity individually, but synthesize all of them onto the same page, screen or viewing, creating new plateaus or forms of composition. Personal computer technology has placed multimedia creation in the hands of any computer user. As multimedia becomes a more prevalent form of communication it is argued that the literacy of 'reading' and 'writing' using multimedia be taught in schools and other education institutions.

The related study of mass media has long been part of the school program in many school systems either as a separate subject option in secondary schools or more often as a part of general literacy learning. Film Study has also been a school subject in many schools for some time using relatively expensive and complicated equipment to make film or video. The rapid development of multimedia via personal computing means that it is becoming a routine form for a widening group of people not only for just "reading" but for creating the media. The line between mass media and personally authored media is becoming much more blurred if not obliterated. Non professional authors on the web already have audiences larger than major commercial publications such as major newspapers and TV stations, whether text based blogs or multimedia podcasts.

Constructivist Learning and Multimedia

Multimedia literacy is a subset of the wider issue of the use of ICT (Information and Communication Technology) in schools. While there is widespread recognition that people need to learn how to use computers effectively in order to function in modern society, there is debate about the nature of that learning. Some see it as a simple but lengthy list of technical skills while others see it as also including recognition of the power of ICT to bring about a major change in learning. Avarim and Talmi identify several groups active in ICT in education, including Technocrats, who see the use of ICT as non-problematic and simply a matter of using the new tools, and Reformists, who see ICT as a major and possibly inexorable agent of change in education.

The reformist group see the rapid growth in the use of ICT in schooling occurring in conjunction with the adoption of the constructivist learning theory. (OECD). This theory supports active, hands-on learning. It is related to Cognitive Apprenticeship and the work of Jerome Bruner.

Some educators see ICT as being a major driver of school reform. This reform is towards a more constructivist approach, using related terms such as: student-centred learning, Problem-based learning and experiential education. Others point to the slow pace of such reform and suggest that ICT may support reform but it is by no means inevitable that it will do so. (eLearning europa).

Supporters of ICT as a powerful tool for constructivist learning point to its capacity to provide:

- Active and highly motivating engagement with students,
- Powerful tools to create text, art, music, sound, models, presentations, movies etc. that produce high quality products and remove much of the tedium normally associated with such creation,
- An error-forgiving environment in which editing of a product fosters learning by trial and error,
- Easy communication in text, voice, video,
- Quick access to information and resources.

Educators are finding, however, that while ICT can provide a technical environment for constructivist learning to occur, there needs to be high quality teaching to develop and sustain an environment that will challenge and inspire students to learn.

Multimedia Literacy in Schools

Teaching literacy has always been the central business of schools. School literacy teaching had tended to focus on written literacy rather than on oral literacy, which is mainly learnt outside school. Literacy has never been a fixed body of skills but has evolved with the development of technology, such as pens and paper, and the needs of society as in the Industrial Revolution. For example, handwriting was a major focus of schooling during the 19th Century as the demand for clerks grew rapidly. Then the invention of the typewriter made neat handwriting a less important business skill. However, important literacy technologies such as the newspaper, the typewriter and the telegraph took decades to spread throughout society, giving schools time to adapt. Schools today are struggling to cope with the teaching of new literacies that are often less than five years old but are widespread in society.

Today the Internet is a major medium of communication and it is increasingly rich in multimedia. Children are regular users of the Internet and educators are recognizing the importance of them being 'literate' in its navigation, searching, authentication and other skills. Most school systems in the developed world are including computer literacy or similarly named programs, into the curriculum.

Film director George Lucas would approve. As he succinctly put it to Elizabeth Daley, Dean of USC's School of Cinema and Television: "In the 21st Century, can you honestly tell me that it is not as important for these students to know as much about Hitchcock as they do about Hemingway? Lucas elaborates on this idea in his conversation with Daley:" Well...I began to realize that the potential for multimedia to enhance the learning process was just astronomical. . . . I'm a big proponent of a new kind of grammar that goes beyond words. To tell a story now means grasping a new kind of language, which includes understanding how graphics, color, lines, music and words combine to convey meaning" (Brown 20). In this conversation with Elizabeth Daley, Lucas asks: "Don't you think that, in the coming decade, students need to be taught to read and write cinematic language, the language of the screen, the language of sound and image, just as they are now taught to read and write text? Otherwise, won't they be as illiterate as you or I would have been if, on leaving college, we were unable to read and write an essay?"(Daley 15)

Children learn much of their mass media literacy, as recipients, quite intuitively from film, television and radio. However, until recently, few have had the opportunity to experience being multimedia authors. Now, with relatively cheap digital cameras, free software and access to powerful multimedia computers, there is both the opportunity and the need, for quite young students to become authors as well as consumers in the new media.

The following sections provide information on skills that students may learn in order to be multimedia literate.

Video

Film making has been a major technology and art form for over a century. Personal video making makes use of many but not all of the techniques of professional film making. Student movie makers need to be familiar with the basic tools and techniques of the art, including familiarity with:

- *Camera shots*: close up, medium, long shot, pan, fade etc. in order to achieve different effects.

- *Story-boarding*: a pictorial frame view of the story line, showing camera views, times and shot sequence which provides the Director with a simple shooting script for a video.
- Editing software replaces tedious and expensive film splicing with digital editing which is quick and forgiving of errors, and allows the insertion of audio tracks in sequence with the video track.
- Sound tracks allow music, sound effects and voice tracks to be added to an existing film (*see* Sound).
- The so called Ken Burns Effect, in which the camera pans across a still image allows still images accompanied by a sound track to create quite powerful presentations.

Sound

Most people are very familiar with the use of sound as a powerful tool in television, radio and film, but have little experience in using it themselves. Digital recording allows the user much greater opportunity to experiment with the effect of sound features such as:

- Voice tone, pace, pitch
- Music as an influence on mood and atmosphere
- Sound effects that provide enrichment and context to a story.

APPENDIX I: FAMOUS ANIMATORS: A BRIEF LISTING

Famous Animators No Longer Living

- Alexandre Alexeieff
- Arthur Babbit
- Berthold Bartosch
- Amadee J. Van Beuren
- Ivo Caprino
- Bob Clampett
- Émile Courtet
- Shamus Culhane
- Jules Engel
- Friz Freleng
- Paul Grimault
- John Halas
- Faith Hubley
- Ub Iwerks
- Chuck Jones
- Kihachirô Kawamoto
- Jean-François Laguionie
- Walter Lantz
- Winsor McCay
- Grim Natwick
- Lotte Reiniger
- Charles Schulz
- Osamu Tezuka
- Jirí Trnka
- Frederico Valle
- Henry Burden
- Tex Avery
- Joseph Barbera
- Joy Batchelor
- Preston Blair
- Osvaldo Cavandoli
- Émile Cohl
- Quirino Cristiani
- Walt Disney
- Max Fleischer
- Oskar Fischinger
- Zlatko Grgić
- William Hanna
- John Hubley
- Ivan Ivanov-Vano
- Milt Kahl
- Yoshifumi Kondô
- Rene Laloux
- Len Lye
- Norman McLaren
- Joe Oriolo
- Émile Reynaud
- Ladislav Starevich
- Frank Thomas
- Bill Tytla
- Karel Zeman
- Ben Lilley

Famous Living Animators

- Aftab Mehboob
- Andreas Deja
- Bill Plympton
- Brad Bird
- Butch Hartman
- Craig McCraken
- Aleksandr Petrov
- Andreas Hykade
- Børge Ring
- Břetislav Pojar
- Chris Shepherd123
- David Crognale

- David Silverman
- Frédéric Back
- Jacques-Rémy Girerd
- Ralph Bakshi
- Peter Chung
- Aryn Hanley
- Piotr Dumala
- Paul Fierlinger
- Pierre Hébert
- Stephen Hillenburg
- Maddisson Hulme
- Mike Judge
- William Kentridge
- John Kricfalusi
- Caroline Leaf
- Wayne Lytle
- Seth MacFarlane
- Yuri Norstein
- Michel Ocelot
- Katsuhiro Otomo
- Nick Park
- Priit Pärn
- Ishu Patel
- Jonti Picking
- Tim Burton
- Brothers Quay
- Linda Bel
- Jan Švankmajer
- Tom Bertino
- Yoshiyuki Tomino
- Dušan Vukotić
- Louis K Wang
- Giselle Wedemire
- Noureddin Zarrinkelk
- Simon Le Marchant-Smith
- Walerian Borowczyk
- Don Bluth
- Isao Takahata
- Michaël Dudok De Wit
- Konstantin Bronzit
- Gene Deitch
- Paul Driessen
- Matt Groening
- Ray Harryhausen
- Don Hertzfeldt
- Melissa Hopkins
- Ollie Johnston
- Glen Keane
- Jean Knoertzer
- John Lasseter
- Guionne Leroy
- Hayao Miyazaki
- Koji Morimoto
- Joe Murray
- Mamoru Oshii
- Nina Paley
- Trey Parker
- Marcel Patel
- Sylvain Chomet
- Terry Gilliam
- Oliver Postgate
- Joanna Quinn
- Matt Stone
- Genndy Tartakovsky
- Bruce Timm
- Will Vinton
- Wan brothers
- Shinichiro Watanabe
- Richard Williams
- Koji Yamamura
- Jankovics Marcell
- Maxwell Atoms

APPENDIX II: FAMOUS ANIMATORS: LISTING

- Animator
- Alexandre Alexeieff and Claire Parker
- John A. Davis
- Peter Avanzino
- Carlos Baeza
- Neil Affleck
- David Anderson (animator)
- Tony Anselmo
- Art Babbitt
- Mark Baker (animator)

- Richard Baneham
- Berthold Bartosch
- Linda Bel
- Tom Bertino
- Milan Blažekovic
- Steve Box
- Bruno Bozzetto
- Frank Braxton
- Laurent de Brunhoff
- Brad Case
- The Brothers Chaps
- Steve Clark (animator)
- Quirino Cristiani
- Gábor Csupó
- Marija Miletic Daïl
- Attila Dargay
- John Dods
- Michaël Dudok de Wit
- George Dunning
- Liz Enthusiasm
- Rick Farmiloe
- Jack Feldstein
- Paul Fierlinger
- Todd John Galda
- Burt Gillett
- Jeff Hall
- Jack Hannah
- Dan Haskett
- Helen Hill
- Mike Hollands
- Jono Howard
- Ron Husband
- Samantha Inoue-Harte
- Chuck Jones
- Jen Kamerman
- Kiyoshi Kohatsu
- Peter Kuber
- Christoph Lauenstein
- Caroline Leaf
- Lela Lee
- Drew Lightfoot
- List of cartoonists
- Lauren MacMullan
- Richard Markle
- Ed Barge
- Joy Batchelor
- Bill Berg (musician)
- Brad Bird
- Geefwee Boedoe
- Ken Boyer (animator)
- Ash Brannon
- Konstantin Bronzit
- Dwayne Carey-Hill
- Osvaldo Cavandoli
- Peter Chung
- Andy Clift
- Sally Cruikshank
- Jill Culton
- Christian Danley
- Ronnie del Carmen
- Paul Driessen (animator)
- John W. Dunn
- Adam Elliot
- Mark Ervin
- James Farr F cont.
- Feltusfeltus
- Randy Fullmer
- Manuel García Ferré
- John Halas
- William Hanna
- Laverne Harding
- John Hench
- Co Hoedeman
- Han Hoogerbrugge
- John Hubley
- Andreas Hykade
- Ivan Ivanov-Vano
- Milt Kahl
- Dick Kelsey
- Nancy Kruse
- Bob Kuwahara
- Wolfgang Lauenstein
- Dan Lee
- Jan Lenica
- List of animators
- Jeffrey Lynch
- April March
- Burny Mattinson

- Robert McKimson
- Michael Marcantel
- Pete Michels
- Fred Mogubgub
- Yuriy Norshteyn
- Nina Paley
- Ishu Patel
- PES (director)
- Rumen Petkov
- Adam Phillips (animator)
- Dominic Polcino
- José Pou
- Adam Reed
- Steve Ressel
- Zsolt Richly
- Christian Roman
- SamBakZa
- Ola Schubert
- Brian Sheesley
- Patrick Smith (artist)
- Aaron Springer
- Art Stevens
- Eva Švankmajerová
- Farkhondeh Torabi
- Dušan Vukotic
- Vincent Waller
- Erik Wernquist
- Tyrus Wong
- Tommy Yune
- Joshua Meador
- Sarah E. Meyer
- Yevgeniy Migunov
- Floyd Norman
- Rony Oren
- Priit Pärn
- Bill Peet
- Karen Peterson
- Petros Papadopoulos
- Bill Plympton
- Oliver Postgate
- Joanna Priestley
- Lotte Reiniger
- Richard Rich (director)
- Ferenc Rófusz
- Carlos Saldanha
- Yusuke Santamaria
- List of Sesame Street animators
- Makoto Shinkai
- John Sparey
- Ladislas Starevich
- Tad Stones
- Martin Taras
- Kara Vallow
- John Walker (animator)
- Keith Waters
- Ben Wheatley
- Ivor Wood
- Noureddin Zarrinkelk

APPENDIX III: FAMOUS FLASH ARTISTS: A LISTING

- Aubrey Ankrum
- The Brothers Chaps
- Neil Cicierega
- Adriana de Barros
- James Farr
- Mike Hollingsworth
- Glenn Ligon
- Kenn Navarro
- Joe Phillips
- Ola Schubert
- Joe Sparks
- Veloso (artist)
- Mod7
- Bruno Bozzetto
- Chris Joseph (writer/artist)
- Joshua Davis (web designer)
- Bernard Derriman
- David Firth
- Andrew Kepple
- Rob Manuel
- Adam Phillips (animator)
- Jonti Picking
- Aaron Simpson
- Joel Veitch
- David Winn

APPENDIX IV: FAMOUS DIGITAL ARTISTS: A LISTING

- AUX MANIR Slobodan Sajin
- Bill Barminski
- Chris Joseph (writer/artist)
- Douglas Anthony Cooper
- Heiko Daxl
- Scott Draves
- Ebon Fisher
- Gary Ferster
- Generative art
- Dieter Grossmann
- Han Hoogerbrugge
- Kagaya Yutaka
- Alan King (artist)
- Roy LaGrone
- Olia Lialina
- Digital matte artist
- N3krozoft Ltd
- Mark Napier (artist)
- Joseph Nechvatal
- Paper Rad
- Don Ritter
- Jason Salavon
- Alexei Shulgin
- Nathaniel Stern
- Tempus Thales
- Jessy Veilleux
- Adrian Ward
- Raymond Wilding-White
- Brian Wood (artist)
- Mod7
- Cory Arcangel
- Stefano Cagol
- Paul Coldwell
- Joshua Davis (web designer)
- Adriana de Barros
- Bernard Dumaine
- David Em
- Ingeborg Fülepp
- Ken Goldberg
- Hugo Heyrman
- Lin Hsin Hsin
- Yael Kanarek
- Myron W. Krueger
- Golan Levin
- MTAA
- Bert Monroy
- Frieder Nake
- Katherine Nash
- Georg Nees
- Eric Paulos
- Buffy Sainte-Marie
- Daniel J. Sandin
- Karl Sims
- Manfred Stumpf
- John Vega
- Addie Wagenknecht
- Peggy Weil
- L. G. Williams
- Zazie (surrealist)

APPENDIX V: FAMOUS DEMOSCENERS: A LISTING

- Fabio Barzagli
- Brothomstates
- Elwood (musician)
- Nino Gauthier
- Olof Gustafsson
- Jochen Hippel
- Mikko Iho
- Alexander Brandon
- Arjan Brussee
- Dan Gardopée
- Gustaf Grefberg
- Peter Hajba
- Hunz
- Jeroen Kimmel

- Mark Knight (sound designer)
- Jesper Kyd
- Michiel van der Leeuw
- Bjørn Lynne
- Karsten Obarski
- Jori Olkkonen
- Paniq
- Ari Pulkkinen
- Thomas Pytel
- Heinz Rudolf
- Andrew Sega
- Janne Suni
- Jeroen Tel
- Jonne Valtonen

APPENDIX VI: FAMOUS ARTSCENE GROUPS: A LISTING

Artscene groups listed here are organized bodies of artists within the underground computer *artscene*. Beginning with *Aces of ANSI Art (<A.A.A>)*, these teams first began to spring up in the IBM PC scene in 1989. During the BBS era, a traditional artscene group would release an artpack on a month-to-month basis. A typical artpack may contain ANSI art and ASCII art, and some times generated from the RIPscrip protocol or VGA-mode art, referred to as *hirez* within the artscene. As the software to create ansi screens improved and the technique became more mature, some groups rose above others in popularity, and their members became highly respected among their peers. Some groups, and their respective members, became rivals of others, both friendly and unfriendly. Some artscene groups survived the transition to the Internet during the 1990s. The surviving groups are either completely dedicated to modern, high resolution graphics, or release ANSI and ASCII art for nostalgic purposes. However, new groups continue to form to this day, adopting many of the habits of the older, BBS-driven artscene.

- ACiD Productions
- Aces of ANSI Art
- Black Maiden
- Blade (artscene group)
- Chemical Reaction (artscene group)
- Creators of Intense Art
- Dark Illustrated
- Fire (artscene group)
- ICE Advertisements
- Impure ASCII
- Mimic ASCII
- Minor artscene groups
- Mistigris
- Remorse ASCII
- Superior Art Creations
- Trank

APPENDIX VII: FAMOUS STOP MOTION ANIMATORS: A LISTING

- Alexandre Alexeieff and Claire Parker
- David W. Allen
- Jirí Barta
- Bruce Bickford
- Katsushi Boda
- Walerian Borowczyk
- Tim Burton
- Christiane Cegavske
- Art Clokey
- Joe Clokey
- Jim Danforth
- Eric Fogel
- Bryce Hallett
- Ray Harryhausen
- Don Hertzfeldt
- Vladimír Jiránek
- Mike Jittlov
- Mike Johnson (animator)

- Christoph Lauenstein
- Jan Lenica
- Tadahito Mochinaga
- Willis O'Brien
- George Pál
- PES (director)
- Brothers Quay
- Henry Selick
- Ladislas Starevich
- Jan Švankmajer
- Jirí Trnka
- Ivor Wood
- Wolfgang Lauenstein
- Norman McLaren
- Yuriy Norshteyn
- Mark Osborne (filmmaker)
- Nick Park
- Bretislav Pojar
- Lotte Reiniger
- Stanislav Sokolov
- Stop Motion Pro
- Doug TenNapel
- User:Joooeeeelllll

APPENDIX VIII: LIST OF INDIAN ANIMATION AND GAMING INSTITUTES

- AAG—Academy of Animation and Gaming
- Accel IT Academy
- Asian Institute of Gaming and Animation
- Animaster
- ANTS—Animation Training School
- Arena Multimedia
- Artlab College of Design and Communication
- Digital Asia School of Animation
- Gecko Animation
- Graphiti School of Animation
- Framebox
- IDC, IIT Mumbai
- Magic Animation Academy
- Maya Academy of Advanced Cinematics
- Maximus India
- MUV Institute of Digital Arts
- National Institute of Design
- Picasso Centennial Canadian Animation College
- Prasad Academy
- Pumpkin Academy of Digital Arts
- SAAMS
- **Takshaa** Featured School
- Webel Animation Academy
- Whistling Woods International
- Xplora Design Skool

APPENDIX IX: LIST OF ANIMATED TELEVISION SERIES

Animated Series are television series produced by means of animation. The following is a list of animated television series listed by decade and country of origin.

1940s

USA

- *Crusader Rabbit* (1949-1952;)

1950s

Germany

- *Das Sandmännchen* (West German version) (1959-1991)
- *Unser Sandmännchen* (East German version) (1959-present)

United Kingdom

- *Captain Pugwash* (1957-1966)

USA

- *Colonel Bleep* (1957)
- *Clutch Cargo* (1959)
- *Felix the Cat* (new TV episodes) (1958-1960)
- *Gumby Show, The* (1956-1967, 1988)
- *Huckleberry Hound* (1958-1962)
- *Pixie & Dixie and Mr. Jinks* (1958-1961)
- *Rocky and Bullwinkle Show, The* (1959-1973)
- *Ruff & Reddy Show, The* (1957-1960)
- *Space Explorers, The* (1958-1960)
- *Tom Terrific* (1957-1959)
- *Yogi Bear* (1958-1988)

1960s

France

- *Colargol* (1967-1974)
- *Magic Roundabout, The* (1964-1971)

Japan

- *8 Man* (1963-1964)
- *The Amazing 3* (1965-1966)
- *Astro Boy* (1963-1966)
- *Attack No. 1* (1969-1971)

- *Big X* (1964-1965)
- *Cyborg 009* (1968)
- *Dororo* (1969)
- *GeGeGe no Kitaro* (1968-1969)
- *Gigantor* (1964-1965)
- *Himitsu no Akko-chan* (1969-1970)
- *Judo Boy* (1969)
- *Kaibutsu-kun* (1968-1969)
- *Kamui the Ninja* (1969)
- *Kimba the White Lion* (1965-1966)
- *Leo the Lion* (1966-1967)
- *Marine Boy* (1968-1969)
- *Obake no Q-tarō* (1965-1967)
- *Ōgon Bat* (1967-1968)
- *Osomatsu-kun* (1966-1967)
- *Otogi Manga Calendar* (1961-1962, 1962-1964)
- *Prince Planet* (1964-1965)
- *Princess Knight* (1965-1966)
- *Sally, the Witch* (1966-1968)
- *Sazae-san* (1969-Present)
- *Sennin Buraku* (1963-1964)
- *Shonen Ninja Kaze no Fujimaru* (1964-1965)
- *Speed Racer* (1966-1968)
- *Star of the Giants* (1968-1971)
- *Tove Jasson no Tanoshii Mūmin Ikka* (1969-1970)
- *Yōkai Ningen Bem* (1968-1969)

Poland

- *Bolek and Lolek* (1964-1986)
- *Reksio* (1967-1988)

Sweden

- *Bamse* (1966-present)

Russia

- *Nu, pogodi!* (1969-present)

United Kingdom

- *Clangers, The* (1969-1974)
- *Mary Mungo & Midge* (1969)

USA

- *Adventures of Batman and Robin the Boy Wonder, The* (1969-1970 CBS)

- *Alvin Show, The* (1961-1962)
- *Aquaman* (1968-1970 CBS)
- *Archie Show, The* (1968-1970)
- *Atom Ant* (1965)
- *Batfink* (1967)
- *Batman/Superman Hour, The* (1968-1969 CBS)
- *Beany and Cecil* (1965-1969)
- *Birdman and their Flying Machines* (1969-1971)
- *Cool McCool* (1966-1969)
- *Courageous Cat and Minute Mouse* (1960-1962)
- *Dick Tracy Show, The* (1960-1961)
- *Fantastic Voyage* (1968)
- *Flintstones, The* (1960-1966)
- *Hardy Boys, The* (1969-1971 ABC)
- *Herculoids, The* (1967-1969)
- *Here Comes the Grump* (1962-1963, 1984-1985, 1987)
- *Jonny Quest* (1964-1965; 1986-1987)
- *Journey to the Center of the Earth* (1967 ABC)
- *King Kong* (1966-1967)
- *Magilla Gorilla* (1964-1967)
- *Mighty Hercules, The* (1964-1966)
- *Mighty Monitor, The* (1967-1969)
- *New Adventures of Superman, The* (1966-1970 CBS)
- *Perils of Penelope Pitstop, The* (1969-1970)
- *Peter Potamus* (1964-1965)
- *Rocket Robin Hood* (1966-1969)
- *Rod Rocket* (1963)
- *Scooby-Doo, Where Are You!* (1969-1972; renewed under various other names through 1986)
- *Shazzan* (1967-1969)
- *Space Ghost* (1966-1968)
- *Spider-Man* (1967-1970)
- *Superman/Aquaman Hour of Adventure, The* (1967-1968 CBS)
- *Top Cat* (1961-1962)
- *Young Samson and Goliath* (1967-1968)
- *Underdog* (1964-1973)
- *Wacky Races* (1969-1970)

1970s

France

- *Il était une fois... l'homme (Once Upon a Time... Man)* (1978)

Germany

- *Vicky the Viking* (1974)

Italy

- *Quaq Quao* (1978)

Japan

- *Candy Candy* (1976-1979)
- *Doraemon* (1979-2005; 2005-present)
- *Conan: The Boy in Future* (1978)
- *Heidi, Girl of the Alps* (1974)
- *Lupin III: Part I* (1971-1972)
- *Lupin III: Part II* (1977-1980)
- *Maya the Bee* (1975)
- *Mazinger Z* (1972-1974)
- *Space Pirate Captain Harlock* (1978)
- *Mobile Suit Gundam* (1979)

United Kingdom

- *Bagpuss* (1974)
- *Sally and Jake (1974)*
- *Roobarb* (1974)
- *The Wombles* (1973-1975; 1998-1999)
- *Grandma Bricks of Swallow Street (1977)*

USA

- *Addams Family, The* (1974)
- *Battle of the Planets* (1978)
- *Brady Kids, The* (1972-1974)
- *Buford and the Galloping Ghost* (1979)
- *Captain Caveman and the Teen Angels* (1977-1980)
- *CB Bears, The* (1977-1978)
- *Clue Club* (1976-1977)
- *Devlin* (1974)
- *Dynomutt, Dog Wonder* (1976-1978)
- *Fangface* (1978-1979)
- *Fat Albert and the Cosby Kids* (1972-1984)
- *Flintstone Comedy Hour, The* (1972-1973)
- *Flintstone Comedy Show, The* (1973-1974)
- *Fred and Barney Meet the Shmoo* (1979-1980)
- *Fred and Barney Meet the Thing* (1979)
- *Fred Flintstone and Friends* (1977-1978)
- *Galaxy Goof-Ups* (1978-1979)
- *Goober and the Ghost Chasers* (1973-1975)
- *Great Grape Ape, The* (1975-1978)
- *Groovie Goolies* (1970)

- *Hanna-Barbera's Cartoon Corral*
- *The Hardy Boys/Nancy Drew Mysteries* (1977-1979)
- *Harlem Globetrotters* (1970-1971)
- *Hong Kong Phooey* (1974-1976)
- *I Am the Greatest: The Adventures of Muhammad Ali* (1977)
- *Inch High, Private Eye* (1973)
- *Jabberjaw* (1976-1978)
- *Jackson 5ive, The* (1971-1973)
- *Jeannie* (1973-1975)
- *Josie and the Pussycats* (1970-1972)
- *Lassie's Rescue Rangers* (1973-1974)
- *Mighty Mouse, Heckle and Jeckle, & Quackula Adventure Hour, The* (1979)
- *Mission: Magic!* (1973)
- *My Favorite Martians* (1973)
- *New Adventures of Batman, The* (1977-1981)
- *New Adventures of Flash Gordon, The* (1979-1980)
- *New Adventures of Gilligan, The* (1974)
- *New Adventures of Mighty Mouse and Heckle & Jeckle, The* (1978-1982)
- *New Fred and Barney Show, The* (1979)
- *Godzilla Power Hour, The* (1978-1980)
- *Partridge Family 2200 A.D.* (1974-1975)
- *Pebbles and Bamm-Bamm Show, The* (1971-1972)
- *Rickety Rocket* (1979-1980)
- *Robonic Stooges, The* (1978)
- *Roman Holidays, The* (1972)
- *Sabrina, the Teenage Witch* (1971-1974)
- *Scooby-Doo/Dynomutt Hour, The* (1976-1977)
- *Scooby's All-Star Laff-A-Lympics* (1977-1978)
- *Scooby's All-Stars* (1978-1979)
- *Schoolhouse Rock!* (1973)
- *Secret Lives of Waldo Kitty, The* (1975)
- *Space Sentinels* (1977)
- *Speed Buggy* (1973-1983)
- *Star Trek: The Animated Series* (1973-1974)
- *Super Friends* (1973-1985)
- *Super Globetrotters, The* (1979)
- *Tarzan and the Super 7* (1978)
- *Tarzan, Lord of the Jungle* (1976)
- *These Are the Days* (1974)
- *Tom and Jerry/Grape Ape/Mumbly Show, The* (1975-1977)
- *Uncle Croc's Block* (1975)
- *Wait Till Your Father Gets Home* (1972-1974)
- *Wheelie and the Chopper Bunch* (1974-1975)
- *Will the Real Jerry Lewis Please Sit Down* (1970)

- *Yogi's Gang* (1973-1975)
- *Yogi's Space Race* (1978-1979)

Uncategorized

- *Fabulous Funnies* (1978)
- *Jetter Mars* (1977)
- *Moomins, The* (1979)
- *M-U-S-H* (1975)
- *Lion, the Witch and the Wardrobe, The (1979)*

1980s

Canada

- *Mona the Vampire* (1983)
- *Care Bears Family Storybook, The* (1986-1990)
- *Ovide and the Gang* (1987-1988)
- *Raccoons, The* (1985-1991)

France

- *Clémentine* (1985-??)
- *Il était une fois... l'espace (Once Upon a Time... Space)* (1982)
- *Il était une fois... la Vie (Once Upon a Time... Life)* (1987)
- *Robo Story* (1985)
- *Seabert* (1985)
- *Spartakus and the Sun Beneath the Sea* (*Les Mondes engloutis*) (1985-1986)

Japan

- *Adventures of the Little Koala* (1984-1988)
- *Astro Boy* (1980-1981)
- *Bosco Adventure* (1986-1987)
- *Dragon Ball* (1986-1989)
- *Dragon Ball Z* (1989-1996)
- *Flying House, The* (1982-1983)
- *Jayce and the Wheeled Warriors* (1985-1986)
- *Lupin III: Part III* (1984-1985)
- *Macron 1* (1986)
- *Macross* (1982-1983)
- *M.A.S.K.* (Mobile Armored Strike Kommand) (1985-1986)
- *Mobile Suit Zeta Gundam* (1985)
- *Monchhichis* (1983)
- *Mysterious Cities of Gold, The* (*Les Mystérieuses Cités d'Or*) (1982)
- *Noozles, The* (1985)
- *Robotech* (1986)

- *Saber Rider and the Star Sheriffs* (1987-1988)
- *Saint Seiya* (1986-1989)
- *Superbook* (1981-1982)
- *Transformers: The Headmasters* (1987-1988)
- *Transformers: Super-God Masterforce* (1988-1989)
- *Transformers: Victory* (1989)
- *Ulysses 31* (1981)
- *Voltron* (1984-1985)
- *Zillion* (1987)

Netherlands

- *Alfred J. Kwak* (1989-1991)

Spain

- *Adventures of Little El Cid* (1980)
- *Around the World with Willy Fog* (1981)
- *Dogtanian and the Three Muskehounds* (1981)
- *Wisdom of the Gnomes* (1987)
- *World of David the Gnome, The* (1985)

Switzerland

- *Pingu* (1986)

United Kingdom

- *Bananaman* (1983-1986)
- *Bertha* (1986-1987)
- *Button Moon*
- *Count Duckula* (1988-1993)
- *Danger Mouse* (1981-1992)
- *Doctor Snuggles* (1980)
- *Family-Ness, The* (1984-1985)
- *Henry's Cat* (1982-1986)
- *Jimbo and the Jet Set* (1986-1987)
- *Murun Buchstansangur* (1984)
- *Postman Pat* (1981-Present)
- *Telebugs* (1986-1987)
- *Trap Door, The* (1984-1986)
- *TUGS* (1988-1989)

United States

- *Adventures of Teddy Ruxpin, The* (1987)
- *Adventures of the Galaxy Rangers, The* (1986-1989)
- *Alvin and the Chipmunks* (1983-1990)

- *A Pup Named Scooby-Doo* (1988-1991)
- *Beetlejuice* (1989-1991)
- *Berenstain Bears, The* (1985)
- *Beverly Hills Teens* (1987)
- *Bill and Ted's Excellent Adventures* (1990-1993)
- *Bionic Six* (1987)
- *Biskitts* (1983-1984)
- *Blackstar* (1981-1982)
- *Bravestarr* (1987-1989)
- *Camp Candy* (1989-1990)
- *Captain N: The Game Master* (1989-1993)
- *Care Bears, The* (DiC series, 1985-1986)
- *Centurions, The* (1985-1987)
- *Charlie Brown & Snoopy Show, The* (1983-1985)
- *Chip 'n Dale Rescue Rangers* (1989-1990)
- *C.O.P.S.* (1988-1989)
- *Comic Strip, The* (1987-1988)
- *Defenders of the Earth* (1986-1987)
- *Dennis the Menace* (1986-1988)
- *Denver, the Last Dinosaur* (1988-1989)
- *Dink, the Little Dinosaur* (1989-1991)
- *Dinosaucers* (1985)
- *Dino-Riders* (1988)
- *Disney's Adventures of the Gummi Bears* (1985-1990)
- *Drak Pack* (1980)
- *DuckTales* (1987-1990)
- *Dungeons & Dragons* (1983-1986)
- *Fantastic Max* (1988-1990)
- *Filmation's Ghostbusters* (1986-1988)
- *The Fonz and the Happy Days Gang* (1980-1982)
- *Galaxy High* (1986-1987)
- *Galtar and the Golden Lance* (1985)
- *Gary Coleman Show, The* (1982-1983)
- *Garfield and Friends* (1988-1994)
- *Get Along Gang, The* (1984-1986)
- *G.I. Joe* (1985-1986; 1989-1992)
- *Gilligan's Planet* (1982-1983)
- *Heathcliff* (1980)
- *He-Man and the Masters of the Universe* (1983-1985)
- *Inhumanoids* (1986)
- *Inspector Gadget* (1983-1986)
- *Jem* (1985-1988)
- *Jetsons, The* (new episodes from 1984-1985 and 1987)
- *Karate Kommandos* (1986)

- *Kidd Video* (1984-1987)
- *Legend of Zelda, The* (1989-1990)
- *Littles, The* (1983-1986)
- *Madballs* (1987)
- *Maxie's World* (1987)
- *Michael Valiant-Heroes of Hot Wheels*
- *Mighty Mouse: The New Adventures* (1987-1988)
- *Muppet Babies* (1984-1990)
- *My Little Pony* (1986-1992)
- *My Pet Monster* (1986)
- *New Adventures of Winnie the Pooh, The* (1988-1991)
- *New Archies, The* (1987-1989)
- *New Yogi Bear Show, The* (1988)
- *Pac-Man* (1982-1984)
- *Pandamonium* (1982-1983)
- *Poochie*
- *Pink Panther and Sons* (1984-1985)
- *Police Academy* (1988-1989)
- *Popples* (1986-1987)
- *Rainbow Brite* (1984-1985)
- *Rambo* (1986)
- *Real Ghostbusters, The* (1986-1991)
- *Richie Rich* (Hanna-Barbera version) (1980-1984)
- *Ring Raiders* (1989)
- *Robocop: The Animated Series* (1988)
- *Rubik, the Amazing Cube* (1983-1984)
- *Rude Dog and the Dweebs* (1989)
- *Scooby-Doo and Scrappy-Doo* (1980-1982)
- *Sectaurs* (1985)
- *Simpsons, The* (1989-present)
- *She-Ra: Princess of Power* (1985-1986)
- *Shirt Tales* (1982-1984)
- *Silverhawks* (1986)
- *Sky Commanders* (1987)
- *Smurfs, The* (1981-1990)
- *Snorks, The* (1984-1988)
- *Spider-Man* (1981-1982)
- *Spider-Man and His Amazing Friends* (1981-1983)
- *Spiral Zone* (1987)
- *Starcom: The U.S. Space Force* (1986)
- *Star Wars: Droids* (1985-1986)
- *Star Wars: Ewoks* (1985-1987)
- *Teenage Mutant Ninja Turtles* (1987-1996)
- *Teen Wolf* (1986-1989)

- *Thundarr the Barbarian* (1980-1982)
- *ThunderCats* (1985-1987)
- *Tom and Jerry Comedy Show, The* (1980-1982)
- *Transformers, The* (1984-1987)
- *Turbo Teen* (1984-1985)
- *Visionaries: Knights of the Magical Light* (1987)
- *Wildfire* (1986-1987)
- *Wuzzles, The* (1985)
- *Yogi's Treasure Hunt* (1985)

Uncategorized

- *City of Gold, The*
- *Moon Dreamers, The*

1990s

- *101 Dalmatians: The Series* (1997-1999)
- *2 Stupid Dogs* (1993-1995)
- *Aaahh!!! Real Monsters* (1994-1998)
- *Addams Family, The* (1992-1993)
- *Adventures of McGee and Me, The* (1989-1992)
- *Adventures of Sam & Max: Freelance Police, The* (1997-1998)
- *Adventures of Sonic the Hedgehog* (1993)
- *Adventures of Super Mario Bros. 3, The* (1990)
- *Adventures of Tintin, The* (1991-1992)
- *Æon Flux* (1991-1995)
- *Aladdin: The Series* (1994-1996)
- *Albert the Fifth Musketeer* (1994)
- *Angela Anaconda* (1999-2002)
- *Angry Beavers, The* (1997-2001)
- *Animals of Farthing Wood, The* (1993-1995)
- *Animaniacs* (1993-1998)
- *Archie's Weird Mysteries* (1999-2000)
- *Around the World in 80 Dreams* (1992)
- *Arthur* (1996-present)
- *Attack of the Killer Tomatoes* (1990-1993)
- *Avenger Penguins* (1993-1994)
- *Avengers: United They Stand, The* (1999-2000)
- *Back to the Future: The Animated Series* (1991-1993)
- *Barnyard Commandos* (1990)
- *Batman: The Animated Series* (1992-1995)
- *Batman Beyond* (1999-2001)
- *Beast Machines* (1999-2000)
- *Beast Wars* (1996-1999)

- *Beavis and Butt-head* (1993-1997)
- *Big Guy and Rusty the Boy Robot* (1999-2001)
- *Biker Mice from Mars* (1993-1996; 2006-present)
- *Blazing Dragons* (1996-1998)
- *Bobby's World* (1990-1998)
- *Bonkers* (1993-1995)
- *Bots Master, The* (1993-1995)
- *Bucky O'Hare and the Toad Wars* (1991-1992)
- *Budgie the Little Helicopter* (1994-1995)
- *Bump in the Night* (1994-1995)
- *Bump in the Night On Nickelodeon* (1994-1996)
- *Busy World of Richard Scarry, The* (1993-1997)
- *Captain Planet and the Planeteers* (1990-1992)
- *Captain Simian & the Space Monkeys* (1996-1997)
- *Captain Star* (1997-1998)
- *Cardcaptor Sakura* (1998-2000)
- *Cartoon Planet* (1995-1999)
- *CatDog* (1998-2002)
- *Celebrity Deathmatch* (1998-2002; 2006-present)
- *Channel Umptee-3* (1997-1998)
- *Conan the Adventurer* (1992-1994)
- *Conan and the Young Warriors* (1994)
- *Country Mouse and the City Mouse Adventures, The* (1998-1999)
- *Courage the Cowardly Dog* (1999-2002)
- *Cow & Chicken* (1997-1999)
- *Cowboy Bebop* (1998-1999)
- *Creepy Crawlers* (1994)
- *Critic, The* (1994-1995)
- *Cro* (1993-1994)
- *Cybersix* (1999-2000)
- *Daria* (1997-2002)
- *Darkwing Duck* (1991-1992)
- *Dennis the Menace* (1996-1998)
- *Detective Conan* (1996-present)
- *Detention* (1999-2000)
- *Dexter's Laboratory* (1996-1998; 2001-2003)
- *Digimon* (1999-present)
- *Dilbert* (1999-2000)
- *Donkey Kong Country* (1998-2000)
- *Doug* (1991-1994; 1996-1999)
- *Dragon Ball GT* (1996-1997)
- *Dragon Flyz* (1996)
- *Dreamstone, The* (1990-1995)
- *Dr. Katz, Professional Therapist* (1995-2000)

- *Dr. Zitbag's Transylvania Pet Shop* (1994-1997)
- *Duckman* (1994-1997)
- *Earthworm Jim* (1995-1996)
- *Ed, Edd n Eddy* (1999-2007)
- *Eek! The Cat* (1992-1997)
- *Exosquad* (1993-1994)
- *Extreme Dinosaurs* (1997)
- *Extreme Ghostbusters* (1997)
- *Family Guy* (1999-2002; 2005-present)
- *Fantastic Four* (1994-1996)
- *Fantastic Voyages of Sinbad the Sailor, The* (1996-1997)
- *Fantomcat* (1995-1996)
- *Flash Gordon* (1996-1997)
- *Flint the Time Detective* (1998-1999)
- *Fly Tales* (1999)
- *Freakazoid!* (1995-1997)
- *Futurama* (1999-2003; 2008-present)
- *Gadget Boy & Heather* (1995)
- *Gadget Boy's Adventures in History* (1998)
- *Gargoyles* (1994-1997)
- *Goof Troop* (1992-1993)
- *Godzilla: The Series* (1998)
- *Gigabyte* (1995)
- *Gravedale High* (1990)
- *Happy-Ness* (1996)
- *Hello Kitty's Paradise* (1993-1994)
- *Hercules: The Animated Series* (1998-1999)
- *Hey Arnold!* (1996-2004)
- *Histeria!* (1998-2001)
- *Home Movies* (1999-2004)
- *I Am Weasel* (1997-1999)
- *The Incredible Dennis the Menace* (1993)
- *Incredible Hulk, The* (1996-1997)
- *Iron Man* (1994-1996)
- *James Bond Jr.* (1991)
- *Johnny Bravo* (1997-2004)
- *Jungle Cubs* (1996-1998)
- *KaBlam!* (1996-2000)
- *Kid 'N Play* (1990-1991)
- *King Arthur & the Knights of Justice* (1992-1993)
- *King of the Hill* (1997-present)
- *Legend of Prince Valiant, The* (1991-1994)
- *Legends of Treasure Island, The* (1993-1995)
- *Little Dracula (1991)*

- *Littlest Pet Shop (1995)*
- *Little Mermaid, The* (1992-1995)
- *Macross 7* (1994-1995)
- *Magic Knight Rayearth* (1994-1995)
- *Magic School Bus, The* (1994-1997)
- *Marsupilami* (1995)
- *Marvel Action Hour, The* (1994-1996)
- *Mask: The Animated Series, The* (1995-1997)
- *Maxx, The* (1995)
- *Mega Man* (1994-1995)
- *Men in Black: The Series* (1997-2001)
- *Mickey Mouse Works* (1999-2001)
- *Mighty Ducks, The* (1996-1997)
- *Mighty Max* (1993-1994)
- *Mike, Lu & Og* (1999-2000)
- *Mobile Suit Gundam Wing* (1995)
- *Monster Force* (1994)
- *Moomin* (1990-1992)
- *Mortal Kombat: Defenders of the Realm* (1996)
- *Mozart Band, The* (1995)
- *Mummies Alive!* (1997)
- *Neon Genesis Evangelion* (1995-1996)
- *New Adventures of Captain Planet, The* (1993-1995)
- *New Batman Adventures, The* (1997-1999)
- *New Adventures of He-Man, The* (1990-1991)
- *Nightmare Ned* (1997)
- *Noah's Island* (1997-1999)
- *Oh Yeah! Cartoons* (anthology series) (1998-2001)
- *Once Upon a Time... The Americas (Il était une fois... les Amériques)* (1991)
- *Once Upon a Time... The Discoverers (Il était une fois... les découvreurs)* (1994)
- *Once Upon a Time... The Explorers (Il était une fois... les explorateurs)* (1996)
- *One Piece* (1999-present)
- *Oz Kids, The*
- *PB&J Otter* (1998-2000)
- *Pepper Ann* (1997-2001)
- *Phantom 2040* (1994-1996)
- *Pink Panther, The* (1993-1995)
- *Pinky and the Brain* (1995-1998)
- *Pirates of Dark Water, The*
- *Pokémon* (1998-present)
- *Powerpuff Girls, The* (1998-2005)
- *Princess Gwenevere and the Jewel Riders* (1995-1996)
- *Princess Sissi* (1998)
- *Project G.e.e.K.e.R.* (1996-1997)

- *Quack Pack* (1996)
- *Quarxs* (1993)
- *Rasmus Klump* (1997-2000)
- *Raw Toonage* (1992)
- *Real Adventures of Jonny Quest, The* (1996-1997)
- *ReBoot* (1994-2001)
- *Recess* (1997-2003)
- *Ren & Stimpy Show, The* (1991-1996)
- *Return of Dogtanian, The* (1990)
- *Richie Rich* (Film Roman version) (1996-1997)
- *Road Rovers* (1996-1997)
- *Rocket Power* (1999-2004)
- *Rocko's Modern Life* (1993-1996)
- *Romeo's Blue Skies* (1995-)
- *Roswell Conspiracies: Aliens, Myths and Legends* (1999)
- *Roughnecks: Starship Troopers Chronicles* (1999)
- *RoboCop: Alpha Commando* (1998-1999)
- *Rugrats* (1991-2005)
- *Sabrina: The Animated Series* (1999-2000)
- *Sailor Moon* (1992-1997)
- *Samurai Pizza Cats* (1990-1991)
- *Santo Bugito* (1995)
- *Savage Dragon, The* (1995-1996)
- *Sheeep* (1998)
- *Secret Files of the Spy Dogs, The* (1998-1999)
- *Shin-chan* (1992-present)
- *Sky Dancers* (1996)
- *Skysurfer Strike Force* (1995-1996)
- *Silver Surfer* (1998)
- *Skeleton Warriors* (1993-1994)
- *Sonic the Hedgehog* (1993-1996)
- *Sonic Underground* (1998-1999)
- *South Park* (1997-present)
- *Schnookums and Meat Funny Cartoon Show, The* (1994)
- *Space Ghost Coast to Coast* (1994-2004)
- *Space Goofs* (1997-1999)
- *Spawn* (1997-1999)
- *Spider-Man: The Animated Series* (1994-1998)
- *Spider-Man: Unlimited* (1999)
- *SpongeBob SquarePants* (1999-present)
- *Street Fighter* (1995-1997)
- *Street Fighter II V* (1995)
- *Street Sharks* (1994-1996)
- *Stressed Eric* (1998, 2000)

- *Super Mario World* (1991)
- *Superman: The Animated Series* (1996-2000)
- *SWAT Kats: The Radical Squadron* (1993-1994)
- *Sylvester and Tweety Mysteries, The* (1995-2000)
- *TaleSpin* (1990-1994)
- *Taz-Mania* (1991-1993)
- *Three Friends and Jerry, The* (1998-1999)
- *Tick, The* (1994-1996)
- *Timon and Pumbaa* (1995-1999)
- *Tiny Toon Adventures* (1991-1994)
- *Toon World* (1998-present)
- *Toxic Crusaders* (1991-1993)
- *Transformers: Zone* (1990)
- *Twisted Tales of Felix the Cat, The* (1995-1997)
- *Vision of Escaflowne, The* (1997)
- *Walter Melon* (1995)
- *What-A-Cartoon! Show, The* (anthology series) (1995-1997)
- *What-a-Mess* (1995)
- *Wheezer Bros., The* (1995-present)
- *Where on Earth is Carmen Sandiego?*
- *Where's Waldo?*
- *Widget, the World Watcher*
- *Wild West C.O.W.-Boys of Moo Mesa* (1992-1994)
- *Wish Kid* (1991)
- *Wizard of Oz, The* (1990)
- *X-Men* (1992-1997)
- *Xyber 9: New Dawn* (1999)
- *Yaiba* (1993-1994)
- *YuYu Hakusho* (1992-1995)

2000s

- *3 South* (2002-2003)
- *6teen* (2004-present)
- *12 oz. Mouse* (2005-2006)
- *Adventures of Chico and Guapo, The*
- *Adventures of Jimmy Neutron: Boy Genius, The* (2002-2006)
- *Alienators: Evolution Continues* (2001-2002)
- *Alien Racers* (2005)
- *All Grown Up!* (2003-2006)
- *American Dad!* (2005-present)
- *American Dragon: Jake Long* (2005-2007)
- *Angelina Ballerina* (2002)
- *Aqua Teen Hunger Force* (2000-present)
- *As Told by Ginger* (2000-2006)

- *Astro Boy* (2003-2004)
- *Atomic Betty* (2004-present)
- *A.T.O.M.: Alpha Teens On Machines* (2005-present)
- *Avatar: The Last Airbender* (2005-present)
- *BB3B* (2005-present)
- *Baby Looney Tunes* (2002-present)
- *Backyardigans, The* (2004-present)
- *Batman, The* (2004-present)
- *Boondocks, The* (2005-present)
- *Ben 10* (2005-present)
- *Bernard* (2004-present)
- *Braceface* (2001-2005)
- *Brandy & Mr. Whiskers* (2004-2006)
- *Bratz* (2005-present)
- *Brak Show, The* (2000-2003)
- *Bromwell High* (2005)
- *Bro'Town* (2005-present)
- *Buzz Lightyear of Star Command* (2000-2001)
- *Buzz on Maggie, The* (2005-2006)
- *Camp Lazlo* (2005-present)
- *Capertown Cops* (2000)
- *Carl²* (2005-present)
- *Catscratch* (2005-present)
- *ChalkZone* (2002-2005)
- *Chaotic* (2006-present)
- *Chowder* (2007-present)
- *Class of the Titans* (2005-present)
- *Class of 3000* (2006-present)
- *Clerks: The Animated Series* (2000)
- *Clic and Kat* (2004)
- *Clone High* (2002-2003)
- *Code Lyoko* (2003-2007)
- *Codename: Kids Next Door* (2002-present)
- *The Cramp Twins* (2003-2006)
- *Cubix: Robots for Everyone* (2001-2003)
- *Curious George* (2006-present)
- *Cyberchase* (2002-present)
- *Da Boom Crew* (2004)
- *Danger Rangers*
- *Danny Phantom* (2004-2007)
- *Dave the Barbarian* (2004-2005)
- *Di-Gata Defenders*
- *Dings & Dongs* (Coming Soon)
- *Dino Squad*

- *Dogsitter Wants*
- *Dogstar* (2007-present)
- *Dragon Booster* (2004-2006)
- *Drawn Together* (2004-present)
- *Duck Dodgers* (2003-2005)
- *Ebb and Flo*
- *El Chavo, la serie animada* (Only in Mexico in 2006-present)
- *El Chapulín Colorado, la serie animada,* (In Mexico 2007)
- *Electronic World* (2004-present)
- *El Tigre: The Adventures of Manny Rivera* (2007-present)
- *Ellen's Acres* (2006-present)
- *The Emperor's New School* (2006-present)
- *Erky Perky* (2006-present)
- *Evil Con Carne* (2003-2004)
- *Fairly OddParents, The* (2001-20 more episodes ordered)
- *Fantastic Four: World's Greatest Heroes* (2006-present)
- *Father of the Pride* (2004)
- *Fighting Foodons* (2002-2003)
- *Fillmore!* (2002-2004)
- *Flipper and Lopaka*
- *Foster's Home for Imaginary Friends* (2004-present)
- *Freak Show* (2006-present)
- *Funky Cops* (2003-2004)
- *F-Zero GP Legend* (2004)
- *Gadget and the Gadgetinis* (2003)
- *Game Over* (2004)
- *Gary & Mike* (2001)
- *Gary the Rat* (2003)
- *Get Ed* (2005-present)
- *G.I. Joe: Sigma 6* (2005)
- *God, the Devil and Bob* (2000)
- *Grim Adventures of Billy & Mandy, The* (2001-present)
- *Grossology* (2006-present)
- *Growing Up Creepie* (2006-present)
- *Happy Tree Friends* (2006-present)
- *Harvey Birdman, Attorney at Law* (2000-2007)
- *Howard Stern, The High School Years* (in development)
- *Hi Hi Puffy AmiYumi* (2004-2006)
- *Horrid Henry* (2006-present)
- *House of Mouse* (2001-2004)
- *Iggy Arbuckle* (2006)
- *I Got a Rocket!* (2007)
- *Invader Zim* (2001-2002, 2005-2006)
- *Jackie Chan Adventures* (2000-2005)

- *Johnny Test* (2005-present)
- *Jozi Zoo* (2001)
- *Justice League* (2001-2004)
- *Justice League Unlimited* (2004-2006)
- *Kappa Mikey* (2006-present)
- *Kaput and Zösky* (ca. 2003)
- *Kim Possible* (2002-present)
- *King* (2006)
- *King Arthur's Disasters* (2005-present)
- *Kirby: Right Back at Ya!* (2002-2006)
- *Korgoth of Barbaria* (2006-present)
- *Kinnikuman Second Generations ULTIMATE MUSCLE* (2004)
- *Kinnikuman Second Generations ULTIMATE MUSCLE 2* (2006)
- *Kong: The Animated Series* (2001)
- *Legion of Super Heroes* (2006-present)
- *Lifeboat Luke* (2006-present)
- *Lloyd in Space* (2001-2004)
- *Legend of Tarzan* (2001-2003)
- *Life and Times of Juniper Lee, The* (2005-2006)
- *Lilo & Stitch: The Series* (2003-2006)
- *Little Einsteins* (2005-present)
- *Loonatics Unleashed* (2005-present)
- *Maya & Miguel* (2004)
- *Martin Mystery* (2003-present)
- *Masters of the Universe* (2002-present)
- *Medabots* (2001-2004)
- *Megaman NT Warrior* (2002-2006)
- *Megaman Star Force* (2006-Present)
- *Megas XLR* (2004-2005)
- *Melancholy of Haruhi Suzumiya* (2006)
- *Metalocalypse* (2006-Present)
- *Monkey Dust* (2003-2005)
- *Monster Allergy* (2006-present)
- *Mr. Bean* (2002)
- *¡Mucha Lucha!* (2002-2005)
- *Mummy Nanny* (2000)
- *Mummy: The Animated Series, The* (2001-2003)
- *My Dad the Rock Star* (2003-2005)
- *My Goldfish is Evil!* (2006)
- *My Gym Partner's a Monkey* (2006-present)
- *My Life as a Teenage Robot* (2003-2006)
- *Naruto* (2002-present)
- *New Toon World* (2007-present)
- *Nico (aka Nicholas)* (2001)

- *Oblongs, The* (2002-2003)
- *Ozzy & Drix* (2002-2004)
- *The Panabaker Show* (Coming Soon)
- *Pelswick* (2000-2001)
- *Perfect Hair Forever* (2005)
- *Pet Alien* (2005)
- *Phineas and Ferb* (2007-present)
- *Pigeon Boy*
- *Pink Panther and Pals* (2008 Coming Soon)
- *Plastic Man*
- *Pocoyo* (At Spain 2005-present)
- *Poochini* (2001)
- *POP!* (Coming Soon)
- *Princess Natasha* (2004-2006)
- *Proud Family, The* (2001-2005)
- *Queer Duck* (2002-2004)
- *Random! Cartoons* (2006-present)
- *Ren & Stimpy "Adult Party Cartoon"* (2003-2004)
- *Ripping Friends, The* (2001-2002)
- *Robotboy* (2005-present)
- *Roobarb and Custard Too* (2005)
- *Ruby Gloom* (2006-present)
- *Sabrina's Secret Life* (2003-2004)
- *Samurai Jack* (2001-2004)
- *Sealab 2021* (2001-2005)
- *The Secret Show*
- *Shorn the Sheep*
- *Sheep in the Big City* (2000-2002)
- *Shuriken School* (2006-present)
- *Silverwing* (2003)
- *Slacker Cats* (2007-present)
- *Sonic X* (2003-2006)
- *Sons of Butcher*
- *Space Cowboys*
- *Spectacular Spider-Man, The* (2008)
- *Spider-Man: The New Animated Series* (2003)
- *Spider Riders* (2006-present)
- *Spooky Sisters, The* (2004)
- *Squirrel Boy* (2006-present)
- *Stargate Infinity* (2002-2003)
- *Star Wars: Clone Wars* (2003-2005)
- *Static Shock* (2000-2004)
- *Storm Hawks* (2007-present)
- *Storyteller Café* (2000-present)

- *Stripperella* (2003-2004)
- *Super Robot Monkey Team Hyperforce Go!* (2004-present)
- *Tamagotchi Toons* (Coming Soon)
- *Team Galaxy* (2006-present)
- *Teamo Supremo* (2002-2004)
- *Teen Titans* (2003-2006)
- *Teenage Mutant Ninja Turtles* (2003-present)
- *Teenage Mutant Ninja Turtles: Fast Forward* (2006-2007)
- *This Just In!* (2004)
- *Time Cracks* (2004)
- *Time Squad* (2001-2003)
- *Time Warp Trio* (2005-2006)
- *Tofus, The* (2004-2007)
- *Total Drama Island* (2007-present)
- *Totally Spies!* (2001-present)
- *Toonimals!* (2000)
- *Transformers: Animated* (2007-present)
- *Transformers: Armada* (2002-2003)
- *Transformers: Cybertron* (2005-2006)
- *Transformers: Energon* (2005)
- *Transformers: Robots in Disguise* (2000)
- *Tripping the Rift* (2004-present)
- *Treasure*
- *Trollz* (2005)
- *Tupu* (2004)
- *Turboman: The Animated Series* (2005-present)
- *Tutenstein* (2003-2007)
- *UBOS* (2001)
- *Vampires, Pirates and Aliens*
- *Venture Bros., The* (2004-present)
- *Viva Piñata* (2006-present)
- *Wayside* (2007-present)
- *Weekenders, The* (2000-2004)
- *What About Mimi?* (2001)
- *What's New, Scooby-Doo?* (2002-2006)
- *What's with Andy?* (2001-2007)
- *Whatever Happened to Robot Jones?* (2002-2004)
- *Where My Dogs At?* (2006-present)
- *Winx Club* (2004-present)
- *W.I.T.C.H.* (2004-present)
- *Wlatcy móch* (2006-present)
- *Wow! Wow! Wubbzy!* (2006-2007)
- *Wrong Coast, The* (2004)
- *X-Men: Evolution* (2000-2006)

- *X's, The* (2005-present)
- *Xiaolin Showdown* (2003-2006)
- *Yin-Yang-Yo!* (2006-present)
- *Yu-Gi-Oh!* (2001-2006)
- *Yu-Gi-Oh! GX* (2005-present)
- *Yvon of the Yukon* (2002)
- *Zeroman* (2004-2005)
- *Zeta Project, The* (2000-2002)

APPENDIX X: LIST OF ANIMATION STUDIOS

This is *list of animation Studios*, animation studio is a studio that is a production facilities, or a financial entitles and is in general similar in organizations to artists studios, and most of them are based in United States of America. But also in Canada and in Europe.

Anime studios (Japanese animations) have many things in common with general animation studios so therefore they are also listed on this list.

Animation Studios of the Past

- Alphanim (French independent animation production and distribution company)
- Amblimation (animation production arm of Steven Spielberg's Amblin Entertainment)
- Barré Studio (1914-1923) (from 1917 renamed Bud Fisher Films Corporation)
- Bray Productions
- Chuck Jones Productions
- Cinar (now Cookie Jar Entertainment)
- Creston Studios (a.k.a. TV Spots)
- DePatie-Freleng Enterprises (1963-1981)
- Ellipse Program
- Filmation (1963-1989)
- Fleischer Studios (1921-1942), Famous Studios (1942-1956) and Paramount Cartoon Studio (1956-1967)
- Format Films
- Fox Animation Studios
- Gaumont British Animation (1946-1950)
- George Pal Studio
- Grantray-Lawrence Animation (1954-1967)
- Halas and Batchelor
- Hanna-Barbera Productions (1957-2001, now Cartoon Network Studios)
- Harman-Ising Productions
- International Film Service (1915-1918)
- Jack Kinney Productions
- Jay Ward Productions (1958-1984)
- John Sutherland Productions
- Laugh-O-Grams (1922-1923)

- Leon Schlesinger Productions/Warner Bros. Cartoons, Inc. (a.k.a. "Termite Terrace" (1933-1964 and 1967-1969), subcontracted to DePatie-Freleng Enterprises 1964-1967, re-opened as Warner Bros. Animation in 1980)
- Metro-Goldwyn-Mayer Cartoon Studio (1937-1957) and MGM Animation/Visual Arts/Sib Tower 12 Productions (1962-1970)
- Pat Sullivan Studio (1915-1933)
- Rankin-Bass
- Rainbow Animation
- Rembrandt Films
- Sullivan-Bluth Studios
- Studio Deitch
- Storyboard Studios/Hubley Studios
- Television Arts Productions (1948-1952)
- Terrytoons (1928-1968)
- Turner Feature Animation
- Ub Iwerks Studio (1930-1936)
- United Productions of America (UPA) (1944-1964)
- Van Beuren Studios (1928-1936)
- Walter Lantz Studio (1929-1940, 1940-1948 and 1950-1972)
- Winkler Pictures (1921-1940) (also known as M.J. Winkler Productions, Charles Mintz Studios and Robert Winkler Productions).

Animation Studios of the Present

- 3lbs Studios
- 3eyegroup Animation Studios
- A. Film
- Aardman Animations
- Act3animation
- AirLex Animation Studio
- Alpamayo Entertainment
- Animafilm
- Animal Logic
- Animation Collective
- Animax Entertainment
- Animedia Arts
- AnimNation
- Anzovin Studio
- Asterisk Animation
- Atomic Cartoons
- Backyard Digital Studios
- Banjax Studios
- Bardel Entertainment
- Bent Image Lab

- Big Idea Productions
- Bird Studios
- Blue Sky Studios
- Blue-Zoo
- Bolexbrothers
- BONES
- Brown Bag Films
- Cartoon Saloon
- Cineteam
- Copernicus Studios
- Collideascope Animation
- CDIT Digital Center, Bokaro
- Crest Animation Studios
- DAGNABIT! Animation Studio
- Dancing Diablo Studio
- Def2shoot
- Delirium Studios
- Designomotion
- D-Rights
- DiC Entertainment
- DreamWorks Animation (animation production arm of DreamWorks)
- DR Movie
- Escobar Studios
- ezGyan InfoTech & Media Solutions
- Factual Fiction
- Fatkat
- Film Roman, Inc.
- Fine Arts Films
- Flinch Studio
- Flash Potatoes
- Folimage
- Future Thought Productions
- Gainax
- GONZO
- GrafKat Oy
- Graphiti Multimedia Pvt. Ltd.
- Grafix Unlimited
- Grand Design Productions
- Graz Entertainment
- Guru Studio
- Hong Ying Animation
- Hyperspective Studios
- J.C. Staff
- JibJab

- Klasky Csupo, Inc.
- Kurtz & Friends
- Kyoto Animation
- Laika Entertainment House
- Linterna Magica Studio
- Longneck Animation Studio
- MADBOX
- Madhouse
- Mainframe Entertainment
- Marathon Studios
- Mbanga Studio
- Melnitsa Animation Studio
- Metaphor Studios
- MGM Animation
- Mike Young Productions
- Mirari Films
- Mifto Productions
- Monster Studios
- Myr Studio Products
- NAS
- NPJB Enterprise, LLC
- National Film Board of Canada
- Nelvana
- Nickelodeon Animation Studios
- Octane Entertainment
- PannóniaFilm
- Pacific Rim Productions
- Pascal Blais Studio
- Pentamedia Graphics
- The People's Republic of Animation
- PES
- Pixar
- Platige Image
- Plus One Animation
- Post Amazers
- Production I.G.
- Rainmaker
- Rhythm and Hues Studios
- Realise Studio
- Record Animations
- Rough Draft Studios
- Saerom
- Sei Young
- Shaded Box

- Skycron
- Smallfilms
- Small Island Productions
- ŠAF
- So! Animation
- Sony Pictures Animation
- Soyuzmultfilm
- Spazco
- Spectrum Animation
- Splitvision Digital
- Spümcø
- Strika Entertainment
- Studio 4°C
- Studio Ghibli
- Sumo Dojo
- Sunrise
- Sunrise Corporation
- Sunwoo Entertainment
- Tata Elxsi Limited—Visual Computing Labs
- Tatsunoko Productions
- Toei Animation
- Tokyo Movie Shinsha
- ToonBangla
- TORTUGA STUDIOS
- Turtle Animation Studios
- Turtle Beach Animations
- Trickompany
- Two Animators! LLP
- TV Tokyo
- Walt Disney Animation Studios
- Walt Disney Television Animation
- Warner Bros. Animation
- Wavescorx Independent
- (W)Holesome Products Inc.
- White Rice Communication
- Williams Street Studios
- We've Inc.
- World Leaders Entertainment
- YUP Productions
- XEBEC
- Xyzoo Animation
- Zagreb Film

APPENDIX XI: LIST OF RECOMMENDED BOOKS AND MAGAZINES BY ALLABOUTANIMATION.COM

Animation Basics & Overview

Animation 101	The Animation Book: A Complete Guide to Animated Filmmaking—From Flip- Books to Sound Cartoons to 3-D Animation	Animation Art: From Pencil to Pixel, the World of Cartoon, Anime, and CGI
The Encyclopedia of Animation Techniques: A Comprehensive Step-by-Step Directory of Techniques, with an Inspirational Gallery of Finished Works	Animation: From Script to Screen	The Complete Animation Course
The Animators Survival Kit	All About Techniques in Drawing for Animation Production	Who's Who in Animated Cartoons: An International Guide to Film and Television's Award-Winning and Legendary Animators
How to Draw Animation: Learn the Art of Animation from Character Design to Storyboards and Layouts	Animated Cartoons: How They Are Made: Their Origin and Development	Animation: The Whole Story
TIMING FOR ANIMATION	Don Bluth's Art of Storyboard	Don Bluth's Art of Animation Drawing
Cartoons: One Hundred Years of Cinema Animation	Character Animation—An Overview	The Best of Draw! Step-by-Step Lessons and Interviews by Top Pros in Comics, Cartooning and Animation.
Designing Sound for Animation with DVD	The Art of the Storyboard: Storyboarding for Film, TV and Animation	Action Anatomy for Gamers, Animators and Digital Artists
Outlaw Animation: Cutting-Edge Cartoons from the Spike and Mike Festivals	Animation Unlimited: Innovative Short Films since 1940	Animating Culture: Hollywood Cartoons from the Sound Era
Cartoon Animation		

Business of Animation

Producing Animation	Producing Independent 2D Character Animation: Making and Selling a Short Film with CDROM	The Animation Business Handbook
Cartoon Monickers: An Insight into the Animation Industry	Serious Business: The Art and Commerce of Animation in America from Betty Boop to Toy Story	Careers in Computer Graphics and Animation
Creating 3D Animation	Stop Motion: Craft Skills for Model Animation	Ray Harryhausen: An Animated Life

Writing for Animation

How to Write for Animation	Gardner's Guide to Animation Scriptwriting: The Writer's Road Map	Storytelling Through Animation

Disney

The Illusion of Life: Disney Animation	Disney's Animation Magic	Walt Disney's Nine Old Men: And the Art of Animation
Disney's Art of Animation	Of Mice and Magic: A History of American Animated Cartoons Revised and Updated	Disney War

(Contd.)

Anime & Manga

Anime Explosion!: The What? Why? and Wow! of Japanese Animation	Anime Mania: How to Draw Characters for Japanese Animation	Anime from Akira to Princess Mononoke: Experiencing Contemporary Japanese Animation
Hayao Miyazaki: Master of Japanese Animation	How to Draw Manga: Making Anime	Cinema Anime: Critical Engagements with Japanese Animation
The Anime Companion: What's Japanese in Japanese Animation?	Anime Companion 2: More What's Japanese in Japanese Animation?	

Behind the Scenes & Making of Art

The Art of Finding Nemo	Art of the Polar Express	The Art of Monsters, Inc.
Batman Animated	Shrek: From the Swamp to the Screen	Making Toons: Inside the Most Popular Animated TV Shows and Movies
Backstage at an Animated Series	Reading the Rabbit: Explorations in Warner Bros. Animation	

Digital Animation

Digital Animation Bible	Mastering 3D Animation	Character Animation in 3D: Use Traditional Drawing Techniques to Produce Stunning CGI Animation
The Art of 3D Computer Animation and Effects	3-D Human Modeling and Animation, 2nd Edition	3D Animation and Filmmaking using Game Engines: The Art of Machinima
Animation in the Home Digital Studio: Creation to Distribution	Making Them Move: Mechanics, Control and Animation of Articulated Figures	Best New Animation Design 2
3D Toons: Creative 3D Design for Cartoonists and Animators	Developing Animation and Games using gmax Bible	3D Game Animation for Dummies with CD
Digital Lighting and Rendering	Gardner's Guide to Colleges for Multimedia and Animation	

Software

Flash 8: Graphics, Animation and Interactivity with CDROM	Macromedia Flash Animation and Cartooning: A Creative Guide	FLASH: AN INTRODUCTION
Flash Cartoon Animation: Learn from the Pros	Hollywood 2D Digital Animation: The New Flash Production Revolution with CDROM	Macromedia Animation Studio
Introduction to 3D Graphics and Animation Using Maya with CDROM	Learning Maya 7: The Modeling and Animation Handbook with DVD	Understanding 3D Animation Using Maya
The Complete Reference Maya 6	Maya Character Creation	3Ds max Animation and Visual Effects Techniques—The Ultimate Reference CD
LightWave 3D 8 Cartoon Character Creation, Volume 1: Modeling and Texturing	LightWave 3D 8 Cartoon Character Creation, Volume 2: Rigging and Animation	

Latest Websites

Tahmima.com is the personal website on Tahmima Anam, the writer of "The Golden Age."
valerieataylor.com is the official website of Valeri Ann Taylor, the founder of CRP.

Drishtipat (New York) is an non-profit, non-political expatriate organization. It is a branch of Drishtipat.

Vanewijck.nl is the personal portfilio site of photographer, Rob van Ewijck (The Natherlands).

Local Content

http://www.advocacyinitiatives.org/ is a podcasting website featuring in online video contents of BRAC program. The website is design by Machizo for BAHRU (BRAC Advocacy and Hudmna rights Unit)

Multimedia CDROM on "PRSP and You" has been produced for SUPRO, a countrywide human rights and development network.

UnnayanVideo: a video content production and publish both online and offline on different development issues of Bangladesh.

Gitanjali, online version of Nobel Laurat Rabindranaṭh Tagore's great work.

Ongoing Projects

http://www.unnayannews.net/is a multimedia and development webzine that actively promotes human rights and development matters through its issue based publications and list serving.

http://www.e-jaban.com/ , is Bangladeshi content in Japanese language. It regularly publish "mail magazine" on different issues of Bangladesh to Japan-Bangla global community

http://total-beauty.org/ is the platform to give webbased consultation for exploring true beauty of human being. The contents of the website as Japanese language.

Hosting and Domain Registration : Latest Offers

Hosting service from US based server, 40, 000 M.B (40 GB))+ free domain + unlimited facilites; price only US$ 72 and service charge.

Hosting service from US based server, 600 M.B + free domain + unlimited facilites; price only US$ 70 and service charge. And domain registration 10 US$/year.

Special hosting from Japanese server, 1 G.B space + all essential facilities, price only Tk. 2500 / year.

Latest video

The web documentary I g **Flood 07** I h portrays the most recent flood situation of Bangladesh. The video contain featured the status of both grassroots and capital city.

APPENDIX XII: ANIMATION LITERATURE REVIEW: AN OVERVIEW

This review is divided into several parts: general animation histories and references; general aesthetics and theory; general silent-era books; the Disney studio and its classical animation (2D); other commercial studios and animators (2D); three-dimensional animation; computer-generated animation; experimental and independent animation; made-for-television animation; related periodicals; and instructional and finding aids.

General Animation Histories and References

A landmark in the development of animation studies was the publication of Giannalberto Bendazzi's book, Cartoons: One Hundred Years of Cinema Animation, by John Libbey in 1994 (it previously had been published in Italian and French language versions). The most comprehensive study of its kind to date, Cartoons provides an encyclopedic history of animation produced worldwide, both at major studios and on a smaller scale. Bendazzi did much of his research at international animation festivals, probably the only place where one could find some of the marginal works he discusses, such as Mongolian animation; to give an idea of the extent of his coverage, the influential Disney studio takes up only 10 of the book's 444 pages of text. Bendazzi covers the period between 1888 and 1990 in five sections, with additional sections devoted to new technologies (ten pages), a bibliography (including national publications and resources related to characters, filmmakers, education, aesthetics and other topics), and indexes to names and titles. As the book's title suggests, filmed animation is of central concern in this book; made-for-television animation and other forms are not given much attention.

A wider view of formats is covered in Charles Solomon's History of Animation: Enchanted Drawings, first published in 1989 and reprinted by Wings Books in 1994. Beginning with a look at the silent era, Solomon's book then proceeds to cover Disney, 1928-1941; the studio cartoon, 1929-1941; wartime animation, 1941-1945; various studios of the period 1946-1960; the "silver age" of Disney, 1945-1960; UPA and the graphic revolution, 1943-1959; television animation; and changes within the industry, 1960-1994. The scope of coverage is broad, encompassing independent work and advertising, along with the 'standards' of animation histories. Particularly noteworthy is Solomon's discussion of made-for-television animation. Though it is not exhaustive, it is far more detailed than most other accounts, which are few.

Earlier books that take a relatively wide view of animation history include Thomas W. Hoffer's Animation: A Reference Guide, published by Greenwood Press in 1981. In the book, the author describes the work as "an encyclopedic survey and guide to the animation literature in cel, stop-action, drawing-on-film, experimental, and computer graphic modes . . ." In addition to an historical overview, the book contains seven appendixes about major research centers, a chronology, sources for collectors, and annotated listings from the trade press. Hoffer's book was ahead of its time in providing reference materials for the field of animation studies.

Bruno Edera's *Full Length Animated Feature Films*, published by Hastings House in 1977, and John Halas's *Masters of Animation*, published by Salem House in 1987, are also relatively broad in scope. Edera's book includes an overview of animation techniques, some general information related to production costs across the world, and discussion of feature films made in various regions. Chapters include pioneers 1916-1945; America (Disney); Middle East, Asia and Australia; Eastern Europe; and Western Europe. A catalog published in the book contains many films, including some future productions, listing English and original titles, year of release, country of origin, running time, technique, basic production credits and a synopsis. Halas's book covers general historical information, as well as brief overviews of national contexts and the 'modern age' of animation (including computers, television and advertising). The majority of the book is devoted to a number of 'masters' of animation from across the world, including Walt Disney, Chuck Jones, John and Faith Hubley, Norman McLaren, Frederic Back, Ishu Patel, Kihachiro Kawamoto, Renzo Kinoshita, and Osamu Tezuka. *Masters of Animation* was created in conjunction with a television series produced by the BBC in England. *Roger Noake's Animation: A Guide to Animated Film Techniques*, published by MacDonald Orbis in 1988, is a book on the production process, but it covers a wide range of techniques and features illustrations of both experimental and commercial films from a number of countries.

In the late 1980s, the American Film Institute published two more anthologies that offer a variety of historical essays in animation studies. The first, *The Art of the Animated Image: An Anthology*, edited by Charles Solomon and published in 1987, contains essays on J. Stuart Blackton; Winsor McCay and personality animation; the Disney multiplane camera; the Walter Lantz Studio (a personal account by Leo Salkin); Norman McLaren; fine art animation; women animators; television and child audiences; and computer animation. The second anthology, Storytelling in Animation: The Art of the Animated Image, edited by John Canemaker and published in 1988, includes essays on non-objective and non-linear animation; animation writers; a personal statement on independent animation by Shamus Culhane; Caroline Leaf and her film The Street, computer animation; studio approaches to story; Disney storytelling; the visual nature of animation; and four Disney films: Pigs is Pigs, Who Framed Roger Rabbit, Snow White and the Seven Dwarfs, and Peter Pan.

More recently, a number of other animation-related references have appeared. Among them is John Lent's 1994 *Animation, Caricature, and Gag and Political Cartoons in the United States and Canada: An International Bibliography*, which is part of the Greenwood Press series, "Bibliographies and Indexes in Popular Culture." One chapter focuses on "US Animation," containing coverage of such categories as legal issues, animation studios, children's press, and syndication.

Jayne Pilling's *Women and Animation: A Compendium*, published by the British Film Institute in 1992, provides another list of animators: in this case, women working internationally, both as pioneers and in recent years. This list, which contains for each name a country of origin, a summary of the woman's style (including, in some cases, quotes), and a list of films with dates of release-caps off a selection of critical essays, interviews and illustrations related to a wide range female artists. Some subjects include Lotte Reiniger, Mary Ellen Bute, Faith Hubley, Evelyn Lambart, Sayoko Kinoshita, Candy Kugel, Leeds Animation, Caroline Leaf, Sally Cruikshank, Joanna Priestley, Jane Aaron, Suzan Pitt, Kathy Rose, Ruth Hayes, Mary Beams, Monique Renault, Alison de Vere, Joanna Quinn, Candy Guard, Vera Neubauer, Joanna Woodward, Sarah Kennedy, Karen Watson, Joan Stabely, Nina Sabnani, and Nina Shorina. Their countries of origin or artistic practice include the US, Canada, France, England, Wales, India, and Russia; Australian animation also is discussed.

Another volume edited by Jayne Pilling focuses on the relationship between Cartoons and the Movies; it was published by Dreamland in 1997 in conjunction with a retrospective at the Annecy International Animation Festival. Part theory and part history, this book contains nine essays covering such subjects as film titles; cross media references (in the work of Frank Tashlin and in general); and the work of Everett Peck (creator of "Duckman"),

Aardman Animation, and Tim Burton. This book represents one of several projects aimed at contextualizing the production of animation within a larger cultural setting: in this case, the film industry as a whole.

The ways in which animation can be used for education is explored in Drawing Insight: Communicating Development through Animation, edited by Joyce Greene and Deborah Reber, a book published by Southbound in 1996. Growing out of special UNICEF projects involving animated programming, this anthology is composed of essays written by industry leaders, development specialists, and animators on the subject of how animation can contribute positive messages in the areas of health and social change. Essay topics include: approaches to creating early childhood development materials, merchandizing program management, the Adolescent Girl Communication Initiative of Eastern and Southern Africa, the Street Kids International project, the training of animators in developing countries, the work of the Children's Television Workshop (producers of the "Sesame Street" series), and African animation.

General Aesthetics and Theory

A general overview of aesthetic issues can be found in Maureen Furniss's book, Art in Motion: Animation Aesthetics, published by John Libbey in 1998. This book, which is designed to be an introductory college course book, is broken into two parts. The first part contains information on animation studies, in general; the foundations of studio practices; 2D alternatives to cel animation; elements of *mise-en-scène*, sound and structural design; the classical-era Disney studio; full and limited animation; 3D animation; and new technologies. The second part of the book contains studies in animation aesthetics focusing on institutional regulators, animation audiences, issues of representation, and form in abstract animation.

More advanced readings on animation aesthetics can be found in a book edited by Jayne Pilling and published by John Libbey in 1996: A Reader in Animation Studies. It contains twenty-one essays divided into five sections: "New Technologies" (three essays), "Text and Context: Analyzes of Individual Films" (eight essays), "Contemporary Cartoons and Cultural Studies" (two essays), "Theoretical Approaches" (four essays), and "Rewriting History" (four essays). Six essays deal with the Disney studio in some respect, while the rest cover a wide range of animated productions from around the world; topics related to American animation include the Bros. Quay (Americans whose studio is located in England), Susan Pitt, Joanna Priestley, The Fleischer Studio and clay animation, Jules Engel, and the "Ren and Stimpy" series.

Two books deal more directly with theoretical elements of animation. Paul Welles's Understanding Animation includes discussions of the evolution of animation, narrative strategies; the construction of comic events (including a 'typology' of 25 gag sequences); the representation of race and gender; and the nature of animation audiences. He includes numerous case studies employing animation produced in the United States and elsewhere. Welles's book was published by Routledge in 1998.

Alan Cholodenko's The Illusion of Life: Essays on Animation, published by Power Publications in 1991, contains essays presented at the Illusion of Life conference held in Sydney, Australia, in 1988. Aside from a transcribed speech by Chuck Jones which begins the volume, essays in the book rely heavily on post-structuralist and post-modernist critiques of French film theory employing semiology, Althusserian Marxism and Lacanian psychoanalysis. Subjects covered include the animation of sound, violence in animation, the notion of the uncanny, and the concept of animation as monstrosity, the bringing to life of dead matter.

Also of general interest to animation scholars is a book of essays written by Russian theorist and filmmaker, Sergei Eisenstein. Eisenstein on Disney, edited by Jay Leyda and published by Methuen in 1988, contains essays in which he discusses his concepts of metamorphosis and explains his theories of 'attraction' in animated work. In addition, a range of illustrations are reproduced in the book, including a number by Eisenstein himself.

General Silent Era Books

The original publication of Donald Crafton's Before Mickey: The Animated Film 1898-1928, by Massachusetts Institute of Technology in 1982, signaled a change in the nature of American animation scholarship (the book was reprinted by MIT in 1984 and 1987). By focusing on not only the silent era but also animation in Europe, this book went beyond the core of 'golden age' Hollywood studios and even the few prominent experimental animators that had constituted the focus of most previous animation scholarship. Delving into the theory of animation in terms of self-figuration (the tendency for animation artists to render an element of themselves in their work), Crafton's book became part of the foundation of the emerging area of animation studies. Significant topics dealt with in this volume include: the genre of 'haunted hotel' trickfilms; the relationship between vaudeville and early animation practice; the pioneering animators Emile Cohl and Winsor McCay; John Randolph Bray, the studio system and the influence of Taylorist management principles; commercial animation in Europe; the development of genre and narrative conventions; and Felix the Cat. In 1990, Crafton published an in-depth study of Emile Cohl, Caricature and Film, through Princeton University Press. Another example of excellent scholarship, this book examines Cohl as a link between the cinema and the field of popular graphic humor (he gained fame as a cartoonist).

Two books by John Canemaker provide in-depth studies of other silent era legends. Winsor McCay: His Life and Art, published by Abbeville in 1987, includes well-researched historical information, as well as numerous illustrations and a bibliography. The same description can be used to characterize Canemaker's 1996 book, Felix: The Tale of the World's Most Famous Cat, published by Da Capo. Its selected filmography contains only titles and years. Both books are based in part on Canemaker's interviews and personal contact with family members, production personnel and collectors who have allowed him to reproduce photos and memorabilia in the books. In 1977, Canemaker published a more general history of animation, The animated Raggedy Ann and Andy: An Intimate Look at the Art of Animation, its History, Techniques, and Artists, through Bobbs-Merrill.

Denis Gifford's American Animated Films: The Silent Era, 1897-1929, published by McFarland in 1990, provides details on the films themselves. It references productions chronologically by 140 series titles, beginning with Blackton Cartoons (1897), Vitagraph

Cartoons (1900-1909), and Winsor McCay Cartoons (1911-1918) and running through the two Mickey Mouse cartoons of 1928 originally recorded as silent films, Plane Crazy and The Gallopin' Goucho. Included with each entry, when applicable, is alternate and British titles, production company name, production credits, distributor, length of film, changes in titles or distributors, and other significant information. Gifford also published a guide to British Animated Films 1895-1985 through McFarland in 1987.

The Disney Studio and its Classical Animation

A useful place to begin to understand the Disney studio is Russell Merritt and J.B. Kaufman's Walt in Wonderland: The Silent Films of Walt Disney, published first in combined English and Italian by Le Giornate del Cinema Muto and La Cineteca del Friuli in 1993 (a later edition in English only was published by Johns Hopkins University Press). This carefully researched study was groundbreaking in its discussion of the Disney studio's output prior to its "Mickey Mouse" films beginning in 1928; early histories of Disney tend to begin with Mickey Mouse, as if Disney never suffered the trials of his early years in business. The extensively-illustrated book covers Walt Disney's early years in Kansas City, his early series, the development of the successful "Alice Comedy" and "Oswald" series in the 1920s, and events leading up to the arrival of "Mickey Mouse." A filmography provides credits, synopses, print sources, and other information.

Bob Thomas's Walt Disney: An American Original is a studio-authorized biography of the company's founder, a true icon of American culture. Thomas's reporting is fairly even-handed; he contends that he was given full access to archives and not censored by the studio in any way. His account of Disney's life briefly extends beyond 1966, the year of his death, to document some of the final accomplishments of his brother Roy, who died in 1971. Thomas's book was first published in 1976 but reprinted by Hyperion in 1994. It was written in part to counteract negative depictions of Disney's life in analyzes such as Richard Schickel's The Disney Version: The Life, Times, Art and Commerce of Walt Disney, originally published 1968 and reprinted by Ivan R. Dee in 1997. Still, negative appraisals continue to be published, for example, Peter and Rochele Schweizer's reactionary Disney—The Mouse Betrayed: Greed, Corruption, and Children at Risk, published by Regnery in 1998 (reviewed following this article).

Kathy Merlock Jackson's Walt Disney: A Bio-Bibliography, published by Greenwood Press in 1993, is an valuable reference listing sources for Disney information in all media, a variety of interviews, articles and speeches given by Disney, and filmographies, award lists, production credits, and other material pertaining to both Disney and his company. The book contains information on the impact of Disney on American culture, including extensive material on the theme parks.

A lot of reference information about the Disney studio has been produced under the company's own publishing label, Hyperion. As might be expected, these books tend to present a positive spin on all details, treading lightly over or ignoring controversial areas; nonetheless, Hyperion books provide varied and useful resources for many applications. Hyperion books include the 608-page Disney A to Z: The Updated Official Encyclopedia, written by Disney archivist Dave Smith and published in 1998. It contains more than 6,500 entries covering noteworthy company employees and visitors, Disney films and television shows, theme parks, and various other Disney ventures. Designed to be an aid for answering common questions asked of the archivists, the book offers short passages containing factual information and bits of trivia as well as air dates and limited production credits.

Leonard Maltin's The Disney Films, was published by Hyperion in a third edition in 1995. It focuses primarily on the live-action and animated features produced under Walt Disney's supervision, from Snow White (1937) to The Luckiest Millionaire (1967). Production credits and a review are provided for each of these films, which are illustrated with one or more photos. Other features are discussed in essays constituting two additional chapters, one focusing on the years 1967 to 1984 and the other continuing from that year until 1994 (the division resting on the 1984 formation of Touchstone Pictures and the changing Disney image as executives were brought in from 'the outside' to turn around the company's relative stagnation). Although the 1995 film Pocahontas is mentioned in an essay, the 'selected credits' listed for all the later features run only through 1994 (excluding that film). Final chapters include essays on the Disney shorts and made-for-television productions (the latter being quite brief); lists of titles by year also are included. A more recent book published by Hyperion, Joe Grant's 1997 The Encyclopedia of Walt Disney's Animated Characters, provides information related to the studio's short and feature length productions. It is divided into three parts, covering shorts, television series, and features, and includes Disney stars as well as generic characters (such as Satan or Neptune, for example). Some descriptions are brief while others, such as Donald Duck (who receives eight pages), are quite lengthy; discussion of voice artists and a filmography are included in some cases.

A deeper look into the Disney company occurs in several anthologies. Eric Smoodin's Disney Discourse: Producing the Magic Kingdom, published by Routledge in 1994, combines some reprints of non-critical articles from the 1940s with recent critical essays. The latter include work on Disney's business history; its relationship with Technicolor; the development of EPCOT Center; Tokyo Disneyland; Latin American themes in films; and merchandizing to children. From Mouse to Mermaid: The Politics of Film, Gender and Culture, edited by Elizabeth Bell and others, examines live-action and animated films produced by the Disney studio from a number of theoretical positions, including feminist, Marxist, post-structuralist and cultural studies. It was published by Indiana University Press in 1995. Animation-related chapters cover such topics as adaptation in Snow White and Pinocchio; the development of female characters types; depictions of nature in Bambi; masculinity in Beauty and the Beast; voice and body in The Little Mermaid; and EPCOT Center. A fascinating Marxist reading of a Disney character, though in the context of print cartoons, occurs in How to Read Donald Duck: Imperialist Ideology in the Disney Comic, written by Ariel Dorfman and Armand Mattelhart and published by International General in 1975.

Multiple facets of the Disney company are investigated in Inside the Mouse: Work and Play at Disney World, a 1995 book by The Project on Disney members Karen Klugman, Jane Kuenz, Shelton Waldrep and Susan Willis. It is published by Duke University Press. This book contains ten essays written over a period of three years, combining personal responses to experiences in the park with more objective scholarly criticism. Essays ranging from employment policies to post-modern architecture result in a work that is not specifically related to animation and yet sheds light on the larger system of operation of one of the world's most influential animation studios. A study of this type also appears in Christopher Anderson's, Hollywood TV: The Studio System in the Fifties, published by the University of Texas Press in 1994. His chapter on "Disneyland" documents the efforts of the Disney studio in combining the company's theme park with a popular television program, a crucial element in the immense success of the company in the post-World War II era.

Several books have documented the art of Disney animation. These include Robert D. Feild's The Art of Walt Disney, published in 1944 by Macmillan and Christopher Finch's The Art of Walt Disney: From Mickey Mouse to The Magic Kingdom, published by Harry N. Abrams, in 1973 and reprinted in 1983. For another take on Disney's art, The Art of Mickey Mouse, a 1995 book edited by Craig Yoe and Janet Morra-Yoe and published by Hyperion, illustrates the many ways in which Disney's most famous character has been incorporated into the work of artists across the world. After a critical introduction by John Updike and a short forward by the editors, over one hundred full color artworks are published without commentary (artist name, title, year, media, and size are included).

While a number of fine artists have been influenced by Disney art, the studio's aesthetics have had an even greater impact on the look of animation across the world. One of the most notable books to document the studio's style is Disney Animation: The Illusion of Life, by veteran Disney animators Frank Thomas and Ollie Johnson. Published by Abbeville in 1983, the book is part instructional text and part a history of the evolution of Disney's style.

To understand the complexity of the production process, one must be familiar with the many individuals who contribute to it. John Canemaker's Before the Animation Begins: The Art and Lives of Disney Inspirational Sketch Artists, published by Hyperion in 1996, sheds light on the complexity of the design process, focusing on the early 1930s through Disney's death in 1966. This extensively illustrated book constitutes original research on an important and largely overlooked area of the creative process, one of the few realms of the Disney studio open to women as well as men. Canemaker documents the work of Bianca Majolie, Sylvia Moberly-Holland, and Mary Blair, as well as several male artists, including Albert Hurter and Ken Anderson. A final chapter of the book overviews recent inspirational artists who have influence Disney animation such as The Lion King, Pocahontas, and Hercules.

Walt Disney's direction of the studio's features, from Snow White to the Jungle Book is the subject of Robin Allan's book, Walt Disney and Europe: European Influences on the Animated Feature Films of Walt Disney, scheduled to be published by John Libbey in 1999. It is based on primary sources, including archival research and interviews with individuals who worked closely with Disney, and also is well illustrated, many images coming from private archives and never before published.

Other Commercial Studios and Animators

A new contribution to American studio animation history is Michael Barrier's Hollywood Cartoons: American Animation in its Golden Age, published by Oxford University Press in 1999. This book, which focuses on short works produced between 1928 and 1966, is based on more than 200 interviews conducted by Barrier and animator Milton Gray beginning in 1969. A substantial portion of the text focuses on the Disney studio; Barrier notes that most of his primary research took place at the Disney archives due to the accessibility of their research materials, though he viewed thousands of films from all the major Hollywood studios in preparing to write the book. Warner Bros. also receives a significant amount of attention, with MGM and UPA each receiving a chapter (other studios are discussed in more generally-focused chapters). Most of this book's 600-plus pages is text; there are few illustrations.

Two 'popular' reference books were revised by their author, Jeff Lenburg, during the early 1990s: The Encyclopedia of Animated Cartoons and The Great Cartoon Directors. The Encyclopedia, originally published by Facts on File, contains "A Nutshell History of the American Animated Cartoon" as of the book's publication date, which is 1991 (reprinting is scheduled for 1999). This overview is followed by a synopsis, production credits, air dates and, when applicable, episode titles for silent cartoon series, theatrical sound cartoon series, full-length animated features, animated television specials, and television cartoon series. A list of awards and honors is also included, along with a bibliography. The Great Cartoon Directors, published by Da Capo in 1993, includes profiles and a filmography for nine of Hollywood's most famous animation directors-Friz Freleng, Ub Iwerks, Chuck Jones, William Hanna, Joseph Barbera, Bob Clampett, Tex Avery, Walter Lantz, and Dave Fleischer. The filmographies containing titles and release dates for each production.

For many years, the standard text of animation history courses was Leonard Maltin's Of Mice and Magic: A History of American Animated Cartoons, a well-illustrated, somewhat popular account of animation history. After an overview of the silent era, its content is organized by chapters on various studios: Disney, Fleischer, Terrytoons, Walter Lantz, Ub Iwerks, Van Beuren, Columbia, Warner Bros., MGM, Paramount/Famous, and UPA. Made-for-television animation is discussed briefly but, on the whole, discounted in its importance to the field. Maltin's approach is reflective of attitudes toward television work in the 1980s, prior to the second 'golden age' of animation following the success of "The Simpsons" and the growth of made-for-television animation during the 1990s.

An earlier collection of essays on animation history was provided by Danny and Gerald Peary, editors of The American Animated Cartoon: A Critical Anthology, which was published by Dutton in 1980. This book contains essays (organized into chapters) dealing with a wide variety of historical issues, including six on early animation history; six on Disney; seven on Warner Bros.; five on other studios, including UPA; and seven on characters. The section on Disney includes his testimony before the House Committee on Un-American Activities while a final chapter of the book contains writing on a variety of subjects, including interviews with Ralph Bakshi and Bill Hanna. Each chapter in the book is followed by a bibliography.

Leslie Carbaga's The Fleischer Story provides a fairly anecdotal account of the studio that provided competition with Disney during the 1920s and 1930s, when it produced the "Ko-Ko the Clown," "Betty Boop," and "Popeye" cartoon series, the feature Gulliver's Travels, and other animated productions. Carbaga's book, first published in 1976 and re-published by Da Capo in 1988, overflows with illustrations, including photos, film stills and production materials. A filmography listing titles and release dates is included as well. Fred M. Grandinetti's Popeye: An Illustrated History of E.C. Segar's Character in Print, Radio, Television and Film Appearances, 1929-1993 focuses on one of the Fleischer studio's most popular stars. A wide variety of illustrations provide examples for each the four chapters suggested by the book's title. A survey of characters associated with "Popeye" in its many forms, as well as an episode guide to animated productions (including title, year of release and a brief synopsis) and various lists of trivia. Selected scripts from animated cartoons appear in the book's Appendix. Grandinetti's book was published by McFarland in 1994.

A number of other directors and studios have been the focus of various publications written in a relatively popular format. For example, Joe Adamson has documented the histories of two legends of animation in Tex Avery: King of Cartoons, published by Popular Library in 1975 (reprinted by Da Capo in 1985), and The Walter Lantz Story, with Woody Woodpecker and Friends, published by G.B. Putnam's in 1985. John Cawley has written on The Animated Films of Don Bluth in a 1991 book by Image Publishing.

Several animators have taken to the keyboard and published their own life and career stories. In Bolt from the Blue: A True Story, Ernest Pintoff focuses largely on his recovery from a stroke in 1986, though he includes some information related to his career in animation and live-action production. Gene Dietch examines life in Czechoslovakia in his 1997 book For the Love of Prague, published by Pragma Press. Pintoff and Dietch's books are not primarily concerned with animation, but rather other aspects of the artists' lives. In That's Not All, Folks! My Life in the Golden Age of Cartoons and Radio, published by Warner Books in 1988, Mel Blanc discusses his career as a voice artist. Chuck Jones's Chuck Amuck-The Life and Times of an Animated Cartoonist, published by Farrar-Straus-Giroux in 1989, is another well-known autobiography within the field. Shamus Culhane's Talking Animals and Other People: The Autobiography of a Legendary Animator originally was published in 1986, though it was reprinted by Da Capo in 1998; following this animator's diverse career, it includes information on the Fleischer, Iwerks, Disney, Lantz, and other studios. Culhane's instructional book, Animation: From Script to Screen, published by St. Martin's Press in 1988, also contains a good deal of the animator's personal philosophy of artistic production.

Live-action and animation director Frank Tashlin is the subject of Tashlin, an anthology edited by Roger Garcia with the assistance of Bernard Eisenschitz and published in 1994 by Éditions du Festival international du film de Locarno in collaboration with the British Film Institute. A fair number of photos, film stills, production materials, and drawings illustrate the eleven critical essays, commentary (by Robert Benayoun, Peter Bogdanovich, and Joe Dante), reprinted writing by Tashlin, and notes on films that fill the book. It is capped by a chronology, filmography (including uncredited and unrealized work) and bibliography, making it an indispensable resource for anyone writing on Tashlin.

Peter Hames edited another valuable anthology, Dark Alchemy: The Films of Jan Svankmajer, published by Praeger in 1995. The aesthetics of this Czech surrealist, who also works in both live-action and animation, are explored in an introduction, four analytical essays and an interview with the artist, who describes his training and the influences of other artists, surrealism and politics on his work. A thorough bibliography and filmography, as well as several illustrations, provide useful additions to the book.

Some relatively dated histories of animation still prove useful to the researcher. For example, Roger Manvell's Art and Animation: The Story of Halas and Batchelor Animation Studio, 1940-1980, though published in 1980 (by Hastings House) offers valuable information about one of England's top studios. The influential animator from the National Film Board of Canada, Norman McLaren, also has been the subject of a number of books published more than twenty years ago. The drawings of Norman McLaren, published by Tundra Books in 1975, contains interviews conducted with Michael White. Other useful books include Maynard Collins's Norman McLaren, published by the Canadian Film Institute published in 1976 and Valliere T. Richard's Norman McLaren, Manipulator of Movement: The National Film Board Years, 1947-1967, published by the University of Delaware Press in 1982. In 1991, Donald McWilliams compiled and edited one of the most recent publications related to the artist: a small book of writings called Norman McLaren on the Creative Process, which accompanies a videotape set, all of which was published by the National Film Board of Canada. It contains technical notes, which McLaren wrote for all his films, as well as personal observations about various aspects of creativity.

Reading the Rabbit: Explorations in Warner Bros. Animation, edited by Kevin S. Sandler, focuses on another of the legendary animation studios of the classical era. The book was published by Rutgers University Press in 1998. Its essays focus on a diverse range of topics, including the influence of Charlie Thorson; caricature and parody; Hillbilly and African American images; cross-dressing; merchandizing; and fan culture. The specific topic of Warner Bros. music is covered in an essay by Scott Curtis, "The Sound of the Early Warner Bros. Cartoons," which appears in Sound Theory/Sound Practice, edited by Rick Altman and published by Routledge in 1992.

Jerry Beck and Will Friedwald's 1989 reference book, Looney Tunes and Merry Melodies: A Complete Illustrated Guide to the Warner Bros. Cartoons, contains a chronological filmography of over nine hundred shorts produced by the studio, as well as lists of its network television series, specials, feature-length films, and government-sponsored cartoons. Entries include release date, main characters, writers, producers, and lead animators. More recently, the authors produced Warner Bros. Animation Art: The Characters, the Creators, the Limited Editions, published by Hugh Lauter Levin in 1997.

Eric Smoodin's Animating Culture: Hollywood Cartoons from the Sound Era provides a contextual analysis of animation produced by Disney and other studios. It was published by Rutgers University Press in 1993. In this book, Smoodin employs various primary documents, such as copyright materials, film bills, and even Federal Bureau of Investigation records to fill in gaps in our understanding of animation history. One chapter examines the press's response to racism and eroticism in Disney's South American themed live-action/and animation features. Other chapters address the links between culture, commerce and government policy; the relationship between cartoons and features on a film bill; the workings of the government's "Private Snafu" series; and the effects of censorship on animation (a limited discussion, focusing primarily on one magazine article published in 1939).

The subject of censorship in animation is examined much more thoroughly in Karl Cohen's Forbidden Animation: Censored Cartoons and Blacklisted Animators in America. Covering both theatrical and made-for-television animation, Cohen investigates the subjects of racist imagery, blacklisting and so-called 'uncensored' adult-oriented animation, and how studios have responded to censorship pressures placed upon them by various institutions. His findings, which were published by McFarland in 1997, primarily are based on anecdotal information, interviews with historians, and textual analysis; primary documentation in this area can be difficult to come by.

Like Smoodin and Cohen, Michael S. Shull and David E. Wilt are interested in the relationship between the animation industry and other American institutions. In Doing Their Bit: Wartime American Animated Short Films, 1939-1945, published by McFarland in 1987, these researchers have focused their attention on the World War II era. Their book provides a content analysis of wartime cartoons released by major American studios, reflecting the way in which war themes were handled in this form of popular culture. Richard Shale's Donald Duck Joins Up, published by UMI Research Press in 1982, provides an account of Disney's production of World War II propaganda.

McFarland's 1998 publication, Film Cartoons: A Guide to 20th Century American Animated Features and Shorts, written by Douglas L. McCall, is divided into three sections. The first section covers 180 animated feature films, mostly American but also some films produced outside the country. It includes general information, production/voice credits and, in some cases, awards. Part two deals with 58 feature-length live-action and animation combination films; it lists the titles and year of release for each film, plus a description of the animation contained in it. Part three covers 1500 animated shorts with brief notes, which include title, year of release, director, studio, various production credits, and in some cases synopses, notes and awards. These shorts are mainly productions of major Hollywood studios. A variety of animation studios are covered in an appendix; they are both large and small and mostly American, though a few studios from Canada and England are included. Entries in this book are uneven in their content, with some being relatively full and others including little.

Strangely enough, despite the great worldwide popularity of Japanese animation, relatively few books have been published that could be considered relatively useful to animation scholars. The recent The Anime Companion: What's Japanese in Japanese Animation?, by Gilles Poitras, is aimed at a fan reader, but takes its subject quite seriously. It provides brief entries covering some 500 subjects related to Japanese culture, from the mundane (such as toilet design and use) to the divine (various facets of Buddhist practice, for example), as well as general information about Japanese animation. It was published by Stone Bridge Press in 1999. In 1996, Stonebridge also published Frederik L. Schodt's Dreamland Japan: Writings on Modern Manga, which contains references to animation among its details on the history and aesthetics of Japanese print comics. A publication of the same year, Antonia Levi's Samurai from Outer Space: Understanding Japanese Animation, published by Open Court, also offers insight into aspects of Japanese animation.

Some of the best publications focusing on animation created outside the United States have been produced by animation festivals to accompany retrospective screenings. Examples include Zagreb 1982: Retrospective Program of Zagreb School of Animation, published by the Zagreb World Festival of Animation in 1982, and Captured in Drifting Sand, published by the Annecy International Festival of Animated Film in 1995. Most of these 'retrospective' books do not find their way into mainstream distribution and must be ordered directly from the festival itself. Along with Nenad Pata's A Life of Animated Fantasy, published by Zagreb Film in 1984, Zagreb 1982 provide interviews and filmographies to help explain the history of Zagreb Film, an innovative leader in the world animation industry beginning in the late 1950s. Zagreb Film subsequently has published other guides to its productions, listing films along with production credits, synopses and illustration; these materials can be ordered directly from the company (PO Box 915, 10000 Zagreb).

Drifting in Sand covers the creative lives and filmmaking of two Swiss artists, Gisèle and Nag Ansorge, who worked largely in the practice of sand animation. A complete filmography as well as many images provide the reader not only with a sense of these artists' history, but also the potential of sand animation.

Festival-produced books often are quite small in scale, being devoted to filmographies and other exhibition-related items. Such is the case with David Curtis's 1983 booklet, Robert Breer, which was published by Cambridge Animation Festival in 1983. Other small books focusing on animation production include Mari Kuttna's Hungarian Animation: A Survey of the Work of the Pannonia Studio, Budapest, published by Hungarofilm, Circa 1970, and Jan Pos's Kratky Film: The Art of Czechoslovak Animation, published by Rutgers in 1991, in conjunction with an exhibition at Jane Voorhees Zimmerli Art Museum.

Three-Dimensional Animation

Throughout the golden era of the 1930s and 1940s, the dominant form of American animation was two-dimensional; specifically, cel animation. During the second 'golden age' of the 1990s, animation has blossomed in many forms. Clay Animation, a book by Michael Frierson, published by Twayne in 1994, documents the long history of this three-dimensional animation technique. It overviews the process of clay animation, as well as the invention of plasticine (the material used to create 'clay' animation) and early clay films, including the work of Willie Hopkins and Helena Smith Dayton. Chapter highlights include clay animation during the 1920s and 1990s, as well as the work of Leonard Tregillus, Art Clokey (and the "Gumby" series), Will Vinton (and Claymation), Bruce Bickford (known for his work with musician Frank Zappa), and David Daniels (and his stratacut technique).

Some of the best known three-dimensional animation is found in horror films featuring models of monsters. Paul M. Jensen's The Men Who Made the Monsters, published by Twayne in 1996, includes chapters on animators Willis O'Brien (probably best known for his work on the 1925 film The Lost World and the 1933 film King Kong) and Ray Harryhausen (known for his work on the 1963 film Jason and the Argonauts and numerous other productions), as well as live-action directors James Whale, Terence Fisher and Freddie Francis. Most of Jensen's information seems to be culled from secondary sources, making this book useful for general information on the subjects, but of less interest to advanced researchers. Ending the book is a selected bibliography, including writing by the subjects themselves, and a filmography, including title, production company, year of release, production credits and running time.

Frank Thompson's The Film, The Art, The Vision: Tim Burton's Nightmare Before Christmas, published by Hyperion in 1993, documents the production process of the influential puppet animation directed by Henry Selick. It reveals how the characters were created and moved before the camera, providing insight into the aesthetics of the film. Although it is certainly a 'picture book,' many of its illustrations offer very useful images of set and character construction. Images of replacement heads and eyes, shot breakdown sheets, and set devices are very helpful for understanding the aesthetics of the film. A related approach is used in a 1996 publication by Hyperion, written by Lucy Dahl, James and the Giant Peach: The

Book and Movie Scrapbook. Taking a much smaller, more personal approach, this books contains several images of production materials and set photos that reveal insight about the film adaptation (also directed by Henry Selick), as told by the daughter of the book's author. However, it is primarily a novelty book.

Peter Lord and Brian Sibley's Creating 3D Animation: The Aardman Book of Filmmaking, published by Harry Abrams in 1998, contains an overview of animation history plus a general introduction to the process of making three-dimensional animation. The authors are animators at Aardman, which is located in Bristol, England; included in their book is information on the making of the studio's "Wallace and Gromit" series. Puppet Animation the Cinema: History and Technique is the focus of a 1975 book by L. Bruce Holman, published by A.S. Barnes. Sections on history and technique are followed by filmographies listing representative films from across the world and the work of seven puppet animators: George Pal, Bretislav Pojar, Ladislas Starevitch, Jirí Trnka, Hermina Tyurlová, Zenon Wasilewski, and Karel Zeman. From the same publisher, in 1980, came S.S. Wilson's Puppets and People: Dimensional Animation Combined with Live Action in the Cinema.

The Edwin Mellen Press also has published a number of titles related to puppetry, in general. For example, James Fisher's The Puppetry Yearbook (1997), which examines the artistry of puppet stage past and present; Henryk Jurkowski's A History of European Puppetry, which is published in two volumes (1996, 1998) and includes history, theory and aesthetics; and Grace Greenleaf Ransome's Puppets and Shadows: A Selective Bibliography to 1930 (1997), which is a reprint of a 1931 sourcebook focusing on Europe and Asia.

Computer-Generated Animation

Most books written on the subject focus on techniques, providing instructions on how to use various software packages. A general discussion of technique is provided by Michael O'Rourke's Principles of Three-Dimensional Computer Animation: Modelling, Rendering and Animating with 3D Computer Graphics, revised in 1998 and published by Norton, which is suitable for college students wanting to learn how to create 3D images with a computer. The Special Interest Group on Computer Graphics (SIGGRAPH) of the Association for Computing Machinery has published a number of guides that will be of use to researchers as well as students. Its Computer Graphics Career Handbook (edited by Ed Ferguson and others), while published in 1991 and therefore outdated, contains 'career profiles' by several professionals who describe their work in the field, a list of universities offering degrees and the technology employed at each, and a list of 'company statistics' that suggests the hardware and software being employed at a number of firms employing computer animation.

A number of books describing recent projects can be helpful for assessing developments in the field. Among them is Rita Street's Computer Animation: A Whole New World, published by Rockport in 1998. Street focuses on work by such companies as ILM (the feature Spawn), Pixar (short films), New Wave International (a ride film), Mainframe Entertainment (the "ReBoot" television series), Colossal Pictures (a commercial), Pacific Data Images (the short Sleepy Guy), Lamb & Company (motion capture) and Medialab (real-time animation in "Donkey Kong"). She also examines the use of CGI in student and personal projects. An historical overview of the field is contained in an introduction by Ed Catmull, who led the development of Pixar within George Lucas's company, Industrial Light and Magic. That company's groundbreaking special effects in Terminator 2: Judgment Day (1991) and other films is the subject of another book, Industrial Light and Magic, written by Mark Cotta Vaz and Patricia Rose Duignan and published by Ballantine in 1996.

A popular Pixar project is detailed in Jeff Kurtti's coffee-table book, A Bug's Life: The Art and Making of an Epic of Miniature Proportion, published by Hyperion in 1998, is certainly promotion and intended for a wide range of readers. However, its sketches, stills and text reveal important considerations in the making of the film and the current state of CGI. For example, one chapter discusses the use of widescreen space while another the design of bugs to overcome the 'ick factor' most people experience when confronted by insects.

Pioneering computer animator John Whitney's book, Digital Harmonies: On the Complimentarity of Music and Visual Art, explains the influence of such figures as Pythagorus (with his theories of harmony) and Arnold Schoenberg (with his twelve-tone compositions) on Whitney's creative process and output as an abstract filmmaker. It was published by McGraw-Hill in 1980. Whitney's detailed description of the design components of Arabesque (1975) and other films are potentially of great value, but will be too technical for all but the most musically and technologically literate readers. Of course, much of the book's technical information is outdated; still, it provides an interesting look at some groundbreaking work in computer animation and a relatively rare examination of the use of music in animation.

General Experimental and Independent Animation

The aesthetics and theory of experimental animation are the focus of William C. Wees's Light Moving in Time: Studies in the Aesthetics of Avant-garde Film, published in 1992 by the University of California Press. Individuals such as Jordan Belson and James Whitney, who employ frame-by-frame animation and real-time techniques, are discussed alongside live-action filmmakers Paul Sharits, Michael Snow, Kenneth Anger and Stan Brakhage. Wees explores the relationship between actual vision and the cinematic form in these artists' works. He discusses operational and metaphorical similarities between the eye/brain and film/camera modes of seeing; although not overly technical, this material will appeal to readers who have an interest in physiological and mechanical processes.

For many years, one of the only sources for information on 'fine art' animated works was Robert Russett and Cecile Starr's Experimental Animation: Origins of a New Art, a revised book published by Da Capo in 1988 (originally published by Litton Educational Publishing in 1976). After an introduction to some new faces and technologies affecting independent animation, a series of short essays and interviews cover twenty-eight individuals considered to be groundbreaking contemporary imagists or pioneers in one of the following categories: abstract and 'pictorial' animation in Europe, abstract animation in America, experimental animated sound, or new technologies. A separate chapter overviews the work of Norman McLaren and the National Film Board of Canada. Other artists covered include Lotte Reiniger, Len Lye, Oskar Fischinger, Mary Ellen Bute, Harry Smith, Larry Jordan, Norman McLaren, John and James Whitney, Stan VanDerBeek, Peter Foldes and

Ed Emshwiller. Its chapters sometimes are composed of interviews. Overall, the book is well-illustrated—a necessity, due to the relative difficulty of seeing some of these artists works, particularly at the time the book was published (the growth of home entertainment formats has made some of them more accessible).

More focused in scope is The German Avant-garde Film of the 1920s, written by Walter Schobert and published by the Göethe Institute in 1989. It includes short overviews, reprinted commentary, and statements related to such animators as Viking Eggeling, Oskar Fischinger, Lotte Reiniger, Hans Richter, and Walter Ruttmann, as well as a number of live-action filmmakers. The variety of independent animation produced during the 1970s can be seen in Frames: A Selection of Drawings and Statements by Independent American Animators, which was self-published by animator George Griffin in 1976. This hard-to-find book contains illustrations and writing submitted by seventy artists, including Jane Aaron, Robert Breer, John Canemaker, Larry Cuba, Jules Engel, Candy Kugel, Caroline Leaf, Frank Mouris, Eliot Noyes, Pat O'Neill, Sara Petty, Maureen Selwood, Stan VanDerBeek and James Whitney. The book also contains a list of names and addresses for the contributors.

Other sources for information on Avant-garde animators include P. Adams Sitney's Visionary Film: The American Avant-garde 1943-1978, originally published by Oxford University Press in 1974 and since reprinted, and David James's Allegories of Cinema: American Film in the Sixties, published by Princeton University Press in 1989. Both these books deal with animation in a relatively marginal way. Other articles on experimental animation can be found in a variety of publications produced by Anthology Film Archives in New York; for example, its recent anthology, First Light, edited by Robert Haller and published in 1998, includes writing on Jordan Belson, Oskar Fischinger, Marie Menken, Hans Richter, James Whitney and others. Malcolm Le Grice's book, Abstract Film and Beyond, published by Massachusetts Institute of Technology in 1977, provides a history of abstract film and a discussion of its interrelation with other arts.

One of the most infamous experimental animators of the American Avant-garde is Harry Smith. Although he was reclusive and secretive in life, friends of his were able to piece together a book overviewing his life and work posthumously. American Magus: Harry Smith, A Modern Alchemist, edited by Paola Igliori and published by Inanout Press in 1996, contains essays, interviews (mostly conducted between 1993 and 1995), reprints of primary documents, photographs and a research guide that provides an appropriately diverse overview of this enigmatic musicologist, anthropologist, painter, filmmaker, occultist and intellectual. For other perspectives, one can consult Noel Carroll's essay, "Mind, Medium and Metaphor in Harry Smith's Heaven and Earth Magic," which was published in Film Quarterly in its Winter 1977 issue, as well as various essays in the June 1992 issue of Film Culture, which contains a 1972 interview with Mary Hill, an essay by Rani Singh, and some of Smith's poems. The publisher of Film Culture, Anthology Film Archives, has a fairly good selection of publications on other experimental animators as well. For example, its 1997 publication, Intersecting Images: The Cinema of Ed Emshwiller, edited by Robert Haller, contains a guide to film and video literature on this innovative artist, along with interviews and critical essays.

Figures in Motion: Len Lye, Selected Writings provides an overview of the accomplishments of the experimental New Zealand animator, who also is known for his work as a sculptor, writer and live-action filmmaker. In this book, published by Auckland University Press in 1984, editors Wystan Curnow and Roger Horrocks have provided a useful introduction as well as a filmography, exhibition list and bibliography, along with reprints of Lye's statements about his work. Lye's essays cover a diverse range of subjects, including his philosophy on color, sound, and motion, as well as his approach to direct-on-film animation, which he sees as being linked to biological issues.

A general discussion of American independent animation can be found in The Current State of American Independent Animation and a Prediction for its Future, an MA thesis written by Maureen Furniss at San Diego State University in 1987. This research was based on questionnaires given to a number of artists and historians. Included are filmographies and resumes from a number of the individuals who participated in the study.

Made-for-Television Animation

Hal Erickson's Television Cartoon Shows: An Illustrated Encyclopedia 1949 through 1993, published by McFarland in 1995, is among the best resources available for made-for-television animation, at least in respect to American exhibition. A 42-page history of television introduces the volume, which contains the titles, networks, airdates, production credits, synopses, and related information (often quite useful) for every animated production aired on American broadcast and cable networks during the forty-four year period. The book concludes with an 8-page chapter on voice artists, covering significant considerations related to the profession as well as a number of individuals who are well-known in the field.

While popular television series generally become the subjects of trivia books or other popular literature, only occasionally does one find a publication such as The World of Hanna-Barbera Cartoons, which was published by the Museum of Radio and Television in 1995, for an exhibit held there June 23—September 24 of that year. Although composed primarily of production art, the book nonetheless provides a useful document of the many series that have emanated from Hanna-Barbera throughout its history. Bill Hanna's A Cast of Friends provides insight into the career of this animator and producer; it also constitutes one of the few histories focusing (in large part) on the made-for-television animation industry, generally, and his own influential company, Hanna-Barbera Productions, specifically.

The bulk of books about made-for-television animation are in the form of audience studies or theoretical discussions of spectator issues. Marsha Kinder's Playing with Power in Movies, Television, and Video Games: From Muppet Babies to Teenage Mutant Ninja Turtles, published by The University of California Press in 1991, serves an example. Using psychoanalytic models of spectatorship and cognitive theory, she examines the way in which children are positioned as both passive consumers and interactive participants. Her study is not specific to animation, but rather addresses media within a broader context; it is more concerned with content than form.

A few books treat animation as a subject related to merchandizing and licensing. For example, both Cy Schneider's Children's Television: The Art, the Business, and How It Works, published by NTC Business Books in 1987 and Ellen Seiter's Sold Separately: Parents and Children in Consumer Culture, published by Rutgers University Press in 1995, treat animation in this manner. Tom Engelhardt's essay, 'The Shortcake Strategy," from the anthology Watching Television, which he edited with Tod Gitlin and published with Pantheon in 1986, is another oft-quoted resource for information on licensing and children's television (again, animation is treated within this context). The ACT Guide to Children's Television, written by Evelyn Kane and published by Beacon Press in 1979, provides insight into the organization's point of view and its recommendations for programming.

However, there are some useful reference works devoted to television. Through Scarecrow Press, George Woolery published a series of such works during the 1980s, including two titles related to animation: Children's Television: The First Thirty-Five Years, 1946-1981, Part I: Animated Cartoon Series, published in 1983, and Animated TV Specials: The Complete Directory to the First Twenty-Five Years, 1962-1987, published in 1988. The Children's Television book contains series synopses, complete production credits, and broadcast schedules for every animated television series from 1946 to 1981. Animated TV Specials contains the broadcast history, principal characters and voices, and synopsis of shows aired on networks or in syndication on American television between 1962 and 1987. Generally it does not include any program identified initially as being a theatrical film. Its appendices include "Most Frequently Aired/Longest Running Network Animated TV Specials," "TV Specials Utilizing Stop-Motion Animated Puppets," "Holiday and Topical Animated TV Specials," and "Animated TV Specials Series." It also contains a "Name Index" to producers, directors, filmmakers, writers, musicians, lyricists, and voices and a "Selected Subject Index" to studios, production companies and distributors.

Related Periodicals

A number of periodicals have devoted themselves to the general topic of animation history, theory, aesthetics and business practices. Among them are Animato!, Animation Magazine, and Funnyworld. Animation World Magazine, an electronic publication, is published on-line at http://www.awn.com; each of its monthly issues focuses on a different topic. More in-depth, researched articles on animation are presented in Animation Journal, published twice a year, which is the only peer-reviewed journal devoted to animation, and Animatrix, a publication of the UCLA graduate animation workshop that comes out more or less once a year. In Spring 1994, Animation Journal published a special issue on women in animation; otherwise, its content, like that of Animatrix, is varied in each issue. A Canadian publication, fps, although focused on the whole of animation, is now highlighting short, independent works.

Worth noting, too, is Film Culture, which includes animators among the avant-garde filmmakers that constitute its focus. For example, its 1974 issue (Nos. 58-59-60) contains a large article on "The Films of Oskar Fischinger" written by William Moritz, who single-handedly took on the task of excavating the extensive and largely dilapidated work of this master of abstract animation, assuring his rightful place in history. A number of Film Culture essays have been collected in Sitney's Film Culture Reader, published by Praeger in 1970; it includes writing by Hans Richter, Parker Tyler, Stan Brakhage, P. Adams Sitney, Gene Youngblood and many others.

Throughout history, periodicals devoted to film or media, in general, have at times published special issues related to animation. The first issue of Hollywood Quarterly, which was dated 1945-1946, while not a special issue, contains essays related to animation; for example, music and the animated cartoon, by Chuck Jones; UPA's film The Brotherhood of Man, by Ring Lardner Jr., Maurice Rapf, John Hubley, and Phil Eastman; and puppets, George Pal and his film on John Henry, by Sondra Gorney. The Spring 1969 issue of Cinema Journal contains two animation-related articles: "The Roadrunner and other Cartoons," an ammended interview with Chuck Jones by Robert Benayoun (which first appeared in the August 1963 issue of Positif), and Howard Rieder's "Memories of Mr. Magoo," based on his 1961 MA thesis, The Development of the Satire of Mr. Magoo, which was written at the University of Southern California.

A December 1988 issue of Griffithiana contains three essays, "The Fantasia that Never Was," by John Canemaker; "Interview with Friz Freleng," by Reg Hartt; and "Mythic Mouse," chronicling the development of the Mickey Mouse character, by Karen and Russell Merritt. The Velvet Light Trap put out a special issue on animation in Fall 1989 (No. 24). It contains interviews with Fleischer animator Myron Waldman and independent animators Paul Glabicki and Robert Breer, as well as essays on the Fleischer's "Popeye" series; Disney's Peter Pan; structure in American studio cartoons; theory and animation; and MTV and post-modernism.

The Winter 1992 (Volume 3, Number 4) issue of Screen contains two animation-related essays, Mark Langer's The Disney-Fleischer Dilemma: Product Differentiation and Technological Change" and David Forgacs "Disney Animation and the Business of Childhood." Paul Welles edited a special issue of Art and Design (May 1997, Volume 53) which included essays on dance animation, documentary aesthetics, the adaptation of Alice in Wonderland, and the Disney Studio (an interview including animators Zach Schwartz and Bob Godfrey). A special issue of Film History from 1993 (Volume 5, Number 2), edited by Mark Langer, contains essays on the subjects of the "Ren and Stimpy" series; early clay animation films; Disney's move into feature filmmaking; phenakistoscopes; the investigation of communism in the animation industry; caricature and parody in Warner Bros. cartoons; and Disney's Cinderella.

A special animation issue published by The Hollywood Reporter every year in winter (for example, in 1999 it was the January 26 issue) presents articles on the current state of the animation industry in terms of economics, business practices, works in progress, studio personnel, and so forth. The Hollywood Reporter also published a "Careers in Animation" special issue in 1998, dated August 14-16.

Instructional and Finding Aids

Researchers wishing to locate specific animated films can consult David Kilmer's The Animated Film Collector's Guide: Worldwide Sources for Cartoons on Videotape and Laserdisc, published by John Libbey in 1997. This reference contains a list of useful books; listings of films by title, author, character, and studio; information on compilations of short films; names of distributors and resources; a worldwide list of chapters of ASIFA (the international animation society); an 'honor roll' of award winning films; and a review of a series of animation released by Pioneer on laserdisc. Although this book is international in its scope, it does not include information on 'anime,' or popular Japanese animation, which the author feels is handled sufficiently in other reference guides. Kilmer indicates that some of the titles he includes can be found on film as well as video and laserdisc.

The Whole Toon Catalog is a useful resource for individuals wishing to purchase a broad range of animated titles on video and laserdisc, as well as audio and books. A Chicago-based distributor of home entertainment, Facets Multimedia, publishes this general animation catalog in addition to a special catalog devoted to only Japanese animation.

Collectors of animation art will find two books by Jeff Lotman of interest: Animation Art: The Early Years, 1911-1953, published in 1995, and Animation Art: The Later Years, 1954-1993, published in 1996, both by Schiffer. Containing thousands of examples of art, these books provide information on fair market prices for various types of animation art.

Individuals interested in college animation programs can consult Ernest Pintoff's The Complete Guide to Animation and Computer Graphics Schools, published by Watson-Guptill Publications in 1995. It contains lists of schools by state, as well as one to two-page essays by a number of individuals working in the field. Educational information also can be found in The ASIFA List of Animation Schools (published by Gunnar Strøm, Volda College, Box 500, Volda N-6101 Norway; E-mail ASIFA@hivolda.no) and Where to Get Multimedia Training in Europe (published by MEDIA/INA, 4, avenue de l'Europe, Bry-sur-Marne Cedex 94366, France; E-mail: colarossi@ina.fr; www.ina.fr). Though somewhat out of date, information on schools, as well as animation equipment suppliers, distributors of animated films, animation literature and other topics can be found in the American Film Institute's Factfile #9: Animation, compiled by Lucinda Travis and Jack Hannah in 1986.

Two useful instructional guides related to the production of animation are Kit Laybourne's The Animation Book, published by Crown in 1979, and Richard Taylor's The Encyclopedia of Animation Techniques, published by Running Press in 1996. The reprint of Edwin G. Lutz's book, Animated Cartoons: How They are Made, Their Origin and Development (originally published in 1920 by Charles Scribners Sons), by Applewood in 1998, is generally of interest to researchers working on Disney, since this is the book that the young Walt used to learn the basic principles of the animation process. The book overviews processes used during the 1910s and provides practical information on principles of movement.

Lists of animators and related companies can be found in such national guides as the 'Directory' published by ASIFA-Canada (contact them at case postale 5226, St. Laurent, Québec) or the "Annuario" published by ASIFA-Italy (contact them at via Cosmo 6, Torino 10131 Italy). Anamú is a directory published group of independent animators in Ireland (contact Anamú at 4-5 Eustace St., Temple Bar, Dublin 2).

Chapter 6

Global Multimedia Projects and Companies: Select Case Studies

CASE STUDY: ABOUT THE PROJECT

Multimedia: From Wagner to Virtual Reality is a unique hybrid publishing project that joins ArtMuseum.net with our partner in print, W.W. Norton & Co., to present an untold history of multimedia. This site is based on the book of the same name, co-edited by Randall Packer and Ken Jordan.

This on-line project was developed in close collaboration with ArtMuseum.net and its Arts and Education program. It is our hope that this site, together with the book, will serve as a valuable resource for students, teachers, artists, and critics probing the interactive media arts, as well as those attempting to make sense of this burgeoning medium that is transforming our art and our culture. We also hope that it will dispel much of the hype surrounding the misunderstood phenomenon of multimedia, and provide a means for illuminating an understanding of its roots, significance and potential.

The Website and the book are meant to work in tandem. The book collects and contextualizes seminal essays from 30 of multimedia's pioneering figures. On-line, *Multimedia: From Wagner to Virtual Reality* is a dynamic, growing resource featuring information, images, and video about the history of this remarkable, emerging medium. The site was launched in June, 2000. Since then, the In Depth section was added to cover the creative work and essays of five of multimedia's pioneers: Douglas Engelbart, Billy Klüver, Alan Kay, Scott Fisher, and Lynn Hershman. There is also a Concepts section, which links artists, engineers and theorists across disciplines according to their contributions to the core concepts that underlie digital multimedia. The Pioneers timeline provides a chronological view of the work of artists and scientists that begins even before Wagner, with the caves of Lascaux. The Overture, a narrative description of the history of multimedia, provides extensive illustrative images of artworks and technological innovation. An extensive collection of video documentation is included throughout the In Depth and Timeline sections. Future plans include the addition of a teacher's guide for using the site in the classroom. *Multimedia: From Wagner to Virtual Reality* will continue to expand over time, and we would appreciate your comments and feedback.

Special thanks to Intel's Kevin Teixeira for his belief in this project from the very beginning, and to Vince Thomas, Irena Rogovsky, and Annie Rodkins of the ArtMuseum.net staff for their expert advice and technical support in helping to shape *Multimedia: From Wagner to Virtual Reality*. To Phyllis Hecht of the National Gallery of Art in Washington, D.C. for her support and guidance in the design of the site. Also to our editor at Norton, Alane Mason, for championing this unorthodox project. To my co-editor Ken Jordan, whose critical feedback has been instrumental in unearthing the many themes and relationships found in this material.

And lastly, to the pioneers of the medium whose contribution to this site has been vast: not only have they graciously provided me with substantial material, but most importantly, their work and vision has been a great inspiration that has fueled the creation of this project.

Board themes mentioned below the underscore an "untold" story behind the evolution of multimedia: its precedents, unsung heroes, and the extraordinary creative work and visionary thinking of artistes and scientists.

Multimedia is emerging as the defining medium of the 21st century. The World Wide Web, CD-ROMs, virtual reality arcade games, and interactive installations only hint at the forms of multimedia to come. Yet the concept of integrated, interactive media has its own long history, an evolution that spans over 150 years. Remarkably, this has been a largely untold story. Discussions of the development of the personal computer and the Internet tend to focus on a few highly successful entrepreneurs, neglecting the less known work of the engineers and artists who first sought to craft a medium that would appeal to all the senses simultaneously—a medium that would mimic and enhance the creative capacities of the human mind. Here, then, is a "secret history" of multimedia: a narrative that includes the pioneering activities of a diverse group of artists, scientists, poets, musicians, and theorists from Richard Wagner to Ivan Sutherland, from Vannevar Bush to Bill Viola.

In the years since World War II, scientists have pursued personal computing and human—computer interactivity as vehicles for transforming consciousness, extending memory, increasing knowledge, amplifying the intellect, and enhancing creativity. The idealistic and ideological aspirations of both groups have resulted in a new medium that emphasizes individual choice, free association, and personal expression.

Birth of a New Medium

New technology has always been used to make media. George Lucas shot his latest Star Wars epic with digital cameras, though the audience experience was no different than if it had been shot on celluloid. But while not all computer-based media is multimedia, today's multimedia starts with the computer, and takes the greatest advantage of the computer's capability for personal expression.

Digital computers were initially designed as calculating machines. The first fully electronic computer, the ENIAC, was built by the U.S. military during World War II to produce ballistics tables for artillery in battle. Computers then were clumsy, hulking devices—the ENIAC had 18,000 vacuum tubes, and measured 50 × 30 feet—that did calculations for scientific research. Only a handful of scientists considered the possibility of personal computing for creative purposes by non-specialists.

The first scientist to think seriously of this potential was Vannevar Bush. In his 1945 article "As We May Think," he outlined "a future device for individual use, which is a sort of mechanized private file and library." Before the ENIAC was completed, Bush was already contemplating how information technology could enhance the individual's capability for creative thought. "The human mind... operates by association," Bush observed. The device that he proposed, which he named the Memex, enabled the associative indexing of information, so that the reader's trail of association would be saved inside the machine, available for reference at a later date. This prefigured the notion of the hyperlink. While Bush never actually built the Memex, and while his description of it relied on technology that predated digital information storage, his ideas had a profound influence on the evolution of the personal computer.

In the years immediately after the War, under the shadow of the atomic bomb, the scientific establishment made a concerted effort to apply recent advancements in technology to humanitarian purposes. In this climate, Norbert Wiener completed his groundbreaking theory on cybernetics. While Wiener did not live to see the birth of the personal computer, his book, The Human Use of Human Beings, has become de rigeur for anyone investigating the psychological and socio-cultural implications of human-machine interaction. Wiener understood that the quality of our communication with machines effects the quality of our inner lives. His approach provided the conceptual basis for human-computer interactivity and for our study of the social impact of electronic media.

Bush and Wiener established a foundation on which a number of computer scientists associated with the Advanced Research Projects Agency (ARPA)—a U.S. government funded program to support defence-related research in the1960s began to build. Leading ARPA's effort to promote the use of computers in defence was the MIT psychologist and computer scientist J.C.R. Licklider, author of the influential article "Man-Computer Symbiosis." Defying the conventional wisdom that computers would eventually rival human intelligence, rather than enhancing it, Licklider proposed that the computer be developed as a creative collaborator, a tool that could extend human intellectual capability and improve a person's ability to work efficiently.

While at ARPA, Licklider put significant resources towards the pursuit of his vision. Among the scientists he supported was Douglas Engelbart, who since the mid-1950s had been seeking support for the development of a digital information retrieval system inspired by Bush's Memex. APRA funding enabled Engelbart to assemble a team of computer scientists and psychologists at the Stanford Research Institute to create a "tool kit" that would, as he phrased it, "augment human intellect." Dubbed the oNLine System (NLS), its public debut in 1968 at the Fall Joint Computer Conference in San Francisco was a landmark event in the history of computing. Engelbart unveiled the NLS before a room of 3,000 computer scientists, who sat in rapt attention for nearly two hours while he demonstrated some of his major innovations, including the mouse, windows for text editing, and electronic mail. Engelbart was making it possible, for the first time, to reach virtually through a computer's interface to manipulate information. Each of his innovations was a key step towards an interface that allowed for intuitive interactivity by a non-specialist. At the end of his presentation, he received a standing ovation.

However, the contributions of the NLS went beyond innovation regarding the computer interface. Engelbart and his colleagues also proposed that creativity could be enhanced by the sharing of ideas and information through computers used as communications devices. The oNLine System had its computers wired into a local network, which enabled them to be used for meaningful collaboration between co-workers. Engelbart understood that the personal computer would not only augment intelligence, but augment communication as well. In 1969 his research in on-line networking came to fruition with the creation of the Internet.

Engelbart's NLS pioneered some of the essential components necessary for the personal computer, but it would be up to a new generation of engineers to advance computing so it could embrace multimedia. As a graduate student in the late 1960s, Alan Kay wrote a highly influential Ph.D. thesis proposing a personal information management device that, in many ways, prefigured the laptop. In 1970, as research in information science was shifting from East Coast universities and military institutions to private digital companies in Silicon Valley, Kay was invited to join the new Xerox PARC in Palo Alto. PARC's mandate was no less than to create "the architecture of information for the future."

At PARC, Alan Kay conceived the idea of the Dynabook—a notebook sized computer that enabled hyperlinking, was fully interactive, and integrated all media. With the Dynabook, digital multimedia came into being. Echoing Licklider, Engelbart and colleagues at PARC, Kay declared the personal computer a medium in its own right. It was a "meta-medium," as he described it in his 1977 essay "Personal Dynamic Media," capable of being "all other media." While the Dynabook remained a prototype that was never built, the work that came from its development, including the invention of the Graphical User Interface (GUI) and subsequent breakthroughs in dynamic computing, was incorporated into the first true multimedia computer, the Xerox Alto.

Integration of the Arts

By proposing that the Dynabook be a "meta-medium" that unifies all media within a single interactive interface, Alan Kay had glimpsed into the future. But he may not have realized that his proposal had roots in the theories of the 19th century German opera composer, Richard Wagner. In 1849, Wagner introduced the concept of the Gesamtkunstwerk, or Total Artwork, in an essay called "The Artwork of the Future." It would be difficult to overstate the power of this idea, or its influence. Wagner's description of the Gesamtkunstwerk is one of the first attempts in modern art to establish a practical, theoretical system for the comprehensive integration of the arts. Wagner sought the idealized union of all the arts through the "totalizing," or synthesizing, effect of music drama Ð the unification of music, song, dance, poetry, visual arts, and stagecraft. His drive to embrace the full range of human experience, and to reflect it in his operas, led him to give equal attention to every aspect of the final production. He was convinced that only through this integration could he attain the expressive powers he desired to transform music drama into a vehicle capable of affecting German culture.

Twentieth century artists have continued the effort to heighten the viewer's experience of art by integrating traditionally separate disciplines into single works. Modern experience, many of these artists believed, could only be evoked through an art that contained within itself the complete range of perception. "Old-fashioned" forms limited to words on a page, paint on a canvas, or music from an instrument, were considered inadequate for capturing the speed, energy and contradictions of contemporary life. In their 1916 manifesto "The Futurist Cinema," F.T. Marinetti and his revolutionary cohorts declared film to be the supreme art because it embraced all other art forms through the use of (then) new media technology. Only cinema, they claimed, had a "totalizing" effect on human consciousness.

Less than a decade later, in his 1924 essay describing the theater of the Bauhaus, "Theater, Circus, Variety," László Moholy-Nagy called for a theater of abstraction that shifted the emphasis away from the actor and the written text, and brought to the fore every other aspect of the theatrical experience. Moholy-Nagy declared that only the synthesis of the theater's essential formal components Ð space, composition, motion, sound, movement, and light Ð into an organic whole could give expression to the full range of human experience.

The performance work of John Cage was a significant catalyst in the continuing breakdown of traditional boundaries between artistic disciplines after World War II. In the late 1940s, during a residency at Black Mountain College in North Carolina, Cage organized a series of events that combined his interest in collaborative performance with his use of indeterminacy and chance operations in musical composition. Together with choreographer Merce Cunningham and artists Robert Rauschenberg and Jasper Johns, Cage devised theatrical experiments that furthered the dissolution of borders between the arts. He was particularly attracted to aesthetic methods that opened the door to greater participation of the audience, especially if these methods encouraged a heightened awareness of subjective experience. Cage's use of indeterminacy and chance-related technique shifted responsibility for the outcome of the work away from the artist, and weakened yet another traditional boundary, the divide between artwork and audience.

Cage's work proved to be extremely influential on the generation of artists that came of age in the late 1950s. Allan Kaprow, Dick Higgins and Nam June Paik were among the most prominent of the artists who, inspired by Cage, developed non-traditional performance techniques that challenged accepted notions of form, categorization, and composition, leading to the emergence of genres such as the Happenings, electronic theater, performance art, and interactive installations.

Allan Kaprow, who coined the term "Happening," was particularly interested in blurring the distinction between artwork and audience. The ultimate integrated art, he reasoned, would be without an audience, because every participant would be an integral part of the work. As he wrote in his 1966 primer, "Untitled Guidelines for Happenings." "The line between art and life should be kept as fluid, and perhaps indistinct, as possible." This approach led to a performance style that pioneered deliberate, aesthetically conceived group interactivity in a composed environment. Happenings artists devised formal elements that allowed participants the freedom to make personal choices and collective decisions that would affect the performance.

In this climate, artists became increasingly interested in integrating technology into their work. While technology clearly played a significant role in 20th century arts (such as photography, film, and video, as well as various fine arts genres), it was not until Bell Labs scientist Billy Klüver placed the potential of advanced engineering into the hands of artists in New York that integrated works of art and technology began to flourish. Klüver conceived the notion of equal collaboration between artist and engineer. He pioneered forms of art and technology that would have been unimaginable to the artist without the engineer's cooperation and creative involvement. With Robert Rauschenberg, Klüver created several of the earliest artworks to integrate electronic media and to encourage a participatory role for the audience, including Oracle (1963-65) and Soundings (1968).

In 1966 Klüver co-founded E.A.T. (Experiments in Art and Technology) to bring artists and engineers together to create new works. E.A.T.'s most ambitious production was the Pepsi-Pavilion, designed for the Osaka Expo 1970 in Japan Ð a tremendously ambitious collaborative, multimedia project that involved over 75 artists and engineers. As Klüver explained, audience participation was at the heart of their interests: "The initial concern of the artists who designed the Pavilion was that the quality of the experience of the visitor should involve choice, responsibility, freedom, and participation. The Pavilion would not tell a story or guide the visitor through a didactic, authoritarian experience. The visitor would be encouraged as an individual to explore the environment and compose his own experience." During this period, the British artist and theorist Roy Ascott began to explore the use of computers in artistic expression. One of the first theoretical attempts to integrate the emerging fields of human-computer interactivity and cybernetics with artistic practice is Ascott's article, "Behavioural Art and the Cybernetic Vision," from 1966-67. Ascott noted that the computer was "the supreme tool that... technology has produced. Used in conjunction with synthetic materials it can be expected to open up paths of radical change in art." Ascott saw that human-computer interaction would profoundly affect aesthetics, leading artists to embrace collaborative and interactive modes of experience.

When Alan Kay arrived in Xerox PARC in 1970, the foundation was in place for a multimedia that synthesized all the existing art forms, and presented them in an environment that allowed for meaningful interactivity. With the Dynabook, the interactive Gesamkunstwerk was brought into the digital realm, and put on-line.

Through the Looking Glass

The fantasy of being transported into another world, to be taken wholly into an imaginary realm, is a primal desire. With computer-based multimedia, encounters with immersive, virtual worlds will soon become commonplace. Virtual reality, after all, is a logical extension of the integration of the arts. It is also an ideal environment for applying our knowledge of human-computer interactivity.

There is an evocative echo in virtual environments of the earliest known form of human expression—the prehistoric cave paintings found at such sites as the caves of Lascaux in the south of France. These immersive environments, dating from 15000 BC, are thought by scholars to have been theaters for the performance of rituals that integrated all forms of media and engaged all the senses. On the walls were painted animal images and shamanist scrawls, but the environment in which the paintings appeared was surely as significant as the paintings themselves. As Joseph Campbell described it, "these magical spots occur far from the natural entrances of the grottos, deep within the dark, wandering chill corridors and vast chambers, so that before reaching them one has to experience the full force of the mystery of the cave itself." To encounter the cave paintings was to immerse the self in an otherworldly domain, which would heighten consciousness and trigger altered states of perception.

There are many examples of immersion in the history of art. The Dyonisian rituals of Greek Theater, and the construction of the great cathedrals of Europe, are two obvious examples. Richard Wagner's Gesamtkunstwerk was driven by a vision of theater in which the audience loses itself in the veracity of the drama, creating an immersive experience. As he wrote in "The Artwork of the Future," "the spectator transplants himself upon the stage, by means of all his visual and aural faculties." To facilitate his vision, Wagner reinvented the conventions of the opera house, and in 1876 opened the Festpielhaus Theater in Bayreuth, Germany, with the first complete production of The Ring cycle. The Festpielhaus, with its employment of Greek amphitheatrical seating, surround-sound acoustics, the darkening of the house, and the placement of musicians in an orchestra pit, focused the audience's undivided attention on the dramatic action. His intent was to maximize the suspension of disbelief, to draw the viewer into an illusionary world staged within the proscenium arch.

In the 1950s, a similar vision inspired the American cinematographer Morton Heilig to propose a "cinema of the future" that would surround the audience with facsimiles of life so convincing they would believe themselves to be transported to another domain. Such a cinema, he wrote, "would faithfully reproduce man's outer world as perceived in his consciousness, it will eventually learn to create totally new sense materials for each of the senses... [that] they have never known before, and to arrange them into forms of consciousness never before experienced by man in his contact with the outer world."

While Heilig devised a theoretical framework that applied the technologies of his day toward the achievement of virtual experience, it was only as a consequence of advances in computer science that the immersion his work suggested became possible. By 1965, Ivan Sutherland had already achieved legendary status among computer scientists as the inventor of Sketchpad, the first interactive graphics software. In a short paper published that year, Sutherland mused over the options available to the engineer to display computer data, to create a "a looking glass" into what he described as a "mathematical wonderland." It seemed reasonable for him to suggest that "The Ultimate Display" (as the paper was titled) would represent this data in 3-dimensional form, allowing the construction of entirely believable 3-dimensional, computer controlled, virtual worlds. However, like Heilig before him, Sutherland took this suggestion one step further. "The ultimate display," he wrote, "would É be a room within which the computer can control the existence of matter." He suggested that such a display could present realities heretofore only imagined, as if seen through Alice's looking glass. Sutherland's proposal was startling, but it launched an entire field of scientific inquiry.

It also fueled the imagination of a generation of artists. One of the first to consider the possibilities of digitally-constructed virtual experiences was Myron Krueger. In the early 1970s, Krueger created the pioneering works Metaplay and Videoplace to explore the potential of computer-mediated interactivity. These works were interactive artistic environments, influenced by Happenings, designed to give participants freedom of choice and opportunities for personal expression. Videoplace also connected participants in different locations through networked technologies, creating the illusion of shared space. As Krueger later wrote about the piece, "our teleconference created a place that consisted of the information we both shared... a world in which full physical participation would be possible. This world is an 'artificial reality.'"

During the 1970s and 1980s, several engineering projects pursued virtual environment display systems that could represent such an "artificial reality". Perhaps the most significant of these in the mid-1980s was led by Scott Fisher at the NASA-Ames Research Center. Fisher's intent was to engage the entire nervous system in a multi-sensory presentation of virtual space Ð extending multimedia beyond the screen. The Ames VIEW system (an acronym for Virtual Interface Environmental Workstation) included a headset with two small liquid crystal display screens, a microphone for speech recognition, earphones for surround-sound effects, a head-tracking device, and dataglove to recognize the user's gestures and place them within the virtual environment. The direction this work pointed in was clear. As Fisher wrote in his 1989 article "Virtual Interface Environments," "with full body tracking capability, it would also be possible for users to be represented in this [virtual] space by life-size virtual representations of themselves in whatever form they choose." Immersive environments, Fisher observed, could give birth to a new form of participatory, interactive electronic theater. The possibility of such a theater had already taken hold of the public's imagination. In Neuromancer, his widely read novel from 1984, William Gibson described in palpable detail a future in which virtual reality was a fact of life. Echoing Myron Krueger's notion that teleconferencing created a "place" that consisted of shared information, Gibson's characters inhabited a virtual environment made possible by the networking of computers, which he named "cyberspace." Gibson's cyberspace provided the first literary definition for the computers, hubs, servers, and databases that make up the matrices of the network. His discussion of cyberspace was so tangible Ð and seductive, with its suggestion that any computer hacker could "jack-in to the matrix" with an encounter with a sexy avatar—it became a touchstone for every engineer, artist and theorist working in the field.

Marcus Novak took Gibson's description of virtual environments as the starting point for his own theoretical and artistic explorations. In his essay from 1991, "Liquid Architecture in Cyberspace," he follows the pioneering work of Sutherland, Fisher, and Gibson, *et al*, to its logical conclusion, and notes its profound implications for architecture, our notions of space, and our attitudes towards the organization of information. He notes that in cyberspace, since all structure is programmable, all environments can be fluid. The artist who designs these immersive digital habitats will be able to transcend the laws of the physical world. As a consequence, architectural forms built in cyberspace can respond to the viewer, encouraging provocative and illuminating interactions. In cyberspace, architecture becomes a form of poetry.

While most research in virtual reality aims to project the viewer into a digital environment by means of a head-mounted display, some engineers have taken an alternative approach. In the early 1990s, Daniel Sandin and Thomas DeFanti conceived of a virtual reality system that places the human body directly inside a computer-generated environment. They describe their system, called the CAVE (an acronym for Cave Automatic Virtual Environment) in their article "Room with a View": "Unlike users of the video-arcade type of virtual reality system, CAVE 'dwellers' do not need to wear helmets, which would limit their view of and mobility in the real world... to experience virtual reality." Instead, participants in the CAVE are surrounded by an immersive, digital "cave painting"—which brings the evolution of immersion full circle, back to the prehistoric caves of Lascaux, and humankind's earliest efforts at personal expression.

Integrated Datawork

Vannevar Bush who, in 1945, determined the chief narrative characteristic of multimedia by proposing a mechanical device that operated literally "as we may think." The challenge, as he saw it, was to create a machine that supported the mind's process of free association. Bush noted how ideas tend to evolve in a non-linear, idiosyncratic fashion. His Memex would be a tool that could supplement this aspect of human creativity by organizing its media elements to reflect the dynamics of the mind at play.

Douglas Engelbart expanded on Bush's premise. His quest to "augment human intelligence," as he aptly phrased it, was based on the insight that the open flow of ideas and information between collaborators was as important to creativity as private free association. The personal computer, as he envisioned it, would not only allow for the arrangement of data in idiosyncratic, non-linear formats. By connecting workstations to a data-sharing network and turning them into communications devices, Engelbart's Online System allowed for a qualitative leap in the collaboration between individuals—almost as if colleagues could peer into one another's minds as part of the creative process. In the early 1960s, experiments with networked personal computing promised the non-linear organization of information on a grand scale.

While few recognized this possibility at the time, it inspired a series of influential theoretical writings by the rogue philosopher Ted Nelson. Working outside of the academic and commercial establishments, following his own strongly held convictions, Nelson devised an elaborate system for the sharing of information across computer networks. Called Xanadu, this system would maximize a computer's creative potential. Central to Nelson's approach was the "hyperlink," a term he coined in 1963, inspired by Bush's notion of the Memex's associative trails. Hyperlinks, he proposed, could connect discrete texts in non-linear sequences. Using hyperlinks, Nelson realized, writers could create "hypertexts," which he described as "non-sequential writing" that let the reader make decisions about how the text could be read in other than linear fashion. As he observed in his landmark book from 1974, Computer Lib/Dream Machines, "the structures of ideas are not sequential." With hypertext, and its multimedia counterpart, "hypermedia," writers and artists could create works that encouraged the user to leap from one idea to the next in a series of provocative juxtapositions that presented alternatives to conventional hierarchies.

Nelson's insights were paralleled by experiments in the literary avant-garde that challenged traditional notions of linear narrative. In his book, he refers to Vladimir Nabokov's Pale Fire and Julio Cortazar's Hopscotch as two novels that use unconventional branching structures to encourage the reader's active collaboration in the construction of the story. As we have already seen, experimental performances inspired by John Cage—including Happenings, interactive installations, and performance art—also gave rise to a variety of non-linear narrative strategies. But perhaps the most prescient explorer of this terrain was the novelist William S. Burroughs.

Like Ted Nelson, Burroughs was deeply suspicious of established hierarchies. He was especially interested in writing techniques that suggest the spontaneous, moment-by-moment movement of the mind, and how non-linear writing might expand the reader's perception of reality. Through his use of the cut-up and fold-in techniques, which he described in his 1964 essay, "The Future of the Novel," Burroughs treated the reading experience as one of entering into a multi-directional web of different voices, ideas, perceptions, and periods of time. He saw the cut-up as a tool that let the writer discover previously undetected connections between things, with potentially enlightening and subversive results. With the cut-up, Burroughs prefigured the essential narrative strategy of hypertext and its ability to allow readers to leap across boundaries in time and space.

Since the invention of the electric telegraph by Samuel Morse in the 1830s, commentators have been noting the transformation of our concepts of space and time by wired technology. From the telegraph to the telephone to television to satellite communications, modern telecommunications has eradicated geographic borders, and made speed a central factor in modern life. This effect was commonly acknowledged as long ago as 1868, when, at a banquet held in honor of Morse's life achievement, he was toasted for having "annihilated both space and time in the transmission of intelligence. The breadth of the Atlantic, with all its waves, is as nothing."

Artists have grappled with the implications of this technology since its inception; the narrative experiments of literary authors reflects this current in modern art. Ted Nelson's concept of hypertext represented a profound effort to put this technology toward the service of personal, idiosyncratic expression. Nelson became an evangelist for hypertext, publishing articles, speaking at conferences, spreading the gospel wherever he could. One of those places was Brown University, which during the 1980s became a hotbed of literary explorations of the form. At Brown, the literary critic George Landow and his colleagues developed hypertext tools, such as Intermedia, which allowed authors with little experience in programming to invent new genres of creative writing. In his own work, Landow applied a trained critical eye to the formal aspects of hypertext, making connections to the post-structural textual analysis of critics like Roland Barthes and Jacques Derrida. Just as academic theoretical discourse was questioning the centrality of the author in the production of texts, hypermedia suggested that, in a future of networked digital media, responsibility would shift from author to reader, actively encouraging.

During this period, media artists whose roots lay in performance and video also began investigating hypermedia as a means of exploring new forms for telling stories. Artists such as Lynn Hershman and Bill Viola were drawn to the computer's ability to break down linear narrative structures. Viola approached the medium as a repository for evocative images that could be projected on screens in installations, "with the viewer wandering through some three-dimensional, possibly life-sized field of prerecorded or simulated scenes evolving in time," as he described it.

Lynn Hershman was among the first to create digital artworks using interactive media, in such pieces as Deep Contact, from 1989. She introduced interactivity into her work to combat the loss of intimacy and control brought about by the dominance of media such as radio and television. Her use of hypermedia allowed the viewer to choose directions inside the artwork's complex branching structure, and shape a personal experience of it.

By the late 1980s, multimedia, which had been at the fringe of the arts and sciences, reached critical mass and went mainstream. Marc Canter, who developed the first commercial multimedia authoring systems, was a chief catalyst. Canter pioneered software tools that artists and designers used to create multimedia on their personal computers. His authoring systems synthesized text, images, animation, video and sound into a single integrated work, using hyperlinks and other hypermedia techniques to connect its various elements.

In 1974, Ted Nelson had declared that "The real dream is for 'everything' to be in the hypertext." It was a proposal that echoed Marshall McLuhan's influential observation that, "after more than a century of electric technology, we have extended our central nervous system itself in a global embrace, abolishing both space and time as far as our planet is concerned." But despite his best efforts, and many advances in the fields of hypermedia and computer-based telecommunications, the global hypermedia library he envisioned remained more dream than reality. Most innovations in hypermedia focused on closed systems, such as the CD-ROM and interactive installations, rather than on open systems using a computer network.

In 1989 Tim Berners-Lee, a young British engineer working at CERN, the particle physics laboratory in Geneva, Switzerland, circulated a proposal for an in-house on-line document sharing system which he described modestly as "a 'web' of notes with links." After getting a grudging go-ahead from his superiors, Berners-Lee dubbed this system the World Wide Web. The Web, as he designed it, combined the communications language of the Internet with Nelson's hypertext and hypermedia, enabling links between files to extend across a global network. It became possible to link every document, sound file or graphic on the Web in an infinite variety of non-linear paths through the network. And instead of being created by a single author, links could be written by anyone participating in the system. Not only did the open nature of the Web lend itself to a wide array of interactive, multimedia experiences, but by hewing to a non-hierarchical structure and open protocols, Berners-Lee's invention became enormously popular, and led to an explosion in the creation of multimedia. By 1993 the Web had truly become an international phenomenon.

The success of the Web seemed to confirm the intuition of artists engaging in digital media that in the future, a global media database would inspire new forms of expression. Roy Ascott, for example, had already been exploring the creative possibilities of networking since the 1980s. He was interested in the notion of "dataspace," a territory of information in which all data exists in a continual present outside the traditional definitions of time and space available for use in endless juxtapositions. Ascott considers dataspace a new type of Gesamtkunstwerk, or a Gesamtdatenwerk as he calls it, in which networked information is integrated into the artwork. In such an environment, Ascott wrote, "meaning is not something created by the artist, distributed through the network, and received by the observer. Meaning is the product of interaction between the observer and the system, the content of which is in a state of flux, of endless change and transformation."

This notion of the artwork as a territory for interaction, as a locus of communications for a community, echoes the Happenings of a previous generation. On-line role-playing games have become laboratories for exploring this form of interactivity. As the social theorist Sherry Turkle has pointed out, on-line communities, such as Multi-User Dungeons (MUD), "are a new genre of collaborative writing, with things in common with performance art, street theater, improvisation theater, Commedia dell'Arte, and script writing." Pavel Curtis created one of the earliest MUDs, LambdaMOO, in 1990 at Xerox PARC. Though it consisted only of text, its interactive quality, made possible through intricate storytelling devices via the Internet, gave participants the illusion of immersion in a virtual environment. Interaction in the on-line environment, Curtis claimed, creates a kind of social behaviour which "in some ways it is a direct mirror of behaviour in real life."

Throughout history, art has often been referred to as a mirror of life. But by building upon the concepts of association and collaboration, computer-based multimedia may well become more than a mirror of life. Already we have seen how multimedia blurs the boundaries between life and art, the personal and the mediated, the real and the virtual. The implications of these tendencies we are only now beginning to grasp.

The Future is Under Construction

The breadth and potential of multimedia lends itself to utopian proposals. The French media theorist Pierre Levy describes multimedia as belonging to a trajectory of planetary evolution that runs from DNA to cyberspace—an arc that follows pure information as it reaches towards its most evolved form of expression. He proposes that today's global networks will usher in an era of "collective intelligence," and suggests that "cyberspace constitutes a vast, unlimited field... designed to interconnect and provide interface for the various methods of creation, recording, communication and simulation." His enthusiastic perspective is full of intriguing possibilities.

At the same time, we are all aware of the dystopian qualities of the 24/7 infotainment juggernaut that is being delivered across the globe through an ever more sophisticated telecommunications network. We read daily about the new media's encroachment on privacy, its opportunity for abuse, and the specter of centralized control that it might make possible. These dangers are real. There is a tension between opposing at the heart of the Internet—between those who prize its potential for an open, freewheeling exchange of art and ideas, and those who see its pervasiveness as an opportunity to expand upon the marketing-driven broadcast model of 20th century media—and it is not at all clear whether utopian or dystopian visions will ultimately prevail.

This project serves as a poignant reminder of the intentions of multimedia's pioneers. Their words, typically written during the heat of invention, convey a passionate involvement with higher ideals. To a remarkable degree, these scientists, artists, and theorists share a commitment to forms of media and communications that are non-hierarchical, open, collaborative, and reflective of the free movement of the mind at play. It is, in sum, an extraordinary vision. But whether we will achieve it is an unresolved question.

CASE STUDY: NEXT WAVE MULTIMEDIA

We are a digital media communications company, providing one-stop, comprehensive digital media solutions for all business communication needs. We make the digital media work for your business.

Whether you want to generate more sales, make a business-to-business presentation, train and motivate your employees, or build your brand through the online media, we will help you successfully address these challenging tasks.

Video Production

We have been helping some of India's top clients enhance their communications through the use of video. Whether delivered on tape, CD-ROM, DVD or through the Web, our experience in this media is extensive.

Game Development

Online/Mobile games are an exciting digital medium. Games on a web site/mobile capture attention and engage the user. Games can be designed to promote brands by incorporating product and marketing themes into the game play.

Website Design and Development

Starting from designing and developing your website to a planned online marketing campaign and e-commerce solutions, we can help you take full advantage of the Internet.

e-Learning

e-Learning brings with it new dimensions in education and training. We use the full potential of the digital media—streaming audio and video, animation and simulations—to offer a unique learning experience.

2D and 3D Animation

We have the creative, technical and production capabilities to create animated short films, television serials and commercials in 2D, 3D or combination.

Multimedia Presentations

Communicate your company's corporate profile, demonstrate your product or service benefits to your clients, we have years of expertise and experience in creating high-end interactive presentations that work.

Overview

Nextwave Multimedia Pvt. Ltd. began operations in 1996 as a video production house. It has since evolved into a company that delivers quality work in Internet, Web Games, Mobile Games, e-Learning, Multimedia Presentations, Animation, Video and also Print for Corporate communication.

The team consists of multi-skilled professionals with high creative talents and sound technical knowledge—writers, art directors, artists, video production executives, editors, animators and programmers.

Senior members of the team have about 10 years of hands-on experience in advertising, brand building, corporate communication, video production and Internet.

Nextwave Multimedia has produced over 500 episodes of television programming for national and regional television channels. About 1000 web and mobile games and over 1000 corporate videos, multimedia presentations and internet projects.

Infrastructure

- All requisite Hardware and Software,
- Numerous mobile handsets for porting and testing,
- Nonlinear Editing Systems,
- Recording Studio,
- High-end Graphic Workstations,
- Lights,
- Cameras,
- Audio Equipment,
- Mikes and accessories, and
- 4000 sq. ft. space.

Skills

Our skill set is wide ranging and includes all major technologies required to design and develop compelling communication solutions in both online, wireless and off-line media:

- Web Application Development,
- Online and Mobile Game Development,
- e-Learning,
- Animation,
- Video,
- Graphic Design, and
- Brand-building.

Video Production

- Business Communication,
- Television Software, and
- Television Commercials.

Nextwave Multimedia has full production and post-production capabilities to create visually exciting and professional videos—from company profiles to training videos, and from 'curtain raisers' at events to internal presentations. Because of our in-house facilities, we are able to keep the cost down and the quality high.

We have a profound understanding of this medium. We meticulously interpret your business and communication objectives and translate them into powerful videos using our creative and technical abilities.

- Business Communication,
- Company Profiles,
- Business Presentations,
- Internal Presentations,
- Campus Recruitment videos,
- New Employee Induction videos,
- Training videos,
- Product Launch videos,
- Event Curtain Raisers, and
- Industrial Safety videos.

Television Software

We have vast experience in producing programs for the television. Nextwave Multimedia has produced over 500 episodes in English, Tamil and Telugu, which were broadcast on Star TV, Star Vijay, Raj TV, E-TV, Splash Channel.

Television Commercials

Our background in advertising, combined with our technical strengths, helps us in producing commercials that are conceptually strong, strategically right on target, and creatively of a high order.

Channel Promos and Show Packaging

Nextwave Multimedia has conceived and produced numerous promotions for Television channels and Television programmes.

Nextwave Multimedia also works with other production houses for packaging of content with graphic design and animation.

Multi-Camera Coverage of Events

Nextwave Multimedia has experience in designing and erecting backdrops and stages for Music concerts, Fashion shows, Product launches and Corporate events.

Nextwave Multimedia has established relationships in the industry to put together a large talented production crew for any demanding event.

Process Steps

- Business needs analysis
- Competitive analysis
- Target audience analysis

- Solution identification
- Project plan
- Prototype
- Development and completion
- Quality check
- Client acceptance
- Implementation
- Maintenance

Although broadly the production of all our creative work goes through the same process (planning, designing and development or production and post-production), it is in the details that the development methodologies differ for each media.

Our development methodologies are adaptable to real world situations where we do not have the luxury of going through detailed steps due to pressing deadlines.

The following are the common steps in the development methodology that we follow for all media.

Objective Analysis

The client brief helps in arriving at a clear understanding of the purpose behind every piece of communication and its targeted audience.

Proposal/website documentation/film treatment note:

- This document is derived from the objective analysis, once agreed upon, forms the basis for starting the first stage of the creative process.
- In the case of the website projects, the proposal or the scope document also contains details about.
- Development tools and technologies to be used.
- Hosting infrastructure requirement.
- The development timeline.
- Cost estimates and payment terms.

Design Prototyping/Details Script or Storyboard

This phase of the work starts after receiving the Work Order alongwith 50 per cent advance payment from the client. During this stage, the work is given the visual shape that the final output will acquire, for web projects, the homepage and a few link pages, and for sometimes, a storyboard, are created for approval.

Development/Production

After approval of the design prototype/script or storyboard, the project enters its most intensive and production phase. Web pages are designed and coded, animation is created, video footage shot and edited, and so on.

The finished work is shown to the client, for approval and animation jobs are now ready for handing over, while web projects enter into their final phase.

Hosting/Billing

Website are ready to be uploaded and tested for bugs, and after correction are billed. Completed video and animation projects are also billed now.

Registration with Search Engine and Directories

This is a free service provided to our clients. The hosted site is manually registered with all the major search engines, search directories and trade directories. This promotion helps in directing traffic to the web site.

Post-Hand Over Maintenance

We provide free maintenance of the websites developed by us, for one year, subject to the condition that the work does not take up more than two hours per month or 24 hours in first year.

For sites which require intensive maintenance, we enter into an annual contract with the client.

Video Production

- Apollo Hospitals Limited
- Explore India, Explore Entity (Polaris Software)
- The Little Rainbow (Van Melle)
- Tidel Park
- Satyam i-way
- Learn At Satyam
- Khel.com—Sydney Olympics
- Electronic Data Systems (EDS)

3D Modelling and Animation

- Ashok Leyland
- Sify Baron Net Devices Ltd
- Satyam i-way TV Commercial
- MRF Corporate Presentation
- Bharathi TV Branding
- 3D Models of Exhibition Stalls
- 3D Gallery

TV Show Packaging

- SS Music
- Marumagal (A Daily series on Star Vijay TV)
- Aarthi (A Daily series on Raj TV)
- Splash
- Star Vijay ("Indru")
- Raj TV

Web (Micro Sites)

- Amco-Yuasa Batteries
- Intel
- Tidel Park
- Game Development
- Iodex Games
- Monkey Business
- Treasure Hunt
- Air Hockey
- Multimedia CD Authoring
- Kris Srikkanth's World Cup '1983
- Direct Edge
- Sify E-Business Offering
- Show Space Profile
- Maveric Systems Limited
- Apollo Hospitals Limited
- Sugal and Damani Jewellers
- Shankar Mahadevan
- Royal Enfield

Web Design

- Krishcricket
- Showspace
- Music Makers
- Amrutanjan
- Timber Homes
- Calmedics
- SM Apparels
- Banyan
- Fordmondeo-india
- Krish Infotek
- HSB Consulting
- Winspire
- Prism-India
- Smart Pages
- IFMR
- Viamore India
- PreMedia Global
- RKKR Group
- Kris-srikkanth
- Apollohospitals
- Apollohospitals/Annanagar
- PORR and Sons

- Ford-India Auto Expo 2002
- PRSI Chennai
- Karma Info
- Cyberpark

MULTIMEDIA

Technology advancement has assured the use of multimedia software by masses. Multimedia presentation services have acquired the vital area in giving instructional trainings, corporate and product presentations, or educational training. Multimedia development is the need for the companies, who aspire to communicate their business needs effectively.

Success of any *multimedia software development* depends on how productively it is developed based on target audiences need. The choice of content, page layouts with the ease in navigation play a major role in development of multimedia software. Shriv ComMedia Solutions Pvt. Ltd. (SCMS), engaged in multimedia development from India offers full range of multimedia presentation services that are custom made as per the requirements of our clients.

We are a professional company that offers innovative, high quality *multimedia presentations* with levelled mixture of simplicity and style. The enormous scope of combining text, visuals together with pictures, graphics, still images, videos, flowcharts and other medias is wondrous. Our team of graphic designers, flash developers, animators, and programming experts applies direct approach and creates creative multimedia presentations aligned to client's strategies.

SCMS deals in areas of CBT/WBT development, 2D/3D animations, Catalogue Design, Product presentation, and Corporate presentation. We keep our resources abreast with the latest and most modern development in required field, to deliver robust products. SCMS also provides expert advice to clients who want to keep themselves abreast with the technically fast progressing field of multimedia.

Computer Based Tutorials (CBT)

The E-learning services, which a little time ago, was looked at as an auxiliary method of teaching and learning strategies have now become the principal technique, for the same. The computer based tutorials (CBT) and the web-based tutorials (WBT) are innovative and effective E-learning solutions.

Shriv ComMedia Solutions (SCMS) provides a superfluity of CBT development that accounts for the varying role of proficient teaching methodology. CBT can be used as a training media for imparting basic information or also for the assessment and analysis. *Computer based tutorials* have their own line of benefits; the biggest being that it can be used at anywhere at any moment of time. Instructors too enjoy a flexible schedule with computer-based tutorials at their disposal.

We as an outsourcing company engaged in CBT development from India work in close association with our clients to deliver robust products. The computer-based tutorials are custom built that SCMS can adjust to the client's framework. Whether it be Toolbook CBT or Authorware, the team involved in computer based tutorials development, designs and deploys creative interfaces to produce seamless learning environment for the learner as well as the instructor.

SCMS offers complete custom computer based tutorials solutions to handle and rationalize the growing training requirements. We have also the first hand experience in converting any standard content formats to SCORM compliant content as for the learning management system (LMS).

2D and 3D Animation

Shriv ComMedia Solutions (SCMS) is a Web Animation Company providing services in 2D and 3D animation software's. Our long-standing experience in crafting 2D and 3D animation software services from India add to our capability of providing end-to-end solutions to our clients.

SCMS is capable of creating and developing the animations, using the correct blend of colors, music, and voice. The product outcome provides a realistic animation that is quite close to live effects. SCMS fits into the scenario of creative edge, to meet the challenges in *2D and 3D animation software's development.*

We bring in the best of 2D and 3D animation services India with the extensive array of technical skills at our base. The animators and graphic designers associated with us, offer our clients a unique multimedia animation experience. A special attention is paid on visual effects, visualization, color, grading, and editing. The use of shadowing, geometrical alignment, and textures are efficiently balanced and spectacularly brought in light.

For us, each organization is unique, and thus we put the best in animation software services with a thoughtful approach. The *2D and 3D animation software's* is so accustomed to clients need that it adds to the say about their organization, products, and services.

Product Presentation

According to experts, first impressions are critical. Communication is the most needed skill for a businesses success. Shriv ComMedia Solutions (SCMS) *product presentation services* convey a lot of information about customer's products and services. The product presentation services from India are basically a form of marketing tool that makes possible, to bring the products and services in limelight. SCMS offers full range of marketing strategies with use of multimedia presentations. This will help our clients to explore new horizons and better market segments for their products.

Product multimedia presentations can actually be considered as the first gateway for the launching of product and services in the market. It is the client's first introduction of their company and potentially their product. Preparation for product presentation services is vital to present a product in the best light possible.

We offer multitudinal service packages, ensuring productivity and longevity of our client's products by making presentation in a lucid and precise manner. We also *develop product presentation* slides with quite a style and difference. We offer:

- Creation or redesigning of product presentation page.
- Listing of product page at popular search engines for maximum traffic.
- Promote the product presentation services.
- Displaying of advertisement banners of client's product at various websites with appropriate links in third party websites.
- Sending volume e-mail's to the targeted customer segments.

Our efforts will surely bring maximum returns as we strive to give a definite meaning to product selling.

Corporate Presentation

Since the origin of Internet and software services, *corporate presentation services* have become a key selling strategy for companies, giving a new perspective to their business opportunities.

We provide our clients corporate presentation design services that are based on philosophy of clarity, lucidity, and simplicity. Shriv ComMedia Solution (SCMS) lays emphasis on content, design, along with technology, such that our patrons are assured of our corporate products presentation services and are contented of its high functionality.

The top-notch expert associated with us develops such multimedia presentations that are eye-catching and easily noticeable. This is fared amid incorporating all available variety of media. We work after listening to your ideas and aims, and then molding it in reality through our expert's advice and experience. There is a perfect fusion of your ideas and our expertise that domino effect in striking *corporate presentation services*.

Have a look at a few of corporate presentation services:

Layout Designing

Be it a legendary author's book or a website of a renowned company, the *layout designing* plays a major role in the overall impression to its viewers. Layout Designing is all related to cognitive arrangement of different objects in media, such that it conveys message to the targeted viewers adeptly. One must have good observation to create layout designing services.

Shriv ComMedia Solution (SCMS) layout designing services India includes not only developing an eye catching, attractive layout, but also extend our services to achieve our client's business improvement targets. We carry this out with help of our experienced, multi-disciplinary teams, and a comprehensive set of services. Our pool of expertise with graphic designers and animators craft stunning *layout designing services* that is sure to leave an unforgettable impression on the viewers. We have experienced professionals that have an eye for details of a perceptible design.

We make sure that our layout designs are interactive and dynamic. We have quiet an experience at working on vast categories of layouts for business, travel related, entertainment, real estate, product promotion, and other businesses. The areas of website layout designing and layout designing for CBT's is a part of our special expertise.

The placement of various elements, in such a fashion that it encourages further reading or browsing, is the ultimate driving factor for our layout designing services.

Catalogue Designing

Shriv ComMedia Solution (SCMS) provides a total solution for *catalogue designing* services from India with the implementation of latest equipment and software's. We provide catalogue designing services for corporate identity as well as individual web catalogue design services. Through our consistent and reliable services we have succeeded in creating a niche for ourself in catalogue designing services India. With our offices in UK, USA, Canada, and India our catalogue designing services have been extended to clients across the world.

A stimulating professional environment, harboring a diverse group of talented and experienced individuals working together as a team, with state-of-art facilities are the basic ingredients for providing correct and timely solutions. All these are basic strength of SCMS. Professionals at SCMS work together to build a creative and workable environment, providing a broad range of catalogue designing services available to our clients, at any time necessary.

While creating a *catalogue designing service* we lay emphasis on the "why's" and "what's" the purpose of the catalogue. These queries respond the very vital stuff—of type of product exposure, whether direct marketing, business reply or any other motive.

We have quite an experience in handling catalogue designing for brochures, flyers, corporate profiles, leaflets, folders, and instructional manuals. Our catalogue designs can be directly put in websites as web catalogue, thus saving time and energy both. We are a firm believer of complete customer satisfaction.

Software's Downloads

Hospital Management System

As the title suggest, this software can single handedly manage hospitals of any size. Equipped with customized features from outdoor patient management to inventory, HMS is truly the software you can be proud of.

Invento Optimizer

This Inventory Management System is tailor made to enhance the way Packers and Movers companies work. It has features to tract and keeps records on transportation, insurance, delivery, reporting by date-wise or month-wise, online confirmation, invoicing, feedback, etc.

Material Management System

This Inventory Management System helps in product analysis, tracking work orders, purchase, sells, payments, maintaining MIS report, etc.

Quotation Management System

Our Quotation Management system quickly and efficiently generates and manages quotations for all of your prospective and manufactured parts.

To save time, you can merge information from a quote that is similar to the one you are currently preparing. After you have put all of the finishing touches on your quote, you may print it on plain paper or a pre-printed form, or fax it directly from your computer.

Our Quotation Management system will save you time, money, and finally put all of your quotation information at your fingertips.

CRM

CRM stands for Customer Relationship Management also known as "front office solutions." This is because it offers a front office interface to customers to deal with.

Many call centers use CRM software to store all of their customer's details. When a customer calls, the system can be used to retrieve and store information relevant to the customer. By serving the customer quickly and efficiently, and also keeping all information on a customer in one place, a company aims to make cost savings, and also encourage new customers.

E-mail Management System

E-mail management system helps companies manage large volume of customer e-mails and web forms, responsively and effectively. With this system, you can differentiate your company from competitors by responding to inbound inquiries promptly and professionally every time.

By using e-mail management software you can help employees by responding to their emails quickly.

Payroll Master

This software is more helpful for analysis of business processes, related to employee and organization.

This system is generated for standard organizations both in U.S. and India. This software is supported by Shriv ComMedia Pvt. Ltd. Organization is able to Create Pension Plan Apply System. This software also helps to manage the holiday plans for employees and calculating tax.

Enterprise Resource Planning (ERP)

Employees can request professional help (to be given by person, online or by phone), take self-assessment tests and access general information on a variety of mental and physical health topics. What exactly is ERP? It is rarely in the context of planning how resources are to be expended. It refers a view of a company and all its parts as connected whole, rather than small silos of activity.

Online Daily Status Report (ODSR)

ODSR assigns multiple tasks, shifts, or clients to your employees or multiple employees to your tasks, shifts, clients, or vehicles for one week. This series of operation is very popular with home care businesses that send caregivers to several client homes each day.

The programme interacts with QuickBooks Pro to transfer employee timesheet information for use in client invoices and employee payroll. This report produces individual and group schedules and comes in sizes for 20, 40, 60, 80, 120 and 160 employees (and 50, 100, 150, 200, 300 and 400 tasks respectively).

Archimedes Business Software (Achieving Financial Control)

Archimedes Business Software is a complete business solution that helps you to streamline your business, be more productive and increase your profit margins. It helps you track all your projects and their related time, tasks and expenses.

It automates workflow and increases productivity. New users enjoy its easy use. Business owners appreciate its power and functions because it clearly focuses on the needs of businesses and users.

CASE STUDY: MACHIZO MULTIMEDIA COMMUNICATION

The name "Machizo" comes from "Machi Ukegazou", a Japanese word means "waiting for change" linked to the mission and vision of Machizo Multimedia Communication. It is a Dhaka based social entrepreneurial media organization. Machizo provides professional media services, local content creation, training, online journalism, advocacy and introducing latest multimedia technology for social development. It actively promotes ethical uses of multimedia, majority access to knowledge and information, online journalism, visual education as well as human rights and human potential development beyond the cultural and geographical boarders.

With the vision to contribute for establishment of the peaceful information society it has launched first South Asian multimedia and development webzine 'UnnayanNews' and establish UnnayanNet—Bangladesh ICT and Development Network. It is famous for its E-Jaban and " Total Beauty" initiatives that promoting Bangladesh contents as Japanese version, which is known as " Bangladesh De Matsu." However Machizo contributes to organize bi-annual "Educational Video Festival for Grassroots Youth and Children." To give ICT and innovative web design supports to grassroots NGOs and development organizations is Machizo's regular project.

As a professional house Machizo has expertise to provide multimedia content creation and communication services as Bangla, English and Japanese languages. Along with social responsibilities it designs creative website, multimedia CD/DVDROM, logo branding, however does action oriented development research, copy writing, online promotion and media consultancy.

'Local content, local voice', 'majority access to information and technology', 'One info Center for One Village' and 'Information for Peace and Unity' are the motto of Machizo's initiatives. All the projects and activities of Machizo are linked to MDG (Mellinnium Development Goals), Culture of Peace and Universal Human Rights declarations. It is committed to produce media kits on development, leadership and human rights issues by focusing MDGs, democratic participation, and conflict resolutions.

Acronyms and Glossary of Terms

.DIB (Device Independent Bitmap)

A Windows graphics file format. Image File Formats.

.FLC

An *animation* or moving picture file format originally created by Animator Pro. FLC files contain one or more frames, so you can see animated pictures from the screen when you display these files. A "FLC" file has an extension .flc.

.FLI

FLI files are also animation files. Although the structure of a FLI file is very similar to that of a FLC file, they are different file formats. A "FLI" file has an extension .fli.

"Sneaker" Net

When all electronic file transfers fail, files are saved to floppies, zip disks or some other removable storage medium and walked or mailed to the destination.

12 Field

An industry standard size for cels, backgrounds and drawings, measuring roughly 10 1/2" by 12 1/2".

16 Field

An industry standard size for cels, backgrounds and drawings, measuring roughly 12 1/2" by 16 1/2".

Acetate Cels

Animation cels made from *cellulose acetate,* a much more stable material which remains the industry standard to this day.

Acrobat

Product from *Adobe Systems, Inc.* which converts text documents, word for word, image for image, into fully-searchable electronic documents. The electronic document, with the exact look and feel of the original but with added hyperlinks, is stored in PDF (Portable Document Format). The PDF document can be viewed and printed with the *free Adobe Acrobat Reader*. The conversion process involves printing, from any word processor or application package, to an Adobe PDF Writer printer *driver*, rather than printing to a physical printer. The driver stops and asks where you wish to store the PDF document. Links, table of contents and other easy-to-create features are done with Adobe's Acrobat Exchange. A wonderful alternative to HTML (Hyper Text Markup Language).

ADC (Analog-to-Digital Converter)

"Recording" feature of sound cards that converts the analog/sound waveforms to digital format, i.e. bits and bytes. This digital representation can then be stored, edited, processed and transferred between media. To playback sound files, the sound card uses a DAC (Digital-to-Analog Converter). The ADC samples the audio at very fast intervals ("sampling rate"), producing a stream of snapshots. When played back by the DAC at the same pace, the samples are perceived as sound.

AIFF Audio Interface File Format

A Mac format for 8-bit and 16-bit digital audio.

Analog

Waveforms, with valleys and ridges, referring to the natural form of sound/audio. To store/ playback on a computer, analog data is converted to *digital* data. Analog-digital comparison.

Animation Cels

The individual painting on celluloid which is photographed along with other cels and a background in a setup, creating the complete image for a single frame of film. Every cel is different, but this does not mean that every cel is unique. Often multiple copies of a cel were created as color models, gifts or as Inker's Tests, which were created by the inkers in their free time to refine their technique and practice their skills.

Animation, Path

The animation software lets you specify a beginning position and an ending position, then calculates the positions in between.

Animation

Drawn motion files, either in 2-D or 3-D. The animated .gif was created using GIF Construction Kit. On the Web, HTML's push-pull animation is very low-end. JAVA, VRML (See Virtus WalkThrough 's "VRML assistant" feature.), DHTML, animated GIF's, Flash, and Shockwave are later adaptations/production tools for Web animation.

Animé

Japanese animation, which in recent years has become popular worldwide. Animé comes in a wide range genres, but a less wide range of styles.

Anonymous

Refers to a generic account username that any user can enter to log-in to a FTP file archive.

ANSI

The American National Standards Institute character set. Used in Windows-based programs. See related **ASCII.**

Anti-Aliasing

Process used to remove jagged edges in computerized graphics.

API (Application Programming Interface)

Set of routines/functions that an application program uses to request and carry out lower-level services performed by the operating system. For Windows, for example, API's help manage icons, windows, menus and other GUI elements. See related—CGI and MCI.

Applets

Small programs, called by application programs, that produce various special effects. WordArt, a Windows applet, lets you produce special effects with text. You can invoke WordArt by selecting Inset from the menu. See related JAVA applets.

Art Corner Setups

Cels sold at Disneyland's Art Corner shop in Tomorrowland from 1955 to the late sixties for a few dollars apiece. These setups were usually trimmed to fit a small mat, and included a litho background or sheet of colored paper and a gold foil authenticating sticker on the back of the mat. Despite the quantities of Art Corner setups sold over the years, good poses continue to be in great demand with collectors.

ASCII

The standard character set for text files.

Aspect Ratio

Height-X-width proportions of graphics. Some programs allow you to maintain the aspect ratio when sizing a picture, i.e. when you change the width, the height changes proportionally so that the resulting image does not look distorted.

Asynchronous Communication

Users communicate/interact, but at different times. These interactions may occur using e-mail, listservs or discussion boards.

AU

Sound file format, originally for SUN UNIX systems, now also supported on PCs and Macs.

Audio

Sound, either synthesized (See MIDI) or digitized, for playback with a computer. File formats: .WAV—Windows, .AU—Unix, playable on both Macs and Windows machines with the right players.

Authoring Software

Programs used to create full, multimedia productions, such as simulations and tutorials. Although most of these programs have some point-and-click features to simplify development, most require some knowledge of programming language concepts. Popular authoring software packages include Asymetrix ToolBook, Microsoft Visual Basic,

Macromedia Director and Authorware. FAQ's—Authoring Packages. At the "lower" end, presentation software, like Microsoft PowerPoint, provide simpler ways to put multimedia into presentations. HyperStudio, sits somewhere in the middle: It provides more interactive capabilities than presentation software, but cannot do all that a fully-robust authoring package can do.

Typical authoring systems:

- Macromedia Authorware and Macromedia Director (Mac and Windows)
- Asymetrix's Multimedia Toolbook/Assistant/Librarian (Windows)
- Apple's Hypercard (Mac and Windows)
- HyperStudio (Mac and Windows)
- Microsoft Visual Basic (Windows)

AVI (Audio Video Interleaved)

Windows format for saving video with sound. See QuickTime—.MOV, the Macintosh counterpart.

AVI Audio Video Interleaved

Microsoft's native video for Windows movie format for storing video with audio.

Background Paintings

A painting or other artwork depicting the environment in which the character operates. First, the Background Stylist made small color sketches called Key Backgrounds, which were created to establish the color scheme and mood. These keys acted as a model for the other background artists to follow. Key backgrounds were also referred to as Preliminary Backgrounds. Backgrounds which were rejected or cut from the film were called *N.G. (No Good) Backgrounds.* Although hundreds of animation drawings and cels would be required for a scene, typically there was only one background. A setup featuring a cel and background from the same scene is often incorrectly referred to as a Key Background Setup, but a more accurate description would be a Matching Background Setup. A cel and background from the same film, but not the same scene is often referred to as a Production Background Setup, while a cel and background from different films is correctly referred to simply as a Background Setup.

Bandwidth

The width of the band over which frequencies are transmitted. So what is a band? A band is a portion of the electromagnetic spectrum, defined by the lowest and highest frequencies in it. The bandwidth is the difference between the highest and lowest frequencies. The greater the bandwidth, the greater the carrying capacity. The Federal Communications Commission allocates portions of the band. For example, the band for VHF television broadcast is defined from 54 to 88 million cycles per second. And, of course, the band contains many "channels."

Big Little Book

A small, square book, usually measuring about 3 inch × 3 inch, with text on the left-hand pages and a single full-page illustration on the right. Big Little Books were originally created in the 1930s, to make use of small pieces of paper that had formerly gone to waste when magazines were trimmed after printing. By running a separate publication on paper that would otherwise go in the trash, the printer was able to create a salable product almost for free. Big Little Books were an ideal way to merchandize comic strip characters, as the drawings could simply be taken directly from the strips themselves. Big Little Books flourished during the days of pulp magazine publishing, which mostly came to an end after World War-II. The form was revived in the 1960s, partly as a nostalgia item, and has been used sporadically ever since. These latter-day Big Little Books are generally printed on better paper, and some, at least, have color illustrations.

Bigfoot

A style of cartoon art characterized by bold, expressive lines, a lack of distracting detail, and humorous exaggeration of bodily features such as noses and feet.

Binary File

A file that can only be read with special software, such as word processors or image viewers. Binary files contain special, embedded codes (i.e. program commands) that create bold or underlined text, for example. Text files, on the other hand, contain no embedded codes.

Bitmap

2-D array of pixels representing video and graphics. A Windows format for storing graphics.

Blackbird

See Microsoft Internet Studio.

Blue Book

CD designed for laserdisc use.

BMP

A Windows native format for a bitmapped graphics file.

Browser

A program that lets you view Web documents. Browser comparisons.

Capture, Video

Video capture cards let you record/digitize pictures for use with a computer. The pictures may be still-images or movies. Once captured, the picture data is compressed using a CODEC, with playback requiring CODEC-decompression. Intel's Smart Video Recorder Board, an excellent capture card, can compress video real-time, or "on the fly", provided you have a fast machine and lots (and lots) of defragmented storage.

Cartoonist

As used here, the word usually means a comics creator who does both major parts of the job, writing and illustrating. Thus, Carl Barks is the cartoonist who created Uncle Scrooge, and Milton Caniff is the cartoonist behind Steve Canyon.

Cascading Style Sheets/CSS

Cascading Style Sheets (CSS) is a mechanism for allowing web authors and readers to attach styles including f‹ ts, colors, etc. to HTML documents. Authors can attach styles to their HTML documents whild readers may have their own personal style sheets. Typically the styles are placed in the HEAD of the document, although they can also be placed in the BODY and often are placed in a separate file.

The basic format of the STYLE tag is:

```
<STYLE TYPE="text/css">
HTML tag.class {special formatting}
....
<SPAN> {special formatting}
</STYLE> (Source: Wayne's World)
```

Casein Based Cel Paints

In an efffort to lower production costs, some studios, most notably the Warner Brothers cartoon studio, used a casein based paint. Made from dairy curd, this binder adhered well to the cel stock for the short-term, but its high level of acidity and its tendency to become severely dehydrated made it very unstable over the long-term. Almost every cel painted with this type of paint at the Warners Studio has cracked and chipped over time. Because of this, casein type of paint is unsuitable for archival restoration.

CAV

"Constant Angular Velocity", as applied to laser discs, permits 30 minutes of recording per side and allows the user to address each frame separately. Contrast with CLV.

CBT

Computer-based training. Used synonymously with computer-assisted training (CAI).

CD-DA

A music CD. See related Red Book.

CDI Compact Disc Digital Interactive

A standard developed by Phillips for CDs containing a mix of sound, images and interaction; for players following the Green Book.

CD-i

Compact Disc-Interactive, developed by Phillips/Sony, includes audio, full-screen video and interactive capabilities. Follows ISO's "Green Book" standard.

CD-R (Recordable CD-ROM, CD-Recordable)

Software/hardware needed to create your own CD's—for backup/archive, catalogs and other large documents, and multimedia! To begin the process, you "pre-master", that is, you use pre-mastering software to decide what data to include on the disc and its best disc arrangement for efficient retrieval. Once pre-mastered, you record. See related: ISO 9660 format.

CD-R Compact Disk-Recordable

A multi-session CD-ROM recording format; requires a multi-session CD-ROM drive.

CD-ROM "Hybrids"

CD-ROM's with embedded Internet links. Although the Web can provide current information, i.e. timely updates and corrections, it lacks the bandwidth to deliver large multimedia files quickly. The "Internet-enabled" CD-ROM, or "cybrid," is being touted as a software solution that will use the strengths of both technologies. The parts of a program that can slow down access time if downloaded from the Internet (multimedia, index searches) are kept on the CD-ROM for faster loading. The Internet side of the equation is used for providing, and for adding new features without the need to send out a new CD-ROM disc. In the near future, look for hybrid DVD's.

CD-ROM Servers

Devices, like *towers, changers* and *jukeboxes,* that allow you to put CD-ROM's on networks: one CD, rather than multiple copies, serves many users. *CD-ROM towers* stack multiple drives, sometimes as many as 40, in a single box. Each drive has a read head for its CD, making access fairly fast. *CD-ROM changers* swap CD's in and out of the one drive. The *jukebox,* the changer's "big brother", can store up to 2,000 CD's and can be as big as a refrigerator. The swapping action can slow CD access, especially for changers. For an interesting Website, see: SIGCAT (Special Interest Group on CD-ROM Applications and Technology)'s report on jukebox performance.

CD-ROM

Compact Disc Read-Only Memory. From single-session, single-speed units, CD-ROM drives are now multi-sessioned, and read information 2X, 4X, 6X, 8X and 10X times as fast as original music CD players. Computer CD-ROM drives can slow down to single-speed to play music CD's: In a pinch, you can play music CD's with Windows' Media Player (Use the Control Panel to add the needed driver), although typically you would use the software that comes with the CD-ROM drive.

CDROM-XA (Extended Architecture)

The standard for pressing CD-ROM disks (See CD-R), which interleaves audio and digital signals for playback on the computer.

CD-RW, CD-ReWritable

An erasable CD-ROM, called CD-RW, or CD-ReWritable. Backers of the new technology say that erasable CDs will become a flexible new storage solution, holding 450 times more data than a typical floppy. Critics point out that CD-RWs can not be played on most of the currently installed CD-ROM drives. CD-RW drives will appear in the first quarter of 1997, and eventually will replace today's CD-ROM drives. Hewlett-Packard hopes to market a temporary solution called "MultiRead" to enable all new CD-ROM drives to handle CD-RW discs. CD-RW technology differs from CD-Recordable (CD-R) technology, which can be recorded on only once. If a mistake is made, the disc is worthless. Meanwhile, the new DVD (digital video disc) drives are able to handle CD-RW discs.

Cel Levels

The individual cels that go together to make up a cel setup. Due to technical considerations, it was very rare for two or more separate characters to be included on a single cel level. Usually, each element was on its own cel, with up to a maximum of five levels to a scene. Because of the added density of the multiple cel levels, the paint colors were corrected for the discoloration caused by the plastic, making the colors on a bottom level cel much brighter than those on a top level cel.

Cel Setups

A combination of two or more cels, with or without a background, which work together to form a complete image. These can be either *Matching* (the way the image appeared in the finished film) or *Non-Matching* (combinations of elements which are pleasing together, but do not appear together in the film).

Cel Washer

At one time, a beginner-level job in animation. Back before animation cels were considered collectible, the ink was usually washed off of a used cel, so the material could be used again. Chuck Jones frequently pointed out that they started in animation as a cel washer.

Cel

In animation, a cel (note that in this usage, the word has only one L) is a transparent sheet containing any part of the individual frame that is intended to move. By putting the action on cel overlays, animators avoid having to re-draw the background in every frame. The word comes from "celluloid", which is what cels were originally made of, although that material was replaced by acetate many years ago. Since animation art has become collectible, cels are now sometimes produced just for sale, rather than as part of the production process.

Cels

Sheets of clear plastic, containing the images of the characters, which are placed over a background, and then photographed in succession to give the illusion of movement in the completed film. The outline of the image, whether hand-inked or xerographed, is applied to the front of the cel. The colors are painted by hand onto the back of the cel to eliminate brushstrokes. Large areas of black paint were sometimes applied to the front of the cel to reduce glare.

CGI (Common Gateway Interface)

Server-side programs, running at the request of the client, that typically perform interactive Web actions. Normally, servers "serve" the content of static files (html, images, movies, sounds). In CGI, clients request a program to be executed and its results to be returned, as in database or search applications. All form-processing requires CGI. (in-depth look)

Character Models

Standardized renderings of characters, expressions, props and costumes. Character Designs would be created by concept artists or lead animators, and once they were approved, photographic stats, called Model Sheets would be produced and distributed to the various departments to insure absolute consistency between the sketches of all of the artists working on a project. Hundreds of photostats would be produced from a single paste-up, consisting of various drawings trimmed and applied to a board. Sometimes animators would create their own model sheets, traced from their own or other artist's drawings.

Chipping and Paint Loss

A portion of paint, from a small chip to an entire section, which has separated completely from the cel.

Clean-Ups

Tracings of the original animation roughs which are often more detailed and refined than the drawings which preceded them. Created by the assisting department, these sketches represent the final stage of animation before the image is transferred to the cel via hand inking or xerography. These sketches often include colored lines to indicate different ink colors, color mark-ups to tell the painters which areas to paint which colors, and notes to the ink and paint department about parts of the character that needed to be registered to other characters or background elements.

Client/Server

Set of computer applications (programs) in which two or more computers work together. Server(s) store data and programs, which they deliver on request to clients. Part of the processing is done on the client, while the server concentrates on storing and delivering the data to be processed. This interaction between the client and server occurs in the background, so users are typically unaware which computer handles what.

Client

Any computer connected to a host computer, or the software used to connect to the host.

Clipart

Collections of pictures/photographs. Many application programs, such as PowerPoint, contain built-in clipart.

CLV

"Constant Linear Velocity", as applied to laser disks, where 60 minutes can be recorded per side. CLV discs cannot display an individual frame. Contrast with CAV.

Codec

Compression/decompression.

CODEC

Program/device that **CO**mpresses/**DEC**ompresses digital video. xxx Cinepak and Indeo (Intel) are examples of CODEC's.

Color Depth

Number of colors in an image: 8-bit (256 colors), 16-bit (32,768 colors), and 24-bit (16.4 million colors).

Color Model Cels

A cel created by the Ink and Paint Department to act as an example for inkers and painters to follow. Color models may be exact duplicates of the cels appearing in the film, or may be test models, exploring various inking techniques or color palettes. Although many collectors assume that color models are less valuable than cels used under the camera, this is not always the case. Since color model cels acted as an example for the inkers and painters to follow, great care was taken to make them absolutely flawless. Cels used under the camera often had flaws due to repairs or corrections quickly done in the heat of production.

Color Palette

Available color selections, ranging from 16 colors to 16.7 million. Color resolution comparison. There are often color shifts from machine to machine that can have "unfortunate" results. See related: dithering. Macintosh and Windows share only 216 out of 256 colors.

Comix

"Underground" comic books. The spelling is often used to distinguish the counter-culture comics, usually intended for adults only, published by such entities as Rip Off Press, The Print Mint, and Last Gasp Eco-Funnies, from the more conventional offerings of such "establishment" companies as *Marvel, DC,* and *Archie Comics.* Examples of comix, as opposed to comics, are *Mr. Natural* and *The Fabulous Furry Freak Brothers.* Comix practitioner Art Spiegelman (author of *Maus*) says it is because the form is a "co-mixing" of words and pictures, but actually it is just a different way of spelling "comics".

Compression (file)

Process for reducing file size, often called "zipping" or "archiving." The resulting, compressed file can be from a single, large file or can contain several files that have been squeezed into a single file. The many-to-one compression makes file group identification, copying, and transporting faster and easier.

Compression (video)

Process which reduces the number of bytes required to store/transmit digital video. Typical schemes involve comparing frames and coding-out, or eliminating, *inter*-frame and *intra*-frame redundancies. The compression may be done by software, hardware or a combination of the two. On playback, the data is decompressed. See CODEC. Why compress video data? To reduce storage space and to playback faster. A full-screen (640 × 480 pixels) image with 16.4 million colors takes up 1 MB of memory. For full-motion, the computer needs to display 30 pictures/frames per second, thus requiring it to "shuffle" 30 MB of data every second. Storing 10 seconds of video would require 300 MB. Jan Ozer, President of Doceo Publishing, is the foremost authority on digital video/CODEC's.

Compression, Lossless

Digitized video containing all the original video information.

Compression, Lossy

Digitized video which, to save space, does not contain all the original video information.

Concept Art

Inspirational sketches or paintings used to establish the situations, color choices or mood of a particular sequence. These were rendered in a wide range of media, from pastels and graphite, to watercolor and cut paper.

Continuous Tone

An image made of blended levels of gray flowing into each other without hard delineations.

Cookie

A "cookie" is a small piece of information, a virtual "sticky note", sent by a Web server to be stored, by your browser, on your hard drive. The cookie stores information about you and can be retrieved by the Website each time you visit there. Without them, sites would not be able to retain information about individual visits; thus, cookies store "state information." Cookies are passive files, typically used in .asp (Active Server Page) programming, and should not be confused with server-side databases that collect personal information you have voluntarily (or unwittingly) submitted.

Copyright

Exclusive ownership of a created work. Given the Web's openness, who owns what?

Courseware

Software containing instructional material, educational software, or audiovisual materials.

Courvoisier Setups

A cel setup marketed through Courvoisier Galleries between 1938 and 1946. Couvoisier setups share several distinctive features: a cream colored mat with the title of the production inscribed in pencil below the mat opening, a simple presentation or wood grain background, and a 3" by 5" label stating the name of the production. Cels in Courvoisier setups were often cut out and attached to the backgrounds, and were occasionally enhanced with airbrushed shading or dry brush effects. The presentation backgrounds ranged from simple air brushed settings depicting dots or stars, to elaborate watercolor paintings created by the Disney background department. Many Courvoisier setups from *Dumbo* and *Fantasia* were laminated using a heat fused process. Courvoisier setups are highly sought after by collectors. Other studios, most notably Walter Lantz, Warner Brothers and Charles Mintz, packaged and marketed artwork in a similar manner between 1938 and 1940.

Cracking

Appears as a series of jagged "breaks" or "tears" in the paint, generally accompanied by some degree of separation.

Crossover

A meeting between characters from two different series, as when *Superman* met *Batman* in *Superman* #76, or when *Alphonse & Gaston* met *Happy Hooligan* on numerous occasions. In recent years, standard crossovers have become so common in comic books, it takes a huge event, such as a mini-series involving most of the company's characters or a meeting between characters belonging to different publishers, to qualify for the name.

Cross-Platform

Files usable/executable with different operating systems. For example, Virtus WalkThrough, a 3-D animator program, can produce "cross-compatible" animation files for Macintosh and DOS/Windows machines. "Power" Mac's let you change to the PC work-mode; "power" PC's can handle Macintosh software/files.

CU SeeMe

A leading desktop videoconferencing software package.

Cut Out or Trimmed Cels

The images on cels were often cut out of the full sheet to make them fit into scrapbooks or small frames; or were carefully trimmed to the outlines of the character, so that the cel could be applied to a background along with other cels without having to worry about where the edges of the cel would fall within the image. In general, aside from those setups produced for sale by the Courvoisier Galleries or the Art Corner, cut out and trimmed cels are worth less than images on full sheets.

Cyberculture

"A collection of cultures and cultural products that exist on and/or are made possible by the Internet, along with the stories told about these cultures and cultural products."

Cycle

A set of animation drawings that are repeated. For example, if a character is walking across a background, there is no need to animate each step he takes—just animate one step, then use the same drawings for the next, etc.

DAC (Digital-to-Analog Converter)

The sound card component that plays sounds stored in a file.

DDE (Dynamic Data Exchange)

Windows' process that supports exchange of commands and data between two application. OLE is a DDE enhancement.

Digest

In the printing/publishing industry, this word, like tabloid, refers to a printed format. "Digest" magazines are those made in approximately the same size and shape as, or perhaps a little smaller than, Reader's Digest. Digests have been a small but noticeable part of the American comics scene since 1968, when Gold Key Comics started publishing its Walt Disney Comics Digest. Archie Comics has had much success with its digest line, sold mainly at supermarket checkout stands, while DC, Harvey and others have experimented with the form.

Digital Signal Processor

A separate processor, built into some sound cards, that offloads/relieves audio processing from the computer's CPU.

Digital/digitalization/digitized

Process of converting video or audio signals, normally in waveform, into 1's and 0's. This digital format (actually patterns of *on*'s/high-voltage (1's) and *off*'s/low voltage (0's) rather than digits) can be processed by a computer.

Digitizing Tablet

Pen-based input system, resembling a sketch pad. The pressure of the pen on the tablet is translated in electronic dot patterns. Many delivery companies, such as UPS, use tablet technology to record signatures upon package receipt. President Clinton used a Wacom graphics tablet and pen to sign the Telecommunication Reform Act of 1996.

Direct Market Distribution

A method of comic book distribution in which wholesalers buy comics from their publishers directly, as opposed to taking the comics on a returnable basis, and sell them directly to retailers. By buying directly, distributors and retailers get a better price. By selling directly, publishers know right away how well a title is doing, and do not have to wait for unsold copies to trickle back in over a period of months. The Direct Market started in the mid-1970s, gained momentum in the early '80s, and since the middle '80s has been the dominant means by which American comic books are distributed.

DirectX

3D graphic programming API written by Microsoft. Allows programs to interface with and use built in high speed 3D graphic routines on graphic cards. Built into Windows 95 and 98.

Distance Education/Learning

Instruction that takes place when the student and instructor are separated by physical space and/or time. Correspondence courses provide one type of "distance learning." Networked computers, especially those linked into the Internet, provide many remote education opportunities. In fact, you can now obtain a degree from a "virtual university."

In North Carolina, there are three major "forces" in distance learning:

1. NCIH (North Carolina Information Highway) the entire statewide 2-way interactive network.
2. NC-REN (NC Research and Education Network)—the protion of NCIH connecting the state's 19 teaching hospital research centers and public universities.
3. MCNC (Microelectronics Center of NC)—Research Triangle organization which functions as a technical resource and central scheduling facility of the NCIH.

Dithering

Blending colors to modify colors or produce new ones.

DLL (Dynamic Link Library)

A Windows' code module that is loaded and linked at runtime, then unloaded when it has finished executing.

DLP

Digital Light Projectors. Contrast with LCD Projectors.

Dot Pitch

The distance between the pixels on the monitor. The smaller the distance, i.e. the denser the pixels, the clearer the picture resolution.

Downlink

Transmission of a signal from a satellite to a receiver on earth.

Download

Process of transferring a file from system to another.

Drivers

Software, typically ending in .DRV in Windows systems, used to 'talk to' or manage hardware, like sound cards, printers ...

Dropped Frames

In digital video, when the computer cannot keep pace with the displayed images, it drops frames in an attempt to catch up.

Dry Brush

To create motion blurs and special textures, inkers would apply paint to the front of the cel using a small amount of thick paint. In some cases, rouge or greasepaint was drybrushed onto the cheeks of characters to simulate blush.

DSP (Digital Signal Processor)

A special processor, additional to the CPU, that is dedicated to processing real-time audio and video signals. For example, the DSP chip on a sound card lets you add echoes, reverb and other special effects.

DVC

Desktop videoconferencing.

DVD's

A new standard for recording video on CD-ROM's using MPEG2, thus boasting better-than-broadcast TV quality. Costing about the same as a CD, DVD-ROM's hold 8 to 40 times more data. Sony/Phillips and Toshiba/Time, the two major developers, predict DVD will replace videocassettes, laserdiscs, CD-ROM's and audio CD's. In June 1997, Hitachi announced a re-writable DVD, which may spell the end to re-writable CD's.

Dynamic HTML/DHTML

A set of recent technologies (HTML, layers, Cascading Style Sheets, Javascript) which, together, enable richer, more interactive content. See: Netscape Developers' Edge Online and a local production done with Macromedia Dreamweaver.

Electronic Mail (e-mail)

Most electronic mail packages provide a method for mailing to other users' electronic mail addresses that are not on the local machine. An e-mail address has two parts, separated by @. The portion before the @ sign is the username, or mailbox name, of a particular user. The portion after the @ is the location adress. The suffix, in this case .gov, denotes what type of organization. Example: mailto:president@whitehouse.gov (By clicking, you can actually send the President some e-mail.)

EPS (Encapsulated Postscript)

Graphics file format often used in desktop publishing packages, like PageMaker.

EPS Encapsulated PostScript File

A file format for describing graphics and page segments for PostScript devices.

Ethernet

A local-area network (LAN) standard.

Extreme

In animation, an extreme is a character's pose at the beginning or end of an action. The poses in-between extremes are called (predictably enough) "In-betweens".

Fanzine

Fan magazine. Fanzines are often, but not always, amateur productions, published not so much to make a profit as simply to provide a vehicle for self-expression on the part of the publisher. The word refers to fan publications of all sorts, but first became widely used in reference to the publications of science fiction fans of the 1930s and later. Probably the first fanzine of that genre was The Time Traveller, published by a pair of science fiction fans named Julie Schwartz and Mort Weisinger, both of whom went on to long careers as editors at DC Comics.

Fielding

Refers to the size of the area on the artwork which falls within the sight of the camera. Thus, a 12 field is roughly 12 inches across and a 9 field is 9 inches across. Even though a drawing or cel may be of a standard 12 or 16 field size, the camera may have been zoomed in to a 8 or 9 field, focusing on a tighter area of the artwork, eliminating the outer margins of the sheet. Most early pictures conformed to a squarish rectangular field referred to as the Academy Format. Later films, which were shot in widescreen or Cinemascope had a more rectangular active area.

File Formats

For graphics/images, movies, sounds/music, text.

File Transport Protocol (FTP)

FTP is an acronym for File Transfer Protocol and is a method for retrieving files from a remote Internet site. Many sites out there allow what is termed an 'anonymous' connection. In other words, there exists a special username called 'anonymous' so that the site can act as a library of useful public domain programs and documents.

Firewire (IEEE-1394)

Emerging serial interface technology that allows connection of devices at speeds up to 50 Mbytes/s. Used for devices such as video cameras so that they can feed real time video to a computer. Also allows devices to be hotswapped (added and removed without rebooting).

Flash

A product from Macromedia (as is Shockwave) that produces interactive vector-based animations called "Flash movies." Like Shockwave movies, Flash movies are intended for web-based distribution to web browsers. Netscape ships with the Flash plug-in. +/-'s of Flash.

FM Synthesis

Creating sounds and musical tones by directly manipulating the frequency of the audio signal.

FM Synthesis

Low-end sound cards create computerized tones using FM—"frequency modulation." The result sounds very unmusical, computer-generated. FM synthesis is being replaced by more lifelike technology called wavetable, where sounds are created from actual recordings of instruments.

Font

A complete set of characters for one style/typeface, including all the letters, numbers and punctuation marks. For example, Times New Roman or Arial.

FPS

Frames per second—the number of picture images displayed per second, giving digital video the illusion of motion. Full-motion video, with no dropped frames, is considered 30 fps (NTSC standard).

Frame Grabber

Video Capture card that captures a single frame from a video stream and stores it as a still image.

Frame Rate

Number of images per second displayed in a stream of video. 30 fps is considered full-motion, television-quality video.

Frame

A single picture in a computerized "movie"/digital video.

Frame

An individual picture in a motion picture film, depicting a small fraction of a second of the action.

Freeware

The software author retains rights to the program, but allows users to copy and use the program without fee. The program thus cannot be resold or relabelled without the consent of the originator.

Full-Motion Video

Digital Video running at 30 fps (NTSC—US standard). It does not necessarily fill the screen.

Full-Screen Video

Digital Video filling the entire screen (use 640 × 480 pixels) for typical graphic, not just a smaller window. Typical video window sizes.

Funny Animal

A genre of fiction which, like superheroes, is found more often in comics and animation than elsewhere, and which is characterized by animals that walk and talk just like humans. Many aficionados of the genre insist that a funny animal no more has to be "funny" than a comic book must be "comic", citing Bucky O'Hare and Teenage Mutant Ninja Turtles, but others disagree. Many of the best funny animals, such as Uncle Scrooge, combine humor with adventure in about equal measure; but some, like Usagi Yojimbo, while not totally eschewing humor, place more emphasis on the dramatic aspects of their stories. And then, of course, there are Pogo, Bugs Bunny and suchlike, that are almost all humor. A surprisingly broad and varied category.

General MIDI

An emerging standard for MIDI.

GET-A-DATE

Cyberdating. Leave an audio messsage for a Web Personal.

GIF (Graphic Interchange Format)

A graphics file format originated by Compuserve, usable for Web pages. Use PaintShop Pro to convert other graphics file formats to .GIF format.

GIF Graphics Interchange Format

A color image transfer protocol developed by CompuServe.

Gopher

A menu-driven system that lets you search for and retrieve files across the Net.

Graphic Novel

A glorified comic book. Graphic novels are distinguished from common, ordinary comic books by their format (they are usually published in book form, with higher production values, rather than as pamphlets, like most comics) and by the fact that they usually contain longer, more complex stories (just as a prose novel is longer and more complex than a short story).

Graphical User Interface (GUI)

A computer interface using point-and-click mouse actions (rather than the keyboard exclusively) and pictures (rather than text exclusively). Windows, Macintosh, Netscape and Mosaic are examples of GUI products.

Graphics Accelerator

A graphics card, used in animation production/creation, that speeds the display/preview of 3D animation.

Graphics, *Bitmap*

Images are laid out in pixels, much like dots of paint on a canvas. As such, bitmap objects are not independent entities, which can be singled out for manipulation, but patterned series of dots. To enlarge (or reduce) bitmap images, the number of pixels is increased (decreased), often giving the resulting image a jagged appearance. (See anti-aliasing.) Scanners produce bitmap images (.TIF), as does Windows' PaintBrush (.BMP, .PCX): Bitmaps are one of the most commonly compatible types of image formats. File formats include: IMB, DIB, GIF, MTX, PCX, TIF, TGA, BMP, WPG, JPG, CUR, CO. (See Image File Formats) PaintShop Pro can be used to convert to/from various formats. Its help menu provides full definitions for all graphics file formats. PaintShop Pro maintains the aspect ratio of pictures when sizing, thus can reduce sizing distortion.

Graphics, *Vector*

Graphics consisting of objects, each of which can be separately manipulated—e.g. sized, moved, (un)grouped, positioned to the back/front. The graphic components are calculated, hence can be sized without distortion. File formats include: AutoCAD, DXF, CBM, EPS, HGL, PIC, DRW, WMF, WPG.

Graphics

Images are typically vector (object-oriented) or bitmap (rastor). See below Graphics, Bitmap and Graphics, Vector. After reading their definitions, test yourself.

Green Book

Format for CD-i.

Gum Arabic Based Cel Paints

The most common type of paint used at the various studios was a rewettable, opaque watercolor with a gum arabic binder. Some studios bought ready-made paint, but MGM and Disney custom manufactured their own paints in-house. Although most studios abandoned this type of paint in the early 1960's when synthetic binders were introduced, the Disney Studios continued to manufacture and use it in production until The Great Mouse Detective was released in 1986.

Hand Inking

Prior to the late 1950's, all animation drawings were traced onto cels by hand using a quill pen or brush. A variety of inks were used, but in general, the colored ink lines were simply cel paint thinned down to the proper consistency. Contrary to popular belief, hand inking is not a lost art. It is still widely used in animated commercials, special effects shots and in publicity artwork.

HDTV

High Definition Television. Because of the larger picture size (16-by-9 display ratio for HDTV versus 4-by-3 for regular TV) and more horizontal picture lines, HDTV will have a higher quality display than conventional TV. Also, HDTV has cd-quality sound and involves digital transmission instead of analog. FAQ's on HDTV. WRAL-TV 5 in Raleigh, NC, is the first television station in the nation to apply for an HDTV license.

High Sierra

ISO 9660: a format for placing files and directories on CD-ROM.

Hit

A match to the criteria you specify in a search.

Home Page

The start-up page for Web documents.

Host

A computer that acts as a file server. Users at remote computers (i.e. client computers) are allowed to access information that is stored on the server, or host computer.

Hotlist

A list of frequently-accessed Web documents. Fun spots!

HTML

Hyper Text Markup Language—the most commonly-used Web programming language. HTML codes are document formatting codes that tell browsers such as Mosaic or Netscape how to display the document you see on the screen.

HTTP

Hyper Text Transfer Protocol—the set of language rules Web users must follow to communicate with each other. The phrase World Wide Web refers to the collective set of servers (computers) speaking HTTP.

Hypermedia

"Hypertext" with links not only to text, but also to other forms of media—sounds, graphics, movies/video, animation.

Hypermedia

Nonlinear multimedia, with hypertext navigational links, nodes, and controls.

Hypertext

"Text" which allows users to "hyper-jump." Hypertext is basically the same as regular text, with one exception: hypertext contains connections within the text to other Web documents. The connections are denoted, generally, as underlined, colored text. The "documents" to which the hypertext connect may be local or remote, perhaps even in a different country.

ICR (Intelligent Character Recognition)

Scanning device/process for hand print recognition.

Image File Formats

.GIF, .JPG, .BMP, .PICT ...

In-Between

In animation, an in-between drawing shows a character's transitional pose between two extremes.

In-Betweener

An animator whose job it is to draw in-betweens. A step up from cel washer, but still a job for someone who has not yet progressed to the level of a journeyman animator. In-betweeners are often called assistant animators.

Indeo

Intel's CODEC for video.

Indeo

Intel's compression/decompression for video; Windows, OS/2, some Mac.

Indicia

A paragraph of small type, found in most magazines (including comic books), indicating the magazine's title, date, publisher, and other relevant information.

Inker

In comics, an inker is the artist who applies ink to the penciller's drawings, making them ready to be photographed and then printed. Inking jobs vary in their complexity according to how tightly the penciller works, but always require the hand and eye of an artist. In animation, an inker was at one time the person who traced an animator's drawings onto cels. Today, the job is usually done with a xerox machine.

Inker's Tests and Clean-Up Tests

Beginning inkers and assistant animators were often given scenes of animation from previous productions to practice and hone their skills on. Also, this category of art also encompasses test pieces given to prospective employees to judge their level of skill. It can sometimes take a skilled eye to recognize the differences between test artwork and production art.

Internet Protocol (IP)

The protocol which provides addresses needed to move packets of information across networks. IP addresses have two parts: a network identifier and a host identifier.

Internet Studio

A Web programming "language", developed by Microsoft, that uses drag-and-drop and OLE—not HTML—to publish Web pages. Internet Studio will support numerous file formats and software programs—VRML, Macromedia Shockwave, Adobe Acrobat, GIF, JPEG, Microsoft Office (Word, Excel, PowerPoint, Access), among others.

Internet

"The network of networks." The Internet originally developed out of the ARPAnet. The ARPAnet model specifies that communication occurs between the source and destination computer in small parcels of data known as Internet Protocol (IP) packets. Each computer transmitting a packet has the responsibility of addressing and delivering it to the destination computer. Berkeley Systems adopted the IP networking system in their version on the UNIX operating system and over the years added many extra network oriented commands to the operating system. Before long, because of the device independence of this protocol, many different vendors adopted the IP system.

In the late 1980s, the National Science Foundation (NSF) created five super-computer centers. They decided to link these centers using the IP protocol as a method of sharing the expensive resources. Academic institutions soon connected their local networks to the central NSF network backbone to be able to access the supercomputer resources. The collection of inter-connected networks became known as the Internet.

Today the Internet has become a global "information highway", connecting almost every country in the world together. Anyone with a computer, modem and the money (or opportunity) to connect into an online service provider (like America Online) can tap into the "network of networks." The World Wide Web (WWW) is one of the most popular Internet services.

Intranet

The World Wide Web documents accessible within a single organization.

ISDN (Integrated Services Digital Network)

A network/telephone connection that transfers data at rates more than 4 times faster than a 28.8Kbps modem. Ordinary modems (non-ISDN) convert computer data to audio tones/analog to transfer over the phone lines. ISDN "modems" connect digitally: Inherently faster digital signals rather than tone signals transfer over the lines. Network transfer speed comparison.

Basic Rate ISDN, often called "2B+D" or BRI, arrives on 3 channels—one Delta ("D") 16 Kbps channel carrying telephone signals and two "Bearer" ("B") channels delivering data at 64 Kbps. Primary Rate ISDN, also known as T1 service, has 23 B channels and one D channel, delivering at a rate of 1.544 Mbps (T3 transmits at an extremely high rate—44.7 Mbps).

ISO 9660

A format for placing files and directories on CD-ROM. Readable by both Macintosh and PC-compatible computers.

ISO 9660

Industry standard multi-platform CD-ROM format.

ISO

International Standards Organization.

JAVA Applets

Small programs written in JAVA that produce various special effects, which are embedded right into the Web pages. When someone accesses a Web page with applets, the applets automatically download with the page: All that is needed to view the effect comes with the page itself, making applets independent of the eccentricities of various operating systems. This design feature makes applets particularly desirable for multimedia applications, which typically are very platform-dependent.

JAVA Beans

Component API's allowing Java applications to run in other frameworks, e.g., Microsoft Word.

JAVA

An , Web programming language, similar to C++, developed by Sun MicroSystems. JAVA applications are compiled into Java bytecode, executable on any java-enabled browser, i.e. browsers which have the "Java Virtual Machine." Thus, JAVA will run the same on any operating system. JAVA applications, technically, are stand-alone programs, whereas JAVA applets (see below) are code snipets, designed to run within Webpages. JAVA is **NOT** Javascript. +/- of Java.

JavaScript

Resembles Java (much easier to learn), but runs (is interpreted) on the client (user) side, not the host/server. (simple code example) +/-'s of Javascript.

Jewel Cases

Plastic carrying cases for CD's.

JPEG (Joint Photographic Experts Group)

Compressed, still-image graphics files. There are two major types of JPEG—progressive, where a fuzzy images emerges into 100 per cent decompression/clarity, and baseline or standard, where a clear image is revealed, part-wise, top-down. Progressive, or interleaved, decompression looks better over networks. See CODEC.

Jukebox

See CD-ROM server.

Key Frame

A "complete" video frame, containing all the image detail, not just the changes from the previous frame.

Kiosk

An electronic "newstand" or booth. Electronic kiosks are often used for mall directories, where users can touch a screen to find the location of a particular shop.

Kodak Photo CD ("PCD's")

Photographs/images are "printed"/digitized on CD's. Your Photo CD comes with a contact sheet, showing small pictures of each image on the disc. You can keep adding pictures to the CD. To view the CD images, you need a viewer. Nowadays, many multimedia programs can import these already-digitized image files into documents.

Lamination

The process of "sandwiching" a cel between sheets of clear plastic in an effort to preserve it. Unfortunately, lamination causes more problems than it solves, because it prevents the paint from absorbing moisture from the atmosphere, making it become brittle and cracked. In addition, the chemicals present in the lamination adhesive can attack pigments over time, causing the colors to mottle and fade. Heat fused lamination was first used by Courvoisier Galleries on cels from Dumbo and Fantasia, and was soon abandoned. The process was revived by the Disney Art Program in the early 1970's, using a laminate similar to a large sheet of scotch tape. All cels sold through the Disney Art Program between The Jungle Book and The Great Mouse Detective were subjected to this process. Haloing is a term which describes the separation of the plastic laminate around the perimeter of the character, common in cels of this type.

LAN (Local Area Network)

A privately-operated communications system interconnecting computers and communications equipment over a limited geographic area, usually 5 miles or less. LAN's enable local resource—sharing (printers, files, etc.).

Laserdisc Player

Like a VCR, this device plays back analog video stored on laserdiscs.

Layout Drawings

A detailed pencil drawing that either indicates the fielding, the character's action, or the design of the background which acts as the scenery behind the character. There are two types of layouts: Character Layouts, which outline the character's path of movement, expressions and action within the scene; and the Background Layout, which generally consists of a line drawing of the environment in which the character exist. These layouts are used as reference by the animator and the background painter, respectively.

LCD Projection Panel

A device to project a computer screen, used with a high-lumen (very bright) overhead projector.

LCD

Liquid Crystal Display panels connected to computers allow the display to be projected on a screen. Always get an active-matrix LCD. If you have a monitor with a video-input, you may be able to use a scan converter as a less expensive alternative to LCD-projection of computer data.

Letterer

In comics, the words are usually put on the page by hand, rather than by typesetting, although computerized lettering is now becoming more common. The letterer positions and draws the word balloons and usually draws display lettering (such as logos and sound effects) as well as transferring words of the script to the balloons and captions.

Limited Edition Cels

A cel created especially for sale to the collector's market, produced in fixed, limited quantities.

Originally intended to re-create original production cels, some studios and artists now create completely new images based on non-production artwork. Although limited edition cels are widely touted as being "good investments", very few editions have ever appreciated in value to any significant degree.

Line Wear

Missing, broken, or smeared lines on either hand inked or xerox cels.

LISTSERV/Mailing Lists

Mailing lists or list servers are a one to many electronic mail conferencing system. Once subscribed to a list, the subscriber receives electronic mail messages from all contributing members of that list. A subscriber can mail to the list e-mail address and the message will be distributed to all subscribed members.

There are a number of different types of lists. An open list is one in which any person with an e-mail address may subscribe and be a part of the conference. A closed list is one in which the list owner will approve or not approve any subscription request. For example, a list may be very specific to a certain profession or group that you must belong to before subscribing. A moderated list is one in which the entries are reviewed by the list owner before being mailed out to the subscribers. The list owner may in fact choose to make a digest out of the submissions, and then post that to the list server. An unmoderated list is one in which all mail coming to the mail server is distributed regardless of the content.

Lossy/Lossless Compression

See compression.

Luminance

A color's brightness.

Magneto-Optical (MO) Drives/cartridges

MO drives store data on removable, rewritable disc cartridges, each with a capacity of 640 MB (soon to be 2.6 Gb). When filled, you swap in another cartridge. Thus, instead of buying a new hard drive (at $500), you buy another cartridge ($30). Get LIM/DOW (Light Intensity Modulation/Direct Overwrite) disks/drive, which re-writes in one pass, resulting in 100 per cent increase in write speed. Contrast with zip drives which store only 100-230 MB.

Manga

The Japanese word for "comic book." In America, the term is applied to translated reprints of Japanese comics, or to homegrown comics that are strongly influenced by the Japanese style.

MCI (Media Control Interface)

Multimedia commands/calls comprising Windows API (Application Program Interface).

Merchandizing Artwork and Book Illustrations

Artwork produced for use on licensed product packaging, educational filmstrips or publications. The quality of these images can vary greatly, since they are rarely created by the same artists that worked on the films themselves. In general, this type of artwork is worth much less than publicity or production art.

Micromoney

Proposed Web-payment scheme where funds are subtracted from your bank account when you buy digital tokens. You then spend this encrypted micromoney at participating Websites without the hassle of a credit card transaction. Ecash and CyberCash are two such digital-cash schemes.

MIDI (Musical Instrument Digital Interface)

Rather than recording sounds, MIDI instruments/software record finger action: what note is being played, when, and for how long. To playback MIDI files, you need a sound card that can interpret the MIDI note data, either by creating the tones themselves (FM-synthesis) or playing back sounds that are stored internally (waveform). "General MIDI" is an emerging standard for MIDI playback. Alphabetical listing of MIDI works by classical composers.

MIDI Musical Instrument Digital Interface

Industry standard connection for digital control of musical devices.

Mini-Comics

Home-made comics, usually amateur productions done by a single individual. Mini-comics are typically made by folding, cutting and stapling xeroxed sheets of paper. They are seldom intended to make a profit, "payment" for the work usually consisting only of the cartoonist's ability to express himself without editorial constraint. Mini-comics characters sometimes "graduate" into regular comics, as did Pam Bliss's "Those Kids"; also, regular comics characters will occasionally guest-star in a mini-comic, as Scott McCloud's *Zot!* did with Matt Feazell's Cynicalman.

Mint

Perfect condition: as highly-regarded a state in comic book collecting as in coins and stamps. No slack is cut for a comic's age or any other factor—mint means perfect, and that is all there is to it. Mint comics often command prices over ten times higher than the same item in "good" condition.

MMX

(Multimedia Extension), a multimedia accelerator in Intel's Pentium processors that speed media and communications processing 40 to 60 per cent. Standard Pentiums move 1 byte of data at a time into the CPU for processing. In contrast MMX Pentiums move 8 bytes, all processed simultaneously. The catch? Not all application programs, as yet, have been written to take advantage of the specialized instruction set for the MMX's, hence you see no performance improvement for most programs currently on the market.

Model Sheet

A set of drawings of a character, showing him in various poses, with various facial expressions, and from various angles, done so that different artists drawing the character can make him look consistent. Model sheets are used in both comics and animation.

Modem

A hardware device that converts waveform (analog) data to digital. MOdulation converts analog to digital; DEModulation converts digital to analog. Hence, MODEM. Network transfer speed comparison.

MOOs, MUDs, MUSHs:

- MUDs = Multi-user Domains
- MOOs = MUD, Object Oriented
- MUSHs = Multi-user Shared Hallucination
- MOOs are Internet accessible, text mediated virtual environments well suited for distance learning. MOOs of interest.

Morphing

Changing one image into another by moving corresponding elements rather than by crossfading.

Motion JPEG MJPEG or MJP

New codec algorithm, particularly in the PC platform.

MPC/MPC2/MPC3 *(Multimedia PC)*

Industry standard for a "minimal" multimedia computer system. (Now outdated; of historical interest)

On June 12, 1995, the Multimedia PC Working Group, an independent special interest group of the Software and Information Industry Association, released the latest standards for multimedia equipment. The MPC3 "does not replace MCP2. It takes multimedia a step further, opening the door for new applications and a vastly improved multimedia experience." Software titles that run under MPC and MPC2-compliant hardware will also run on MPC3-compliant hardware.

MPC-2

Spec for a multimedia PC, based on a 486SX.

MPEG (Motion Picture Experts Group)

A hardware CODEC for compressing video files.

Current ISO Standards:

1. MPEG1—1/4 broadcast quality translating to 352x240pixels (consumer-quality video).
2. MPEG2—Full-motion quality translating to 704x480 pixels and 30 fps (broadcast-quality video).
3. MPEG3—The latest.

MPEG Moving Pictures Experts Group

Codec technology for moving images using inter-and intra-frame compression.

MSCDEX.EXE

The "translater" program that lets DOS talk to a CD-ROM drive.

Multi-Session

A CD-ROM drive that can read CD's that have been updated/changed. As CDs are updated, new directories are written, with the newer directories written further and further out to the edge. Multi-session CD-ROM drives begin searching for directories by reading out to in, thus can find the furthermost directory. Single-session CD-ROM drives begin searching for directories from the inside out, thus only the first directory nearest the hub would be encountered.

Multi-Thread

Describes a program that is designed to have parts of its code execute concurrently.

Mutant

The basic meaning is simply a thing which has changed. In biology, a mutant is an organism that differs from its parents as a result of a random change in one or more of the genes passed on to it. In Marvel Comics, a mutant is a person who, as a result of genetic mutation, is born with a special power of one sort or another. Usually (but not always), the power (and any unusual physical appearance that might go with it, such as The Angel's wings) manifests itself during puberty. In the Marvel Universe, mutants have been with the human race for a long time, but their rate of appearance has accelerated drastically since nuclear power started increasing the amount of radiation in the world. Normal humans in Marvel comics tend to hate and fear mutants, who are seen as a danger to them—and some of whom, using their powers for evil purposes, actually are dangerous. It was to combat the threat of such evil mutants, and to help other mutants deal with their differences, that Professor X formed The X-Men in 1963.

Network Computer

An inexpensive PC "box", used with your television monitor, which is dedicated for use with the Internet.

Newsgroups

A newsgroup is like a bulletin board: any subscriber can post a message to the newsgroup, and each subscriber can read any or all of the messages. Newsgroups can be useful for gathering information on subjects that are popular among other Internet users. The most active newsgroups are usually those focused on high-tech topics, topics of concern to academics or students. However, newsgroups devoted to entertainment and non-technical professional topics often have a significant number of regular participants. You can read news using the Netscape browser, or through a variety of news reading programs.

Nitrate Cels

Animation cels made from cellulose nitrate, a flammable, unstable material prone to wrinkling, yellowing and shrinkage over long periods of time. Decomposing nitrate emits fumes and resins which can accelerate the rate of decomposition of any cel in close proximity. Nitrate cel stock was used throughout the 1920's, '30s and the early 40's at the Disney Studios, and well into the 1950's at other studios.

NTSC National Television Standards Committee

Composite signal standard adopted by TV and videos in the US and Japan, with a frame rate of 30fps actually 29.97 fps.

NTSC, PAL, SECAM

NTSC is the standard for video signals in the US, Japan and Canada. NTSC uses 30 fps. PAL and SECAM are international/European standards, using 25 fps.

Object-Oriented

A programming technique that focuses design on the data (=objects) and on the user interfaces to it.

To make an analogy with carpentry, an "object-oriented" carpenter would be mostly concerned with the chair he was building, and secondarily with the tools used to make it; a "non-object-oriented" carpenter would think primarily of his tools. Object-oriented design is also the mechanism for defining how modules "plug and play." (from Sun MicroSystems)

OCR (Optical Character Recognition)

Scanning/process for machine print recognition. Compare to ICR.

OLE (Object Linking and Embedding)

Windows' "magic" to transfer objects from one program "document" to another. The process involves copying the selected object to the clipboard, then switching over to the receiving document and pasting. Paste Linking (available as a Paste Special option), plants a trail back to the original/source document so that when the original changes, you see the changes in the receiver. Paste Embedding, the default paste mode, places a copy of the original into the receiver. Because the two programs are not linked, any changes to the original are not reflected in the receiver.

OpenGL

3D graphic programming API written by Silicon Graphics. Allows programs to interface and use built in high speed 3D graphic routines on graphic cards. The standard for high end 3D modeling and recently adopted by Apple Computers as their standard 3D interface.

Optical Storage Unit

CD-ROM drive.

Orange Book

Standard for WORM (Write Once Read Many) CD's. Used for archiving/backing up catalogs, directories and other computerized paperwork.

Painter

In animation, the painter is the person who applies color to the inked cel.

PAL

Video format used in Australia and western Europe.
In comics, a panel is an individual picture. The story is told in the form of a sequence of panels. There are also one-panel cartoon features, such as Hazel and They'll Do It Every Time.

Panning Shots

Wider cels, backgrounds and drawings were used in moving camera shots. Pans were often referred to as a 12 field double pan (10 1/2" by 25") or a 16 field 1 1/2 pan (12 1/2" by 24 1/"). In films shot in Cinemascope or Technirama (like Lady & the Tramp or Sleeping Beauty), panning cels were used in many scenes to accommodate the wider fields needed for the widescreen process.

Parallel Ports

Also called "printer ports", parallel ports transfer several bits simultaneously. Thus, they are faster than serial ports. However, they can only send, not receive, information; whereas serial posts can handle 2-way transmission.

PCI

Peripheral Component Interface, very fast I/O bus (with potential of 132 Mbps transfer rate).

PCMCIA

Personal Computer Memory Card International Association.

PCX

Graphic format originally used by PC Paintbrush; the newest version supports 8-bit and 16-bit color images; supported by most PC and some Mac graphic programs.

PDF (Portable Document Format)

A platform independent Post Script based file format; part of Adobe Acrobat.

Penciller

In comics, a penciller is the artist who does the basic drawing. Usually, the penciller lays out the page, positions the figures, sketches in poses, facial expressions, backgrounds, etc. The inker follows, rendering the drawing in high-contrast black and white for the camera.

Photo CD

Kodak's technology for storing images on CDs, in five resolutions — for printing, computer display, HDTV display, and thumbnails.

Photographic Lines

The Disney Studios developed a method of reproducing animation drawings to cel by means of a photographic process as early as 1936, for use on Snow White & the Seven Dwarfs. The technique continued to be used as late as the early 1950's. In scenes where the camera was required to focus in tight on a very small character, this process was able to produce a fine hairline which was much more accurate than could be achieved by hand inking. The animation was rendered at full size, and then would be reduced photographically to fit the scene. The photographic lines could be dyed several colors as well, but on close inspection, they sometimes appears to be slightly translucent. This technique was discontinued after the development of xerography, and very little information on how it was accomplished has survived.

PICT

A Macintosh graphic image format; the newest version can be compressed and supports 24-bit color images; supported by most Mac and PC graphic programs.

Pixels

PICture ELements = Pixel. The tiny dots comprising a picture.

PNG

Standing for "Portable Network Graphics" and pronounced "ping", is a proposed replacement/improvement for the GIF format. It allows for both up to 8-bit and 8 × 8 × 8 palettes, variable transparency, gamma correction, better interlacing and better compression than GIF. It does not, however, allow for animation. PNG has only recently seen support from Netscape and IE, neither one supports the PNG standard fully, though plug-ins are available for most platforms to allow both browsers to be more PNG compliant. Macromedia's Fireworks uses PNG as its native format. See: http://www.libpng.org/pub/png/

Polyphony

The total number of sounds a sound card can reproduce at the same time. A 32-note card can play 32 notes at a time.

PostScript

De facto standard page description language (PDL).

POTS

"Plain Old Telephone Service", analog telephone service.

Presentation Setups

After the contract with Courvoisier Galleries expired in 1946, the Disney Studios continued to assemble cel setups in nearly identical packaging to give as gifts to clients, VIP's and studio guests. Since the production cels were often imperfect, damaged or unavailable, these cel setups were created to order by the ink and paint department using poses taken from original animation drawings. These cels were usually combined with a production background, or a simple complementary painting created by the background department in down-time.

Presentation Software

Packages, such as Microsoft Powerpoint, which allow users to create "electronic overhead transparencies." Typically easy to use, presentation software does have all the full multimedia capabilities that you will find in authoring software.

Typical presentation systems:

- Gold Disk's Astound (Mac and Windows)
- Microsoft's PowerPoint (Mac and Windows)
- Kai's Power Show (Mac and Windows)
- Harvard Graphics (Windows)
- Lotus Freelance Graphics (Windows)

Production Artwork

Any cel, drawing or painting used in any part of the making of a film. (*Note*: Production does not mean Under The Camera.) Many types of art created for the production of the film were not photographed, but instead acted as a guide for artists to follow.

Protocol

A set of rules.

Public Domain

Software is available for unrestricted use, and can be copied freely and even renamed and resold.

Publicity and Promotional Artwork

"Perfect poses" used to promote the release of an animated film. Publicity artwork produced for the original release of a film may often closely resemble production art, while cels and backgrounds created for later re-releases may look quite different. In general, publicity images from the original release are worth much more than ones from later re-releases.

Push Web Technology

Also referred to as "Web-casting" or "channel-casting", this technology publishes/broadcasts personalized information to subscribers. Then, instead of using bookmarks and search engines to pull down information, users would run a client application that gets updated with data that is "pushed" down by a server.

QuickTime (.MOV)

A CROSS-PLATFORM real-time video and multimedia data format developed by Apple Computer. QuickTime files can include text, sound and video.

QuickTime

System-level software architecture supporting timebased media, giving a seamless integration of video, sound, and animation. For Macs and Windows.

RAID

"Redundant Array of Independent Disks", stacked hard drives.

RAM

"Random Access Memory"—cache RAM (fast RAM to match the speed of microporcessors); flash RAM (fast, permanent memory on PCMCIA cards); DRAM (dynamic RAM); SRAM (static RAM); SDRAM (synchornized DRAM); VRAM (video RAM); CDRAM (cached DRAM) ... RAMbo.

RealAudio

Real-time, live audio on the Web. RealAudio highly compresses sound files to ship down the network. After front-loading a portion of the recording, the receiving player starts, pulling in remaining portions. This lets users begin listening as the sound file is being downloaded, hence "real-time", rather having to wait until downloading is complete. You can take a closer look/"listen" at http://www.real.com/.

Real-Time Compression

Compression of movies as soon as they come into the computer—also known as one-step capture.

RealVideo

Delivers "broadcast-quality" video over the Internet in real-time. The software operates over modems operating at 28.8 Kbps and up. The beta version is available at http://www.real.com/

Reboot

To restart an entire series from the beginning, as if the characters had never been seen before. This is sometimes done when past continuity gets so complicated that new readers have a hard time following it. For example, Superman was rebooted in 1986 and The Legion of Super Heroes in 1994. It's also sometimes done in conjunction with a basic change in publishing strategy. For example, The Fantastic Four was rebooted in 1996.

Recent Art Packaging

Since 1973, cels sold at the Disney theme parks, studio stores and authorized dealerships have all been packaged with a certificate of authenticity and a certifying seal. Most other studio art programs, like those of Warner Brothers and Hanna-Barbera use a similar format for their artwork. Desirability and value on recent cel setups varies widely, depending on the quality of the image and the relative scarcity of similar artwork on the market. Cels which do not carry these seals and certificates are not necessarily forgeries, however. Most unpackaged artwork on the market comes from artists and technicians who received the artwork as a gift from the studio for doing a good job on the production.

Red Book

A music CD.

Resolution

The clarity of the displayed/printed image. The more pixels/dots per square inch (dpi), the finer the detail (higher resolution). Color resolution comparison.

Retcon

Retroactive continuity. Many comic book fans are very concerned that each story about a character be consistent with every story that has been published in the past. For example, it is no longer possible to do a story about Lois Lane trying to prove Clark Kent is Superman, because DC Comics has published stories in which she found out for sure. Sometimes, to make stories work, it is necessary to "tweak" the past a little bit, so they do a "retcon." For example, Marvel Comics established that the man using the name of Captain America in the 1950s was not the same as the one in the '40s, to stay consistent with the story in which The Avengers found the original Captain America had been frozen in Arctic ice since 1945. The term also applies to wholesale revisions of continuity, for example, DC's mid-1980s complete revamping of its entire fictional history.

RGB (Red Green Blue)

The additive colors used by computers to display colors. White is 100 per cent of all three colors, black is 0 per cent of all three.

RIFF (Resource Interchange File Format)

File format for storing sound and graphics so they can be played by different types of computers.

RIFF Resource Interchange File Format

A file format for multimedia data on PCs; can contain bitmapped graphics, animation, digital audio, and MIDI files.

RLE (Run Length Encoding)

Microsoft's CODEC used for no more than 256 colors.

Rotoscope

A device that enables animators to trace the movement of live actors, frame by frame, into an animation sequence. The rotoscope is decried by some animation purists, but has often been used to good effect (for example, in enabling actor Hans Conried to perform the part of Disney's Captain Hook, as well as provide Hook's voice). The device was invented by Max Fleischer, who used it in his series "Out of the Inkwell" before World War I.

Rough Animation Drawings

The original, first generation sketch by the animators in creating the movement in a scene. Roughs can be divided into three basic types: Key Drawings, which were drawn by the principal animators themselves, Break-Downs, which were drawn by both animator and his assistant, and Inbetweens which were the work of the assistant animators alone. Generally, the animator would sketch out a key drawing for every five or six frames and leave the drawings between his keys for the assistants to fill in. Once the rough animation was approved, the drawings would be delivered to the assisting department for Clean Up. Many collectors prefer roughs to clean ups, because they are often more spontaneous and full of life, and they are more likely to be the work of a lead animator.

Sampling

When coverting video or audio waves to digital format, digitizing software picks out points along the wave and records or "snapshots" these points. These "snapshots" can then be replayed in much the same way that motion pictures are recreated from the individual frames. The higher the sampling rate, i.e. the more snapshots/points, per unit time, the more accurate the computer's representation of the wave.

Scan Converter

See *Video Scan Converter.*

Scanner

Computer device which "reads" text or graphics and converts them into digitized documents/ files. Most scanners work by lighting an image and measuring the light reflected through it. The scanner them converts the reflections into distinct voltages which are, in turn, transformed into patterns of dots. The resolution or clarity of the image is measured in dots per inch.

Screen Saver

A visual program using moving graphics to prevent monitor burn-in.

ScriptX

An object-oriented authoring language and multi-platform standard for multimedia software development.

SCSI Small Computer Systems Interface

A fast general-purpose system interface for connecting computer peripherals such as hard drives, scanners, printers, CDROM drives, and so on.

SCSI

"Small Computer Systems Interface", a very fast, versatile parallel port allowing a computer to connect (or "daisychain") up to 7 peripheral devices, like laser printers, CD-ROM drives.

Sealant

Lacquer or nail polish applied to the back side of the paint, in an effort to prevent paint from cracking, or to hold already loose paint in place. Over a long period of time, sealants hasten paint loss, and can also cause pigment mottling and fading.

Search "Engines"/tools

Programs which allow you to search through Web pages by keyword or subject.

SECAM (Sequential Color with Memory)

Video format used mostly in France.

Self Paced

The student can start and finish the program at any time, at his/her convenience. It typically involves no moderation/interaction with an expert/instructor. Examples include most CD-ROMs, video-tapes, cassettes, etc.

Separation, Lifting, or Glassing

Refers to separation of paint from the back of the cel, with or without cracking. Separated sections have a discolored appearance.

Sequential Art

Will Eisner (The Spirit) coined this expression, which means a series of illustrations which are intended to be viewed in consecutive order to create a coherent narrative. Actually, it is a hifalutin term for comics.

Serial Ports

Used for 2-way communication, serial ports transfer data one bit at a time. Many devices, including modems, scanners and laser printers, connect to serial ports. Contrast to parallel ports.

Serigraphs

A mass produced cel created by means of a printing process similar to silk screening. No hand painting or inking is involved. These cels are produced in large quantities and are marketed as a low-cost alternative to production and limited edition cels. They have very little value on the secondary market.

Server-Side Markup (SSM)

A "tag" embedded in the Webpage that gets interpreted "on the fly"/processed by the server each time the page is requested. For example, a "last modified" time/date stamp, e.g. producing Monday, 12-Apr-1999 08:00:16 EDT, is done with the tag <!—#flastmod file="*name_of_file*.htm" —> (an in-depth look). Related: Active Server Pages, Cold Fusion.

Shareware

"Try before you buy" software. The author retains full rights to the package. It may be copied at will, but shareware cannot be used at will. There is generally a limited period of use granted without fee, commonly 30 or 60 days. After that period, the user pays a licensing fee to continue using the software.

Shockwave

Add-in to MacroMedia Director that lets you create highly-compressed interactive animations and movies for Web pages. Director supports Java applets. (in-depth look) An easier-to-use, vector-based Web-animation program is Flash, also from Macromedia. +/-'s of Shockwave.

SND

A standard Mac resource format for sounds; now widely supported.

Sound Blaster-Compatible

Works with software written for the Sound Blaster video card, the sound standard.

Sound Card

An add-in circuit board that once installed, enables the computer to accept audio input from a microphone, edit/trim/mix recordings, play sound files stored on disks or CD-ROM's, and produce audio output through speakers or earphones. For output, sound cards can (1) create or synthesize sounds, like a keyboard/synthesizer, and (2) play previously-recorded sounds, like a tape recorder/player.

Splash Panel

A large comic book panel, usually half a page or more (in fact, sometimes spread over two facing pages), and usually coming at the beginning of a story. In modern comics, the splash panel is usually part of the story. In older comics, the splash usually functioned as a sort of interior cover, showing a highlight from the story it introduced, or a picture in some way symbolic of the story's theme.

Story Boards

A precise description detailing how each multimedia element is going to be used and screen-by-screen planning of what is available to the enduser.

Storyboard

A sequence of still drawings, used in animation to display the key points of a story—that is, a script of sorts, done with pictures instead of words. Using storyboards, directors are better able to control pacing, among other things. After being brought to a modern level of sophistication by the Disney organization (to early glimmerings had been seen even in the pre-Felix days), storyboards were adopted throughout the animation industry, and soon started being used by live-action directors, as well. Today, they are seen everywhere in film production, from TV commercials to mega-blockbuster feature films.

Streaming Audio/Video

Capability to begin playing media on the client side before it has fully downloaded from the server side, i.e. begins playing as it is coming in, "in real-time." The major players are RealNetworks (RealAudio—the industry standard), Microsoft (Netshow—avoid this!) and Apple ("streaming" QuickTime). +/-'s of streaming media (an in-depth look).

Sunday Page

Before World War II, it was the norm for newspaper cartoonists to have an entire page of their own on Sundays. Some used the whole page for one series, as Hal Foster did with his Prince Valiant; whereas others split theirs between the main feature and a topper—for example, Chic Young's page contained both Blondie and Col. Potterby & the Duchess. In the early 1940s, wartime paper shortages forced papers to start cutting back on the size of comics, starting an appalling trend that has, by now, brought newspaper comics down to postage-stamp size.

Superhero

A genre of fantasy fiction, found most often in American comic books and TV cartoons (but spilling over into prose novels, film, popular music, and just about everywhere else, at least occasionally). The superhero genre is generally characterized by a stylized form of gaudy costume and/or extraordinary abilities on the part of some characters. Tho the word was in use earlier, the genre is generally considered to have started with Superman, published by DC Comics beginning in 1938. Superheroes have been a part of the comic book scene ever since—and have at various times (including the present) been American comic books' dominant genre. Since 1981, DC and Marvel Comics have claimed a joint trademark on the term, but have made only spotty attempts to keep others from using it, and it is anybody's guess whether or not it would stand if it were ever seriously challenged in court.

SVGA (Super-VGA)

Video monitor/card supporting 640 × 480 resolution (or greater) with 256 colors or more.

Synchronous

Communication/interaction in real time, i.e. at the same time, thus lending itself to the kind of immediacy of communication experienced in a classroom. This may be done using the telephone, chat rooms, whiteboards, etc.

Synthesized

Sounds created by computer circuitry.

SyQuest

An older but proven removable data storage technology in 44MB, 88MB, and 200MB 5.5 inch cartridges or 105MB and 270MB 3.5 inch cartridges. Initial cost is much lower than for MO drives.

Tabloid

Before it was a style of journalism, "tabloid" meant a style of newspaper—physical style, that is, not content style. A tabloid publication is half the size of a regular newspaper, about 11" × 17". The reason it is come to refer to a less-than-savory source of news is simply that the cheapest papers, usually the ones published in the less-expensive smaller size, were usually the ones with the most sensational and least trustworthy news. In the publishing industry, however, "tabloid" is a neutral term, referring only to the actual size of a publication's pages.

TCP/IP

"Transmission Control Protocol/Internet Protocol"; a set of communication standards through which different kinds of computers on the Internet communicate together; the "language" of the Internet.

Teleconference

A phone meeting where callers can both see and hear each other. Network transfer speed comparison.

Text Files

Files that contains no special codes or commands—such as bold, italics or graphics—only text. Text files, unlike binary files, can be read without any special software.

Text-to-Speech

Voice synthesizers that "read" computer text. First used to read screens for blind computer users, text-to-speech is becoming increasingly popular for children's games. For more information: Visit AT&T's Advanced Speech Products Group (http://www.att.com/aspg)

TIFF (Tagged Image File Format)

Cross-Platform file for storing high-quality graphics.

Title Cards

A background painting which acts as part of the credits for an animated film. The text is often on a cel overlay. Title cards can be divided into several categories. Series title, main title and cost and crew credits.

Tool

Program, following defined protocols, that provides a service.

Topper

A small Sunday comic strip that accompanied another strip. The first toppers (which came from King Features in the 1920s) ran across the top of the page, hence the name, to different syndicates put them in different places. Toppers are no longer in use, now that cartoonists are no longer given a whole page to work with, but before World War II, they were common—encouraged by newspaper editors who wanted to advertise having more comics, but did not want to add pages to the comics section. A few examples of toppers are Jungle Jim (topper to Flash Gordon), Cicero's Cat (topper to Mutt & Jeff), and Maw Green (topper to Little Orphan Annie).

Touch Screen

Monitor input where you can use your finger to draw on a screen or select an on-screen object. Touch screen technology is often used in ATM machines or in malls, for example, in electronic information kiosks/directories.

Trackball

Operating like a mouse, a trackball remains stationary while a ball on its top is rolled with the fingers. Because you do not move it around the desk/mousepad like a mouse, it takes up less space.

True-Type

Window's built-in "outline" font technology. It works by taking a mathematical description of a font's outline and using it to "paint in" on-the-fly screen and printer representations. The printed appearance is true to the displayed appearance, hence "true-type." True-type fonts are stored in two files, with the extensions .TTF and .FOT. To install a TTfont, copy the .TTF file into the directory where the font files are stored (C:\WINDOWS\SYSTEM). Then use Control Panel to ADD the font: Control Panel creates the .FOT file and adds a line to WIN.INI that enables Windows to initialize the font at start-up. A typical font-entry looks like: Arial (TrueType)=ARIAL.FOT.

Turnkey

Refers to a complete system designed, integrated, installed and tested, so that all the user has to do is "turn the key" to start it.

Universe

The milieu in which a large number of characters (mostly superheroes) from related but separate series operate, usually preceded with a qualifier indicating how the characters are related (the two major examples being "Marvel Universe" and "DC Universe", denoting characters owned by Marvel and DC Comics, respectively). A comic book universe may have a history different from that of the real world, such as the "fact" that in the Marvel Universe, Hitler was killed by The Human Torch. Its geography may be different—for example, in the DC Universe, there are major U.S. cities named Metropolis and Gotham City. Even scientific laws may be different, manifest, for example, in the ability of some DC Universe characters to travel in time by exceeding the speed of light. The important thing, in the eyes of many readers, is that everything be consistent—if a particular "fact" is "true" in one Marvel comic, then while it need not apply to DC comics, it must be "true" in all other Marvels.

URL (Uniform Resource Locator)

The addressing scheme used to link resources on the Web. Like the post office, which must have addresses to deliver mail, Internet users—and their computers—must have addresses in order to send and receive messages. A URL has two parts, separated by://. Example: http://www.whitehouse.gov/

The portion before the "://" is the web protocol, which could be http://, gopher://...

The after portion is the name of the computer the person is using—the host.

The name of this host computer may consist of several parts, each separated by a period. The last part tells you what kind of organization owns the computer. For example, **gov** stands for government, **com** for commercial organizations, **edu** for educational institutions, **mil** for the military, and so forth. Occasionally you see names which end with country codes. The United States designation is **US**.

USB (Universal Serial Bus)

Serial interface that allows connection of up to 127 devices at speeds of either 1.5 or 12Mbits/s. It supplies power for those devices and allows the devices to be hotswaped (added and removed without rebooting). Currently used to connect keyboards, mice, printers and scanners.

VGA

Video monitor/card supporting 640 × 480 resolution with 16 colors. (Also covers resolutions of 320 × 240 with 256 colors.)

Video CD-ROM

A CD-ROM standard that uses MPEG to store up to 74 minutes of digital video on one CD-ROM.

Video for Windows

Microsoft's system-level Windows software architecture; similar to QuickTime.

Video RAM

Special memory chips residing fast video cards. The more memory, the higher the resolution. For example, to put out 256 colors you need 512K of video RAM; for 16.7 million colors, you need 2 Mb. (See VRAM).

Video Scan Converters

Convert computer RGB signals to NTSC, PAL or SECAM video signals. Once converted, these signals may be videotaped or shown on a television monitor.

Video, Analog

True full-motion video from laser discs, videotapes. Formats: Hi8, 8mm, S-VHS, VHS.

Video, Component

Used in Hi8 and SuperVHS cameras, component video splits the single composite video signal into colors (RGB) and improves the quality by adding a luminance or brightness (Y) channel and a color/chroma intensity (C) channel. Superior to composite video.

Video, Composite

Single-signal video, used in VHS. Inferior to component video.

Video, Digital

Digitized video, i.e. video converted/compressed to file format. Formats: .AVI (Video for Windows) and .MOV (QuickTime—cross-platform for both Macintosh and Windows).

Videoconferencing

Transporting real-time voice and video over telecommunications services. Nowadays, "Web conferencing" is the fashion, thanks to various desktop videoconferencing (DVC) products like Enhanced Cu-SeeMe.

Vinyl and Acrylic Based Cel Paints

Since the early 1960's, non-rewettable opaque watercolor paints with a synthetic plastic binder have become the industry standard. Although these commercially available paints are more durable and permanent than vintage gum arabic based paint formulas, they do not have as wide a variety of pigments as the traditional Disney paint formula. In most cases, the original Disney gum arabic paint formula is preferable for archival restoration.

Voice Recognition

Software which recognizes spoken commands. Most software has to be individually trained for each voice, making its general usage limited. For a good example of voice-recognized commands, dial 1-800-ATT-COLLECT.

VRML

Virtual Reality Markup Language, the "next stage" in HTML, permitting 3-D animation browsing. The VRML server works by transmitting an object command, such as "cone", and the mathematical description of its dimensions, location, color and texture to the client. The client then handles rendering and manipulation. See: http://www.vrml.org/. Free VRML tools.

For interesting Websites, see:

1. fr
2. VRML specifications, reports, information and links at http://www.sdsc.edu/vrml

WAN

Wide Area Network.

WAV

Popular format for storing audio files in Windows.

Wavetable

Sound synthesis using a built-in selection/table of actual recordings. The output is more realistic than that produced by the older technology, FM synthesis.

Whiteboard

Document-teleconference function that lets multiple users simultaneously view and annotate electronic documents with pens, highlighters and drawing tools.

Word Balloon

The area in which a comics character's speech appears, usually with a "tail" pointing to the one speaking. Usually, balloons are both positioned and drawn by the letterer. Sometimes called "word bubble" "speech bubble" or "dialog bubble", especially in Europe.

World Wide Web (WWW)

Provides the glitziest on-line information on the Internet. The Web or WWW or W3 or WaWaWa, as it is familiarly called, consists of a system of pages where the information is linked together like hypertext. As you click on each underlined word, it takes you to the next page of related information, and so on. In the Web, however, the links jump from one information source to another, where the sources may be in different countries.

WORM

(Write Once Read Many) CDs. Used for archiving/backing up catalogs, directories and other computerized paperwork.

WPG

WordPerfect graphic file format.

Xerography

In the late 1950's, the Disney Studios developed a xerographic process to transfer the animator's drawings directly onto cels. Sleeping Beauty was the first film to include scenes utilizing this process. At first, only black toner was used, but in the early 1970's, browns, greys and other colors were developed. Xeroxed lines appear to be more sketchy than hand inked lines, but since they are transferred directly from the animator's drawings they often retain a sense of "life" and spontaneity that hand inking often lacks.

XML (Extensible Markup Language)

XML is younger sister to hypertext markup language (HTML). The difference is that XML is a "metadata language", i.e. it carries information about information. XML allows reuse of learning objects, and assembly of objects on demand as a learner asks for information. XML also allows the same learning object—for example, a definition with a test question about the definition—to change with context.

Some sites to check for information about XML include:

http://www.xml.com/xml/pub/98/10/guide1.html
http://www.xmlu.com/
http://www.scripting.com/
http://www.geocities.com/SiliconValley/Peaks/5957/xml.html

Yellow Book

CDs for computer programs and data.

Zip drives

Removable, floppy-disk drive alternatives. Iomega's (http://www.iomega.com/) zip (low-end) and Jaz (high-end) disks accommodate 100MB and 1Gb of storage, respectively. The drives cost about $200 and $500, respectively, and individual cartridges cost $20. With speeds close to hard disk rates, zip/jaz cartridges/drives can replace hard disks for many uses, including large video file storage.

Bibliography

Abbott, L. (1987). *Active Acting: Exercises and Improvisations Leading to Performance.* Star Publishing Company: Belmont, CA.

Abel, Sam (1995). The rabbit in drag: Camp and gender construction in the American animated cartoon. *Journal of Popular Culture* 29(3): 183.

Abocar, Amran (1999). CINAR sells Arthur series to Chinese television [animation]. *Reuters* (December 9).

Adalian, Josef (2000). NBC Orders Six Episodes of Steve Martin Show ["the downer channel" animation]. *Reuters/Variety* (August 16).

Adalian, Josef (2000). WB Berths 'Baby' ["Baby Blues" animated TV show based on comic strip]. *Reuters/Variety* (June 28).

Adams, Noah (1994). Snow White [Disney animated movie compared to original German story]. National Public Radio's All Things Considered (October 31).

Adams, Noah (1996). Dalmatians [dog breeding due to Disney animated movie]. National Public Radio's All Things Considered (November 21).

Adams, Noah (1998). Rugrats' Voices [animated movie]. National Public Radio's All Things Considered (November 24).

Adams, Noah (1999). New IMAX Version of 'The Old Man and the Sea' [by Russian animator Alexander Petrov]. National Public Radio's All Things Considered (October 1).

Adamson, Joe. *Tex Avery: King of Cartoons*. 1975. New York: Da Capo, 1985.

————. *The Walter Lantz Story, with Woody Woodpecker and Friends*. New York: G.B. Putnam, 1985.

Ahrens, Frank (1999). Toying with Tarzan: Mattel secures doll's suggestive hand [animated movie merchandising] *Washington Post* (June 19): C5.

Allan, Robin. *Walt Disney and Europe: European Influences on the Animated Feature Films of Walt Disney*. London: John Libbey, 1999.

Anderson, Christopher. *Hollywood TV: The Studio System in the Fifties*. Austin: University of Texas Press, 1994.

Andre, E. (ed.) (1997). Notes of the IJCAI-97 Symposium on Animated Interface Agents: Making Them Intelligent, Nagoya, Japan, August. *Representative survey of current work on animated agents, covering issues in effective presentation, affective modelling, social impact, and character design.*

Angeli, Mike. (1998). Oh my God! They made a movie [South Park animators Matt Stone & Trey Parker]. *Details* (August): 116-121.

Anonymous. *Where to Get Multimedia Training in Europe.* Bry-sur-Marne: INA, various dates.

———. *The Whole Toon Catalog.* Chicago: Facets Multimedia, various dates.

———. *The World of Hanna-Barbera Cartoons.* New York: Museum of Radio and Television, 1995.

———. *Zagreb 1982: Retrospective Program of Zagreb School of Animation.* Zagreb: Zagreb World Festival of Animation, 1982.

Ansen, David (1999). Further proof: Toys "r" us [Toy Story 2 animation review]. *Newsweek* (November 29): 94.

Ansen, David (1999). Take that! The creme de la crude [South Park animated movie]. *Newsweek* (July 5): 58.

Ansen, David and Yahlin Chang (2000). Building a better dinosaur: The first movie to emerge from Disney's digital studio brings the prehistoric age to virtual life [Disney computer-animated movie]. *Newsweek* (May 15): 58-64.

Archer, Peter; Harvey Eisenberg and Samuel Armstrong (1954). MGM's Tom and Jerry's Merry Christmas [Little Golden Book for children based on animation]. Racine, WI: Western Publishing Company/New York: Golden Press.

Arthur, Nicole (1999). 'The Iron Giant': Heavy metal [Warner Bros. animated movie]. *Washington Post* (August 6): Weekend 44-45.

Associated Press (1998). Actress Mae Questel dies: Lent voice to Betty Boop [animation]. *Washington Post* (January 9): B6.

Associated Press (1999). Cartoon theft no laughing matter [animation cels]. Associated Press (August 14).

Ault, Alicia (1999). A Virtual Reality That's Best Escaped [computer animation of schizophrenia]. *New York Times* (July 8).

Avasthi, Su (1997). Fox to Challenge Disney in All-Out Animation War. *New York Post* (October 27).

Badler, N. "Real-Time Virtual Humans," in Proc. (1997). Pacific Graphics Conf., Seoul, Korea, 1997. *Survey of issues in creating real-time animated human figures, with focus on design of Jack architecture and discussion of systems that employ it. Used by: Rickel and Johnson, 1997.*

Baldwin, Kristen (1998). Cooked cook [South Park animated TV show]. *Entertainment Weekly* (December 11): 16.

Baldwin, Kristen (1999). Park prophets? [animated TV show South Park]. *Entertainment Weekly* (April 30): 12.

Ball, G., D. Kurlander, J. Miller, D. Pugh, T. Skelly, A. Stankosky, D. Thiel, M. Van Dantzich, and T. Wax, "Lifelike Computer Characters: the Personal Project at Microsoft Research," in Software Agents, J. Bradshaw, Ed. AAAI Press: Menlo Park, CA, (1997). *Overview of Microsoft work on building animated, conversational assistants. Focus on Peedy, a parrot that processes spoken requests for music. Emphasis on technical issues (e.g., voice recognition, animation, etc.).*

Barnes, Clive (1997). 'Lion King' is Ext-Roar-Dinary [Play Based on Animated Movie]. *New York Post* (November 14).

Barnes, Deborah, Debbie Beyer, Kim Lochart and Cherie Spino (1994). The kingdom behind The Lion King [animation]. *Disney Adventures* 4(10; July 30): 37-47.

Barrier, Michael (1999). *Hollywood Cartoons: American Animation in its Golden Age.* Oxford. Oxford University Press.

Bates, J. "The Nature of Characters in Interactive Worlds and The Oz Project," Tech. Report CMU-CS-92-200, School of Computer Science, Carnegie Mellon University, Pittsburgh, October (1992). *Summarizes the Oz project's motivation and goals. Discusses possible types of interaction between users and believable agents. Primarily of historical interest.*

Bauder, David (2000). 'South Park' Parodies Reno on Raid [in animated TV show]. Associated Press (April 28).

Baumbach, Nico (1999). Inspector Gadget [movie based on animated TV series]. *Village Voice* (July 28). online at http://www.villagevoice.com/issues/9930/baumbach.shtml

Bayles, Martha (1999). Go Hollywood, Moses [review of Solomon book on The Prince of Egypt: A New Vision in Animation]. *New York Times Book Review* (January 3).

Beck, Jerry & Will Friedwald (1997). *Warner Bros. Animation Art: The Characters,* the *Creators, the Limited Editions*. Levin Associates.

Beck, Jerry (1994). The fifty greatest cartoons: As selected by 1,000 animation professionals. Atlanta, GA: Turner.

Beck, Jerry and Will Friedwald. *Warner Bros. Animation Art: The Characters, the Creators,* the Limited Editions. New York: Hugh Lauter Levin, 1997.

————. Looney Tunes and Merry Melodies: *A Complete Illustrated Guide to the Warner Bros. Cartoons*. New York: Henry Holt, 1989.

Beifuss, John (1997). There's no shortage of tragic history to animate [Anastasia]. *Nashville Tennessean* (Dec 20): 54-55.

Bell, Elizabeth (ed.) (1995). *From Mouse to Mermaid: The Politics of Film, Gender, and Culture [in Disney animated movies*]. Bloomington: Indiana University Press.

Bell, Jerry and Shalom Auslander (1991). "I Tawt I Saw a Puddy Tat:" Fifty Years of Sylvester and Tweety [animation]. New York: Henry Holt.

Bendazzi, Giannalberto (1994). *Cartoons: One Hundred Years of Cinema Animation.* Bloomington, Ind.: Indiana University Press.

Benesch, Connie (1995). Holy cartoons, Batman! *Animation Magazine* (August 8): 10.

Bennett, Ralph K. (1999). Tycoon tips from C. Montgomery Burns [from the Simpsons animated TV show]. *Regardie's Power* (November-December): 52-53.

Benning, Victoria (1999). Youths pack Tysons Corner for pointers on 'Pocket Monsters' [Pokemon Japanese animation]. *Washington Post* (August 8): C4.

Bennis, Warren G. and Patricia Ward Biederman (1997). Organizing Genius: The Secrets of Creative Collaboration [chapter on Disney animation team]. Reading, MA: Addison-Wesley.

Berger, Arion (2000). Why do the heathen rage [animated movie "The Road to El Dorado"]. *Washington City Paper* (March 31): 40.

Berlin, Michael (1998). North of Hollywood [Pixar Animation Studios]. *Icon Thoughtstyle Magazine* (December): 42-43.

Bernadin, Marc (1997). Superzero [Spawn movie and animated cartoon]. *Entertainment Weekly* (Dec 19): 81-82.

Bernard, Jami (1989). Looney Tunes and Friz Freleng [animation]. *Comics Scene* (7): 17-20, 41.

Bernstein, Jonathan (1997). The worst years of our lives: High school heroine Daria is the girl with the most hate [animation]. *Spin* (May): 30.

Bernstein, Paula (1999). Fox Kids goes Psycho ["Joe Psycho & MooFrog Cartoonshow" animation]. *Reuters/Variety* (December 29).

Bernstein, Paula (1999). MTV to Broaden Daria Into Animated TV Movie. *Reuters* (December 16).

Beyer, Debbie (1995). Inside Spidey's web [Spiderman animation]. *Disney Adventures* (September 30): 29-31.

Beyer, Debbie and Chris Golden (1995). The man behind the web [Spiderman animation]. *Disney Adventures* (September 30): 26-28.

Bianculli, David (1999). New Toon 'Mission': Implausible ['Mission Hill' animated TV show]. *New York Daily News* (September 21).

Binswanger, C. K. and Jeca Taudte (1997). Urp. Pass the Cheesy Poofs [South Park animated TV series]. *Newsweek* (Aug 25): 8.

Bishop, JM and DR Krause (1984). Depictions of aging and old age on Saturday morning television [animation]. *Gerontologist* 24 (1; Feb.): 91-4.

Blanc, Mel. *That's Not All, Folks! My Life in the Golden Age of Cartoons and Radio.* New York: Warner, 1988.

Blevins, Bret (2000). How to Draw the WB Animated Style. *Wizard* (101).

Block, Melissa (1995). Pocahontas in Park [Disney animated movie premier]. National Public Radio's All Things Considered (June 9).

Blumberg, B. "Action-Selection in Hamsterdam: Lessons from Ethology," in Proc. Third Int. Conf. on Simulation of Adaptive Behaviour, Brighton, England, (1994). *Presents computational model of agent behaviour based on biological factors, e.g. hunger, fear. Interesting alternative to psychological and artistic metaphors.*

Bobbin, Jay (1999). "Olive, the Other Reindeer": The title character tries to help Santa Claus save Christmas in the new, animated Fox special [based on J. Otto Siebold children's book]. *Bergen Record's Your Time TV* (December 12): 6.

Bohlen, Celestine (2000). Pride projected on the big screen: Filmmaker's Oscar becomes a victory for Russian culture [animator Aleksandr Petrov and "The Old Man and the Sea"]. *New York Times* (May 10): B1, 3.

Bond, Paul (2000). Jones cries 'Timber' over Net [Chuck Jones animated internet series]. *The Hollywood Reporter* (August 15).

Bond, Paul (2000). Kricfalusi chills at Icebox.com ["Ren & Stimpy" creator John Kricfalusi doing internet animation]. *The Hollywood Reporter* (May 31).

Boon, Mike (1999). Doug's 1st Movie is undeniably charming [animation]. *Calgary Herald* (March 26).

Borders.com (2000). The kings of clay [Aardman Animation co-founder David Sproxton interview]. *Inside Borders* (January): 27.

Borow, Zev (1999). Mystery Science Theater 3000 [Matt Groening animated TV show Futurama]. *Spin* (May): 94-100.

Brown, Corie & Laura Shapiro (1998). Woman warrior [Disney's animated movie Mulan]. *Newsweek* (June 8): 64-5.

Brown, DeNeen L. (1999). MTV, where the mighty take a fall; 'Celebrity Deathmatch' pits clay stars in the ring a laugh [animation]. *Washington Post* (August 26): C1, 7.

Brown, Scott & Doug Rand (1998). Reality check [animated movies Antz and A Bug's Life]. *Entertainment Weekly* (December 11): 16.

Browne, Ray B. (1994). Animation, Caricature and Gag and Political Cartoons in the United States and Canada: An International Bibliography by John A. Lent [Book Review]. *Journal of Popular Culture* 28(2; Fall).

Brownstein, Charles (1997). C. Scott Morse [animator interview]. *Feature* 3(3; Fall): 47-54.

Burke, Timothy & Kevin Burke (1999). Saturday Morning Fever: Growing Up with Cartoon Culture [animation]. New York: St. Martin's Griffin.

Burr, Ty. (1998). Special 'Delivery' [Japanese animator Hayao Miyazaki's Kiki's Delivery Service released in US by Disney]. *Entertainment Weekly* (September 4): 88.

Burr, Ty. (1999). Smaller is better [Rugrats animation]. *Entertainment Weekly* (April 2): 97-8.

Canemaker, John (ed.). *Storytelling in Animation: The Art of the Animated Image.* Los Angeles: American Film Institute, 1988.

Canemaker, John. *Before the Animation Begins: The Art and Lives of Disney Inspirational Sketch Artists.* New York: Hyperion, 1996.

————, Felix. *The Twisted Tales of the World's Most Famous Cat.* New York: Da Capo, 1996.

————, Winsor McCay. *His Life and Art.* New York: Abbeville, 1987.

Carbaga, Leslie. *The Fleischer Story.* 1976. New York: Da Capo, 1988.

Carroll, Noel. "Mind, Medium and Metaphor in Harry Smith's Heaven and Earth Magic. *Film Quarterly* 31:2 (Winter 1977-78): 37-44.

Carter, Bill (1999). Priest Takes Aim at 'Family Guy' [Animated TV Series]. *New York Times* (July 1).

Catlin, Roger (2000). Powerpuffs: Curtesy, campy and cashing in [animation]. *Hartford Courant* (June 7): D1, 4.

Cawley, John. *The Animated Films of Don Bluth.* New York: Image, 1991.

Chambers, Veronica (1999). A superstar from under the sea ['Sponge Bob Squarepants' animated TV series]. *Newsweek* (September 13): 67.

Chang, Elizabeth (1998). My Disney Kitchen [Disney animated computer game review]. *Washington Post* (November 27): Weekend 90.

Cholodenko, Alan (ed.). *The Illusion of Life.* Sydney: Power Publications, 1991.

Chong, Don (1998). Work in Progress: Erick Stough, Comedy Central/South Park [TV computer animation]. *Alias Wavefront Assistant* (5): 30-1.

Christie's (1984). *The John Basmajian Collection of Walt Disney Animation Art* [Disney]. New York: Christie's East.

Christie's (1986). *Animation and Comic Art [Disney; Winsor McCay; EC Comics].* New York: Christie's East.

Chunovic, Louis (1997). *The Rockey and Bullwinkle Book [animation].* New York: Bantam.

Clark, Tanya (1997). 'Spirit Princess' moves Japan [animation]. *USA Today* (Aug 28).

Clements, Marcelle (2000). What's it all about? The kids know. Do you? [animation and licensing]. *New York Times* (May 21): 23, 32-33.

Clemetson, Lynette (2000). Trying to right Mr. Wong [Icebox.com internet animation and charges of racism]. *Newsweek* (July 31): 55.

Cochran, Jason (1997). Shadow of a doubt [Casper: A Spirited Beginning animated movie]. *Entertainment Weekly* (September 12).

Cochran, Jason (1998). Sum of their parts [Disney animation]? *Entertainment Weekly* (Feb. 6): 64-65.

Cohen, Karl. *Forbidden Animation: Censored Cartoons and Blacklisted Animators in America.* Jefferson, NC: McFarland, 1997.

Cohen, L.L., R.L. Blount and G. Panopoulos (1997). Nurse coaching and cartoon distraction: an effective and practical intervention to reduce child, parent, and nurse distress during immunizations [animation]. *Journal of Pediatric Psychology* 22 (3; June): 355-70.

Cole, Stephen (1998). Bob's your dentist: And adults will appreciate him more than children [Bob and Margaret animated TV show]. *National Post* (December 16).

Collins, Maynard. Norman McLaren. Ottawa: Canadian Film Institute, 1976.

Colton, Michael (1998). The Dancing Baby's mainstream boogie: Icon leaps from web to 'Ally' to t-shirts [computer animation]. *Washington Post* (April 13): D1, D7.

Cooper, Douglas (1994). Toon town: If Brian Boigon has his way, cartoon-filled Spillville will be one of the first cities on the infobahn [computer animation]. *Wired* (Dec): 94-103.

Cooper, Matthew (1998). Hollywood and Divine [Prince of Egypt animated movie]. *Newsweek* (March 30): 62.

Crafton, Donald (1982). *Before Mickey: The Animated Film 1898-1928.* Cambridge, Mass.: The MIT Press.

Crafton, Donald. Emile Cohl, Caricature and Film. Princeton: Princeton University Press, 1990.

-----. *Before Mickey: The Animated Film*, 1898-1928. 1982. Cambridge, MA: MIT, 1987.

Culhane, Shamus. *Talking Animals and Other People: The Autobiography of a Legendary Animator.* 1986. New York: Da Capo, 1998.

-----. *Animation: From Script to Screen.* New York: St. Martin's, 1988.

Curnow, Wystan and Roger Horrocks (eds.). *Figures in Motion: Len Lye, Selected Writings.* Auckland: Auckland University Press, 1984.

Curtis, David. Robert Breer. Cambridge: Cambridge Animation Festival, 1983.

-----. *Experimental Cinema.* New York: Universe, 1971.

Curtis, Scott. "The Sound of the Early Warner Bros. Cartoons." *Sound Theory/Sound Practice.* Ed. Rick Altman. New York: Routledge, 1992. 191-203.

Dahl, Lucy. James and the Giant Peach: The Book and Movie Scrapbook. New York: Hyperion, 1996.

Daly, Steve (1998). Disney serves potluck [review of The Black Cauldron animated movie]. *Entertainment Weekly* (August 7): 82.

Daly, Steve (1998). Tobacco Bill vetoed: Childproofing 'Melody Time' [Disney censoring Pecos Bill animated short]. *Entertainment Weekly* (July 10): 79.

Daly, Steve (1999). Bug screen TV; Rather than accept television's limitations for the video release of A Bug's Life, Disney and Pixar have reworked the film's ant's-eye vistas—and made a visual mountain out of a molehill [animation]. *Entertainment Weekly* (April 23): 64-5.

Daly, Steve (1999). Deconstructing Woody: From caterpillar cameos to a Van Gogh homage we uncover Toy Story 2's secret jokes [animation]. *Entertainment Weekly* (December 10): 12-13.

Daly, Steve (1999). Making prophets ['The Prince of Egypt' animated movie's video release]. *Entertainment Weekly* (September 17): 82-84.

Daly, Steve (1999). Re-animated: The hilariously offensive South Park: Bigger, Longer & Uncut and the gloriously bighearted The Iron Giant breathe colorful new life into non-Disney cartoon features. *Entertainment Weekly* (November 26): 102-103.

Daly, Steve (1999). The vine king [Disney computer animation in Tarzan movie]. *Entertainment Weekly* (July 9): 36-38

Daly, Steve and Anne Thompson (1996). A Tight Squeeze [Batman and Robin movie]. *Entertainment Weekly* (March 8).

Dampf, Andrew (1999). *Sotheby's Auctions 'Mulan' Artwork [from Disney animated movie].* Associated Press (March 6).

Dargis, Manohla (1998). Holy Moses! DreamWorks spins the Bible [The Prince of Egypt animated movie]. *LA Weekly* (December 18). online at http://www.laweekly.com/ink/99/04/film-dargis.shtml

Dauphin, Gary (1999). Japanimation's All-ages Show ["Studio Ghibli, Japan" anime show at the Museum of Modern Art]. *Village Voice* (September 15). online at http://www.villagevoice.com/issues/9937/dauphin.shtml

Dauphin, Gary (1999). South Park: Bigger, Longer & Uncut [animation]. *Village Voice* (June 30). online at http://www.villagevoice.com/issues/9926/dauphin.shtml

Davis, Alisha (2000). No sympathy for 'Devil' ["God, the Devil and Bob" animated TV series]. *Newsweek* (March 20): 80

Day, R.C. and M. Ghandour (1984). The effect of television-mediated aggression and real-life aggression on the behaviour of Lebanese children [including animated violence]. *Journal of Experimental Child Psychology* 38 (1; August): 7-18.

Dempsey, John (1999). Audiences killing Kenny [South Park animated TV show]. *Reuters* (April 27).

Dempsey, John (2000). Powerpuff pic on tap at WB [animated TV series]. *Reuters/Variety* (June 11).

DeWitt, David (2000). Slackers, now animated, in color and a wee bit cute ['Clerks' by Kevin Smith]. *New York Times* (May 30): B5.

Dickinson, Amy (1997). The Sound of the Simpsons [animated TV show]. National Public Radio's All Things Considered (May 1).

Dietch, Gene. *For the Love of Prague*. Prague: Pragma Press, 1997.

Dini, Paul (1997). A view from above: Superman producer Paul Dini talks about comics, animation, and everything in-between. *Diamond's Kid Stuff* (1): 2-3.

Dirda, Michael (1998). A new Homeric Age [review of The Simpsons: A Complete Guide to Our Favorite Family; animation]. *Washington Post Book World* (January 11): 5.

Dixon, Chuck and John Calmette (illus.) (1996). *Batman: The Joker's Apprentice* [childrens' book based on Batman: The animated series]. Boston: Little, Brown.

Doherty, Mike (1998). No nudity or violence, unless it's essential: In Canada, Bob and Margaret's creators struck a deal they could live with [animated TV show]. *National Post* (December 2).

Dorfman, Ariel and Armand Mattelhart. *How to Read Donald Duck: Imperialist Ideology in the Disney Comic*. New York: International General, 1975.

Dowell, Pat (1995). [Merchandising of the new Disney animated film "Pocahontas"]. National Public Radio's Morning Edition (June 23).

Dowell, Pat (1995). [Rediscovery of films by Jiri Zrnka, a famous Czech puppet animator]. National Public Radio's Morning Edition (February 2).

Dowell, Pat (1998). The Making of Prince of Egypt [animated movie]. National Public Radio's Morning Edition (December 18).

Doyle, Audrey (1997). TV special: steve.oedekerk.com [computer animation]. *Digital Magic* (October): 47-8.

Drennan, Danny. (1998). South Park for dummies: The first season [animated TV show]. *Spin* 14 (3; March) 70-72.

Duke, Paul F. (2000). Fox Tooning Out, Closing Phoenix Studio [animation]. *Reuters/Variety* (June 27).

Duke, Paul F. (2000). Twentieth Century Fox Slashing Cartoon Studio Staff [animation]. *Reuters/Variety* (February 14).

Dunning, Jennifer (2000). Tatiana Riabouchinska, 83, ballerina and Disney model [obituary; animation]. *New York Times* (September 3): NE 31.

Ebert, Roger (1999). Guy's a regular Swiss army knife [animation; Inspector Gadget movie]. *Bergen Record* (July 23): Previews 4.

Edera, Bruno. *Full Length Animated Feature Films*. New York: Hastings House, 1977.

Edwards, Bob (1995). [Charles Schulz interview about the Charlie Brown Christmas animated TV show]. National Public Radio's Morning Edition (December 6).

Edwards, Bob (1995). [Disney's computer-animated film "Toy Story"]. National Public Radio's Morning Edition (November 24).

Edwards, Bob (1995). [Obit of Friz Freleng, the Warner Brothers' animator responsible for Bugs Bunny (2:00)] National Public Radio's Morning Edition (May 29).

Edwards, Bob (1996). [interview with animator Chuck Jones about "How the Grinch Stole Christmas" TV show]. National Public Radio's Morning Edition (December 18).

Edwards, Bob (1997). [death of Snow White actress Adriana Caselotti from animated Disney film]. National Public Radio's Morning Edition (January 21).

Edwards, Ellen (1997). Arthur! Arthur [animation]! *Washington Post* (May 7): D1.

Egri, L. The Art of Dramatic Writing. Simon & Schuster: New York, (1949). *Discussion of effective techniques for writing drama, particularly applicable to scripts and playwriting.*

Eisenstein, Sergei. *Eisenstein on Disney* (ed.). Jay Leyda. Trans. Alan Upchurch. London: Methuen, 1988.

Elber, Lynn (1999). *Voice Actor Plays Woody Woodpecker* [animation voice Billy West]. Associated Press (July 7).

Elber, Lynn (2000). 'Simpsons' Character To Die Off [animation]. Associated Press (February 1).

Elber, Lynn (2000). Faith Hubley Gets TV Showcase [pioneer woman animator]. Associated Press (March 16).

Eller, Claudia (1999). Celebrity voice-overs make big noise at box office [animation]. *Los Angeles Times* (December 2).

Emery, Gene (2000). Fun and Games with Racers, Army Men, Flintstones [video game based on Hanna Barbera animation]. *Reuters* (August 30).

Endreson, Lisa (1998). 'South Park' Rules [letter on animated tv show]? *Newsweek* (April 13): 18.

Engelhardt, Tom. 'The Shortcake Strategy.' *Watching Television*. New York: Pantheon, 1986. 68-110.

Erickson, Hal (1998). *Television Cartoons* [animation].

Erickson, Hal. *Television Cartoon Shows: An Illustrated Encyclopedia 1949 through 1993*. Jefferson, NC: McFarland, 1995.

Evans, J.H. (1998). Using multimedia for patient information—a programme about nocturnal enuresis [cartoon and animation used]. *British Journal of Urology 81* (Suppl 3; May): 120-2.

Facinoli, Dave (1999). A nostalgic look back at 'Schoolhouse Rock' [live theater based on animated television shorts]. *Northern Virginia Sun Weekly* (July 15): 14.

Farber, Jim (1998). Cashing in their clips [Pearl Jam music video animation by Todd McFarland]. *Entertainment Weekly* (October 2): 73.

Farhi, Paul (1997). Animation's new battle lines: With 'Anastasia' marketing blitz, 20th Century tries to out-fox Disney. *Washington Post* (Nov 21): G1, G2.

Feeney, F.X. (2000). All the World's a Farm: Chicken Run and other delights from abroad [Aardman Animation movie]. *LA Weekly* (June 23). online at http://www.laweekly.com/ink/00/31/film-feeney.shtml.

Fehr, Stephen C. (1998). Invasion of the money snatchers: Kids under attack by bugs, pigs and other must-have movie tie-ins [animation]. *Washington Post* (November 27): A1, A22-3.

Feiffer, Jules (1998). Robin Williams: An Interview [animation]. *Civilization* (Jun/Jul).

Feild, Robert D. *The Art of Walt Disney*. New York: Macmillan, 1944.

Feiwell, Jill (1999). "Iron Giant" stands tall at cartoon awards [animation]. *Reuters* (November 7).

Ferguson (ed.) *et al. Computer Graphics Career Handbook*. New York: ACM SIGGRAPH, 1991.

Feschuk, Scott (1998). Holy Moses! It delivers: It's DreamWorks' biggest gamble, it's the biggest movie opening ever, and, amazingly, it's a big success [Prince of Eygypt animated movie]. *National Post* (December 18).

Fierman, Daniel (1998). The odyssey of Homer: The Simpsons began its journey 11 years ago [animation]. *Entertainment Weekly* (April 17): 84.

Finch, Christopher and Linda Rosenkrantz (1998). *Sotheby's Guide to Animation Art*. New York: Henry Holt & Company.

Finch, Christopher. *The Art of Walt Disney: From Mickey Mouse to the Magic Kingdom*. 1973. New York: Harry N. Abrams, 1983.

Fisher, James. *The Puppetry Yearbook*. Lewiston, NY: Edwin Mellen Press, 1997.

Fiske, S. and S. Taylor, *Social Cognition*. McGraw-Hill: New York (1991). *Chapter 7 discusses people's desire to use schemas in dealing with one another in order to predict/understand behaviour.*

Flaherty, Mike (2000). Girl power: Tiny heroines the Powerpuff Girls are taking a big bite out of crime—and toy sales [animation]. *Entertainment Weekly* (545; June 16): 23.

Flamini, Roland (1976). Television and the Magoo factor [testing TV pilots against old animated show]. *American Film* (May): 50-53.

Flatow, Ira (1997). Science Is Fun [Tom Snyder, co-creator, executive producer, and writer "Dr. Katz: Professional Therapist" animated TV show]. National Public Radio's Talk of the Nation (September 12).

Fleming, Michael (2000). Vintage flicks to return as cartoons [RKO Pictures animation]. *Reuters/Variety* (August 25).

Fleming, Michael, (1997). Fox 'Toons in to New Sci-fi Film [animated feature "Planet Ice"]. *New York Post* (November 26).

Flint, Joe (1999) 'Tisn't the season [PJ's animated series] *Entertainment Weekly* (June 11): 51.

Flint, Joe (1999). Just the facts [Family Guy animated TV show used a real person's name]. *Entertainment Weekly* (July 9): 53.

Flynn, Gillian (1999). Cosmic thing [illustrated by animator David Sheldon]. *Entertainment Weekly* (August 13): 84.

Frierson, Michael. *Clay Animation: American Highlights 1908 to the Present*. New York: Twayne, 1994.

Fries, Laura (1999). "Mission Hill" funniest new show of season [animated television show]. *Variety* (September 19).

Frum, David (1996). [review of Disney's animated movie 'The Hunchback of Notre Dame']. National Public Radio's Morning Edition (June 19).

Fung, Shirliey (1998). Aye, there's the sub [Beatles' 1968 animated movie Yellow Submarine rerelease and merchandising]. *Entertainment Weekly* (November 20): 22.

Furniss, Maureen. *Art in Motion: Animation Aesthetics*. Sidney: John Libbey, 1998.

————, *The Current State of American Independent Animation and a Prediction for its Future*. Master of Arts thesis, San Diego State University, 1987. V. Garcia, Roger, ed. Frank Tashlin: A Retrospective. Locarno: Locarno Film Festival, 1994.

Furusho, J. *et al.* (1998). Patient background of the Pokemon phenomenon: questionnaire studies in multiple pediatric clinics [Japanese animation]. *Acta Paediatrica Japonica* 40 (6; December): 550-4.

Gardner, Elysa (2000). Roll over, Beethoven: Breaking out of their traditional modes, artists chisel out new passions from classical music to theater to film scores [animation]. *USA Today* (August 25): 1-2E.

Gavin, William F. (1998). Tweety talks tough [Warner Brothers animated character's marketing]. *Washington Post* (August 30): C7.

Gehr, Richard (1999). Darkside Toons [Cartoon Noir" animation movie]. *Village Voice* (December 1). online at http://www.villagevoice.com/issues/9948/gehr.shtml

Gehr, Richard (1999). Turn on, toon in, watch out; Richard Gehr looks at the Cartoon Network and wonders, what about the children? [animation]. *Feed* (December 2): http://www.feedmag.com/essay/es273_master.html

Germain, David (1999). *Pixar Hopes for Third Straight Hit* [computer animation]. Associated Press (November 22).

Germain, David (2000). *Study: G-Rated [animated] Films are Violent*. Associated Press (May 24).

Giammarco, David (1999). Changing his 'toon: Filmmaker Katzenberg takes animation to a new level. *National Post* (January 16).

Gibbs, Hope Katz (1998). Rugrats Adventure Game [review of videogame based on animated TV show]. *Washington Post* (November 20): Weekend 82.

Gifford, Denis (1987). *British Animated Films, 1895-1985: A Filmography*. McFarland and Company.

Gifford, Denis. *American Animated Films: The Silent Era*. Jefferson, NC: McFarland, 1990.

————. *British Animated Films 1895-1985*. Jefferson, NC: McFarland.

Gitlin, Tod and Tom Engelhardt (ed.). *Watching Television*. New York: Pantheon, 1986.

Gleiberman, Owen (1998). Scoring dopes [South Park TV show animators Trey Parker and Matt Stone]. *Entertainment Weekly* (August 7): 47-8.

Gleiberman, Owen (1998). The Red Sea diaries [The Prince of Egypt animated movie]. *Entertainment Weekly* (December 18): 50.

Gleiberman, Owen (1999). Aye, robot; The story of a boy and his heavy metal friend, The Iron Giant animates a luminous retro fairy tale. *Entertainment Weekly* (August 13): 50.

Gleiberman, Owen (1999). Device squad: Matthew Broderick overextends himself as a gizmo-sprouting cop in the gimmicky Inspector Gadget [animation]. *Entertainment Weekly* (July 30): 46.

Gleiberman, Owen (1999). My little monsters [Pokemon animated movie]. *Entertainment Weekly* (November 19): 106.

Gleiberman, Owen (1999). Quicktakes: Doug's 1st Movie [animation review]. *Entertainment Weekly* (April 2).

Gloeckner, Phoebe (1989). Comic books: a medium deserving another look. Etc. 46(Fall): 246-7.

Golden, Christie (1998). *Invasion America* [animated miniseries novelization]. New York: Roc.

Golden, Christopher (1998). *Invasion America: On the Run* [novel based on animated TV series]. New York: Roc.

Goldfarb, Michael (1996). [English animators the Brothers Quay interview]. National Public Radio's Morning Edition (April 2).

Goldstein, Adam O., Rachel A. Sobel and Glen R. Newman (1999). Tobacco and alcohol use in G-rated children's animated films. *Journal of the American Medical Association* 281 (12; March 24): 1131-1136.

Grandinetti, Fred M. *Popeye: An Illustrated History of E.C. Segar's Character in Print, Radio, Television and Film Appearances, 1929-1993*. Jefferson, NC: McFarland, 1994.

Grandmont, Charles (2000). Troubled Canadian producer drops another bombshell [Canadian animation company]. *Reuters* (March 12).

Grant, J. (1998). *Encyclopedia of Walt Disney's Animated Characters*. New York: Hyperion.

Graser, Marc (1999). Pixar set to abet 'toon boom [computer animation]. *Variety/Reuters* (December 22).

Graser, Marc (2000). Burton Toons Up Web Pact [Director Tim Burton to create a series of animated short films based on his character Stainboy]. *Reuters/Variety* (January 28).

Graser, Marc (2000). Lucas' effects house 'toons up its plans [Industrial Light & Magic and animation]. *Reuters/Variety* (June 13).

Green, Howard E. (1999). *The Tarzan Chronicles* [Disney animated film history]. Hyperion.

Green, Joyce and Deborah Reber (ed.). *Drawing Insight: Communicating Development through Animation*. Penang: Southbound, 1996.

Greppi, Michele (1998). 'Eric' Feeble? You Bet He Is! ['Stressed Eric' British Animated Television Show]. *New York Post* (August 12).

Greppi, Michele (1998). 'June Bugs': Cartoon Network's Hare-Raising Marathon [Animated Television Show]. *New York Post* (June 19).

Greppi, Michele (1998). Prime-Time 'Katz' and Dogs ['Bob and Margaret' animated television show]. *New York Post* (June 22).

Greppi, Michele (1999). 'Dilbert:' He's Not Great (Even Nude) [animated television show]. *New York Post* (January 25).

Grice, Bonnie (1998). ['Dancing Baby' computer animation interview]. National Public Radio's Anthem (January 31).

Griffin, George. *Frames: A Selection of Drawings and Statements by Independent American Animators*. New York: George Griffin, 1978.

Griffin, Nancy (1998). TV land: How Bart and Homer Simpson almost lost their voices [animation]. *New Yorker* (April 20): 46-7.

Groening, Matt (1993). *Matt Groening's Cartooning with the Simpsons [animation]*. New York: Harperperennial.

Groer, Annie (1999). Tarzan's desk-top cast of characters [Disney animated movie merchandise]. *Washington Post* (July 1): Home 5, 8.

Gropper, M., Z. Liraz, D. Portowicz and M. Schindler (1995). Computer integrated drug prevention: a new approach to teach lower socioeconomic 5th and 6th grade Israeli children to say no to drugs [using computer animation]. *Social Work in Health Care* 22 (2): 87-103.

Gross, John (1986). Books of the Times [Review of Talking Animals and Other People by animator Shamus Culhane]. *New York Times* (April 29).

Grove, Lloyd (2000). The reliable source [Al Gore on 'Futurama' animated TV show]. *Washington Post* (May 16): C3.

Grove, Lloyd (2000). The reliable source [Kristin Gore writing on 'Futurama' animated TV show]. *Washington Post* (May 17): C3.

Gutfeld, Greg (1999). Monster rally [children's animation]. *TV Guide* (October 30).

Guthmann, Edward (1995). Frank and Ollie: Walt Disney's Soul-Mate Animators. *San Francisco Chronicle* (Apr 21).

Halas, J. (1947). Animated film. *Art and Industry* 43 (Jul-Aug): 2.

Halas, John and Roger Manvell (1959). *The Technique of Film Animation.* New York: Communication Arts Books.

Halas, John. *Masters of Animation*. Topsfield, MA: Salem House, 1987.

Hall, Wayne V. (1997). Lovely Anastasia welcome threat to Disney hegemony [animation]. *Pentagram* [Military Division of Washington] (Nov 28): 26.

Haller, Robert (ed.). *First Light*. New York: Anthology Film Archives, 1998.

————. *Intersecting Images: The Cinema of Ed Emshwiller* (New York: Anthology Film Archives, 1997).

Hames, Peter (ed.). *Dark Alchemy: The Films of Jan Svankmajer*. Westport, CT: Praeger, 1995.

Hamilton, Kendall (1998). On MTV, a star is slain [Celebrity Deathmatch clay animation TV show; caricature]. *Newsweek* (November 23): 63.

Hamilton, Kendall (1999). Another day, another indignity: Dilbert hits prime time—and gets the job done [animated TV series]. *Newsweek* (January 25): 62.

Hamilton, M.C. (1998). 'South Park' Rules [letter on animated TV show]? *Newsweek* (April 13): 18.

Hamilton, Martha M. (1998). Mobil pumps life into its flying red horse [computer animation for advertising]. *Washington Post* (September 15): C1, C4.

Hanna, Bill and Tom Ito. *A Cast of Friends*. Dallas, TX: Taylor, 1996.

Hanna, Junko (2000). Japan pays tribute to its animation heritage [museum exhibit]. *The Daily Yomiuri* (July 27): 7.

Hansen, Liane (1995). Beau Hunks Play Raymond Scott [animation soundtrack music]. National Public Radio's Weekend Edition Sunday (August 27).

Hardy, Ernest (1999). Animating the Century; Princess Mononoke taps the Zeitgeist [anime]. *LA Weekly* (October 29). online at http://www.laweekly.com/ink/99/49/film-hardy.shtml

Hargreaves, Darron (2000). You've come a long way, Baby [development of animation and anime]. *Daily Yomiuri* (July 27): 7.

Havranek, Carrie (2000). Ay Caramba! ["Go Simpsonic with the Simpsons" animated TV show music]. *Village Voice* (December 29). online at http://www.villagevoice.com/issues/9952/havranek.shtml.

Hearn, Michael Patrick (1975). The Animated Art of Winsor. *McClay American Artist* 39(394): 28.

Helber, Annabelle Massey (1999). Quick, draw: After years of talking and hoping, DNA Productions finally inks a big-time deal [animated Christmas special "Olive, the Other Reindeer"]. *Dallas Observer* (December 16). online at http://www.dallasobserver.com/issues/1999-12-16/sketches.html

Heller, RB, AR Dobbs and BG Rule (1992). Communicative function in patients with questionable Alzheimer's disease [using silent animation]. Psychology and Aging 7 (3; Sep): 395-400.

Henkin, Stephen (1998). Universal appeal: Orlando theme park plays nostalgia card [Marvel Comics, animation characters]. The World & I 13(3, March): 86-93.

Heraldson, Donald (1975). *Creators of Life: A History of Animation*. New York: Drake Publishers.

Herskovitz, Jon (2000). Japanese videogamers look beyond Pokemon [animation]. *Reuters/ Variety* (January 2).

Hettrick, Scott (2000). Movie franchises mine video gold [direct to video animation]. *Reuters/ Variety* (June 23).

Hettrick, Scott, (2000). Straight-to-vid cartoon Buzz-ing to No. 1 [Disney's animated "Buzz Lightyear of the Star Command: The Adventure Begins"]. *Reuters/Variety* (August 17).

Hill, Michael (1991). The Silly Symphony: Animism and anthropomorphism in animation land. Humanities Postgraduate Conference, UTS, Sydney.

Hochman, David (1998). Epics and insects [animated movies The Prince of Eypt and A Bug's Life]. *Entertainment Weekly* (November 20): 62-8.

Hochman, David (1998). Reel World: Foley tracks [Disney's A Bug's Life animated movie toys]. *Entertainment Weekly* (December 4): 62.

Hochman, David (1999). Putting the 'R' in 'Park' [rating South Park animated movie]. *Entertainment Weekly* (July 9): 15-16.

Hoffer, Thomas W. *Animation: A Reference Guide.* Westport, CT: Greenwood, 1981.

Hofman, Mike (1999). It's my potty [on-line scatalogical computer animation]. *Entertainment Weekly* (April 23): 69.

Holden, Stephen (2000). May a slightly different force be with you ["Titan A.E." animated movie by Don Bluth]. *New York Times* (June 16): B12.

Holman, Bruce. *Puppet Animation the Cinema: History and Technique.* South Brunswick, NJ: A.S. Barnes, 1975.

Hontz, Jenny (1998). Animated Dilbert coming on UPN. *Washington Post* (Feb 12): E6.

Hopps, Jason (2000). Britain Animated About 'Chicken Run' But No Sequel. *Reuters* (July 4).

Horn, John (1998). Do dreams come true [DreamWorks animation including Prince of Egypt movie]? *Premiere* (December): 106-114.

Hornaday, Ann (1998). A charming view of Chinese myth; Review: 'Mulan' is fun to watch. Disney does it again [animation]. *Baltimore Sun* (June 19).

Horovitz, Bruce (1998). McDonald's going after the small fry [by selling animated Ronald McDonald videos]. *USA Today* (October 8): 3B.

Horton, A. Writing the character-centered screenplay. University of California Press: Berkeley, CA (1994). *Process and recommendations for developing strong characters, then building a narrative around them. Draws examples from contemporary film.*

Horwitz, Jane (2000). 'Blue's Clues': Nice Doggy! Touring Show Brings Preschool TV Hit to Life [theater based on animated TV show]. *Washington Post* (March 7): C1.

Horwitz, Jane (2000). 'Blue's Clues': Nice Doggy!: Touring Show Brings Preschool TV Hit to Life [theater show based on animated tv series]. *Washington Post* (March 7): C1.

Horwitz, Jane (2000). Filmfest for the younger set [animation]. *Washington Post Weekend* (April 7).

Howard, R.J. *et al.* (1995). Activation of area V5 by visual perception of motion demonstrated with echoplanar MR imaging [by viewing animation]. *Magnetic Resonance Imaging* 13 (6): 907-9.

Howe, Desson (1996). Leave It to 'Beavis' ["Beavis and Butt-head Do America" animated movie]. *Washington Post* (December 20): Weekend 44.

Huard, R. and B. Hayes-Roth. "Character mastery with improvisational puppets," in Notes of the IJCAI '97 Workshop on Animated Interface Agents, Nagoya, Japan, Aug (1997), pp. 85-90. *Experimental study of children's play with three kinds of toys: commercial art software, traditional puppets, and improvisational puppets that have animate minds and animated bodies. Results show that children enjoy all three kinds of toys, but only play with improvisational improves their master of characters and their performance on associated measures of social understanding, story comprehension, and storycrafting.*

Hubley, John and Zachary Schwartz. "Animation Learns a New Language." *Hollywood Quarterly* 1 (1945-1946): 360-63.

Huhn, Mary (1998). 'South Park' creators want fans to spurn Spin [animation]. *New York Post* (February 13).

Hulett, Ralph (1955). Artist's part in the production of an animated cartoon. *American Artist* 19(May): 33.

Hull, Dana (1997). Bye-bye, 'B&B' [Beavis and Butthead animation]. *Washington Post* (Aug 2): A17.

Hunter, Stephen (1997). 'Anastasia:' A magical ride unfettered by facts [animation]. *Washington Post* (Nov 21): C1, C6.

Igliori, Paola (ed.). *American Magus: Harry Smith, A Modern Alchemist*. New York: Inanout, 1996.

Inge, M. Thomas. *Perspectives on American Culture: Essays on Humor, Literature, and the Popular Arts.* West Cornwall, CT: Locust Hill, 1994.

Ingerto, Craig (1989). [Letter; Teenage Ninja Mutant Turtles; animation]. *Comics Scene* (7): 43.

Isbister, K. "Personality in Interactive Computer Characters: The Importance of Consistency," unpublished manuscript. *Reports evidence that people prefer consistent personality traits to inconsistent personality traits, even when the consistent value is not preferred. Consistency refers to similarity of passive/dominant mode in verbal and physical behaviours.*

Isbister, K. and B. Hayes-Roth. Social Interaction with Characters. Submitted to J. of Applied AI, Special Issue on Animated Interface Agents, (1998). *Analysis of transcripts from web site visitors interacting with an animate character, Erin the Bartender. Results indicate that a character's role-appropriate behaviour can induce role-appropriate behaviour in users.*

Isherwood, Charles (2000). "Lobster" loses taste [play about Disney animators and Salvador Dali]. *Reuters/Variety* (January 10).

Ishida, S. *et al.* (1998). Photosensitive seizures provoked while viewing "Pocket Monsters," a made-for-television animation programme in Japan. *Epilepsia* 39 (12; December): 1340-4.

Jackson, David (1998). A sound track to success: Ex-Devo member scores a cartoon hit [music for Rug Rats animated TV show]. *Washington Post* (April 18): B1-2.

Jackson, Kathy Merlock. *Walt Disney: A Bio-Bibliography.* Westport, CT: Greenwood, 1993.

Jacobs, A. J (1998). Gross, point blank [South Park animated TV show]. *Entertainment Weekly* (Jan 23): 32-34.

James, Caryn (1999). 'Dilbert': Made for People Who Hate Their Jobs [animated TV series]. *New York Times* (January 25).

James, David. *Allegories of Cinema: American Film in the Sixties*. Princeton: Princeton University Press, 1989.

Jensen, Paul M. *The Men Who Made the Monsters*. New York: Twayne, 1996.

Johnson, L. and B. Hayes-Roth (Eds.) Proc. 1st Int. Conf. on Autonomous Agents, Marina del Rey, CA, Feb (1997). *Broad survey of current work on autonomous agents, but several sessions focus specifically on believable agents and actors. Good general view of current work.*

Johnston, Ollie and Frank Thomas (1993). *The Disney Villain* [animation]. New York; Hyperion.

Johnstone, K. IMPRO: Improvisation and the Theater. Routledge: New York, (1992). *Describes issues and methods in improvisational theater. Presents clear theory for modeling certain improvisational interactions. Excellent background reading for issues in character interaction.*

Jones, C. Chuck Amuck: The Life and Times of an Animated Cartoonist. Avon Books: New York, (1990). *Biography of author of Road Runner cartoons et al. Survey and anecdotes of character design, early problems and evolved solutions in creating believable animated characters. Widely cited artistic reference.*

Jones, Chuck. Chuck Amuck-*The Life and Times of an Animated Cartoonist.* New York: Farrar-Straus-Giroux, 1989.

Jones, Steve (1998). 'Chef Aid' CD puts Hayes back on front burner [South Park animated TV show]. *USA Today* (November 24): 5D.

Jurkowski, Henryk. *A History of European Puppetry from its Origins to the End of the 19th Century.* Lewiston, NY: Edwin Mellen Press, 1996.

————, *A History of European Puppetry* Volume Two: The Twentieth Century. Lewiston, NY: Edwin Mellen Press, 1998.

Kakutani, Michiko (1997). Behind the Mouse, a Subtle Huckster [Review of The Magic Kingdom: Walt Disney and the American Way of Life by Steven Watts; animation] *New York Times* (December 26).

Kaltenbach, Chris (1998). 'Rugrats Movie' adds little to the television cartoons [animation]. *Baltimore Sun* (November 20).

Kaltenbach, Chris (2000). Cartoon 'Titan' is small in every way; Review: Animated sci-fi adventure is all mayhem and very little else. *Baltimore Sun* (June 16).

Kaltenbach, Chris (2000). What's up, doc? Classic 'toons, that's what; Television: Warner Bros. shows off the early history of some much-loved cartoon characters [animation]. *Baltimore Sun* (June 10).

Kane, Courtney (2000). Advertising: M&M/Mars conclues, after 46 years, that 'Plain' does not do justice to the original M&M's candy [cartoon mascots/animation]. *New York Times* (June 29): C8.

Kane, Evelyn. *The ACT Guide to Children's Television*. Boston: Beacon Press, 1979.

Kanfer, Stefan (1997). Serious Business: *The Art and Commerce of Animation in America from Betty Boop to Toy Story*. New York: Scribner.

Kannenberg, Gene Jr. (1999). Proving "Silas" was an artist: Winsor McCay's formal experiments in comics and animation. *International Journal of Comic* Art 1 (1; Spring/Summer): 57-75.

Kaplan, David A. and Adam Rogers (1999). It's a Pokemon planet [Japanese animation]. *Newsweek* (March 1): 48.

Kaplan, James, Jason Cohen and Moira McCormick. Top ten new Kid's shows [animation]. *TV Guide* (October 30): 17-26.

Karger, Dave (1998). 'Toon time [Tom & Jerry; animation]. *Entertainment Weekly* (April 3): 17.

Kelly, Kevin (1999). One-Eyed Aliens! Suicide Booths! Mom's Old-Fashioned Robot Oil! [Matt Groening's "Futurama" animated television show]. Wired 7(2; February).

Kelso, M. T., P. Weyhrauch, and J. Bates, "Dramatic Presence," PRESENCE: *The Journal of Teleoperators and Virtual Environments,* Vol. 1(1), pp. 133-138, 1992. *Preliminary paper on the Oz project. Introduces concept of "interactive drama," theory of plot construction, principles of interactive story design. Describes real-world tests measuring engagement in acted stories with limited sophistication, including transcripts and commentary. Best paper motivating principles of the Oz project.*

Kempley, Rita (2000). 'Chicken Run': Welcome to the fryers club [animation]. *Washington Post* (June 23): C1, 12.

Kempley, Rita (2000). 'Rocky and Bullwinkle': Moosterpiece theater [animated movie]. *Washington Post* (June 30): C1, 12.

Kempley, Rita (2000). The wonderful thing about 'Tigger' [Disney animated movie]. *Washington Post* (February 12): C1, 5.

Kennedy, Joseph and John Canemaker (1998). *Lucy Goes to the Country* [gay-themed children's book by animation historian]. Alyson Wonderland.

Kenny, Glenn (1999). "She's available for interviews.": Man's quest for the perfect woman gets down and digitized as cybermodels strut their stuff [computer animation]. *Details* (October): 164-169.

Kepel, Bruce (1986). Cadence selling comic book, animation unit; New World Pictures to acquire Marvel. *Los Angeles Times* (November 21): 4-2.

Kilday, Greg (1999). Trial and error [Katzenberg *vs.* Disney over animation profits]. *Premiere* (September): 47-51.

Kilmer, David (1999). *The Animated Film Collector's Guide: Worldwide Sources for Cartoons on Videotape and Laserdisc.* John Libbey & Co. Ltd.

Kilmer, David. *The Animated Film Collector's Guide: Worldwide Sources for Cartoons on Videotape and Laserdisc.* Sidney: John Libbey, 1997.

Kimura, Jennifer (2000). *Clay Animation Studio Teaches* Art [Brad Schiff, lead animator for Portland's Will Vinton Studios makes Claymation]. Associated Press (May 9).

Kinder, Marsha. *Playing with Power in Movies, Television, and Video Games: From Muppet Babies to Teenage Mutant Ninja Turtles.* Berkeley, CA: U California P, 1991.

Kitano, H. (ed.). Notes of the (1996) AAAI Workshop on Entertainment and AI/A-Life, Portland, OR, Aug. 1996. *Range of papers on entertainment issues not limited to agents; include theater, pedagogy, logical formalisms for believability, environments to support characters, social aspects of AI. Some unusual points of view.*

Kitman, Marvin (1999). Taking a look into our 'Futurama' [Groening animated TV show]. *CNN Interactive* (April 7): http://cnn.com/SHOWBIZ/TV/9904/07/marvin.kitman.lat/

Klein, Andy (1999). Bigger, longer, and almost as funny: South Park parents battle the hideous threat of potty-mouth [animated movie]. *Dallas Observer* (July 1). online at http://www.dallasobserver.com/issues/1999-07-01/film2.html

Klein, Jeff Z. (2000). A new neighbourhood for the black sitcom ["The P.J.'s" animated TV show]. *New York Times* (August 27): AR 21, 28.

Klein, Joshua (2000). Faith Hubley: The veteran animator talks to the Onion A.V. Club about technology, funding, children, art and her new piece Witch Madness [interview]. The Onion A.V. Club: http://avclub.theonion.com/avclub3610/avfeature_3610.html

Koehler, Robert (2000). "Alien Adventure" underwhelms [Belgian animator Ben Stassen]. *Reuters/Variety* (August 25).

Koehler, Robert (2000). "Pokemon" sequel better than original [Pokemon 2000 the Movie: The Power of One (Poketto Monsutaa: Maboroshi No Pokemon X: Lugia Bakudan) animated Japanese movie]. *Reuters/Variety* (July 21).

Koehler, Robert (2000). "Titan A.E." terrific [animation]. *Reuters/Variety* (June 11).

Korkis, Jim (2000). Everything old is new again [computer animation and Pixar]. Hogan's Alley (7; Winter): 19-21.

Kornblum, Janet (2000). Kelsey Grammer gives metamorphosis a trial ["Gary the Rat" animated internet show]. *USA Today* (August 22): 3D.

Kuchwara, Michael (2000). 'Lobster Alice' a Confusing Tale [play about Disney animators and Salvador Dali]. Associated Press (January 9).

Kurtti, Jeff. *A Bug's Life: The Art and Making of an Epic of Miniature Proportion.* New York: Hyperion, 1998.

Kushner, David (1998). Play that 'toon [computer animation]. *Entertainment Weekly* (September 25): 117.

Kuttna, Mari. *Hungarian Animation: A Survey of the Work of the Pannonia Studio,* Budapest. Budapest: Hungarofilm, CA. 1970.

Lane, Anthony (2000). High times: A lady's flight of fancy, and "Fantasia 2000." [Disney animated movie review]. *New Yorker* (January 17): 86-87.

Laris, Michael (1999). Mickey gets China's ear; Beijing lifts its ban on Disney films [animation]. *Washington Post* (February 8): A1, 12.

Laski, Beth (2000). Fox Animation Studios in Phoenix draws to a close. *The Hollywood Reporter* (June 27).

Lasseter, J. "Principles of traditional animation applied to 3D animation," in Proc. SIGGRAPH '87, Anaheim, FL, July (1987), pp. 35-44. *Summary of Disney animation principles and explanation of how they apply to computationally generated 3D believable characters. Examples and images drawn from "Luxo Jr." short film et al. Excellent bridge between traditional and computational character animation.*

Lasswell, Mark (1999). 'Family' feud ['Family Guy' animated TV show]. *TV Guide* (August 7): 30-31, 34.

Laurel, B. "Interface Agents: Metaphors with Character," in The Art of Human-Computer Interaction Design, B. Laurel (ed.). Addison-Wesley: Reading, MA, 1990. *Presents key characteristics of interface agents. Examines arguments pro and con; emphasis on anthropomorphism, dramatic character of agents. Considers motivations for building such agents.*

Laurel, B. Computers as Theatre. Addison-Wesley: Reading, MA, 1993. *Explores metaphor of computer as theatrical device. Computational context for engagement, drama, story. Widely cited support for interactive agents in computing.*

Laybourne, Kit (1999). *The Animation Book: A Complete Guide to Animated Filmmaking from Flip-Books to Sound Cartoons to 3-D Animation.* Three Rivers Press.

Laybourne, Kit. *The Animation Book*. New York: Crown, 1979.

Le Grice, Malcolm. *Abstract Film and Beyond*. Cambridge, MA: MIT, 1977.

Lee, Will (1999). Mouse droppings [recall of The Rescuers animated movie] *Entertainment Weekly* (January 22-29): 9.

Leibman, James (1998). 'South Park' Rules [letter on animated TV show]? *Newsweek* (April 13): 18.

Leiby, Richard (2000). Cartoons That Make Guys Click: Web Entertainment Sites Use Animation to Draw a Crowd. *Washington Post* (February 17): C1.

Lenatti, Chuck (1998). King of the "Antz" [computer animated movie]. *Upside Magazine* (October): http://www.upside.com/Magazine/

Lenburg, Jeff (1983). *The Great Cartoon Directors* [animation]. London: McFarland.

———. *The Encyclopedia of Animated Cartoons*. New York: Facts on File, 1991.

Lent, John, Comp. *Caricature and Gag and Political Cartoons in the U.S. and Canada.* Westport, CT: Greenwood, 1994.

Levi, Antonia (1996). *Samurai from Outer Space: Understanding Japanese Animation.* Open Court Publishing Company.

Levi, Antonia. *Samurai from outer Space: Understanding Japanese Animation.* Chicago: Open Court, 1996.

Levy, Shawn (2000). Tarzan [Disney animated movie review]. *Pulse!* (February): 37.

Leydon, Joe (1999). "Bartok the Magnificent" true to its name [Animated direct-to-video movie prequel to 'Anastasia']. *Reuters* (November 28).

Leydon, Joe (2000). "Flintstones" prequel hits rock bottom ["The Flintstones in Viva Rock Vegas" based on Hanna Barbera animated TV series]. *Reuters/Variety* (April 27).

Leydon, Joe (2000). Misadventures with "Rocky & Bullwinkle" [movie based on Jay Ward's animation]. *Reuters/Variety* (June 30).

Lickteig, Mary Ann (2000). *New 'Peanuts' Shows in Production* [animation]. Associated Press (March 1).

Lim, Dennis (2000). Auto Ban ["Titan A.E." animation]. *Village Voice* (June 14). online at http://www.villagevoice.com/issues/0024/lim.shtml

Limpert, Ann (2000). Muffin to it [Miss Muffy and the Muff Mob" internet animation]. *Entertainment Weekly* (545; June 16): 95.

Littleton, Cynthia (2000). Buzz Lightyear lands on ABC's Saturday sked [Disney animated TV series]. *The Hollywood Reporter* (July 6).

Lloyd, Robert (1998). Forward Into the Past: The terrifying togs of That '70s Show; the retro robots of Rolie Polie Olie [computer-animated series by William Joyce produced for the Disney Channel by Canada's Nelvana Ltd. in concert with France's Metal Hurlant]. *LA Weekly* (October 2). online at http://www.laweekly.com/ink/98/45/tv-lloyd.shtml

Lloyd, Robert (1999). Hoops, Hogs and High Speeds ["The Three Little Pigs," in HBO's animated series Happily Ever After: Fairy Tales for Every Child]. *LA Weekly* (June 25). online at http://www.laweekly.com/ink/99/31/TV-lloyd.shtml

Lloyd, Robert (2000). God, the Devil and NBC: One show cancelled, one show begun ['God, the Devil and Bob' animated TV series]. *LA Weekly* (March 31). online at http://www.laweekly.com/ink/00/19/tv-lloyd.shtml

Lobdell, Scott (1989). Why no Elfquest [television cartoon animation]? *Comics Scene* (8): 68.

Lofficier, Jean-Marc and Randy Lofficier (2000). *French Science Fiction, Fantasy, Horror & Pulp Fiction: A Guide to Cinema, Television, Radio, Animation, Comic Books & Literature from the Middle Ages to the Present.* McFarland.

Logan, Michael (1999). Betty Lou Gerson tribute [obituary for actress from Disney's animated movie "101 Dalmations"]. *TV Guide* (April 3): 4.

Long, Chris (1996). Hot list: Cartoons and animation [cartoon and comics websites online]. *Online Access* 11(7; Jul 1): 77-80.

Lord, Peter and Brian Sibley. *Creating 3D Animation: The Aardman Book of Filmmaking.* New York: Harry Abrams, 1998.

Los Angeles Daily News (2000). Hot 'Powerpuffs' Born in School [animation]. *Arizona Republic* (March 29).

Lotman, Jeff & Jonathan Smith (1995). *Animation Art: The Early Years 1911-1953.* Schiffer Publishing Ltd.

Lotman, Jeff & Jonathan Smith (1995). *Animation Art: The Later Years 1954-1993.* Schiffer Publishing Ltd.

Lotman, Jeff (1998). *Animation Art at Auction: Since 1994.* Schiffer Publishing Ltd.

Lotman, Jeff. *Animation Art: The Early Years, 1911-1953.* Atglen, PA: Schiffer, 1996.

Lotman, Jeff. *Animation Art: The Later Years 1954-1993.* Atglen, PA: Schiffer, 1996.

Lutz, Edwin G. *Animated Cartoons: How They are Made, Their Origin and Development.* 1920. Bedford, MA: Applewood, 1998.

Mack, Bob (1997). Hot buttered soul man [Isaac Hayes on South Park animated TV show]. *Details* (November): 91-2.

MacLachan, Suzanne L. (1993). Economy: Cartoon characters animate check sales. *Christian Science Monitor* 85(185; Aug 19): 9.

Maddox, Garry (1999). Animators give world a taste of our pudding [Norman Lindsay's children's classic "The Magic Pudding" into an Australian animated feature film]. *Sydney Morning Herald* (October 30).

Maestri, George (1998). Animation workshop: Building skeletons. *Digital Magic* (Feb): 34-35.

Maggio, Joe (1997). Mean Spirit [Space Ghose animation revival]. *Icon* (Dec): 114-115, 122.

Majendie, Paul (1999). UK Plasticine Manin Giant Hollywood Film Deal [Wallace and Gromit animator Nick Park]. *Reuters* (October 30).

Malcolm, Shawna (1999). Futurama [Matt Groening's animated TV series]. *Entertainment Weekly* (January 22-29): 30.

Malkin, Mark S. (1999). 'Inspector Gadget' searches for a clue [movie based on animated TV series]. *Premiere* (March): 35-6.

Mallory, Michael (1999). *Hanna-barbera Cartoons* [animation]. Hugh Lauter Levin Associates.

Maltin, Leonard (1981). Making drawings move [Review of Disney Animation: The Illusion of Life by Frank Thomas and Ollie Johnston *New York Times* (November 29).

Maltin, Leonard (1987). *Of Mice and Magic: A History of American Animated Cartoons*. Rev. edition New York: New American Library.

Maltin, Leonard. *The Disney Films*. New York: Hyperion, 1995.

————. *Of Mice and Magic: A History of American Animated Cartoons*. 1980. New York: Plume, 1987.

Manvell, Roger. *Art and Animation: The Story of Halas and Batchelor Animation Studio, 1940-1980*. New York: Hastings House, 1980.

Marden, Keith (1994). 'Far Side' fans facing suspended animation. *Albany Times Union* (Oct. 4): A1.

Marin, Rick (1998). The rude tube [South Park animated TV show]. *Newsweek* (March 23): 56-62.

Marling, Karal A. (1995). Norman Klein's Seven Minutes: The Life and Death of the American Animated Cartoon [review]. *American Historical Review* 100(1; Feb): 225.

Marlowe, Chris (2000). Backstreet Boys' cyber egos ready to rock [Stan Lee Media animated internet show]. *The Hollywood Reporter* (August 22).

Marlowe, Chris (2000). Grammer takes the Internet bait with 'Rat' series ["Gary the Rat" animated internet show]. *The Hollywood Reporter* (August 22).

Masers, Brooke A. (1998). Character's creator sues party company [animated TV character Arthur]. *Washington Post* (August 8): B3.

Maslin, Janet (1998). 'Prince of Egypt': Fairy Tale? Musical Comedy? Nope, Biblical Epic [animated movie review]. *New York Times* (December 18).

Matthews, Charles (1999). Celluloid dreams [review of Barrier's Hollywood Cartoons: American Animation in its Golden Age]. *Washington Post Book World* (April 11): 3.

Matthews, Karen (1999). *Kids' TV Show Getting Theatrical* ["Blue's Clues" animated television show]. Associated Press (November 8).

Mauldin, M. "ChatterBots, TinyMUDs, and the Turing test: Entering the Loebner prize competition," in Proc. 12th Natl. Conf. on Artif. Intell., Seattle, WA, July 1994, pp. 16-21. *Description of ChatterBot "Julia," a MUD agent capable of limited conversation. Details conversational model and response design. Analysis of interaction in a limited Turing test, with comparisons to ELIZA and PARRY. Provides useful insights into heuristics for conversational believability.*

Mazzeo, Henry (1987). Whatever happened to Prince Buckethead? [animation]. Snow White and the Seven Dwarfs Golden Anniversary (1; Fall): 11-12.

McCall, Douglas L. *Film Cartoons: A Guide to 20th-Century American Animated Features and Shorts*. Jefferson, NC: McFarland, 1998.

McLaren, Norman. *The Drawings of Norman McLaren*. Montreal: Tundra Books, 1975.

McWilliams, Donald, Comp. and ed. Norman McLaren on the Creative Process. Ottawa: National Film Board of Canada, 1991.

Melnbardis, Robert (2000). Cinar's founding couple defiant after firing [Canadian animation firm]. *Reuters* (August 18).

Merritt, Russell and J.B. Kaufman. *Walt in Wonderland: The Silent Films of Walt Disney.* Pordenone: Le Giornate del Cinema Muto/La Cineteca del Friuli, 1993.

Michaud, Christopher (1999). Blood Flows, But Beautifully, in [Tim] Burton's World [Disney animation work]. *Reuters* (November 17).

Miller, Bob (1989). The lure of 'Laputa' [Japanese animation movie]. *Comics Scene* (7): 69.

Miller, Jeff (1996). Re-reading Steve Canyon, Part I. International Comics and Animation Festival.

Miller, Jeff (1997). A Barthesian reading of Frank Miller's Sin City. National Communication Association.

Milvy, Erika (2000). 'Toon talk show with a twist; 'The God & Devil Show' puts guests on the hot seat [animated internet show]. *Access Magazine* (Jan. 9-Jan. 15).

Mohr, Ian (2000). Linklater 'Life' animates cast. *The Hollywood Reporter* (July 7).

Mondello, Bob (1998). 'Mulan' Storms China, Box Office [Disney animated film]. National Public Radio's Weekend All Things Considered (June 21).

Mondello, Bob (1998). Animated Films. National Public Radio's Weekend All Things Considered (November 28).

Mondello, Bob (1998). Winter Movies [animated children's film "Prince of Egypt"]. National Public Radio's All Things Considered (November 27).

Montagne, Renee (1998). Space Ghost [rebroadcast of interview with Mike Lazzo of animated TV show]. National Public Radio's Weekly Edition (October 3).

Montagne, Renee (1998). Space Ghost Coast to Coast [interview with Mike Lazzo of animated TV show]. National Public Radio's Anthem (August 29/repeated November 28).

Montagne, Renee (1999). Animation & TV. National Public Radio's Anthem (May 8).

Moon, Y. "Can computer personalities be human personalities?" in *Int. Journal of Human-Computer Studies*, Vol. 43, pp. 223-239, 1995. *Summarizes evidence that people prefer individuals with personality attributes similar to their own. Includes review of studies of a range of relationships, e.g. marital satisfaction, roommate relationships, interest in strangers.*

Moore, Frazier (2000). Daria Stars in Her First TV Film [animation]. Associated Press (August 24).

Moorhead, M.V. (2000). Mesozoic mess: The Disney formula goes disturbingly awry in the off-putting Dinosaur [animation]. *Dallas Observer* (May 18). online at http://www.dallasobserver.com/issues/2000-05-18/film3.html

Moraes, Lisa de. (1999). At the networks: Toon in tomorrow [animation]. *Washington Post* (February 25): C7.

Moraes, Lisa de. (1999). Fatal Friday: Fox Dumps Its Failing Lineup ["Harsh Realm" and animated sitcom "Family Guy"]. *Washington Post* (October 26): C1.

Moraes, Lisa de. (1999). The TV Column [animated TV show South Park merchandise cancelled by J.C. Penney]. *Washington Post* (May 3): C7.

Moraes, Lisa de. (1999). TV's uncivil servants; Study finds portrayals no laughing manner [animation]. *Washington Post* (May 5): C1, 3.

Moritz, William. "The Films of Oskar Fischinger," *Film Culture* (58-59-60). 37-188.

Morrison, Eileen (1998). Something everyone can cash in on [The Rugrats Movie; animation]. *National Post* (November 20).

Morton, Victor (2000). Zingers in 'Clerks' deadly accurate [animated TV series by Kevin Smith]. *Washington Times* (May 27): D5.

Musgrove, Mike (1997). Virtual Springfield, Fox Interactive [Simpons' animated series CD-ROM review]. *Washington Post* (Oct. 17):Weekend 62.

Nachmanovitch, S. Free Play: Improvisation in Life and Art. Jeremy P. Tarcher, Inc.: Los Angeles, (1991). *Explores the origins of the creative process, arguing that improvisation is the key to creative expression. Broadly motivating, non-technical.*

Nass, C., J. Steuer, and E. Tauber, "Computers are Social Actors," in Proc. CHI '94 Conf., Boston, MA, Apr. 1994. *Introduces thesis that interaction with computers is fundamentally social. Brief analysis of experiments in which users work with and then evaluate computer tutoring systems. Often cited psychological justification for character-based interfaces. Expanded by: Nass et al., 1995.*

Nass, C., Y. Moon, B. J. Fogg, B. Reees, and C. Dryer, "Can computer personalities be human personalities?" in *Int. Journal of Human-Computer Studies,* Vol. 43, pp. 223-239, 1995. *Study supporting thesis that people prefer to interact with others of similar personality. Results indicate personality can be conveyed by simple, superficial cues. Some summary of psychological literature. Expands on: Nass et al., 1994.*

Nesselson, Lisa (2000). "Heavy Metal 2000" blasts off [animated film]. *Reuters/Variety* (May 31).

Neumaier, Joe (1998). A dog has his day [Scooby-Doo animation]. *Entertainment Weekly* (September 25): 113.

Neumaier, Joe (1998). Just Scooby-Doo it [animated TV series]. *Entertainment Weekly* (July 31): 9.

Newell, A. *Unified Theories of Cognition*. Harvard University Press: Cambridge, MA, 1990. *Newell puts forth the proposition that the field of AI should focus on building integrated intelligent agents. He illustrates the goal and process with a detailed report of his own group's work on the Soar architecture.*

Noake, Roger. *Animation: A Guide to Animated Film Techniques*. London: Macdonald Orbis, 1988.

Nolan, Sara (1998). This month, The Simpson's Mr. Smithers feels the burns [animated TV show]. *Details* (October): 196.

Norman, D. Things That Make Us Smart. Addison-Wesley: Reading, MA, (1993). *Emphasizes design of systems to match human strengths, rather than adapting humans to computers. Many concepts apply to design of spaces for intelligent characters. Widely cited HCI reference.*

Norris, Chris (1998). Welcome to South Park... fat-ass [animated TV show]. Spin 14 (3; March) 66-67.

O'Rourke, Michael. *Principles of Three-Dimensional Computer Animation: Modeling, Rendering and Animating with 3D Computer Graphics.* 1995. New York: Norton, 1998.

O'Sullivan, Michael (2000). 'Rocky and Bullwinkle': pun for all [animated movie]. *Washington Post* (June 30): Weekend 45.

O'Sullivan, Michael (2000). Yabba Dabba dud ['The Flinstones in Viva Rock Vegas' based on Hanna-Barbera animated TV series]. *Washington Post* (April 28): Weekend 53.

Oldenburg, Don (1999). Beyond the family film g-rating [animation]. *Washington Post* (January 12): C4.

Oldenburg, Don (1999). Beyond the family film g-rating [animation]. *Washington Post* (January 12): C4.

Oren, T., G. Salomon, K. Krietman, and A. Don, "Guides: Characterizing the Interface," in *The Art of Human-Computer Interface Design*, B. Laurel, Ed. Addison-Wesley: Reading, MA (1990). *Describes personality-based interface to encyclopedic survey of American history. Issues of designing personalities, incorporating multiple guides with distinct interests, user response to distinct characters, experiments in several presentation modes. Detailed examination of how believable agents might be used in pedagogy. In: Laurel, 1990.*

Owen, David (2000). Taking humor seriously: George Meyer, the funniest man behind the funnies TV show on TV [The Simpsons animation]. *New Yorker* (March 13): 64-75.

Owen, Rob (2000). Down at the Quick Stop: 'Clerks' clocks in as a cartoon tonight on ABC [animation by Kevin Smith]. *Nashville Tennessean* (May 31): 3D.

Pacheco, Nathan (1997). Web-toons: Hot flash [animator John Kricfalusi's Spumco website]? *Washington Post* (Nov 7): Weekend 70.

Pata, Nenad. *A Life of Animated Fantasy.* Zagreb: Zagreb Film, 1984.

Patoski, Joe Nick (1997). Hank Hill; Like other suburban Texans, he's a real character. ['King of the Hill' animated TV show by Mike Judge]. *Texas Monthly* (September).

Patterson, John (1998). Scanners: Bill Plympton's head trip [animation]. *LA Weekly* (August 28). online at http://www.laweekly.com/ink/98/40/film-patterson.shtml

Patterson, Robert and Charles Weijer (1998). D'oh! An analysis of the medical care provided to the family of Homer J. Simpson [television animation]. *Canadian Medical Association Journal* 159 (12; December 15): 1480-1481.

Pearlman, Cindy (1998). News from Frostbite Falls [Rocky and Bullwinkle animated movie]. *Entertainment Weekly* (Jan 23): 13.

Peary, Danny and Gerald Peary (ed.). *The American Animated Cartoon.* New York: Dutton, 1980.

Pener, Degen (1996). Racer's Edge [Volkswagon's Speed Racer commercial; animation]. *Entertainment Weekly* (Sept. 20): 12.

Pepoon, Steve (2000). Homer *vs.* Lisa and the Eight Commandment [Simpsons animation script excerpt]. *Washington Post* (January 1): M10.

Perlin, K. "Real time responsive animation with personality," *IEEE Transactions on Visualization and Computer Graphics*, Vol. 1, (1995). *Technical details of character animation system. System is concerned with physics and dynamics of representing animated characters, rather than internal motivation. Extended in: Perlin, 1996.*

Perlin, K. and A. Goldberg, "Improv: A System for Scripting Interactive Actors in Virtual Worlds," *Computer Graphics*, Vol. 29, 1996. *Presents an authoring system for movement and action of graphical characters. Behaviour engine uses simple scripting language to control cues, character behaviours; animation engine translates programmed canonical motions into natural noisy movement. Focus on physical action without high-level intelligent control. Used in: Hayes-Roth et al., 1996. Related work: Badler 1997.*

Phillips, Debra (1997). It's a wrap: This fall, kids could turn the new cartoon series 'Mummies Alive' into a licencees's dream [animation]. *Entrepeneur* (Sept.): 125-130.

Phipps, Keith (2000). The Powerpuff Girls: Creator and animator Craig McCracken talks about the cult hit [interview]. The Onion A.V. Club: http://avclub.theonion.com/avclub3623/bonusfeature1_3623.html

Picard, R. *Affective Computing*. MIT Press: Boston, MA, 1997. *Argues the need for emotion in computing applications. Describes design requirements of emotional computers, technical and social issues of affective computing, instances of fielded applications.*

Pilling, Jayne (ed.). *A Reader in Animation Studies.* Sydney: John Libbey, 1997.

————. *Cartoons and the Movies*. Paris: Dreamland, 1997.

————. *Women in Animation: A Compendium*. London: BFI, 1992.

Pinsky, Robert (1998). My favourite show: The Simpsons [The Poet Laureate of the United States' animated TV choice]. *New York Times Magazine* (September 20): 55.

Pintoff, Ernest. *The Complete Guide to Animation and Computer Graphics Schools.* New York: Watson-Guptill Publications, 1995.

————. *Bolt from the Blue: A True Story.* Salt Lake City, UT: Northwest, 1992.

Pixar, Luxo Jr., (film), (1986). *Classic short film about adventures of two animated lamps. Excellent example of animation principles in practice; extremely believable characters despite lack of facial features or speech.*

Podhoretz, John (1997). 'South Park': What's left to subvert [animation]? *New York Post* (December 23).

Poitras, Gilles (1998). *The Anime Companion: What's Japanese in Japanese Animation.* Stone Bridge Press.

Polk, James (1997). Highly animated [review of Chunovic's Rocky and Bullwinkle Book]. *New York Times Book Review* (March 9).

Pos, Jan. Kratky Film: *The Art of Czechoslovak Animation*. New Brunswick, NJ: Rutgers, 1991.

Project on Disney, The. *Inside the Mouse: Work and Play at Disney World.* Durham, NC: Duke UP, 1995.

Ransome, Grace Greenleaf, Comp. *Puppets and Shadows: A Selective Bibliography to 1930.* Lewiston, NY: Edwin Mellen Press, 1997.

Rees, Christina (1998). This cartoon is X-rated [anime/"Japanimation"]. *Dallas Observer* (September 3). online at http://www.dallasobserver.com/issues/1998-09-03/nightday2.html

Reeves, B. and C. Nass. *The Media Equation: How People Treat Computers, Televisions, and New Media Like Real People and Places.* Cambridge University Press: New York, 1996. *Full treatment of thesis that people treat computers as social entities. Extensive material drawn from psychological experiments, analysis. Extends: Nass et al., 1994; Nass et al., 1995.*

Reilly, W. S. "A Methodology for Building Believable Social Agents," in Proc. First Int. Conf. on Autonomous Agents, Marina del Rey, CA, Feb. 1997, pp. 114-121. *Presents simple approach for modeling believable characters. Provides transcripts and analysis of user interactions to evaluate robustness and believability of agents in testbed environment. More useful for conceptual approach than practical results. Extended by: Reilly, 1996.*

Reilly, W. S. "The Art of Creating Emotional and Robust Interactive Characters," in Working Notes of the AAAI Spring Symposium on Interactive Story Systems, Stanford, CA,

1995. *Briefly presents the major issues in character design. Displaying emotions, robustness, scale of interactivity. Short but informative.*

Reilly, W. S. N. "Believable Social and Emotional Agents." Ph.D. Thesis, School of Computer Science, Carnegie Mellon University, 1996. *Describes details of Em emotional model, illustrated with user testing over several scenarios with multiple autonomous emotional agents. Summary of character design methods and heuristics used.*

Renan, Sheldon. *An Introduction to the American Underground Film.* New York: E.P. Dutton, 1967.

Resnik, Andy (1999). *Animation Business Moves Eastward* [Character Builders in Ohio, co-founded by Jeff Smith of 'Bone']. Associated Press (August 10).

Reuters (1999). Actress Jean Vander Pyl dies; was voice of Wilma Flintstone [animation]. *Washington Post* (April 15): B6.

Rhodes, B. "PHISH-Nets: Planning Heuristically in Situated Hybrid Networks." Master's Thesis, Media Lab., Massachusetts Inst. Technol., (1996). *Presents architecture for action-selection under multiple interacting goals. Architecture is used to implement the "Big Bad Wolf" in several variations of the Three Little Pigs tale. Describes technical details, models of character and goals, and experimental outcomes. Significant attempt to build an architecture for believable characters.*

Richard, Valliere T. Norman McLaren, *Manipulator of Movement: The National Film Board* Years, 1947-1967. New York, NJ: University of Delaware Press, 1982.

Richmond, Ray and Antonia Coffman [eds.] (1998). *The Simpsons: A Complete Guide to Our Favourite Family* [animation]. New York: HarperPerennial.

Rickel, J. and W. L. Johnson, "Integrating Pedagogical Capabilities in a Virtual Environment Agent," in Proc. 1st Int. Conf. on Autonomous Agents, Marina del Rey, CA, Feb. 1997, pp. 30-38. *Describes Steve, an animated, autonomous agent that demonstrates procedural skills in a graphical environment. Agent may appear in several forms depending on design needs. Uses the Jack character architecture.*

Rieder, Howard. The Development of the Satire of Mr. Magoo. Master of Arts thesis, University of Southern California, 1961.

Riff, Reb (1989). *Dis Bonjour a la Dame* [animated flip book]. Paris: Rackam Productions.

Ringle, Ken (1997). A rollicking ride on the high c's: B. J. Ward found the right note in her spoofs of opera plots [animation]. *Washington Post* (Nov. 5):D1, D6.

Rist, T., E. Andre, and J. Muller, "Adding animated presentation agents to the interface," in Proc. Int. Conf. on Intelligent User Interfaces, Orlando, FL, Jan. (1997), pp. 21-28. *Describes PPP Persona, a system for building animated characters to present multimedia information. High-level overview; emphasis on architecture rather than character behaviours.*

Ritter, Malcolm (1999). *At the Movies: 'Toy Story 2'* [animation]. Associated Press (November 23).

Roberts, Victoria (1999). Dept. of Equitation: A visit to the National Horse Show at Madison Square Garden: Ladies Side Saddle Under Saddle Event, November 5, 1999 [comic strip journalism]. New Yorker (November 22): 68.

Robertson, Barbara (1994). Digital toons [digital animation tools]. *Computer Graphics World* 17(6; Jun): 40.

Roundy, Bill (2000). On the air ["Daria: Is It Fall Yet?" animated movie and lesbianism]. *Washington Blade* (September 8): 41.

Roundy, Bill (2000). On the air [gay-themed Mission Hill animated TV show]. *Washington Blade* (June 23): 39.

Roundy, Bill (2000). On the air [gay-themed MTV animated TV show "Spy Groove" by Glen Hanson]. *Washington Blade* (July 28): 38.

Roundy, Bill (2000). TV references increase: Watchdog group decries boost in gay content ['The Simpsons' animated series]. *Washington Blade* (April 7): 16.

Roush, Matt (1997). Inspired 'Simpsons' hands out triple treats [The Simpsons: Treehouse of Horror VIII; animation]. *USA Today* (Oct. 24): 3D.

Roush, Matt (2000). Parent traps: New 'toons go the family way ["Sammy" by David Spade and "Baby Blues" animated tv series]. *TV Guide* (July 29): 10.

Rousseau, D. and B. Hayes-Roth, "Improvisational synthetic actors with flexible personalities," Tech. Report KSL-97-08, Knowledge Systems Lab., Stanford Univ., Stanford, CA, Sept. (1997). *Presents social-psychological model for character interaction. Represents several characters using this approach, and evaluates user interactions in the "Cybercafe" scenario. Comprehensive description of a well-founded approach to character mentality. Expands: Rousseau, 1997b.*

Rousseau, D. and B. Hayes-Roth, "La personalité dans les acteurs synthétiques," to appear in Analyse de Systemes, (1998). *Threads literature in psychology, AI, and theater in discussion of computational improvisation. Description of personality model and implementation in Cybercafe system. In French.*

Rousseau, D. and B. Hayes-Roth, "Personality in synthetic agents," Tech. Report KSL-96-21, Knowledge Systems Lab., Stanford Univ., Stanford, CA, July 1997. *Describes model for building psychologies of intelligent actors, based upon psychology, AI, and drama theory. Provides survey of supporting research, outline of model, and examples of user interaction in "Cybercafe" scenario. Extended by: Rousseau, 1997c.*

Russakoff, Dale (1998). On children's TV, an unusual new character: cool parent [Nickelodeon animated TV shows]. *Washington Post* (December 13): A1, 18.

Russett, Robert and Cecile Starr. *Experimental Animation: Origins of a New Art. 1976.* New York: Da Capo, 1988.

Sample, Ann (1998). Dream baby [Ally McBeal TV show computer animation]. *Entertainment Weekly* (Jan 30): 73.

Sandler, Kevin S. (ed.) (1999). *Reading the Rabbit: Explorations in Warner Bros. Animation.* Rutgers University Press.

Sandler, Kevin S. *Reading the Rabbit: Explorations in Warner Bros. Animation.* New Brunswick, NJ: Rutgers University Press, 1998.

Satran, Richard (2000). Pixar earnings jump on "Toy Story 2" [computer animated movie]. *Reuters* (February 3).

Schickel, Richard. *The Disney Version: The Life, Times, Art and Commerce of Walt Disney.* 1968. New York: Ivan R. Dee, 1997.

Schiff, W., H. Blackburn, F. Cohen, G. Furman, A. Jackson, E. Lapidos, H. Rotkin and S. Thayer (1980). Does sex make a difference? Gender, age, and stimulus realism in perception and evaluation of aggression [animation]. *American Journal of Psychology* 93 (1; March): 53-78.

Schneider, Cy. *Children's Television: The Art, the Business, and How It Works.* Chicago: NTC Business Books, 1987.

Schneider, Michael (2000). 'Pet' Adopted by ABC [animated TV series "Teacher's Pet" by Gary Baseman]. *Reuters/Variety* (April 19).

Schneider, Michael (2000). 'Weekenders' Wend Way to ABC [animated TV series]. *Reuters/ Variety* (January 7).

Schneider, Michael (2000). Nick, WB tops among kids [TV animation, Nickelodeon, Warner Bros.]. *Reuters/Variety* (May 26).

Schneider, Michael and Josef Adalian (2000). NBC Flies with 'Chicken' [animation rights sold to TV]. *Reuters/Variety* (June 20).

Schobert, Walter. *The German Avantgarde Film of the 1920s.* Munich: Göethe Institute, 1989.

Schodt, Frederik L. *Dreamland Japan: Writings on Modern Manga.* Berkeley, CA: Stonebridge, 1996.

Schweizer, Peter and Rochele Schweizer. *Disney—The Mouse Betrayed: Greed, Corruption, and Children at Risk.* Washington D.C.: Regnery, 1998.

Scott, A.O. (2000). Jurassic lark: Rex of the cartoon jungle [Disney computer animated film 'Dinosaur' review]. *New York Times* (May 19): B10.

Seiter, Ellen. *Sold Separately: Parents and Children in Consumer Culture.* New Brunswick, NJ: Rutgers UP, 1995.

Shale, Richard. *Donald Duck Joins Up.* Ann Arbor, MI: UMI Research Press, 1982

Shales, Tom (1999). 'Dilbert': What memos are made of [animated TV show]. *Washington Post* (January 25): C1, 9.

Shales, Tom (1999). 'Family Guy': Time to take out the garbage, dear [animated TV series]. *Washington Post* (January 30): C1, 8.

Shales, Tom (1999). 'Futurama': Watch this space [animated TV series by Groening]. *Washington Post* (March 27): C1, 7.

Shales, Tom (1999). Fox's flimsy house of cards [The PJs animated TV series]. *Washington Post* (January 9): C1, 7.

Shales, Tom (2000). 'God, the Devil': Sinfully unfunny [animation]. *Washington Post* (March 9): C1, 7.

Shales, Tom (2000). ABC's Easter: Claymation on Golgotha ["The Miracle Maker", religious animation TV special]. *Washington Post* (April 23): G1, 5.

Shull, Michael S. and David E. Wilt. *Doing Their Bit: Wartime American Animated Short Films, 1939-1945.* Jefferson, NC: McFarland, 1987.

Simak, Steven A. (1998). The magic behind Mulan [computer animation]. *Digital Magic* (June): 16-21.

Sitney, P. Adams (ed.). *Film Culture Reader*. New York: Praeger, 1970.

Sitney, P. Adams. *Visionary Film: The American Avantgarde 1974.* Oxford: Oxford University Press, 1979.

Skully, Michael (1989). [Letter; Who Framed Roger Rabbit movie; animation]. *Comics Scene* (7): 42-43.

Smith, C. (1977). The early history of animation: Saturday morning TV discovers 1915. *Journal of the University Film Association* 29(3): 23-30.

Smith, Dave. *Disney A to Z: The Updated Official Encyclopedia.* New York: Hyperion, 1998.

Smith, Sean M. (1999). Disney killed my Mom! [animated movies death statistics]. *Premier* (July): 41.

Smith, T. J., J. Shi, J. Granieri, and N. Badler, "JackMOO: An Integration of Jack and LambdaMOO," in Proc. Pacific Graphics (1997), Seoul, Korea, 1997. *Describes integration of Jack as an avatar animation system and LambdaMOO as a control platform for creating virtual training scenarios. Technical details on client design and interface between Jack and LambdaMOO. Novel approach for combining proven technologies.*

Smoodin, E. and R. W. McEachern (1996). Animating culture: Hollywood cartoons from the sound era. *Journal of Popular Culture* 29(4): 253.

Smoodin, Eric (ed.). *Disney Discourse: Producing the Magic Kingdom.* New York: Routledge, 1994.

Smoodin, Eric Loren (1993). *Animating Culture: Hollywood Cartoons from the Sound Era.* Rutgers University Press.

Smoodin, Eric. *Animating Culture: Hollywood Cartoons from the Sound Era.* New Brunswick, NJ: Rutgers, 1993.

Snead, Elizabeth (1998). Here comes merchandise in 'toon with 'South Park' [animated TV show]. *USA Today* (June 26): 5E.

Snierson, Dan (1998). Welcome, Matt [new Groening animated show]. *Entertainment Weekly* (August 21/28): 103.

Snierson, Dan and Carrie Bell (1999). Toying around ['Toy Story' animated film opening]. *Entertainment Weekly* (November 26).

Snyder, Janet (1997). Japan seeks cause of convulsions [Pocket Monsters animation]. *Washington Post* (Dec. 18): C16.

Solomon, Charles (ed.). *The Art of the Animated Image: An Anthology.* Los Angeles: American Film Institute, 1987.

Solomon, Charles. *History of Animation: Enchanted Drawings.* 1989. New York: Wings Books, 1994.

Span, Paula (1997). Wither Daria: Meet The Teen Terminator. MTV's Hot New Toon is Sharp, Funny—and Female [animated television show, spun off of Mike Judge's 'Beavis and Butthead']. *Washington Post* (June 1): G1.

Sprafkin, J., K.D. Gadow and P. Grayson (1987). Effects of viewing aggressive cartoons on the behaviour of learning disabled children [animation]. *Journal of Child Psychology & Psychiatry and Allied Disciplines* 28 (3; May): 387-98.

Sragow, Michael (1997). Muscle bound; Disney's Hercules is all brawn, no brain [animation]. *Dallas Observer* (June 26). online at http://www.dallasobserver.com/issues/1997-06-26/film3.html

Sragow, Michael (1998). Making a mountain out of an anthill; The craftsmen at Pixar delight with the inventive and enchanting A Bug's Life [Disney animation]. *Dallas Observer* (November 26). online at http://www.dallasobserver.com/issues/1998-11-26/film4.html

Stauffacher, Frank (ed.). *Art in Cinema: A Symposium on the Avantgarde Film Together with Program Notes and References.* San Francisco: San Francisco Museum of Art, 1947.

Stephens, Chuck (2000). Space Junk: Titan A.E. [Don Bluth and Fox animated movie]. *LA Weekly* (June 16). online at http://www.laweekly.com/ink/00/30/film-stephens.shtml

Stepp, Laura Sessions (1999). The 'Pokemon' phenomenon [Japanese animation]. *Washington Post* (April 9): C4.

Sternberg, R. and P. Ruzgis (eds.). *Personality and Intelligence.* Cambridge University Press: Cambridge, 1994.

Stockwell, Jamie (1999). Taming the Pokemon craze: The animated creatures are all the rage, but parents should set limits. *Washington Post* (August 29): H5.

Strauss, Bob (1998). Surf park [South Park animated TV show]. Yahoo! Internet Life (February): 66-68.

Street, Rita (1995). Sunbow: Turning comics into TV hits. *Animation Magazine* 8 (August): 15.

Street, Rita. *Computer Animation: A Whole New World.* Glouster, MA: Rockport, 1998.

Strøm, Gunnar, Comp. *The ASIFA List of Animation Schools.* Volda: Volda College, various dates.

Stuever, Hank (2000). The little merman [satire on use of real-life tragedy as animated musicals, illustrated by caricaturist Roman Genn]. *Washington Post* (January 29): C1, 4.

Stuever, Hank (2000). What Would Godzilla Say? At the Japanese Animation Festival, a Brave New World of Hot Pink and Cool Kids. *Washington Post* (February 14): C1.

Sturm, James and Art Baxter (1999). A Response to Chapter Nine: Build a Beach Head [of Scott McCloud's 'Understanding Comics']. *Comics Journal* (211; April): 93-99.

Styles, Betsy (1998). 'South Park' Rules [letter on animated TV show]? *Newsweek* (April 13): 18.

Sullivan, Kevin (1997). Japan's cartoon violence: TV networks criticized after children's seizures [Pocket Monsters animation]. *Washington Post* (Dec. 19): D1, D6.

Sullivan, Kevin (1997). The Wolf-Girl from Japan: 'Princess Monoke' Fans Fill the Movie Theaters [animation]. *Washington Post* (Sept. 17): D1.

Sutel, Seth (1999). TBS Pulls Plug on Women's Network [while starting network for company's]:

Talbots (2000). Remember how she just pressed a button and got a complete outfit? [advertisement using The Jetson animated Hanna-Barbera TV series]. *Washington Post* (April 28); (May 4): A10.

Tanahey (ed.) (1999). A New 'Batman' Takes Wing [Batman Beyond animated TV series; Paul Dini]. *New York Daily News* (January 11).

Tannen, D. Talking From 9 to 5: Women and Men in the Workplace: Language, Sex, and Power. Avon Books: New York, (1997). *Analysis of communication in the workplace, with focus on social and cultural impediments to communication.*

Taylor, Charles (2000). "Fantasia 2000": Beethoven, Gershwin, Respighi and Stravinsky meet Disney kitsch in this sequel to the not-quite-classic animated feature. *Salon* (June 23): http://www.salon.com/ent/movies/review/2000/06/23/fantasia/index.html

Taylor, Charles (2000). "The Adventures of Rocky and Bullwinkle": Robert De Niro's whip-fast Fearless Leader blurs the line between humans and cartoons, but the rest of this clunky TV remake is stiffer than an iron curtain [movie based on Jay Ward animation]. *Salon* (June 30): http://www.salon.com/ent/movies/review/2000/06/30/bullwinkle/index.html

Taylor, Richard. *The Encyclopedia of Animation Techniques.* London: Running Press, 1996.

Thomas, Bob. *Walt Disney: An American Original.* 1976. New York: Hyperion, 1994.

Thomas, Frank & Ollie Johnston (1981). *Disney Animation: The Illusion of Life*. New York: Abbeville Press.

Thomas, Frank and Ollie Johnston. *Disney Animation: The Illusion of Life.* New York: Abbeville, 1984.

Thomas, Susan Gregory (1994). Toontown Tricksters: For Animators, Gig is Up as Laser Disc Exposes Dirty Deeds. *Washington Post* (March 18).

Thompson, Frank. *The Film, The Art, The Vision: Tim Burton's Nightmare Before Christmas.* New York: Hyperion, 1993.

Thompson, Luke Y. (2000). Crash of the Titan: Disney-esque characters and anime stylings don't mix, but at least the battles are cool [Bluth animated movie "Titan A.E." from Fox]. *Dallas Observer* (June 15). online at http://www.dallasobserver.com/issues/2000-06-15/film2.html

Thompson, Stephen (2000). Chuck Jones [animator interview]. The Onion A.V. Club: http://avclub.theonion.com/avclub3313/avfeature3313.html

Thompson, T. L. and E. Zerbinos (1995). Gender roles in animated cartoons: Has the picture changed in 20 years? *Sex Roles* 32(9-10): 651.

Tippit, Sarah (2000). Playful, vintage looks dominate Oscar fashion ["South Park" animator Trey Parker]. *Reuters* (March 27).

Tobias, Scott (2000). Aardman Animations: Directors Peter Lord and Nick Park talk about stop-motion animation and the new Chicken Run [interview]. The Onion A.V. Club: http://avclub.theonion.com/avclub3623/avfeature_3623.html

Tourtellotte, Bob (1999). Pixar [Animation Studio] shares jump on strong video sales. *Reuters* (October 26).

Tourtellotte, Bob (2000). English Animators Go Hollywood for 'Chicken Run'. *Reuters* (June 20).

Tourtellotte, Bob (2000). Pixar posts strong quarter, ups guidance [computer animation]. *Reuters/Variety* (May 4).

Townson, Don and Charles Lyons (2000). Disney closes Canuck shops, lays off 200 [animation]. *Reuters/Variety* (February 15).

Travis, Lucinda and Jack Hannah, Comp. Factfile #9: Animation. Los Angeles: American Film Institute, 1986.

Tyler, Parker. *Underground Film: A Critical History.* New York: Grove, 1969.

Urycki, Mark (1995). Balto [animated movie]. National Public Radio's All Things Considered (December 26).

Van Boven, Sarah with Devin Gordon and Esther Pan (1998). The 'Veggies' that kids actually like: A bumper crop of animated Bible Videos. *Newsweek* (December 7): 67.

Van Oss, Alex (1997). [controversy about remaking animated TV show as Mr. Magoo movie]. National Public Radio's Morning Edition (August 6).

Vaz, Mark Cotta and Patricia Rose Duignan. *Industrial Light and Magic.* New York: Ballantine, 1996.

Verrall, Robert (1954). Making an animated cartoon: The romance of transportation. *Canadian Art* 11 : 148-150.

Vitale, Tom (1997). Lion King on Broadway [play based on Disney's animated movie]. National Public Radio's Morning Edition (November 13).

Vogel, Mark R. (1998). A cat and two dads: New children's book presents a very nontraditional family [animator John Canemaker gay-themed book]. *Washington Blade* (May 15): 39.

Vogel, Traci (2000). The Dark Side of Pop Culture: Disturbing Animation [Satoshi Kon's Japanese anime film, Perfect Blue]. *The Stranger* (September 30).

Walk, Gary Eng. 1998. Poking fun [Japanese animation and game character Pokemon]. *Entertainment Weekly* (November 6): 96.

Walker, Leslie (1999). An internet dress address [Miss Boo animated computer character]. *Washington Post* (July 1): E1, 6.

Walker, M. A., J. E. Cahn, and S. J. Whittaker, "Improvising Linguistic Style: Social and Affective Bases of Agent Personality," in Proc. 1st Int. Conf. on Autonomous Agents, Marina del Rey, CA, Feb (1997), pp. 96-105. *Presents details of system for improvising specific forms of character utterances based on mood, personality, and social status. Provides examples of variability in "Casablanca" dialog. Interesting approach to generating vocal behaviours based upon social models of interaction.*

Walt Disney Productions, Snow White (film), (1937). *The world's first full-length animated film. Early example of then-new Disney animation principles used to make cartoon characters with depth and life. A classic.*

Walt Disney Productions, Toy Story (film), (1995). *First full-length computer animated cartoon. Disney principles applied to graphic design. Comparable to "Snow White" for redefining animated film.*

Walters, Barry (1996). Artful animation from Japan. *San Francisco Examiner* (April 12).

Wartofsky, Alona (1999). Pop Notes ["Tomorrow night MTV premiers its new animated series, 'Station Zero'"]. *Washington Post* (March 7): G2

Wartofsky, Alona (2000). Masters of the speeding pullets; The creators of Wallace and Gromit move to the eggs-press lane with 'Chicken Run' [Claymation, Nick Parks, Peter Lord, Aardman Animation, Dreamworks]. *Washington Post* (June 18): G1, 6.

Wax, Emily (2000). School beckoning, girls 'power' up: Superhero cartoon fuels demand for fashionable supplies [Powerpuff Girls animated TV show marketing]. *Washington Post* (August 20): C1, 4.

Waxman, Sharon (1998). 'Rangers' dispute settled [animation]. *Washington Post* (Feb. 6): B7.

Waxman, Sharon (1998). Actors' Guild faces off against 'Power Rangers' [Saban Entertainment; animation]. *Washington Post* (Jan 31).

Waxman, Sharon (1999). That's Show Buzz: For the Guys Behind 'Mission Hill,' a Long, Hard Climb [animated television series]. *Washington Post* (October 7): C1, C7.

Waxman, Sharon (2000). Animation grows up: The new generation of Hollywood cartoons isn't just for kiddies. *Washington Post* (May 20): C1, 4.

Wees, William C. *Light Moving in Time: Studies in the Visual Aesthetics of Avantgarde Film.* Berkeley: U California, p. 1992.

Weinkauf, Gregory (2000). Coop de grace: These British filmmakers do Chicken right ['Chicken Run' animated movie]. Dallas Observer (June 22). online at http://www.dallasobserver.com/issues/2000-06-22/film2.html

Weinraub, Bernard (1999), Loosening a Strict Film Rating for 'South Park' [animated movie]. *New York Times* (June 29).

Weir, William (2000). Hope Springs Eternal [adaptations of Jay Ward's animation including 'The Adventures of Rocky and Bullwinkle']. *The Hartford Courant* (July 15).

Weiss, Jeffrey (2000). Scooby-Doo's new adventure: The latest mystery facing his friends involves Wicca [animation]. *The Dallas Morning News* (January 7).

Weizenbaum, J. "ELIZA—A Computer Programme for the Study of Natural Language Communication between Man and Machine," in *Comm. of the ACM*, vol. 9(1), pp. 36-45, (1966). *Describes ELIZA, a text-based interactive Rogerian psychologist. Emphasis is on issues of parsing and text generation, not believability. Classic reference for early character design.*

Welles, Paul. *Understanding Animation*. London: Routledge, 1998.

Wells, Paul (1998). *Understanding Animation*. Routledge.

Wertheimer, Linda (1997). Cartoon seizures [Pokemon Japanese animated cartoon causes medical problem]. National Public Radio's All Things Considered (December 18).

Wertheimer, Linda or Noah Adams. 1994. Bill Frisell [wrote music score for Gary Larson's Far Side animated TV show]. National Public Radio's All Things Considered (October 26).

Werts, Diane (2000). Animation machinations: How 'The Simpsons' redrew the television map. *Newsday* (January 2).

Whitney, John. *Digital Harmony: On the Complementarity of Music and Visual Art.* Peterborough, NH: McGraw-Hill, 1980.

Whitty, Stephen (1998). Hakuna it's notta [review of Disney's animated video The Lion King II: Simba's pride]. *Entertainment Weekly* (October 30): 119-120.

Whitty, Stephen (1999). Adults only [animation reviews of Who Framed Roger Rabbit, Antz, Yellow Submarine]. *Entertainment Weekly* (February 12): 84-5.

Wickstrom, Andy (1991). 'Japanimation' adult cartoons come to U.S. [Manga]. *Albany Times Union* (Oct. 24): T27.

Wild, David (1997). I need a hill [Mike Judges' animated series King of the Hill]. *Rolling Stone* (Feb. 20): 79.

Wild, David (1998). South Park's evil geniuses and the triumph of no-brow culture [animation]. *Rolling Stone* (February 19): 32-61.

Williams, Robin (1998). Robin Williams: An Interview (Williams reflects on animated cartoons from Daffy Duck to South Park) *Civilization* (June-July) http://www.civmag.com/articles/C9807F05.html

Willis, Heather (2000). Fight the power [animated 'The Powerpuff Girls' music merchandising]. *Pulse!* (August): cover, 24-26.

Willman, Chris (1998). (Not so) fresh 'Prince' [The Prince of Eygypt animated movie's 3 soundtracks]. *Entertainment Weekly* (November 20): 128.

Wilonsky, Robert (2000). Squirrel meat: Animated duo return in a very Rockroad movie [Jay Ward's Bullwinkle]. *Dallas Observer* (June 29). online at http://www.dallasobserver.com/issues/2000-06-29/film3.html

Wilson, S. S. *Puppets and People: Dimensional Animation Combined with Live Action in the Cinema.* San Diego: A. S. Barnes, 1980.

Wloszczyna, Susan (2000). Talk is cheap for expressive horse Altivo [animated movie "The Road to El Dorado"]. *USA Today* (March 24): 1E.

Woolery, George. *Children's Television: The First Thirty-Five Years, 1946-1981*, Part I: Animated Cartoon Series. Metuchen, NJ: Scarecrow, 1983.

————. *Animated TV Specials: The Complete Directory to the First Twenty-Five Years, 1962-1987.* Metuchen, NJ: Scarecrow, 1988.

Worth, Larry (1997). 'Lion' Share of the Credit [Disney's 'The Lion King' play adaptation of animated movie]. *New York Post* (November 13).

Worth, Larry (1997). 'Triumph' for ex-"Beauty' [Susan Egan, Meg, in "Hercules" Disney animated movie]. *New York Post* (October 23).

Worth, Larry (1998). Fire-Breathing Is Draggin'. ["Quest for Camelot" Animated Movie Review]. *New York Post* (May 15).

Xiberras, Jean-Luc. *Captured in Drifting Sand: Gisèle.and Nag Ansorge.* Annecy: International Animated Film Festival of Annecy, 1995.

Yeo, Michael (1998). To boldly go: we have to look beyond the Simpsons for a true medical hero [animation]. *Canadian Medical Association Journal* 159 (12; December 15): 1476-1477.

Yoe, Craig and Janet Morra-Yoe (ed.). *The Art of Mickey Mouse.* New York: Hyperion, 1995.

Yokota, Fumie and Kimberly M. Thompson (2000). Violence in G-rated animated films. *Journal of the American Medical Association* 283 (20; May 24/31): 2716-2720.

York, Julie (1999). 'South Park' adds to teen worries [animation]. *South Bend Tribune* (July 1).

Young, Charles M. (1994). Meet the Beavis [animation]! *Rolling Stone* (Mar 24): 38-42.

Young, Josh (1998). A better mousetrap [Nickelodeon *vs.* Disney's animation efforts]. *Entertainment Weekly* (December 4): 26, 30.

Youngblood, Gene. *Expanded Cinema.* New York: E.P. Dutton, 1970.

Zahed, Ramin (2000). "Bob" moves heaven, earth to win yucks ["God, the Devil and Bob" animat ed TV series]. *Reuters/Variety* (March 7).

Zahed, Ramin (2000). HBO sets sail with "Odyssey" cartoon [animation by Vilanima Studios of Lithuania]. *Reuters/Variety* (January 5).

Zahed, Ramin (2000). Jesus comes to life on ABC [The Miracle Maker review; clay animation]. *Reuters/Variety* (April 19).

Zarroli, Jim (1995). [stock offering by computer animation firm who did Disney film 'Toy Story']. National Public Radio's Morning Edition (November 30).

Zimbardo, P. and M. Leippe. *The Psychology of Attitude Change and Social Influence.* McGraw-Hill: New York, (1991).

Index